World Music

World Music

A Global Journey

Terry E. Miller & Andrew Shahriari

Routledge
Taylor & Francis Group
New York   London

Cover photos from top to bottom: Gypsy musicians perform for visitors to the Great Plain near Bugac, Hungary (Terry E. Miller); Flamenco dancers and guitarists perform in a club in Cadiz, Spain (Robert Garfias); Tseyen Tserendorj playing the Mongolian *morinhuur* (two stringed, "horse-head" fiddle), New York City (© Jack Vartoogian/FrontRowPhotos); Indian street musician "charms" two cobra snakes with his *punji* double clarinet consisting of gourd windchest, drone pipe, and melody pipe with finger holes (Max T. Miller); The Chinese *pipa* (pear shaped lute) played by Lai Wah-Chiu (Terry E. Miller); *Atumpan* drums from Ghana, often used as a speech surrogate (Amy Unruh); Playing for a New York audience, Mingo Saldivar (accordion) with Los Cuatro Espadas play *conjunto* music (© Jack Vartoogian/FrontRowPhotos); The *ntahera* ivory horn ensemble of the Asantehene, Kumase, Ghana (Joseph S. Kaminski); A young boy in traditional costume dances to the accompaniment of a Balinese gamelan (Amy Unruh); Mr. Ken Somjindah plays the Northeastern Thai *khaen paet* with sixteen pipes in Ban See-Kaeo, Roi-et province (Terry E. Miller)

Published in 2006 by
Routledge
Taylor & Francis Group
270 Madison Avenue
New York, NY 10016

Published in Great Britain by
Routledge
Taylor & Francis Group
2 Park Square
Milton Park, Abingdon
Oxon OX14 4RN

Printed in the United States of America on acid-free paper
10 9 8 7 6 5 4 3 2

International Standard Book Number-10: 0-415-96892-5 (Softcover)
International Standard Book Number-13: 978-0-415-96892-8 (Softcover)
Library of Congress Card Number 2005025908

Library of Congress Cataloging-in-Publication Data

Miller, Terry E.
    World music : a global journey / Terry E. Miller and Andrew Shahriari.
       p. cm.
    Includes bibliographical references (p.   ), discography (p.   ), and index.
    ISBN 0-415-96892-5 (pbk. : alk. paper)
    1. Ethnomusicology. I. Shahriari, Andrew C. II. Title.

ML3798.M53 2006
780.9--dc22   2005025908

informa
Taylor & Francis Group
is the Academic Division of Informa plc.

Visit the Taylor & Francis Web site at
http://www.taylorandfrancis.com

and the Routledge Web site at
http://www.routledge-ny.com

Table of Contents

Acknowledgements

None of us acquires our knowledge in isolation, and all of us are indebted to the many people we have encountered during our lives. Certainly we are indebted to our own formal teachers at all levels, but our knowledge of the world's musics is only possible thanks to innumerable individuals, some known first-hand, others known through performances, who have—wittingly or unwittingly—taught us what we know. We, not they, are responsible for that which remains unknown or misunderstood.

In particular we are indebted to the many individuals who have made it possible to offer an unprecedented seventy tracks of music, especially those who did so without payment. Similarly, we are indebted to those who allowed us to use their photographs. Their names are to be found in the credits for each track and each photo. All photos not credited were taken by Terry E. Miller. Photos appearing with a ⒸC are also found in the color insert.

Perhaps ironically, we are also indebted to our many students—the good, the bad, and the ugly—who over the years have made us increasingly aware of the challenges of teaching world musics. While some of our students have been music majors, the vast majority are "non-music majors" satisfying requirements for their Liberal Education Core and for Diversity courses. As such, few have a special interest in the world's musics, so inspiring enthusiasm in the subject matter is an ongoing challenge. The insights brought from teaching students with a variety of majors and levels of interest (or disinterest) in studying the world's musics and cultures have been the greatest resource. It is these students who inspired much of our writing throughout the book.

Another motivating factor was to create a book for non-specialist teachers. Based on several years experience with the College Music Society, we are grateful to the many non-ethnomusicologist teachers who, having been pressed into service to teach a world music survey, shared with us their concerns and wishes.

Before this book was completed a great number of individuals kindly offered feedback for four sample chapters. We find in these a remarkable amount of helpful criticism, even from those who have many "issues" with what we have done. Unfortunately, because these comments came at the end of the process, and many require a fairly thorough reexamination of the manuscript, there is not enough time for such revisions to the first edition. We have made those changes that we could in a short time, but the rest will be saved for a hoped-for revised second edition down the road.

Last but not least we must thank our families for their forbearance and tolerance of our long periods sitting before the computer writing this book. Preceding that were many long and often demanding research trips to the field, usually with our spouses or with them left to "hold the fort" at home.

In addition Terry would like to acknowledge the good humor shown by his children, Sonia and Esther, who, dragged along on numerous field trips, at least contributed their charms on his "research subjects." Esther in particular thought her family's trip to Trinidad was to visit beaches but soon discovered that they were spending up to eight hours on Sunday in Spiritual Baptist churches. Andrew apologizes in advance, expecting that his son, Cyrus, will have similar experiences in the future, but he promises to visit the beach at least once per field trip for his wife's sanity.

An Open Letter
to Our Readers

W hy another world music textbook? First, the short answer: In spite of modern air travel and the Internet, and even in the face of the latest phase of globalization, our planet's music remains overwhelmingly diverse. Acknowledging a growing library of materials pertaining to the musics of the world's peoples, and the availability of several fine world music textbooks, there is always room for one more book, as no single study can capture the planet's musical essence.

The long answer is more complex.

For Whom Has This Book Been Written?

Despite increasing budgetary restrictions on college campuses, there has been a steady growth in the number of "world music survey" classes taught across North America. Several factors are driving this process. One is the rise of "diversity" as an educational priority. Another is the striking demographic shift occurring in the United States through the growth of immigration from non-European countries. Yet another is the growing realization that our population has always been diverse, and that the curriculum has hitherto failed to take this into account. In spite of the fact that music is not a "universal language"—indeed, each musical system must be studied according to its own merits and principles—it is an excellent means by which students can enter into and experience other cultures. Although many "cultural diversity" courses are expected to include politically loaded discussions of current problems, it is possible to study music without having to take sides. From a relatively neutral space, one can observe how music acts both to reinforce hegemonic power and to challenge or subvert it.

While many of our colleagues in the field of ethnomusicology believe that ethnomusicologists should teach world music survey courses, the reality is that most institutions either cannot or will not spare the money for a new position dedicated to ethnomusicology. As a result, music departments across the land in all sorts of institutions—great and small—

attempt to offer such courses using existing faculty. While few of these teachers have any training in ethnomusicology, many in fact do throw themselves into their teaching with enthusiasm. Unfortunately, their institutional libraries rarely have adequate collections of books, journals, or media materials to support such courses. We have had conversations with colleagues working in small liberal arts colleges, community colleges, and even small state institutions who have expressed a strong desire for a comprehensive world music survey textbook that includes enough resources to make the course effective even when their libraries lack materials. We have attempted to design this book to meet these goals.

Scope

Anyone who attempts a book such as this must first answer the question: Breadth or depth? You cannot have both, unless you want a tome that could hold down your loose papers through a hurricane. We have chosen breadth. While we recognize the impossibility of doing justice to all the world's notable and interesting musics, we also feel that doing what you can is better than doing nothing. The second major question is: Geographical or topical organization? As ethnomusicologists we are tempted to organize our studies topically, in order to explore such issues as identity, gender, representation, meaning, and so on, but we have found that this approach leaves most students in a state of geographical disorientation. While such a plan would make it easier to discuss many of the issues at stake in "cultural diversity" courses, it makes it nearly impossible to communicate a coherent view of the music of a given area. Thus, we have chosen a geographical organization. This we have framed as an imaginary "global journey" of the Earth.

A third question is: Should the concentration be on music as sound or music as culture? Our field has long had a fascination with the anthropological aspects of the musics studied—what we used to call "the context"—but some of our critics have noted a growing reluctance to discuss musical sound at all, complaining that we do "everything but the music." Others have scoffed at ethnomusicology as eth-NO-MUSIC-ology. We have chosen to emphasize music as sound because we suspect that many of the professors who will use this book are situated in music departments and are naturally inclined to focus on music in this way. We believe that what attracts people to world music first is its sound; only later do they become interested in its cultural aspects. In keeping with that idea, we have naturally included the cultural context as well. Teachers using this book can choose which to emphasize.

In constructing such a book, one must choose between using one author or multiple specialist authors. The latter approach has the distinct advantage of bringing the best thinking to bear on each particular area, but also has the disadvantage of inconsistent style and approach. We have chosen a two-author plan. The limitation of this approach is that neither of us has real expertise in a number of the areas covered in this book. Both of us, however, have had extensive experience teaching world music surveys, have acquired broad knowledge through study and travel, and have availed ourselves of recent research available in both print and audio-video form. For the purposes of a world survey, it is not necessary to know everything about a given area, however desirable that might be.

While ethnomusicology began as the study of "traditional" music and, at least in its early days, viewed popular culture and the beginnings of globalization as threats, it has changed its focus considerably. Today scholars are as likely to study the many stages of musical hybridization as well as urban popular music as they are traditional types of music. We have chosen not to focus on these for several reasons. First and foremost is that the book is written around seventy tracks of music, a tiny number considering the diversity of the world's musics but generous in comparison to many textbooks. With these we only provide minimal coverage for each continent. We know our colleagues, with full justification, will argue that we should have included certain others. We cop the plea that to add a track, we would have also had to delete a track. Second, to include any track, we have to gain permission, usually paying fees to the recording owner. Licensing any kind of commercially viable music (i.e., popular and many hybrid musics) is expensive. Indeed, the complications of copyright and licensing fees on these kinds of music has been a major stumbling block for scholars concentrating in these areas. Therefore, we are forced to work within the bounds of fiscal and practical realities and cannot realize the ideal of representing everything that's out there. We wanted a book that would be affordable for today's working student.

Organization

Our book has been written using travel as its central metaphor. After three introductory chapters in which we discuss the elements of music from a worldwide perspective, we present ten chapters on specific areas, be they continent (e.g., Europe) or subcontinent (e.g., South Asia). As with any major trip, some preparation is necessary before a specific area can be considered in depth. The section called "Background Preparation" seeks to provide the big picture, and should be approached as if you were pouring over books and maps at the kitchen table. We need first to get a handle on the general lay of the land, discuss some of an area's history, and raise certain issues related to music-making in the region. Then we run through some of the "must-see sites"—that is, some of the most significant types of music the area has to offer. As with any trip, one must be selective. After circling around in order to get an overview of the place, we then land in a particular country or area. Here we review the background information pertinent to this particular place, and give the reader some feel for the area's history and culture.

After this, we begin visiting our individual "sites." These are the music examples and CD tracks we have chosen to represent the area—though you should always bear in mind that we have had to leave out many others of equal significance. As with travel, so with music: we simply cannot visit everything. Hopefully you will come back to some areas later and experience more on your own. Each site is explored in three steps. In the section called "First Impressions" we approach the site as if without prior knowledge, attempting to convey the impressions and associations the music might inspire in a first-time listener from the West. In the next section, "Aural Analysis," we focus on the site in terms of musical sound, discussing whatever is most relevant. This could include the medium (instruments and/or voices) and any of the prominent musical elements that define an example. Because we recognize that many readers of this book are not going to be students majoring in music, we avoid becoming overly technical. A full musical analysis of each site would increase this book's size to that of an unabridged dictionary. We also avoid using musical notation, because we feel the added space and expense it would require is not justified for a study at the beginning level. Instructors may wish to bring in some examples, based on their own focus, as a supplement to the materials provided here. In a final section, we offer "Cultural Considerations" in which relevant cultural matters are raised. Here you can find the "contexts" and "issues" that have differentiated ethnomusicology from most other music disciplines.

How to Expand Course Coverage

"Teaching a textbook" is a widely and often effectively used method, but also one that raises thorny issues. The problem with any world survey is that the authors must of necessity choose a certain set of examples and ideas based on their own experience—but course instructors may have had a different set of experiences. We suggest therefore that teachers consider the following ideas when using this book:

1. Be selective. If you find that seventy-odd music examples are too many for your class, then select those that suit your needs. We have attempted to provide reasonably good surveys of each area—considering the limitations of space—but for some this will be too much and for others too little.

2. Use our plan as a model. Just as you can exclude specific sites, you can also add your own. These additions can be accomplished by either professor or student. An excellent assignment would be for the students to write about a music track not selected by us, using the three approaches employed in this book: first impressions, aural analysis, and cultural considerations. Such exercises could become class presentations as well.

3. Go further on your own. Just as easily as further sites can be researched and written about, existing ones can be developed by

students into class presentations that include audio examples, video/DVD clips, and even performances on substitute instruments or on the real ones. Students and teachers can find living representatives of a culture—or even musicians from the tradition under study who can come to class and present the music live.

4. Music teachers who wish to give their students more analysis than we provide can take what is presented here and expand on it through careful classroom listening, transcription, and attempts to apply various analytical tools to specific tracks.

To further your study, we have prepared a website to accompany this book, **www.routledge-ny.com/textbooks/worldmusic**. On it, you'll find more photos, articles, and listening examples, plus teaching aids. This textbook should be seen as just the beginning of each individual's personal journey. We would be extremely pleased to learn that as a result of this book, our readers pursued further study of sites discussed here. We would be delighted to find that you actually traveled to some of these sites and experienced them for yourselves or that you met someone who represents the tradition living in your end of town.

Our Own Journey (Thus Far)

Neither author, of course, has been everywhere or heard every kind of music the world has to offer. Writing this book has been a humbling experience—only fools think they can cover the world's musics in a single volume. Regardless of our qualms, however, world music courses have become a normal part of the academic environment, and the need for such surveys is not going to go away because of our philosophical reservations. If anything, the demand for them will be growing. We have attempted to play to our strengths while recognizing our limitations. In so doing we hope to have met the expectations of the medical profession's Hippocratic Oath: "first, do no harm." In the following pages of this preface we engage in a kind of "truth in advertising," by revealing some of our own personal histories with regard to the musics of the world. Perhaps after having read of our experiences, which we present separately, you will better understand what we have chosen, how we have approached it, and why we wrote what we wrote.

Terry E. Miller

My first experience hearing a non-Western music came during my undergraduate years at the College of Wooster (in Ohio), where I was majoring in organ performance. Ravi Shankar, still India's most famous sitar player, came to the campus as part of the Community Music Series in 1964, several years before he became famous in his own right and as the teacher of George Harrison. After his performance the music majors met with Shankar, but our attempts to understand the concept of raga were mostly unsuccessful. We simply had no conceptual categories with which to understand modal improvisation. Further, we had never seen a musician perform seated on the floor, or encountered incense at a music event, and we also failed to understand the significance of the tambura lute player and tabla drummer. In those days there were virtually no world music courses anywhere, and recordings other than those on the Folkways label were virtually nonexistent.

My next encounter with an "exotic" music did not come until after I had been drafted into the U.S. Army in 1968 and sent to the Republic of Vietnam in 1969 to help fight the war from a swivel chair in front of a Remington typewriter. As a "chairborne" soldier working at a huge

Co-author Terry Miller (on right)
with fellow soldier while serving in the
United States Army in Vietnam (1969)

base about twenty miles from Saigon (now Ho Chi Minh City), I could have ignored Vietnam entirely. For some odd reason I decided to find out about Vietnamese music. To do so, however, required trips to Saigon, but having no official business there and no authorization, I had to go illegally on weekends. In Saigon, I attended performances of two kinds of theater, bought instruments and recordings, and visited the Saigon Conservatory of Music, where my language abilities were too limited for effective communication. A one-week leave to Bangkok, Thailand, in January 1970 brought me into contact with Thai music. During a visit to Thailand's TIMland tourist venue, I purchased a long, bamboo mouth–organ instrument called the *khaen* simply because it resembled a pipe organ. I did not know how significant this instrument would become for me later.

After returning to the United States, I enrolled in a Western historical musicology graduate degree program at Indiana University. Despite the program I was in, however, I decided to write my doctoral dissertation on the music of northeast Thailand. With a generous grant in hand, I went with my family to northeast Thailand in late 1972, for a fourteen-month stay during which I researched that region's music. The resulting dissertation completed my Ph.D and luckily I stumbled into a teaching position at Kent State University just as they were starting a graduate program in ethnomusicology. I have been teaching at Kent State since that time.

To make a long story short, I've kept up my interest in Thailand during my tenure at Kent, but my interests have also expanded in other directions. With the help of a succession of "native musician" graduate students, I started two ensembles, one to play traditional Thai music, the other to play Chinese music, and I have played in both since 1979 and

1987 respectively. In 1998 the Thai Ensemble toured Thailand, performing in six cities and on most television channels. The musics of mainland Southeast Asia—Thailand, Laos, Cambodia, Vietnam, Burma, and Malaysia—remain my core interest, with the greatest emphasis being on Thailand and Laos. Readers of this book may notice a certain inclination to cite examples from this region. I also developed a now long-standing interest in orally transmitted hymnody in the West, which has led to extensive and continuing fieldwork in the United States, Scotland, Jamaica, Trinidad, and St. Vincent, the latter three being part of the English-speaking Caribbean. My third area of interest has been Chinese music, and I have done fieldwork in China itself but much more in the overseas Chinese community of Thailand.

Lastly, I have collected material and experienced live music when possible in each country I've visited. In addition to Vietnam, Thailand, and China, these include the United Kingdom, Ireland, France, Germany, Spain, Hungary, Slovakia, Greece, Israel, Nepal, Japan, Korea, and South Africa. In South Africa my wife and I investigated the music of an America-related church. All of these experiences have contributed to my bank of knowledge. Even so, they have exposed me to only a small percentage of the world's musics. The rest have thus far been experienced, if at all, only vicariously through audio and video recordings. Naturally, knowledge gained through first-hand experience goes deeper than that gained from books and CDs, but even an introductory book like this and carefully listened-to recordings can shed some light on a corner of the world that would otherwise remain totally unfamiliar.

Andrew Shahriari

My first recollection of an interest in "world music" is actually associated with a music that I knew quite well. As an undergraduate, I was fortunate to study abroad and to visit Russia on a two-week tour of Moscow and Leningrad (now St. Petersburg—again) in 1990, during the last days of the Soviet Union. My first revelation was that what I had previously believed about Russians was completely untrue: I had been misled all my life into thinking they were evil, American-hating Communists who would sooner spit on me than shake my hand. To the contrary, I found the people I met in Russia to be the most friendly, helpful people in Europe, with a great respect for Americans. My misconceptions were based on ignorance and on the stereotyping of people I hadn't known.

My second revelation came in a Moscow jazz club, where I realized that music can cross cultural barriers as effectively as speech. While music is not a "universal language," it nonetheless generally draws more on emotion than intellect. Music has the uncanny power to enable those who speak the same musical language to "connect" on a different level than is possible with the spoken word. Though conversations I had with Russians fluent in English were friendly, they were mostly superficial exchanges. In contrast, the twenty-minute "jam" my American friends and I played with the jazz club's Russian house band resulted in genuine laughter, bear hugs, and toasts in our honor for the rest of the night—without our ever even learning the names of our comrades. All of us knew we would never meet again, but for that night we were the best of friends because we spoke through music.

My Russian encounter inspired my interest in ethnomusicology and continues to motivate my core concerns as a scholar, educator, and musician. Cultural ignorance is the source of many stereotypes about other peoples. A primary goal of my own study and certainly of my teaching, as well as of this textbook, is to encourage an awareness of our cultural biases. You cannot learn about the world from only the nightly news and cable television. While the United States has "free" media, the stories that get presented are highly selective and strongly biased toward American interests. To think otherwise is naïve. Politics and business influence the content of newspapers, books, television, movies, radio, even the Internet, all of which then shape our attitudes

Co-author Andrew Shahriari (seated at piano) and friends perform in a jazz club with local university students in Moscow, Russia (1989)

about others and ourselves. We cannot avoid being culturally biased, but an awareness of this reality is important to keeping an open mind, which encourages understanding of other perspectives and fosters communication rather than conflict.

By studying world music, I learn about people's passions. I learn what they value, and I learn how they think. Music can reveal the deepest emotions of a people, their philosophies of life, their conceptions of death, their hopes and fears, anger and affections, desires and dreams. Music says what cannot be put into words and often adds to words what cannot be merely spoken. I hope that each person who reads this textbook will approach each site visited with an open mind and appreciate each tradition on its own terms. Remember that appreciation is not necessarily the same thing as enjoyment. Some music is like sugar, sweet to taste and easy to take from the start. Other music is an acquired taste, and may only ever be appreciated at an intellectual level. I myself do not find all music aurally appealing, yet I strive to keep an open mind and accept that all musics (or musical sounds) are worthwhile because they are significant to someone—otherwise they would not exist. If you have read this far, I am certain you will do the same.

The writing of a world music survey is a daunting task, so unrealistic that no human (or even two humans) should try it. But that is the "perfect world" syndrome. It is a fact of life that well-meaning professors are teaching such courses all over the United States and elsewhere and they need textbooks. We have read many excellent suggestions for improvement, and more will surely follow publication. Later editions can be improved, but some of the basic philosophical issues simply cannot be solved. World music survey texts have limitations. To the extent that we have succeeded in creating a useful textbook, we are thankful to our own teachers, informants, and experiences.

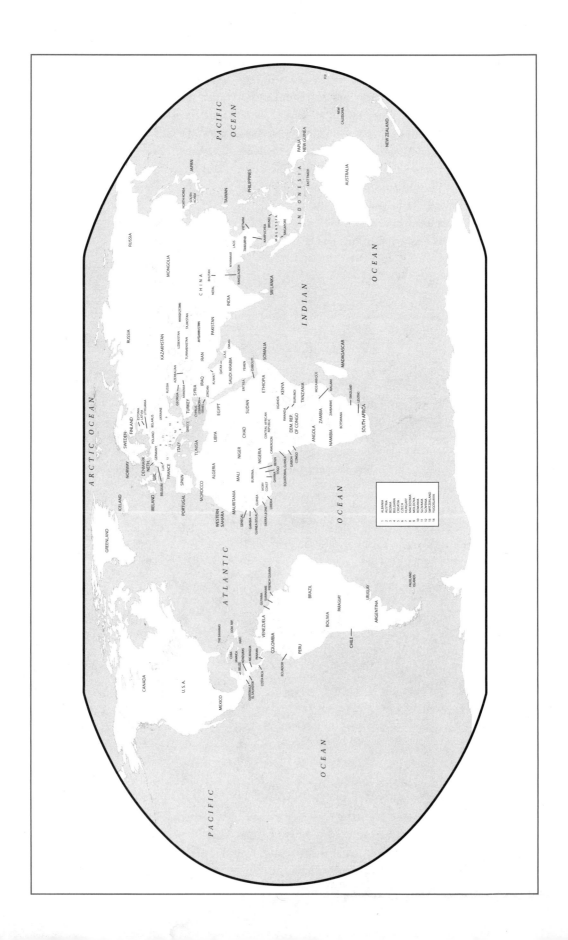

Co-author (TM) playing *yangqin* dulcimer (right) with an unknown musician playing *yeh hu* fiddle (left), Shantou, China (Sara Stone Miller)

CHAPTER 1

Before the Trip Begins: Fundamental Issues

What Is Music?

Although virtually every library includes numerous books on "music," humankind's music is notoriously difficult to describe and discuss. While music is in a literal sense only a kind of sound vibration, it is distinguished from others not considered to be music. This distinction is based not on observable acoustical differences, but on the meanings we assign music. Music is thus a conceptual phenomenon that exists only in the mind; at least that is where the distinctions between "noise" and "music" occur. Graphic representations of music—notations of any sort—are only that, representations. A score is not "the music" because music is a series of sonic vibrations transmitted through the ears to the brain, where we begin the process of making sense of and finding order in these sounds.

We are normally surrounded by sounds—the sounds of nature, the sounds of man's inventions, our own voices—but for most of us most of the time distinguishing "music" from the totality of ambient sounds around us comes "naturally." We recognize "noise" when we hear it; we recognize "music" when we hear it. The difference between the two derives from our lifetime of conditioning. This conditioning is cultural in origin. Our own concept of what distinguishes music from noise is more or less the same as our overall "culture's" concept, since we were raised in an environment that conveyed to us general notions about the distinction between the two. Therefore, definitions of "music" are of necessity culturally determined.

We use the term *music* broadly to include both vocal phenomena and instrumental sounds. But that is not the case for everyone. Many people make a distinction between music and singing; for them, the word *music* refers only to instrumental sounds. Some years ago we wrote to a Primitive Baptist elder (a church leader) in North Carolina regarding that denomination's orally transmitted hymn singing. We asked—naively—"when you sing, do you use music?" The answer was totally logical within the elder's own world: "We don't have any music in our church. All we do is sing." By *music* we meant *notation;* but for the elder music meant *instruments.* The concept of "music" in this book, however, encompasses both instrumental and vocal phenomena.

Within the vocal realm, one of the most intriguing distinctions is that between speech and song. At what point on the speech-song continuum does speech become song? The answers to this question vary widely from place to place. Listeners from one culture may easily misjudge sounds from another culture, by assuming, based on their own experience, that this or that performance is "song" when the people performing consider it other than "song." A general term for such "in-between" phenomena is "heightened speech." One is most likely to have trouble differentiating "speech" and "song" when experiencing the heightened speech of religious and ritual performances, especially those associated with religions that discourage or even ban the performance of "song."

In the Buddhist tradition of Thailand, for example, ordained monks are not permitted to perform song. But if you were to attend a "reading" of the great tale of Prince Wetsandawn, during which a robed monk intones a long poem describing the prince's life before his reincarnation as the Buddha, you would probably, like most Westerners, describe the performance as "singing." After all, the monk performing the story clearly requires considerable vocal talents to negotiate such elaborate strings of pitches. From our perspective this performance sounds convincingly like song. From the monk's perspective, however—indeed, from that of most Thai—what he is performing cannot be song because monks are prohibited from singing. The monk's performance is described by the verb *thet,* which means, "to preach." Why is this performance not song, when it sounds like song to us? Because there is consensus among Thai that it is not song but rather is preaching. Thus, chanted poetry is simultaneously "music" from our perspective and definitely "not music" from that of the performer. Neither perspective is right or wrong in a universal sense; rather, each is "correct" according to respective cultural norms.

Thai Buddhist monks chant in an afternoon service, Roi-et, Thailand

Music: Universal Language or Culturally Specific Activity?

It is frequently asserted that "music is a universal [or international] language," a "meta-language" that expresses universal human emotions and transcends the barriers of language and culture.

The problems with this analogy are many. First, music is not a language, at least not in the sense of conveying specific meanings through specific symbols, in standard patterns analogous to syntax, and governed by rules of structure analogous to grammar. While attempts have been made to analyze music in linguistic terms, these ultimately fail because music is of a totally different realm than language. Second, it is questionable whether music really can transcend linguistic barriers and culturally determined behaviors, through some form of emotional communication so fundamentally human that all respond the same way. What we have seen does not support this idea, unfortunately, and we do not believe such a concept to be useful in examining the world's musics.

As will become increasingly clear as you begin your exploration of the world's vast array of musics, musical expression is both culturally determined and culturally encoded with meaning. The field of *semiotics,* which deals with signs—systems of symbols and their meanings—offers an explanation of how music works. Although semiotics was not created specifically for music, it has been adapted by Canadian scholar Jean-Jacques Nattiez and others for this purpose.

SEMIOTICS
The study of "signs" and systems of signs, including in music.

A semiotic view of music asserts that the musical sound itself is a "neutral" symbol that has no inherent meaning. Music is thus thought of as a "text" or "trace" that has to be interpreted. In a process called the *poietic,* the creator of the music encodes meanings and emotions into the "neutral" composition or performance, which is then interpreted by anyone listening to the music, a process called the *esthesic.* Each individual listener's interpretation is entirely the result of cultural conditioning and life experience. When a group of people sharing similar backgrounds encounters a work or performance of music, there is the possibility that all (or most) will interpret what they hear similarly—but it is also possible that there will be as many interpretations as there are hearers. In short, meaning is not passed from the creator through the music to the hearer. Instead, the hearer applies an interpretation that is independent of the creator. However, when both creator and hearer share similar backgrounds, there is a greater likelihood that the hearer's interpretation will be consistent with the creator's intended meaning.

Obviously, then, when the creator and listener are from completely different backgrounds, miscommunication is almost inevitable. When, for example, an Indian musician performs what is called a *raga,* he or she is aware of certain emotional feelings or meanings associated with that raga. An audience of Europeans with little knowledge of Indian music or culture must necessarily interpret the music according to their own experience and by the norms of their society's music. They are unlikely to hear things as an Indian audience would, being unaware of culturally determined associations between, say, specific ragas and particular times of the day. Such miscommunication inevitably contributes to the problem of *ethnocentrism:* the assumption that one's own cultural patterns are normative and that those that differ are "strange," "exotic," or "abnormal."

Whenever we encounter something new, we subconsciously compare it with all our previous experiences. We are strongly inclined to associate each new experience with the most similar thing we have encountered previously. People with a narrow range of life experience have less data in their memory bank, and when something is truly new, none of us has any direct way to compare it to a known experience. Misunderstandings easily occur at this point. We attempt to rationalize the unfamiliar in terms of our own experience, and "assume" the unknown is consistent with what we already know. Even if a newly encountered music sounds like something we know, we cannot be sure it is similar in any way. Sometimes a lullaby from another culture may sound like a war chant in our culture. Knowing about this potential pitfall is the first step in avoiding the trapdoor of ethnocentrism.

ETHNOCENTRISM

The unconscious assumption that one's own cultural background is "normal," while others are "strange" or "exotic."

Beware of Labels

The German philosopher Ludwig Wittgenstein (1889–1951) famously warned that labels "terminate thinking." But because world music is such a vast subject, it must be broken down into manageable subcategories, which are labeled for the purpose of identification. While such labels are useful, they can also mislead. In teaching the musics of the world it is often tempting to use labels as shorthand. Unfortunately, not everyone understands their meanings and limitations; furthermore, these labels are employed in a variety of ways depending on the user's background. Thus, while we prefer not to employ such labels here, we recognize that they *are* difficult to avoid. When we do use them, we will attempt to limit them to particular circumstances.

Anyone who aspires to write a music survey, especially one covering the entire planet, cannot avoid being caught on the horns of the label/generalization dilemma. On the one hand, we recognize the problems inherent in such labels, the danger of stereotyping, the inevitability of making over-generalized statements. At the other end of the spectrum, phenomenology allows no possibility for generalizations, emphasizing the individuality of each experience. It would be difficult for any course or textbook that attempts to survey the world's musics to avoid drawing a larger picture, to see individual things as part of a bigger whole. Recognizing the dangers of labels and generalizations, we still see no way around many of them. In attempting to make sense of a broad area, we sometimes resort to overarching ideas, and we do accept that some of these amount to a kind of stereotyping.

Terms that can cause trouble when studying the musics of the world include *folk, traditional, classical, art, popular,* and *neotraditional.* For example, the term *folk* (from the German *volk)* carries with it a set of meanings and attitudes derived from the Romantic movement in literature, which flourished in Europe during the late eighteenth and early nineteenth centuries. During this period German scholars, in particular, sought to explore their own culture's roots in opposition to the dominant "classical" culture imported from France and Italy. Romanticism championed the common people over the elite, and in the early nineteenth century writers such as the Grimm brothers and the pair Arnim von Achim and Clemens Brentano began collecting stories and song texts from the "peasants," whose wisdom was seen as equal to that of learned scholars. Folktales, folksongs, and ballads were collected and published, and composers such as Franz Joseph Haydn, Carl Friedrich Zelter, Johann Rudolf Zumsteeg, and Franz Schubert sometimes set these texts to music as folk-like "art songs." What this means is that the term *folk music* carries with it a lot of nineteenth-century European baggage that can clutter our thinking when it is applied to other musics.

Folk, classical, and *popular* are the trio of words most commonly used to categorize and distinguish among various types of music. Defining them individually is one issue; taken together they are problematic because they assert a hierarchical value system in which *classical* is typically considered highest, *folk* of a much lower value, and *popular* at the lowest level. We would much prefer to have value-neutral terms with universally applicable definitions, but this is a difficult, if not impossible, goal within any single language. However, when the terms *folk, classical,* and *popular* are used in this text, they are meant to represent points on various kinds of continua, rather than distinct categories.

The term *classical* has several meanings, and thus carries with it the potential for confusion. It may suggest connection with or influence from the styles of ancient Greece and Rome, though this usage is rarely associated with music. It also denotes a revered model or the epitome of a style or type. Thus we describe a 1956 Thunderbird as a "classic" car or certain films as "classics." In a sense many of the so-called classical musics of the world, be they European, Arabic, or Asian, conform to this second definition. A third definition, however, suggests value: it identifies *classical* as the highest form, the best. Such a usage, particularly with reference to European "classical music," implies a problematical belief in a canon of "great works" created by a pantheon of "great" composers—

An Inside Look

Gerhard Kubik

I became a scientist at age nine. My first exercise in data gathering was the documentation of the allied air raids on Vienna in World War II. I began to write my war diary when I was exactly eight and three-quarters years old, on August 13, 1943, under the impression of the devastating air raid on Wiener Neustadt, a small town south of Vienna. I completed my little book on April 15, 1945, just after the Russian Army had occupied the city.

In 1947, when I was thirteen, I took the next step: I wrote a novel called *Im Schloss* (In the Castle) exploring my adventures with a youth gang. A year later I embarked on writing my second novel, with its plot set in China. Those original manuscripts are preserved.

Gerhard Kubik with his nephew.

Music did not yet play a significant role in my life. But when it began to do so, it was jazz. By 1948 I was addicted to Lionel Hampton, Woody Herman's "Four Brothers," Cab Calloway, Glenn Miller, and then, in 1952, I fell in love with Charlie Parker, Dizzy Gillespie, Stan Getz, Gerry Mulligan, "Bop" and "Cool." Around 1951 I began to take lessons on the clarinet. Intellectually, I was attracted to Sigmund Freud, Ludwig Klages, the poetry of Arthur Rimbaud (in French) and, somewhat later, Stefan Zweig, Arthur Schopenhauer, and George Orwell.

After completing high school in 1953, I became a professional jazz musician. My band won the First Prize at the 1959 Jazz Festival in Vienna. But then it dissolved

a belief that has led to charges of cultural domination by "dead, white, European males." Finally, for commercial purposes and in the minds of many non-musicians, the word *classical* is used to refer to anything orchestral, even soundtracks and Broadway shows.

Perhaps the words *folk, classical,* and *popular* would be more useful if defined in economic terms. *Classical,* in that case, would denote music created in contexts where there is enough surplus wealth to release musicians from the necessity of providing their own food and shelter, so that they may

Gypsy musicians perform for visitors to the Ⓒ Great Plain near Bugac, Hungary

and I set out on my first long trip to Africa, walking and hitchhiking from Europe. It took one year from October 1959 to October 1960, and I passed through twelve African countries. Studying the court music in the Kingdom of Buganda, East Africa, I made some discoveries in the field of audiopsychology, e.g., the perceptual phenomenon I termed "inherent patterns" or I.P. effect. That is how I became known in the field of ethnomusicology. After many other long field trips, I completed university studies in 1971 with a Ph.D. in Cultural Anthropology (Ethnology). My dissertation was on the mukanda boys' initiation schools I had studied in eastern Angola in 1965.

In 1972 I was back to jazz, playing *kwela,* a South African jazz derivative in the band of Daniel and Donald Kachamoa of Malawi. During the 1970s we toured no less than 33 countries of the world with our music: in Africa, Europe, and South America. My first visit to the United States was in 1977, thanks to an invitation by blues researcher David Evans to speak on his panel at the Musicology Congress in Berkeley, California.

Ever since the 1960s I have spent about half a year's time on fieldwork in Africa or elsewhere, and the other half in Europe, writing up my notes and teaching. I have written many books on anthropological, ethnomusicological, and ethnopsychological topics, and published extensively in scholarly magazines. One of my recent works is *Africa and the Blues,* published in 1999 by the University of Mississippi Press in Jackson. You might like to study it or see my video, *African Guitar,* released in 1995 by Stefan Grossman's Guitar Workshop in New Jersey.

spend their lives practicing their art and thinking up increasingly complex and technically challenging ways of creating and performing music. Competent performances of classical music produced under these conditions generally require specialized training and years of practice. *Folk* might denote music created and performed by people of modest means whose main occupation leaves limited time for practice and whose limited income leaves little money for expensive instruments. Such music is usually simpler in process and technically less demanding because its practitioners cannot devote the time and energy to it that classical musicians devote to their type of music. As such, folk music usually requires less rehearsal to be performed proficiently and is usually learned through observation, recordings, and informal instruction.

Popular, a term that also means many things to different people, would, in economic terms, denote music that is widely disseminated by various types of media and supported by a broad base of relatively casual consumers, whose purchases make possible productions of spectacular proportions. Popular music, therefore, needs to appeal to a broad spectrum of the population to achieve financial success. Critics of popular music may see it as merely reflecting current fashions in music, but we should remember that popular music, like all music, has the potential to be politically challenging when the sentiments expressed oppose the status quo or unifying when the words express widely held feelings.

Our discussion has to this point avoided the term *traditional*. Music that is spoken of as "traditional" is often contrasted with the individually innovative music of European classicism. It is also frequently contrasted with popular music or modernized music and is therefore considered synonymous with "folk." Traditional music is assumed to change little over time, and to thereby preserve values long held by the community. Although the implication is that a special characteristic of "traditional" music is its emphasis on continuity over innovation, a great deal of music otherwise labeled as "classical" or "popular" is equally conservative or continuous in style. However, while we admit there are numerous problems with the term *traditional,* we doubt that any text on world musics can avoid its use entirely. At the very least, it can be said to be a more descriptive and less value-laden term than *folk.*

Knowing the World's Musics

What can we know about the world's musics and how do we obtain this knowledge? These are basic questions in the field of ethnomusicology, but there is rarely a single answer to any question. If music is a part of the culture that produces it, and both the makers and hearers of the music share similar lifetimes of experience that give the music meaning, then how can we as outsiders experience this music?

Obviously, upon first encounter with new sounds, our own personal life experience is all we have to draw on and the ethnocentrism we referred to earlier may take over. The sound quality of an unfamiliar instrument may seem "grating" to someone whose experience has been limited to Western orchestral instruments, or a singer may sound unpleasantly nasal compared to vocalists trained in a Western conservatory. One of the assumptions of those who study the musics of the world is that, with additional knowledge, we can gradually overcome our ethnocentrism and accept each music on its own terms. This is each individual student's challenge.

While several fields of scholarship have included music as part of their purview, including anthropology, sociology, and folklore, the main field devoted to world musics is *ethnomusicology*. In its earlier days, at the end of the nineteenth century, the field was called Comparative Musicology, or in German, *Vergleichende Musikwissenschaft*. At the time, many European colonial powers sent researchers to their growing empires to gather materials for what became the great ethnographic museums of Europe. Early ethnomusicologists worked in these museums and in archives, using as their primary source materials recordings and other artifacts brought back from the "field" by collectors. Sometimes, however, scholars were able to work directly with foreign musicians on tour, such as when Germans Carl Stumpf and Erich Moritz von Hornbostel recorded Siamese musicians in Berlin in 1900 for the Phonogrammarchiv, the first international archive of recordings.

Early ethnomusicologists focused on description and classification, using the rapidly accumulating materials found in European museums. Germans Curt Sachs and Erich M. von Hornbostel, for example, using earlier models, evolved a comprehensive system for classifying musical instruments based on *what* vibrates to make musical sound. (This system will be discussed in Chapter 2.) Scholars throughout Europe transcribed recorded music into notation and attempted classifications based on genre, scale, and other observable characteristics. This was the era of the "armchair" scholar who practiced the "science" *(Wissenschaft)* of music.

Over time scholars began doing their own fieldwork during which they recorded music in the field on cylinder, disc, wire, and later magnetic acetate tape. Many of these scholars thought of themselves as ethnographers or anthropologists. Among the greatest of these was an American woman, Frances Densmore (1867–1957), who, working directly with Native American singers and instrumentalists, wrote fifteen books and numerous articles, and released seven commercial recordings, mostly through the Smithsonian Institution in Washington, D.C.

American ethnomusicology began changing dramatically in the 1960s, especially because of five men and the academic programs they influenced. Alan Merriam (1923–1980)—of Indiana University's Department of Anthropology—published in 1964 *The Anthropology of Music,* one of the most influential books ever written on the subject, in which he defined ethnomusicology as "the study of music in culture." Unlike the older school of Europeans who viewed music as sounds to be analyzed apart from their cultural context, Merriam saw music as a human behavior. Similarly, British anthropologist John Blacking

ETHNOMUSICOLOGY

The scholarly study of any music within its contemporary cultural context.

FOLKLORE

The study of orally transmitted folk knowledge and culture.

FIELDWORK

The first-hand study of music in its original context, a technique derived from anthropology.

Frances Densmore recording a Piegan Indian c. 1916 (Library of Congress)

(1928–1990) has defined music as "humanly organized sound." Ki Mantle Hood (b. 1918), originally a composer, provided a musicological alternative at the University of California, Los Angeles's Institute of Ethnomusicology, by emphasizing what he calls *bi-musicality*. In this approach researchers combine learning to play the music under study with field observation. David Park McAllester (b. 1916) and others at Wesleyan University in Middletown, Connecticut, created a program in "world musics" that emphasized performance and composition taught by masters of musical traditions from around the world, especially India, Africa, and Indonesia. Finally, Bruno Nettl (b. 1930), both through his teaching at the University of Illinois and his numerous publications, has influenced the course of ethnomusicology over the last fifty years, and continues to help guide this field through a period of increasing diversification. For many, Nettl and his work represent both common sense and the mainstream of the profession.

Thus, ethnomusicology has long been pulled in two directions, the anthropological and the musicological, the first centering on the study of human behavior and cultural context, the second emphasizing the sonic artifacts of human music-making. Regardless of orientation, however, most ethnomusicology programs are found in college and university departments of music. Typical programs include courses for non-majors, especially world music surveys, and more specialized courses on both broad and specific areas of the world as well as courses in research methodology. In many cases the opportunity to play in world music performance ensembles is offered as well.

Ethnomusicology today, however, has been much influenced by the new ways of thinking generally subsumed under the heading *postmodernism.* A reaction against *modernism* or *positivism,* in which the establishment of "truth" is based on verifiable "facts," postmodernism de-emphasizes description and the search for absolute truth in favor of interpretation and the acceptance of the relativity of truth. A great variety of intellectual approaches, mostly borrowed from other disciplines, offer ethnomusicologists new ways to interpret the meaning of music. These include gender studies and feminist theories; Marxist interpretations; semiotic approaches; attention to such issues as identity, postcolonialism, and the political ramifications of music; and, especially, popular music studies. The latter has risen rapidly since about 1980 under the influence of the "Manchester School" in England, and is associated with the term *cultural studies,* which denotes several postmodern theoretical approaches used to interpret popular culture. The study of popular music, however, has recently led to an apparent decrease of interest in fieldwork and a parallel de-emphasis of the techniques that are appropriate to the study of "traditional" music, because popular musics are more easily studied through the media than are traditional musics.

The Life of an Ethnomusicologist

What do ethnomusicologists actually do? How do they learn about the world's musics? We view the process as having four basic phases: 1) preparation, 2) fieldwork, 3) analysis, and 4) dissemination. Before going to the field, whether it be an obscure nation in Central Asia, a region of Indonesia, or a nearby town, ethnomusicologists must *prepare* themselves by learning everything they can about that area, the kinds of music they will encounter, and the conditions under which they will do their study. This is best accomplished through library, media, and Internet resources and through interaction with others who know the area, especially people who grew up there or perhaps still live there. In many cases researchers must spend years studying the language of their area, which often is one that is rarely taught. Well-prepared field researchers will need not only a good deal of expensive recording equipment but the wits and maturity to deal with all sorts of unexpected situations, some technical, some social.

Besides doing research, ethnomusicologists must also live and eat, and the latter requirement may present great challenges when unfamiliar food is on the menu. In doing research they may need to create professional documents through still photography, videography, audio recording, interviews, and participation in various rituals, festivals, and other events. A detailed journal becomes important, not to mention the logs that retain the details of recordings and photographs. The *field phase* can last anywhere from a few weeks to several years. Based on experience, we can say that the longer one stays in the field, the more one will know but the less one will understand. This apparent irony stems from the increasing perception of complexity that accompanies prolonged exposure to any culture: the more you experience, the more you realize how much more there is to learn. Firsthand experience teaches us that all cultures are deep and complex, and that understanding a music is far more demanding than simply collecting it.

What do ethnomusicologists do with the material and knowledge they acquire? It is a standing joke among ethnomusicologists that they spend thousands of dollars and six months of their lives, braving tough weather and strange foods, to bring back a few videotapes that they look at only once. The material collected in the field is considered "raw." After it is collected, ethnomusicologists must find ways to *interpret* and *disseminate* what they have learned. This is done primarily through teaching, writing and reading "papers" at professional meetings, writing books and journal articles, and, perhaps, compiling CDs, videotapes, or DVDs for commercial release. As they acquire expertise in an area, they may be called upon to referee articles submitted to journals, write reviews of books and CDs, or serve on panels for public arts organizations. Most ethnomusicologists work as professors in colleges and universities, but some hold positions in publicly funded agencies such as the National Endowment for the Arts, while others work for museums, community programs, and art centers. A few work as freelance scholars and musicians. Few can afford to be just ethnomusicologists—that is, researchers—full time. Most spend the majority of their time doing other kinds of work.

Co-author (AS) blessed by a spirit dancer in northern Thailand (Christina Shahriari)

Representation:
What Musics Does One Study?

A survey course on the musics of the world presents a challenge far different from that presented by a course covering the classical musics of Europe. In the latter case there is a rough consensus on who the "great composers" are and what the "great works" are. These make up what is called a *canon*—that is, a foundation list of core composers and works that every music student should know. World music courses have no such canon, and certainly no list of great composers. The world is too large and there are too many choices for much consensus to form. Therefore one must consider not only how to organize such a course but what to include. What should every world music student know? If the organization is geographical, what genres and particular examples should "represent" a country or culture? Our choices reveal our biases and assumptions about what constitutes the music of a given place. Some might choose to emphasize contemporary culture, by including a greater proportion of urban-based popular musics than of "traditional" ones. Others would argue that the essence of a culture is in its traditional music. There is no way to resolve these questions except by agreeing that any world music course is only the beginning, the first few steps of a learning journey that can last a lifetime. In a way, it does not matter *how* one begins as much as it matters that one *actually* begins.

Resources for the Study of the World's Musics

Today's students are fortunate to live in a time when resources for the study of world musics are growing exponentially. The proliferation of publications, both print and recorded, has been astounding. We suggest the following as likely the most comprehensive and readily available resources for further study.

Reference works. Two major reference works have recently appeared. The first of these is the ten-volume *Garland Encyclopedia of World Music,* nine volumes of which cover geographically defined areas of the world, with the tenth volume being a compilation of resources. Each volume is between 1,000 and 1,500 pages and includes both general and specific articles, hundreds of photos and musical examples, a CD, and an extensive list of bibliographic and recorded resources. The second major reference work is *The New Grove Dictionary of Music and Musicians,* 2nd edition, in twenty-nine volumes. This offers extensive coverage of the world's musics, primarily through articles on specific countries. Also worth consulting is the two-volume edition of *World Music: The Rough Guide,* which includes articles on musics throughout the world, often with emphasis on popular styles. While the Garland and Grove series were both written by specialists, most Rough Guide articles were written by nonspecialists for a more general audience.

Video. The variety of world musics on video is growing rapidly. Two collections deserve special mention. First is the *JVC Anthology of the World's Music and Dance,* a series of video clips with accompanying booklets. One drawback of this collection is that it consists in large part of preexisting and readily available footage, which means that for some areas the coverage is uneven and unrepresentative. Also worth mentioning is the *Beats of the Heart* documentary series produced by Jeremy Marre for the world music label Shanachie.

Compact Discs. A great variety of companies in the United States, Europe, and Japan produce commercial CDs available in the United States. Unfortunately, the majority of them are produced by nonspecialists, and therefore the information provided in liner notes must be approached with caution. What is perhaps the most significant series of recordings was originally released on Moses Asch's old Folkways label, and is now being reissued on CD in expanded form by Smithsonian-Folkways in Washington, D.C. Other important series have been produced by Lyrichord, Nonesuch, World Music Library, Pan, Rounder, Multicultural Media, and many other record companies both in the United States and Europe.

Journals. Most journals are produced by scholarly societies, and therefore the articles in them tend to be specialized, and at times obscure. Serious students, however, can gain much from such material. The most significant journals to consider include *Ethnomusicology, Yearbook for Traditional Music, American Music, Asian Music, Journal of African Music, Ethnomusicology Forum, The World of Music, The Journal of Popular Culture,* and a variety of other journals dedicated to specific areas of the world, such as *Chime* (focused on China).

Questions to Consider

1. What do ethnomusicologists mean when they say, "Music is universal, but it is not a universal language"?

2. What are the potential problems in classifying music as "classical," "folk," or "popular"?

3. How might an ethnomusicologist approach the study of Western classical music differently from a musicologist?

4. What is "fieldwork"? What is its importance to the study of world music?

5. In what ways does world music study require an interdisciplinary approach?

6. What is ethnocentrism? Have you ever experienced it?

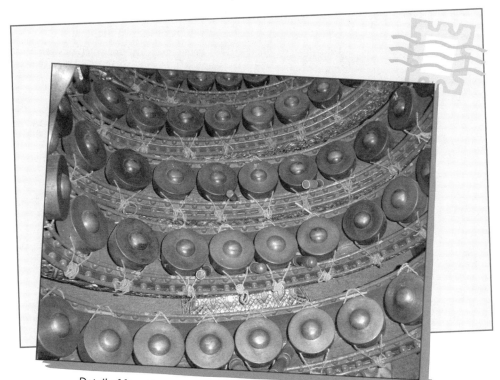

Detail of four *khong mon* (bossed gong circles) from Thailand

CHAPTER 2

Aural Analysis:
Listening to the World's Music

How to Listen to World Music

The primary objective of this book is to expose you to some musical traditions from several cultures around the globe. Learning something about the music of other people is like gaining a window into another world and is a chance to explore the creative power of humanity. The ability to recognize various musical traditions and express some knowledge about them is a good start toward crossing the cultural boundaries that often divide us. This book is not only world music; it is about people and cultures as well.

Some music traditions are easy to recognize, whereas others require you to develop a systematic method for identifying what you hear. Each person's method will undoubtedly be different, but here are some initial suggestions as to how to listen to unfamiliar world music:

- Begin by listening to the music examples included with this text before reading any of the material.
- Remember your initial gut feeling. Often times your first impression of a musical sound helps you remember that sound in the future. Is the music familiar sounding or completely alien? Do you like it or does it make you want to skip to the next track? Does the music seem busy, cold, happy, relaxing, heavy? Does it sound like rain, whale calls, a screeching owl, a music box? Any image you can use later to help you recognize the music will be helpful.
- Make the music samples part of your daily life, even if you don't like every example. Many new musical sounds require you to develop a taste for them before they can be appreciated. Listen in your car, before you go to bed, or while exercising, walking the dog, cooking, and so on.
- Use the book to help you better understand the form and intent of each example. It is necessary to read each chapter to connect what you hear with what you know. If you don't know anything about the type of music you're listening to, what you hear won't mean much. You may enjoy the music, but you can't fully appreciate it unless you understand what's happening and why.
- You'll know you are "familiar" with a particular musical example when you can recognize it after just a few seconds of listening, and answer "yes" to the following questions: Do you know which country the example comes from? Can you visualize the instruments, imitate the sound of the music, and anticipate changes in rhythm? Immediately knowing in what contexts the music is performed, or with which religion it is associated, is also an indication that you are becoming familiar with the tradition it represents.
- Don't limit yourself to the musical examples provided with this text. Find other recordings of the same types of music and compare them with the given ones. Identify the commonalities in musical sound so that you're able to recognize the tradition, not just the example.

Remember, music is universal, but it is not a universal language. Understanding world music requires an open mind and a willingness to acknowledge that other perspectives, ideas, and attitudes are equally as valid as your own. Our world is "smaller" than it has ever been in history. You will undoubtedly meet people from many of the places discussed in this book. Knowing something about their music can help you communicate with them, and may lead to cultural experiences you would never have anticipated. So, listen with your mind and your emotions, as well as your ears.

"Talking" about Music

Every discipline, be it physics, economics, or art, has its own jargon, a vocabulary that must be learned. Music is no exception. Because music is conceptual, its components require names in order for discussion to occur. Music terms such as *melody* and *rhythm* are familiar to most readers, musician and nonmusician alike. Other terms, such as *heterophony, idiophone,* or *rhythmic density* usually require some explanation. This chapter seeks to put all readers on an equal footing by explaining basic music concepts, as well as introducing certain terms peculiar to the discipline of ethnomusicology.

A musical sound has four basic components: timbre, pitch, duration, and dynamics. *Timbre,* or the quality of a musical sound, is inherently linked to a *medium*—that is, to the object or person producing the sound. *Pitch* is most often expressed as a frequency, such as A = 440 Hertz (Hz). Your ear recognizes discrete pitches based on their specific frequencies. *Rhythm* depends on durations of sounds, which are often organized into regular patterns. Finally, *dynamics* denotes the volume, or relative loudness or softness, of a sound, and can be measured in decibels (dBs).

Timbre and Medium

The easiest way to learn to recognize a world music tradition is to become familiar with its media—that is, with the sounds of its typical instruments and vocal styles. In order to identify a specific medium, we must first become familiar with its characteristic timbre or "color." Most terms used to describe timbre are based on analogies between musical sound and everyday physical and sensory experience. Terms such as *nasal, dark, mellow, strained, rough, soothing,* and so on, are highly subjective when applied to music, but are nevertheless helpful in describing "aural color."

Just as we distinguish visually between red, blue, and green, so too we distinguish between different aural "colors"—that is, between the characteristic timbral qualities that define the sounds of, say, the trumpet, the violin, and the flute. (Compare CD I, track 1 and CD II tracks 25 and 36.) In the case of "visual color," determining the differences among red, yellow, and green is fairly easy. In order to differentiate between evergreen, lime, and emerald, however, one must possess a sharper eye. Similarly, while it may be easy to hear the difference between a violin and a trumpet, learning to distinguish among the similar sounds of a banjo, koto, and sitar may take some time even for an attentive listener. (Compare CD I, tracks 5 and 16.) Fortunately, in addition to timbre there are other elements that can help you identify what you are hearing: such as pitch, rhythm, dynamics, style, and various extramusical factors.

When listening to an example of an unfamiliar music tradition for the first time, you must first determine whether you hear voices, instruments, or a combination of both. (Compare CD II tracks 15, 27, and 31.) The next step is to identify how many voices or instruments you hear. Either you will hear a soloist or an ensemble. (Compare CD I,

MEDIUM
The source of a sound, be it instrument or voice.

TIMBRE
The tone quality or "color" of a musical sound.

tracks 16 and 17.) If what you hear is an ensemble, determine whether it is a small group, such as an instrumental trio or vocal duet, or a large ensemble, such as an orchestra or choir. (Compare CD II, track 1 and CD I, track 31.) The larger the ensemble, the more difficult it will be to distinguish specific media. However, this very difficulty may help you hear the ensemble as a whole rather than as individual performers. Once you have determined roughly how many performers there are, the next step is to try to identify each medium specifically.

Vocal Timbre

In the case of voices, you should be able to distinguish between male and female voices fairly easily, primarily based on their ranges.

An Inside Look
Bruno Nettl

Dr. Bruno Nettl, Professor Emeritus, University of Illinois

I got into ethnomusicology in the most conventional way—by taking an elective course in 1949 at Indiana University—in one of the very few schools offering such courses. I think what turned me on to this field was the immense variety of musical sounds produced by the world's cultures; and the many different kinds of ideas about music—what it is and what it can do—that one finds in the world. I began by studying the music of Native American societies, particularly of the Northern Plains, and then went on years later to do fieldwork in Iran, and eventually found my way to India, all the while teaching undergraduates and graduates at the University of Illinois in Urbana. I've been in this profession for a half century and so have had, over the years, to change my mind about many things, and to learn new ways of studying and doing research.

Today's younger students can hardly believe the kinds of technology we had (or didn't have) in the 1950s. But I think I can identify three questions that have motivated me all these years. They are related, as you'll see. About the musics of the world, I keep wondering what it is that causes a society to have, or maybe to select, a particular kind of music for itself. Why does Native American music sound as it does? Why is the music of Iran so different from the music of Japan? When it comes to doing research, I've been concerned with understanding the differences between the ways the people in a society perceive their music, and the cultural outsider's perspective, and ways to reconcile the inevitable differences. As a teacher, I've been particularly concerned with finding ways for helping students of Western, mainly classical, music to see this music in the context of a world of musics, trying to understand why it developed the way it did, learning to value it as an expression of its culture while learning to appreciate and comprehend the world of musical sounds and musical cultures.

(Compare CD II, tracks 11 and 19.) While range is a concept related to pitch, voices can also have timbral qualities that will help you to identify what you hear. Certain traditions feature distinctive vocal timbres that make them as easily distinguishable from other traditions as bluegrass is from European opera.

Instrumental Timbre

In the case of instruments, timbre is closely related to instrument construction. The study of musical instruments is known as *organology*. Essential to organological study is the classification of instruments. In the European art music tradition, instruments are classified into five basic categories: strings, wind, brass, percussion, and keyboards. This system, however, does not work well when applied to the rest of the world's musical instruments.

In the field of ethnomusicology, the *Sachs-Hornbostel* system, created by German musicologists Curt Sachs and Eric M. von Hornbostel, is the dominant system used to describe and classify instruments. The four primary categories are *aerophones, chordophones, idiophones,* and *membranophones; electrophones* have become a fifth category. An instrument is classified according to what part of the instrument vibrates to produce the sound. Within each of these primary categories are several subcategories. Knowledge of only the more common subcategories is usually enough to help you perceive the timbre of a musical instrument. The more discretely you can subcategorize an instrument's construction, however, the more accurately you will understand how the construction affects the unique timbre of the instrument.

SACHS-HORNBOSTEL SYSTEM
Standard classification system for musical instruments created by Curt Sachs and Erik M. von Hornbostel.

ORGANOLOGY
The study of musical instruments.

AEROPHONE
Instruments that require air to produce sound—namely, flutes, reeds, trumpets, and bellows-driven instruments.

CHORDOPHONE
Four types of stringed instruments: lutes, zithers, harps, lyres.

Aerophones: Flutes, Reeds, and Trumpets

Aerophones are defined as those instruments that produce sound through the direct vibration of air, rather than through the vibration of air by another medium such as a string or membrane. Aerophones are typically divided into three categories: *flute, reed,* and *trumpet* instruments. Flutes are defined as instruments in which a column of air is split on an edge. (Listen to CD II, track 36.) Reed instruments have one or two small pieces of material, such as cane, bamboo, or metal, that vibrate when air is blown over or through them. (Listen to CD II, track 9.) Trumpets require the performer to vibrate the lips, rather than a reed, as they blow air into the instrument. (Listen to CD I, track 24.) Recognition of the characteristic timbre of flutes, reeds, and trumpets is an important first step toward becoming a discriminating listener. Keep

A Japanese *noh kan* horizontal flute

in mind, however, that these terms refer to general categories, not specific instruments such as the European ("silver") flute or brass trumpet.

Double-reed aerophone *(pi)* from Thailand

Chordophones: Lutes and Zithers

Chordophones are defined as having one or more strings stretched between two points. Sound is produced when a string vibrates. There are many chordophones in the world of music, but two basic types, *lutes* and *zithers,* comprise the majority. The relative size of the resonating body is the key feature that distinguishes a lute from a zither. The strings of a zither are stretched parallel to the entire sounding board, as with a piano. Thus the whole instrument acts as a resonator. (Listen to CD I, track 27.) In addition to a resonating body, a lute has a neck, which allows a performer to vary the acoustical length of a string to produce different pitches, as with a guitar. Because its neck does not act as a resonator, a lute generally has less resonance than a zither of the same size and its sound dissipates more quickly. (Listen to CD II, track 32.)

The most common zithers are either

The *ntahera* ivory horn ensemble of the Asantehene, Kumase, Ghana
(Joseph S. Kaminski)

The Finnish *kantele* zither

hammered, as with the piano, or plucked, as with the Japanese *koto,* while lutes are generally either plucked, as with a guitar, or bowed, as with a violin. A hammered zither tends to have a more reverberant sound timbre than other types of chordophones. The resonance of a plucked lute will die away almost immediately as the vibration amplification of each note diminishes. (Listen to CD I, track 26.) The sounds of a plucked lute or zither are further distinguishable by whether a plectrum or a finger plucks the string.

FRET

A bar or ridge found on chordophones that enables performers to produce different melodic pitches with consistent frequency levels.

IDIOPHONE

Instruments that themselves vibrate to produce sound, such as rattles, bells, and various other kinds of percussion.

MEMBRANOPHONE

Instruments, such as drums, that use a vibrating stretched membrane as the principle means of sound production.

The string vibration of a bowed lute is continuous for as long as the bow is pulled across the string; thus, the sound does not immediately fade until the bowing stops. (Listen to CD II, track 25.)

In addition to being plucked or bowed, lutes are either *fretted* or *fretless.* A fret is a straight bar of wood, bamboo, or metal placed on the neck of a lute so that it runs perpendicular to the direction of the strings, as seen on a guitar. This enables an exact pitch to be played each time the performer presses the string against the fret. A fretless lute allows the performer to slide the finger between pitches, potentially sounding all of the frequencies between two distinct tones. (Listen to CD I, track 5.) Fretted lutes are more likely to be plucked than fretless lutes, which are more frequently bowed. This is due to the fact that plucked lutes sound tones of short duration, while bowed lutes can sustain longer tones.

Based on their construction, other major chordophones fall into the *lyre* and *harp* categories. The strings of lyres

The Turkish *tanbur* lute

and harps are suspended by an open frame and are most often plucked. The string plane of a harp, in particular, runs perpendicular to the

L to r: Fretless lute *(sarod)* and fretted lute *(sitar)*
from India

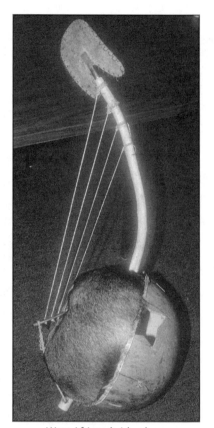

West African bridge harp

Ethiopian Lyre

resonating body. The timbre of lyres and harps is generally difficult to distinguish from that of lutes and zithers, though visually the construction is quite distinct.

Idiophones: Plucked, Struck, and Shaken

Idiophones are defined as those instruments that produce sound through the instrument itself vibrating *(idio* meaning "itself"). A good sound can be easily produced on most idiophones. Practically anything can be considered an idiophone, from bottles, to slamming doors, to change in your pocket. Bells, rattles, and a variety of other percussion instruments are common idiophones in a musical context. Most idiophones fall into one of three categories: *plucked, struck,* or *shaken.*

Small, plucked idiophones are often a type of *lamellophone,* meaning that they have a *lamella* (tongue or prong) that is flexed, and then released, causing a brief sound before the vibrations of the *lamella* come to rest. (Listen to CD II, track 1.) The music box, with its prongs, or keys, is probably the most familiar example of a *lamellophone.*

Struck idiophones comprise the most varied category and include gongs, bells, wood blocks, and just about anything else that can be struck. (Listen to CD I, track 9.) The great many timbres associated with such instruments are not easily generalized, though the sharp initial attack of the sound is a typical feature. Shaken idiophones are most often rattles. (Listen to CD II, track 1.) Most rattles have a hollowed center that

Three lamellophones from sub-Saharan Africa

is filled with small objects, such as pebbles, seeds, or sand. When the instrument is shaken, the particles bounce against the outer instrument causing it to vibrate. Other rattles are constructed so that the small particles are loosely fixed to the outside of the object, such as with leg rattles.

Membranophones

Membranophones are defined by having a vibrating membrane, usually animal skin, that is stretched over a frame. This category encompasses the majority of drums found in the

Gourd rattle *(shekere)* from sub-Saharan Africa

world. The different types of drums are categorized on the basis of body shape—some, for example, are goblet-shaped, while others are barrel-shaped—and according to whether they are single- or double-headed. Most drums are struck with either the hand or some implement, usually a stick. (Compare CD I, tracks 5 and 32). There are too many kinds of drums throughout the world to make generalizations about

Goblet drums *(djembe)* from sub-Saharan Africa

timbre; however, smaller drums usually have a higher, tighter sound, while larger membranophones are deeper and earthier in character. Becoming familiar with the unique sounds of different drums takes time and effort. The essential first step is being able to distinguish between struck membranophones and struck idiophones. Not all membranophones are struck, however; those that are not—such as friction drums and "singing membranes" (i.e., kazoos) —are less common but particularly unique in timbre. (Listen to CD II, track 23.)

Summary

Learning to distinguish among aerophones, chordophones, idiophones, and membranophones is the first step in training your ear to listen attentively to world music. Being able to recognize subcategories within these instrument groups greatly enhances your appreciation of sound and helps you to identify the music you hear more quickly. You will encounter many similar types of instruments, such as the Japanese *shakuhachi* and the Native American flute, that are hard to distinguish from each other based on timbre alone. Fortunately, other aspects of musical performance such as pitch, rhythm, and dynamics can help you identify the tradition you are hearing. Differences in timbre, however, are most often what distinguish the sound of two instruments, even when all other aspects are identical. Familiarize yourself with the unique "aural colors" of each recorded example supplied with this text before trying to tackle the often more complicated issues associated with musical creation.

PITCH
A tone's specific frequency level, measured in Hertz (Hz).

Pitch

Every sound can be described as having either a *definite* or *indefinite* pitch. A definite pitch is determined by the dominance of a specific frequency level; for example, the Euro-American "concert pitch," A above middle C, has 440 Hz as its dominant frequency. Definite pitches are those used to produce melody and harmony. (Listen to CD II, track 26.) An indefinite pitch is one made up of a cluster of more or less equal frequency levels—that is, no one level dominates. Indefinite pitches, such as those produced by handclaps or rattles, are most often used in a rhythmic capacity. (Listen to CD I, track 4.) While indefinite pitches are regularly found in music traditions throughout the world, the varied uses of definite pitch is more often the primary focus of musical activity; therefore, the term *pitch* hereafter refers specifically to definite pitches.

Tuning System

The term *tuning system* denotes the entire collection of pitch frequencies commonly used in a given music tradition. Tuning systems are culturally determined. Our ears become accustomed to the tuning system of the music we hear on a regular basis. When we hear an unfamiliar tuning system, certain of its pitches may sound "out of tune" because we have been culturally conditioned to accept other frequency levels as "correct." Pitches with frequency levels significantly different from those in our accepted tuning system often sound strange.

The basis for most tuning systems around the world is the *octave*. An octave is produced when the frequency level of a specific pitch is either doubled or halved. Pitches that are an octave apart (or a series of octaves apart) are considered to be the "same" even though they have different frequencies. The easiest way to understand this concept is to listen to a man with a "low" voice and a woman with a "high" voice sing the "same" pitch. Our ears sense that the two pitches are equivalent even though the man may be singing at a frequency level of 220Hz, while the woman sings at 880Hz, two octaves higher.

In the most commonly used European tuning system (equal-tempered tuning), the octave is divided into twelve equal parts. In the Thai classical music tradition, however, the same octave is divided into only seven equal parts. (Compare CD I, track 11, and CD II, track 8.) Consequently, the pitches common to the European tuning system sound different than the pitches common to the Thai tuning system. The tuning systems common to some traditions use more than thirty discrete pitches within a single octave. After extended exposure to a different tuning system, your ear will become accustomed to its standard frequency levels. Even before this, however, the very "oddness" of an unfamiliar tuning system may help you recognize the musical tradition to which it belongs.

TUNING SYSTEM
The pitches common to a musical tradition.

Scale

While a tuning system encompasses all of the pitches commonly used in a music tradition, a *scale* consists of a set of pitches (generally expressed in ascending order) used in particular performances. For example, a pentatonic scale (*penta* meaning "five," and *tonic* meaning "tone") uses only five tones. (Listen to CD I, track 17.) Different pentatonic scales can be derived from a single tuning system, as long as

Tuning pegs and micro-tone tuners of the Turkish *kanun* zither

the number of pitches available within a tuning system is greater than five. Thus, pitches 1, 2, 3, 5, and 6 from a particular tuning system may constitute the pentatonic scale for one performance, while pitches 2, 4, 6, 8, and 9 from that same system may form the pentatonic scale for a different performance. Scales, in some music traditions, are limited to as few as two or three pitches, while other traditions regularly use a greater number of pitches.

Interval

An *interval* is perhaps best thought of as the "distance" between two pitches. Intervals are described as either wide or narrow. A wide interval—such as that from *A* ascending to *G*—is one with a large difference in frequency levels, while a narrow interval—such as that between *A* and *B*—is one with a relatively smaller difference. Likewise, the interval between the bottom and top pitches of an octave is wider than the interval distance of any two pitches within the octave. The difference between narrow and wide intervals can be both seen and heard. On a piano, for example, the size of an interval can be understood visually in terms of the distance between a pair of keys, and aurally in terms of the frequency levels the keys sound. A tradition that prefers either wide or narrow intervals may be easier to recognize as a result.

Range

Range refers to the span of pitches a given instrument or voice is capable of producing. It is described as being wide or narrow, as well as high or low. An instrument with a narrow range is capable of producing fewer pitches than an instrument with a wide range. Instruments with wide ranges, such as the piano, are typically, though not always, larger than those with narrower ranges, such as the harmonica. Vocal ranges can vary substantially: trained professionals practice to extend their range, sometimes to more than three octaves, while an average person has a narrower vocal range of roughly two octaves or less.

Ranges are also characterized in terms of where they fall on the spectrum from very low-pitched sounds to very high-pitched sounds. An instrument or voice may have a relatively high or low range in comparison to other musical media. A female, for example, generally has a higher vocal range than a male. Instruments also often have characteristic ranges; a violin, for example, uses a high range, while a tuba plays in a low range. (Compare CD I, tracks 18 and 24.)

Melody

A *melody* is defined as an organized succession of pitches forming a musical idea. These are the "tunes" that characterize a specific composition, such as "Twinkle, Twinkle Little Star." Because pitches exist in real time—that is, because they have a duration—rhythm also is always a key component of melody. Ask your teacher to play a descending C major scale on any instrument. Do you recognize a melody? Not unless you consider a scale a melody. Now ask your teacher to play the beginning of "Joy to the World." The addition of rhythm to the same pitches creates a recognizable musical idea, or melody.

Melodic Contour

A melody can be described in terms of its *melodic contour,* or shape. "Joy to the World," for example, has a "descending" melodic contour as the pitches descend from high to low (see figure 1). Melodic contours are typically drawn as a graph representing the direction of the melody. It is often useful to graph the contour of a melody to identify regularly occurring features characteristic of a music tradition. For example, our graph of a Native American Plains Indian chant reveals a characteristic "cascading" melodic contour, reflecting the Plains Indian practice of holding certain pitches longer than others in the course of a descending melodic line (see figure 2; listen to CD II, track 35.) Drone pitches can be represented as horizontal lines, while chords (several pitches played at once) may be represented with vertical lines, as in our graph of Irish bagpipe performance (see figure 3; listen to CD II, track 9.)

MELODY
An organized succession
of pitches forming
a musical idea.

MELODIC CONTOUR
The general direction and
shape of a melody.

DRONE
A continuous or
repeating sound.

Figure 1. Descending Melodic Contour.

Figure 2. Cascading Melodic Contour.

Melody:

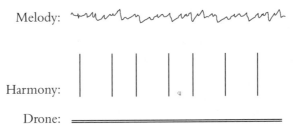

Harmony:

Drone:

Figure 3. "Irish Bagpipe Melodic Contour."

Ornamentation

Ornamentation consists of embellishments or decorations that are applied to a melody, and thus modify the original musical idea. Some traditions have elaborate systematic procedures for ornamenting a melody, while others place less emphasis on ornamentation or shun it altogether. Ornamentation can consist of just a few added notes or of a long series of tones meant to display a performer's skills or make the basic melody more interesting. (Listen to CD I, track 6.)

Text Setting

Text setting, a term limited to vocal performance, is the process of combining music and words. Settings can be one of two broad types, depending on the relationship they establish between syllables of text and individual sung pitches. If each syllable of a text corresponds to one pitch, the text setting is considered *syllabic.* If, however, several pitches are sounded for a single syllable of text, the setting is considered *melismatic.* It is perhaps best, however, to think of most text settings as being on a continuum between the purely syllabic and the purely melismatic. Most vocal performance falls somewhere on this continuum, most frequently toward the syllabic side. (Compare CD I, track 25, and CD II, track 3.) However, some traditions strongly emphasize either syllabic settings, as with popular rap music, or melismatic settings, as with African-American spirituals.

TEXT SETTING
The rhythmic relationship of words to melody; can be syllabic (one pitch per syllable) or melismatic (more than one pitch per syllable).

Rhythm

Rhythm is essentially the relationship of sound durations. Some rhythms fall into regular patterns, while others are less predictable.

Beat and Tempo

Beat is a regular pulsation of sound. The simplest example is your heartbeat, which pulsates at a relatively fixed rate. (Listen to CD II, track 25.) This rate, or speed, is called *tempo*. The tempo of your heartbeat increases when you become more physically active, whereas its speed decreases when you sleep. In the same way, musical tempo can be described as relatively fast or slow in relation to a basic beat.

RHYTHM
The lengths, or durations, of sounds as patterns in time.

Accent and Meter

An *accent* is an emphasized beat. Accents frequently signal a particular kind of musical activity or a specific stage in a performance or piece. For example, the louder sound of accented beats may correspond to dance steps or signal the end of a performance. Accents are often used to indicate the underlying rhythmic structure of a musical performance. In many traditions, this structure is based on a system of grouping beats into regular units. Such grouping of beats is known as *meter.*

Most meters can be considered as either *duple* or *triple.* When groups of beats are divided by two, the meter is duple; when the beats can be divided by three, it is triple. (Compare audio CD II, tracks 10 and 22.) Meter may be articulated aurally by a single instrument, such as a woodblock, sounding the basic beat. More typically, however, the meter is implied through the use of rhythms that elaborate on the basic beat to make the music more interesting. In some musical traditions meter can be asymmetrical; in others, it can be organized into long cycles. (Listen to CD I, track 21). Understanding these meters is important, but hearing them is often difficult. In other cases, musicians do not think in terms of meter, but how rhythms relate. Ascribing a meter to such traditions can detract from appreciating the musician's approach to music-making.

The opposite of metered music is music in *free rhythm.* (Listen to CD II, track 27.) Such music has no regular pulse, as is the case with speech. Without a beat to follow, a meter cannot be established. If you cannot easily snap your fingers to a piece of music, it is probably in free rhythm. Such freely rhythmic music is usually highly ornamented, and when performed vocally tends to have melismatic text settings.

Rhythmic Density

The term *rhythmic density* refers to the relative quantity of notes between periodic accents or within a specific unit of time. Rhythmic

Xylophones *(gyil)* from Ghana (Amy Unruh)

density can be described as a continuum between low and high (or thin and thick). Long sustained tones in free rhythm with little melodic activity have a low rhythmic density in contrast to music with a steady, usually quick, tempo and numerous notes of short duration. (Compare CD I, track 16, and CD II, track 2.) If the music sounds "busy," the rhythmic density is generally high (thick); if it sounds "relaxed," the density is most likely low (thin).

PHONIC STRUCTURE

The relationship between different sounds in a given piece; it can be either monophony or some form of polyphony.

MONOPHONY

Music with a single melodic line.

POLYPHONY

The juxtaposition or overlapping of multiple lines of music; the three types of polyphony are homophony, independent polyphony, and heterophony.

Phonic Structure

The term *phonic structure* (also described as *texture)* refers to the organizational relationship between or among musical sounds. A single line of music, whether performed by a soloist or in unison by an ensemble, is described as *monophonic* (adj.) or *monophony* (n.), mono meaning "one," as long as the performers play the same pitches with the same rhythms. (Listen to CD I, track 25.) Music featuring melodic lines performed an octave apart, as when a male and female voice sing the same line of music in different ranges, is still considered monophonic.

Multiple lines of music (or parts) performed simultaneously are considered *polyphonic. Polyphony* has three primary subsets: *homophony, independent polyphony,* and *heterophony.* The term *homophony* refers to multiple lines of music expressing the same musical idea in the same meter, *homo* meaning "the same." Music that is homophonic requires the use of at least two pitches played simultaneously at an interval other than an octave. In Euro-American musical traditions such music is referred to as *harmonic,* a description that generally implies the use of *chords,* or combinations of three or more tones that are blended together simultaneously to produce *harmony.* Because harmony generally supports a melody, most homophony can be described as melody with chordal accompaniment. (Listen to CD II, track 29.)

Independent polyphony consists of two or more lines of music expressing independent musical ideas. Each line of music is played or sung in relation to the others without any single line dominating. (Listen to CD I, track 34.) This concept covers a variety of possibilities from European strict counterpoint to styles in which the voice and instrumental accompaniment are melodically independent.

The term *heterophony* refers to simultaneous variations of the same line of music, *hetero* meaning "different" or "variant." As such, heterophonic music requires more than one performer, each performing the same melody, but differently either in terms of pitch, rhythm, or both. (Listen to CD I, track 17.) Each manifestation of the melody is shaped by the idiomatic characteristics associated with the performance style of each instrument or voice. A single melody played by two performers, one of whom adds frequent ornaments to the melody, is considered heterophonic in structure. Complex heterophonic structures are especially common throughout much of Asia.

Dynamics

The term *dynamics* simply refers to the relative volume of a musical sound. The relative loudness or softness of a music can be a distinguishing characteristic of its performance. (Listen to CD I, track 15.) A gradual increase in volume is known as a *crescendo,* while a gradual decrease in volume is called a *decrescendo.* These and other terms related to dynamics are often derived from the European art music tradition. Most others, such as *forte* (loud) or *pianissimo* (very quiet), are not commonly used in ethnomusicological writing.

Form

Another important feature of music is *form.* This term refers to the overall pattern of a piece of music as it unfolds in time. Form may be likened to architectural design, in that it provides the underlying structure over time that gives a musical performance a predictable or coherent shape. Some kinds of music follow a preexisting form, with, for example, an established beginning, middle, and ending section, while others have less obvious organization. The forms used in one world music tradition may vary greatly from those used in another tradition. Becoming familiar with some of these forms will help you recognize certain traditions, and will also help you understand how particular performances are conceived of by performers and audiences alike.

HOMOPHONY
Multiple lines of music expressing the same musical idea in the same meter.

INDEPENDENT POLYPHONY
Multiple lines of music expressing independent musical ideas as a cohesive whole.

HETEROPHONY
Multiple performers playing simultaneous variations of the same line of music.

Fundamentals of Music

Here's a summary of the basic terms we introduced in this chapter.

TIMBRE. The tone quality or "color" of a musical sound.

MEDIUM. The object that produces a sound. Can be: vocal, instrumental, or both; solo or ensemble (duet, trio, choir, orchestra, etc.); one of various instrument types (aerophone, chordophone, idiophone, membranophone).

PITCH. A tone determined by its frequency level. Related concepts include:

Tuning system. The pitches common to a particular musical tradition.

Scale. The pitches used in a particular performance arranged in order.

Interval. The difference between two pitches.

Range. All the pitches that a voice or instrument can potentially produce.

Melody. An organized succession of pitches forming a musical idea.

Melodic contour. The general direction and shape of a melody.

Ornamentation. An embellishment or decoration of the melody.

Text setting. The rhythmic relationship of words to melody. Text settings can be *syllabic* (one pitch per syllable) or *melismatic* (several pitches per syllable).

RHYTHM. The relationship of durations. Related concepts include:

Beat. A regular pulsation.

Accent. An emphasized beat.

Tempo. The relative rate of speed of the beat.

Meter. A system of grouping beats into individual units.

Free rhythm. Music with no regular pulsation.

Rhythmic density. The quantity of notes between periodic accents or over a specific unit of time.

PHONIC STRUCTURE. The organizational relationship between or among musical sounds. Related concepts include:

Monophony. A single line of music.

Polyphony. Multiple lines of music.

Homophony. Multiple lines of music expressing the same musical idea.

Independent polyphony. Two or more lines of music expressing independent musical ideas.

Heterophony. Multiple performers playing simultaneous variations of the same line of music.

DYNAMICS. The volume of a musical sound.

FORM. The underlying temporal structure of a musical performance.

Questions to Consider

1. Which of the four basic components of music is most helpful in identifying a world music tradition? Why?

2. In the Sachs-Hornbostel system, name at least three examples from each instrument category. In which subcategories do these belong?

3. How does *pitch* differ from *tuning system?* How does *tuning system* differ from *scale?* How does *scale* differ from *range?*

4. How does *homophony* differ from *independent polyphony?* How does *independent polyphony* differ from *heterophony?*

5. What are some difficulties in using English terminology to describe the world's musics?

6. When music is represented graphically in notation, what are some of the limitations? How is Western staff notation limited in its ability to describe world music?

Istanbul's impressive "Blue Mosque,"
built in the sixteenth century by the Ottoman Turks

CHAPTER 3

Cultural Considerations:
Beyond the Sounds Themselves

In a technical sense, music is just organized sound and can be analyzed through concentration on its elements, such as melody, rhythm, phonic structure, form, and so forth. But no music exists in a vacuum, free from social context, even if it primarily lives on concert stages or in recordings. All music manifests itself within a "culture," however defined, and has meanings for those who create, perform, or consume it that go far beyond the sounds themselves. This chapter briefly discusses some of the perspectives that may be brought to bear on a given musical type or style. This list of ideas, however incomplete, at least suggests that a full understanding of any music would require multiple approaches. Obviously, with only limited space we cannot apply these concepts with any degree of thoroughness or consistency, but those concepts that are most relevant will be introduced when appropriate.

Music and the Environment

Music, it is often said, is "everywhere." One might conclude that this "everywhereness" means that modern societies place a high value on music. For many musicians, however, music's omnipresence is more of a curse than a blessing. Music has become the "auditory aspirin" of modern society. Especially with the development of media capable of delivering it anywhere, anyplace, anytime, music has come to be used more and more as a drug. People use music to get themselves going, to facilitate relaxation, to enter meditative states, or to dispel boredom. The music business, in cahoots with psychologists, has developed the means to use music as a manipulative tool. Muzak, the company, promotes its "product" as a means of achieving increased sales, moving people in and out of rapid-turnover restaurants (or keeping them there to buy more drinks), and maintaining productivity in the workplace by altering the natural daily cycle of human energy. Some people drown their concerns in a tidal wave of sound, especially in their "speakers on wheels"—cars whose sounds can sometimes be heard for hundreds of feet *with their windows closed.* Indeed, loud parties and booming cars have brought about "noise" laws in many cities, in an attempt to curb "noise pollution."

Other forms of environmental degradation have also had an effect on music-making. As numerous plant and animal species have become endangered, many long-time musical practices have been lost or altered. Traditionally, many musical instruments were made of natural materials such as now-rare hardwoods or ivory. Dancers used feathers from now-endangered birds or skins from now-endangered mammals. As a result, many old instruments are refused entry into countries enforcing international environmental laws, and in fact may be confiscated and destroyed. New materials have been developed to substitute for restricted substances; for example, plastic or bone are now often used in place of ivory. Some instruments, though, cannot be made of substitute materials, such as the ivory elephant tusk horns used in West Africa. In certain situations, governments permit the hunting and use of certain endangered animals that are part of the ritual tradition of a given people.

Cultural Knowledge

Every individual absorbs a certain amount of cultural knowledge while growing up. Just being somewhere makes you a member of a "cultural group," whether at the level of family, "tribe," community, nation, continent, or global cultural sphere (such as "the West"). Who you are depends on where you are and with whom you are living.

The experience of growing up within a given society creates a sense of normalcy; individuals develop expectations that typical patterns will continue. This sense that one's own culture is "normal," and that cultures which exhibit differences, both great and small, are "abnormal," "weird," or "exotic," is a natural perspective known as "ethnocentrism."

ETIC
The perspective of a cultural outsider.

EMIC
The perspective of a cultural insider.

Frederick Verney, Secretary to the Siamese (Thai) Legation in London, wrote in 1885 that a great "stumbling-block" for many in the West when attempting to appreciate non-Western music is Western education, which "precludes the possibility of a full appreciation of music of a foreign and distinct school." In order for a Westerner to fully appreciate Asian music it would be necessary "to forget all that one has experienced in the West." Ethnocentric reactions are natural and perhaps inevitable—but an

Ivory tusk horns in Ghana are essential to the Ashante court in Komasi, but African elephants are endangered and transporting such instruments across national boundaries is forbidden (Joseph S. Kaminski)

awareness of ethnocentrism makes it more likely that one will come to accept and understand music that is "different."

Scholars attempting to understand how music is experienced and "known" have developed a distinction between "outsider" and "insider" knowledge. They have dubbed the "outsider" perspective *etic* (from "phonetic"), and the "insider" perspective *emic* (from "phonemic"). Insiders are assumed to react to their own culture's music in ways that draw on a lifetime of unconsciously absorbed cultural knowledge and attitudes. Outsiders, because they come to a given culture after their perceptions are formed, are assumed not just to inject ethnocentrisms into their interpretations, but also to prefer to dwell only on those aspects of music that are observable to outsiders, such as objects and sonic structures.

French ethnomusicologist Alain Weber performs with The Musicians of the Nile from Upper Egypt

The major drawback to this concept of "insider" and "outsider" is that it doesn't allow for middle ground: there's no room conceptually for the sympathetic "outsider" who has acquired "insider" knowledge. Do we value the views of an insider, simply because he or she grew up in a given culture, over those of an outsider, no matter how knowledgeable that person is? Can individuals shift identities by living among a "foreign" people? If so, for how long must they live among them? When I (TM) studied the pre-cented (lined out) psalm singing done in the Scottish Gaelic language in Edinburgh in 1982, the worshippers at Greyfriar's Kirk (church) pre-sented a problem for the folklorists at the University of Edinburgh. Some years earlier a young French woman had gone to live on the Hebridean island of North Uist, learned Gaelic, and became excep-tionally skilled in psalm singing. After moving to Edinburgh, she attend-ed Greyfriar's and provided the strongest voice of the Gaelic-speaking congregation. Some of the folklorists contended that her singing was not "authentic" because she had come to Gael life as an adult—even though she was the group's best singer. In their view, an outsider could *never* attain insider status, even after many years of life amongst a new group and the attainment of a high level of cultural knowledge and skill. On the other hand, Western audiences have no problem in accepting

An Inside Look

Ki Mantle Hood

My father was a violinist, singer, easel painter, and architect. As a young man he worked with Frank Lloyd Wright. My mother was preparing for the concert stage as a pianist, but when she married at eighteen, she became instead a teacher of piano. She told me that at age five I was put to bed afternoons so I could join them in evening concerts [in Springfield and Chicago, Illinois]. Years later she said, "Whenever they played a piano concerto [which starts with an orchestral exposition], you jumped physically when the piano entered." I learned as an adult that this was the moment when two different tuning systems collide. There are other stories that indicate I was born with an unusual sensitivity to sound, especially musical sound.

Ki Mantle Hood, Professor Emeritus, UCLA; composer and ethnomusicologist with his wife, Hazel.

The first time I heard very early recordings of Javanese and Balinese music, I was ecstatic to hear more, to know more, to go to Indonesia to try to comprehend the logic I sensed as a young composer but didn't understand. That same sensitivity to exotic sounds all over the world has been present all my life. At UCLA, in the Fall of 1954, I was privileged to establish the very first university program of training in ethnomusicology.

I didn't realize until I was about 40 that apparently I hear things in musical sound that others either do not hear or unconsciously ignore. That led to the develop-ment of a series of melographs, laboratory instruments that show in continuous display the pitch, loudness, and quality (by including a printout of overtones) of musical sounds.

orchestral conductors and musicians who grew up outside Western culture, people such as Japan's Seiji Ozawa, India's Zubin Mehta, and New Zealand's Kiri TeKanawa, a Maori ethnic minority. We would argue for a more fluid and nuanced view that does not automatically privilege "insiders" over "outsiders."

Value Systems and Hierarchies

Within any given culture, people tend to evolve value systems that dictate what kinds of music, which performers, and which instrument-makers are considered "better" than others. Although in the West many accept and others assert that "classical" music is superior to "popular" music, such a ranking begs the question of *authority*—that is, the complex question of who gets to make such judgments. What, after all, are the criteria that make one music tradition superior to another? And who decides? Is it done by some kind of consensus, by appointed critics, or by *self*-appointed critics? What are the implications of such hierarchies?

Essentially, the question is whether expressions of value are to be taken as matters of truth, opinion, or perspective. In the United States, value systems and hierarchies are now understood more in political than aesthetic terms. Many ask whether a value system can be taken seriously when it asserts that the musical heritage of a dominant group, such as European-derived peoples, is inherently superior to that of, for example, African-Americans. Music is necessarily part of the current debates in our society over *canons*, *diversity*, and *hegemony*. As with the canon of

When I was about 50, I visited an aunt I hadn't seen for many years. She told me that I avoided family reunions beginning at age 12. She said, "We used to worry that you didn't really belong to us. Now we understand, you never did. You belong to the world." Exposure to the indigenous music of many cultures of the world has enriched my lifelong pleasure in many different traditions of music and afforded a penetrating understanding of the cultures that produced them. By now I must agree with my insightful Aunt. As a musician, I never belonged to my roots in Illinois but to the riches of music worldwide.

I retired from teaching in 1998 and began a series of semi-fiction novels. My wife and I have lived in many parts of the world and learned as performers (she as a dancer, I as a musician) that the arts are a sure and immediate door to the identity of a different culture. Knowing I would no longer be teaching in a university regularly I decided to write books that helped the reader learn things we had learned as performers in the arts of other cultures. To keep them turning pages I decided to make them thrillers. The bookstore Borders handled the first one and dubbed me the writer of thrillers "with an education." The label has stuck through seven books. Recently I also published an autobiography.

"great books," the canons of "great composers" and "great works" are essentially European. Calls for "diversity" challenge not just the canons but also hitherto accepted standards of greatness. Some feel threatened by these challenges to the hegemony of European tradition, others feel liberated.

Courses in "world musics" (and textbooks like this one) have been part of this essentially political process. Until relatively recently, the study of "music" in education at most levels focused almost exclusively on the Western "classics." Courses on the musics of the rest of the world, which have now become common, still do not create many problems as long as they are restricted to studies of compositional style and "exotic" instruments. But scholarly assertions that all musics are potentially valid, or as William Malm often said, "different but equally logical," are seen as threatening in some quarters.

Music and Identity

A person expresses their identity in a variety of ways. The clothes we wear, the foods we eat, and the language we speak are all outward projections of "who we are," or more accurately, "who we *think* we are." Biological factors, namely race and sex, are often cited as the source of a person's identity; however, cultural factors are equally, if not more important determinants.

For example, what makes a person "African?" Must he or she have "black" skin? That can't be the answer, because Africans come in an array of skin pigmentations, including "olive" and "white." Likewise, would it make sense to consider Australian aborigines or the Trobrianders of Papua New Guinea "African" because many of them have a dark skin color? Certainly not. Rather, people are "African" because they think they are. And because they think this way, they behave as "Africans" do.

How others interpret the behaviors of an individual or group is also important to the formation of identity. If, for example, a person's behaviors are considered by others to be representative of the qualities of being "African," then this self-perception as an "African" is reinforced. However, if others do not agree that the person's behaviors are typical of an "African," then a conflict arises in which either the individual must modify these behaviors, thereby altering this self-perception, or the atypical behaviors must be accepted by the others as properly "African." If the conflict is not resolved, then the "African" identity of our hypothetical person would be continually questioned.

Music plays a vital role in expressions of ethnic identity. Groups and individuals often use music as a way to assert their unique ethnic qualities in relation to others. Outside perceptions of particular musical activities as normative behavior for a group or individual reinforce the sense of ethnic identity expressed through the music. Along with other cultural elements, such as language, religion, dress, diet, and so on, music shapes

how people [...] at
themselves [...] ole
within a so[...]

In mar[...] es, the
expression [...] ic iden-
tity throu[...] ic is an
essential [...] of daily
life, so u[...] ling and
appreciat[...] al activ-
ities is a [...] ant part
of gettir[...] ow how
people f[...] cultures
think. [...] cultures
where [...] s consid-
ered a specialized activity,
much is expressed and
revealed through the

Japanese tourists watch a Thai Cultural Show at a Bangkok ©
restaurant that caters strictly to tourists

types of music common to the culture. For example, the glitz and glamour of Super Bowl halftime shows reveals the emphasis our culture places on entertainment, even though these music performances are certainly not representative of all the music found in the United States.

Use versus Function

The anthropologist Alan Merriam spent an entire chapter of his landmark 1964 book *The Anthropology of Music* differentiating *use* from *function*. Whereas use, defined as "the ways in which music is employed in human society" (p. 210), can be easily observed, function requires much deeper inquiry into the meanings of music. Most studies of music's use are descriptive and are based on the observations of the researcher. The study of music's function, however, requires deep-level cultural knowledge and can entail much interpretation; for this reason, the perspectives of "insiders" are often privileged over those of "outsiders." Recently, however, there has been a trend in what is called "postmodern" scholarship to conceptualize function in the broadest way possible.

Music and Ritual

One of the most important contexts for music is its use in a ritual context. While the term ritual obviously encompasses religious services, it is more broadly applied to all situations in which patterns of behavior are repeated without question because they are seen to have meaning. Ritual may also include sporting events, graduations, Memorial Day parades, Christmas dinners, and many other occasions when music is desired as part of the "pomp and circumstance." For example, the singing of the American national anthem occurs before virtually all sporting events in the United States. Casually, this is merely a step in a longer sequence of requisite events, but its function is to reaffirm national identity and solidarity.

When music's use in ritual contexts is considered, questions inevitably arise about the relationship between music and trance states. In rituals in which trance occurs, such as those associated with the African-derived religious systems found in the Western hemisphere

Spiritual Baptists in the tiny Caribbean nation of St. Vincent and the Grenadines sing a hymn in a trance state called "doption" (from the "adoption of the Holy Spirit")

(e.g., Cuban *Santeria*), does music cause trance? Gilbert Rouget, in his seminal 1980 book *Music and Trance: A Theory of the Relations between Music and Possession*, demonstrates that seemingly trance-inducing music does not in fact cause trance, because if it did, it would automatically affect all who hear it, including the musicians and researchers. Music instead acts to stimulate, regulate, or end trance states, which are not possible without the expectation of possession. Music may be *used* in a given possession ritual to "call the gods"—but its *function* is to regulate trance.

Music and Spirituality

In addition to having a significant role to play in many long-established religious rituals, music can serve a spiritual role in the lives of individuals. In recent times, for example, many in the so-called "New Age" movement have asserted that music can heal, directly affect the mind and its many moods, or enhance contact with the spiritual world. These views have resulted in everything from belief in the so-called "Mozart effect"—an alleged increase in intelligence among infants exposed to the music of Wolfgang Amadeus Mozart—to books that claim that listening to specific compositions will cure certain ailments. While the field of music therapy has come to be accepted as a legitimate professional use of music, certain other applications coming from the "New Age" sensibility probably remain little more than wishful thinking.

Music and Ethics

Music has also been thought of in ethical terms. For Plato, in the fourth century before the Christian era, the ideal ruler was one shaped by an array of ethical forces, including music performed in the appropriate musical modes. (Conversely, Plato saw great ethical peril in music performed in the "wrong" modes.) China's great philosopher Kong Fuzi (also known as Confucius), who lived five hundred years before the Christian era, also taught that the harmonious operation of the universe, down to the lives of individual humans, was directly affected by music. In his thinking, music must reflect the same order, balance, and restraint expected of human behavior.

Plato's student, Aristotle, founded this school near Vergina, Greece, about 338 B.C., where he tutored Alexander the Great and the other children of Philip of Macedonia

New Theoretical Perspectives

Although we cannot offer a complete history of recent scholarship, we believe that some discussion of it is required in any essay on holistic approaches to music. The original work of the musicologist was to create authoritative musical scores based on manuscripts or prints, as close to the original as possible. Musicologists also sought to write histories of music and musicians based on "primary sources," namely firsthand documents such as letters. This concern for "sticking to the facts" and "establishing verifiable truth" is the core of what is called *modernist* scholarship.

Such work continues to be the focus of the majority of musicologists, but a countertrend has arisen as a result of new kinds of scholarship in other fields such as literature. Whereas modernism taught that (capital T) Truth could be established, what is now called *postmodernism* teaches that "truth" is relative and has little validity beyond the person attempting to establish it. Instead of "describing facts," postmodern scholars seek to "interpret texts," a text being anything, including a book, painting, sculpture, or a piece of music. There are other new directions in ethnomusicological scholarship as well, including those focusing on political and economic perspectives (e.g., Marxist interpretation), gender issues, such as feminism, and non-heterosexual perspectives (e.g., "Queer Theory," which examines music-making from a gay or lesbian viewpoint). While some of this scholarship has proved to be provocative and stimulating, the specialized vocabularies common to such writing can seem impenetrable to those not familiar with the jargon or theories involved.

Music Technologies and Media

Technology has played a key role in the development of ethnomusicology. Wire recordings and the Edison wax cylinders of the late 1800s and early 1900s were important to the research of comparative musicologists who focused much of their attention on transcription and on the tuning systems of world music traditions. Throughout the twentieth century, technological advances enabled ethnomusicologists to record music in increasingly remote locations with greater and greater ease. While early field researchers traveled with heavy loads of equipment and numerous boxes of cylinders, reel-to-reel tapes, and eventually cassettes, today's ethnomusicologist can get pristine digital recordings with equipment that fits easily into a shirt pocket.

The media through which music is disseminated have also vastly changed over the last one-hundred-plus years. They have evolved from radio and vinyl records to television and CDs to the Internet and MP3s—and each new development has made dissemination of the world's music easier and faster. This evolution has created greater opportunities for ethnomusicologists to disseminate their research in both academic and mass-market arenas.

The ease with which recording can be done today has resulted in a proliferation of world music recordings for sale to the general public. While many of these are well researched and come with accurate liner notes, others are simply tourist trinkets slapped together to make a quick buck. Oftentimes what seems to be a poor-quality recording is actually an attempt to capture music in its original context, such as a crowded festival. Conversely, a studio recording with excellent sound quality may misrepresent a tradition, by, for example, leaving out instruments from an ensemble or incorporating inauthentic rhythms or melodies. It is generally best to stick to well-known labels, such as Smithsonian-Folkways or Lyrichord, although sometimes even a carelessly put together CD can provide an enjoyable listening experience.

Music and the Arts

The relationships between music and the other arts—including dance, theater, the fine arts, and literature—are varied and complex. While there certainly is music that stands alone for its own sake, a surprisingly great part of the world's music exists in relation to other arts.

The relationship with dance is the most obvious. Dance without music is almost unthinkable. Dance music provides far more than just a beat: it must also have a character appropriate to the kind of dance it

A street performance of Chinese Chaozhou regional opera with percussion accompaniment in [C] Shantou, Guangdong province, People's Republic of China

accompanies, whether the dance occurs in the world of classical ballet, folk music, opera, traditional theater, or in a ballroom. A great deal of dance music may be heard—indeed, normally is heard—separately from dance, causing us to sometimes forget that a particular song or piece was actually conceived to accompany movement.

Theater in the Western world is usually thought of as spoken drama, opera being a separate category of sung theater. The West also has theater types that include both speaking and singing such as the old German *Singspiel* of Mozart's time (the eighteenth century), the English ballad opera, and the American outgrowth of the latter, the Broadway musical. But throughout the rest of the world, theater without music is often unthinkable. This is particularly true in Asia, which has some of the world's most distinctive theatrical traditions, including Indian *Kathakali*, Thai *Khon*, Indonesian *Wayang*, and Chinese Jingju (Bejing Opera).

Music tends to have one of two relationships with the visual arts. The first is found in the field of *musical iconography,* the study of music history—and particularly musical instruments—through pictures. The second occurs when a composer, especially in the Western classical tradition, creates a work that is at least said to have been inspired by a work of visual art. Perhaps the most obvious example is Russian composer Modest Mussorgsky's famous *Pictures at an Exhibition*, composed

The altar for a Thai *wai khru* (teacher greeting ceremony) is extremely elaborate ⓒ

in 1874 based on a series of paintings by Viktor Hartmann.

Music can also be related to literature—primarily by association—through title, text setting, or allusion. The general term for this phenomenon is *programmatic music*, meaning music that alludes to something outside itself, be it a story, a great literary work, a poem, a painting, or, even more broadly, an emotion or aspect of nature. Chinese music titles commonly allude to well-known stories from novels, "Chinese opera," and famous poems. Most pieces have titles that suggest an image, emotion, or place—such as "Meditation at the Dressing Table," "Suzhou Scenery," or "Winter Ravens Sporting over the Water."

Transmission and Pedagogy

Musical knowledge can be acquired in various ways: intuitively by living in a given culture, directly from a teacher, from a book, or by observation. When teaching is involved, many issues arise—such as the nature of the student/teacher relationship and the question of what educational methodologies are employed. When technologies are used in instruction, questions concerning memory, notation, and recording also arise. Some cultures have developed formal institutions that transmit music to anyone willing to learn (the conservatory, for example) and others have created institutions for preserving it within a closed system (the Japanese Imperial Household, for example). In some societies, especially those of East, South, and Southeast Asia, the music teacher is a revered individual who offers knowledge as a privilege. The Indian *guru* (and by extension, the Thai, Cambodian, and Lao *khru*) dispenses knowledge in a somewhat unsystematic fashion over a long apprenticeship; in the past, students lived with teachers and acted as their servants. In these Asian societies, rituals that honor the teacher and the teacher's lineage are often required before learning is permitted.

In contrast, in the past music teachers in Europe were sometimes seen as odd characters deserving of ridicule, as with Don Basilio in Rossini's famous opera, *The Barber of Seville* (1816). As for students, many societies offer titles or other forms of recognition such as certificates or degrees when students attain certain levels of skill.

Notation Systems and the Creation of Music

Students of Western music are accustomed to thinking in terms of a "composition" and a "composer." In the popular culture the composer is usually depicted as a male seated at the piano, left hand on the keys, right hand writing on manuscript paper. This image more often than not comes with an assertion that composing involves "inspiration" and "genius." Perhaps the best-known icon-composer is Ludwig van Beethoven (1770–1827), with his intense eyes, furrowed brow, and wild hair.

Western classical music developed a division of labor between the creator/composer and the realizer/performer. Composers are assumed to have the genius that leads to a work's creation. In order to maintain control over all aspects of a work, the composer represents his ideas through graphic symbols called musical notation—which must be played "as written" by subservient performers. Performers may add nuances but may not violate the composer's intentions. As a result, formal music education in the West tends to privilege "musical literacy,"

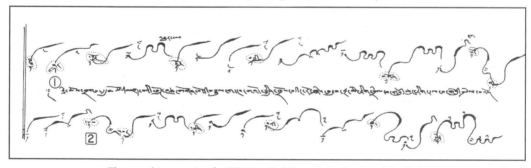

The graphic notation for Tibetan Buddhist chant is enough to help informed practitioners remember the chants

with the unspoken implication that cultures without notation suffer from "musical illiteracy." It is important to realize, however, that only certain aspects of music—such as pitch, melody, rhythm, meter, and texture—can be depicted in notation; aspects such as ornamental nuance, slight gradations of pitch, timbre, and mood cannot be indicated.

Musical notation exists elsewhere in the world, but most often only to preserve compositions for posterity or as a reminder to performers. Few cultures outside the West use music notation prescriptively, that is, as a guide to live performance. And even where there is notation, it is usually skeletal because its function is to provide only what is necessary to cause performance. This notation is viewed as a point of departure, much as you find with jazz improvisation.

Exchange and Adaptation

Although disparate musical categories like *kabuki* and *bluegrass* suggest that musical systems are isolated from each other, the reality is much more complex. As distinctive as a given musical culture can be— and many are quite distinctive—none developed without outside influence. Some borrowed or loaned aspects travel better than others, however. Instruments, because they are objects, can be easily adopted by other cultures, though they are usually *adapted* as well to make them serve the aesthetic ideals of the borrower. On the other hand, even neighboring cultures can have dramatically differing musical concepts, timbre preferences, decorative styles, and tuning systems.

To give a specific example, few would debate that Vietnam's musical culture is distinctive, that it can be quickly recognized even by min-

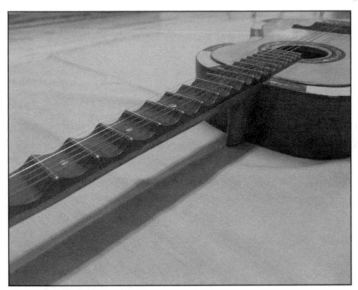

Notice the wood has been scraped away from the neck of this "Vietnamized" guitar

imally experienced listeners. But it is also true that Vietnam was virtually a Chinese colony for nearly 1,000 years and adopted many aspects of Chinese music, especially its instruments. However, the Vietnamese transformed these instruments to satisfy the requirements of their own sonic world. The most striking difference is the use of noticeably higher frets on the lutes with loosely strung strings. While Chinese instruments were built primarily to produce fixed pitches, the Vietnamese system uses many "in-between" pitches and thus

requires tone-bending created by pulling the strings downward. The Vietnamese guitar, for example, has an unusual neck, with the wood between the frets scooped out to give the player the space in which to pull the strings.

Cultural Intersections

To the extent that the world ever had any isolated, unique cultures, the modern world in which we live has certainly breached most of the old walls. Culture contact between and among distinctly named cultural groups is the norm. Whereas in the past this contact occurred through personal interaction as people from one group visited, encountered, traded with, fought with, or expanded into other groups, today there are also pervasive media bringing music, film, and dance to almost anyone living anywhere.

In 1991, I (TM) visited a remote village in central Laos accessible by Landrover over miles of dirt roads through other pre-modern villages. As we approached the village, we had to disembark from the vehicle and walk the last mile because the bridge had been destroyed during the Vietnam War some twenty years earlier and was not yet replaced. As we approached one of the larger houses, owned by the village headman, a group of traditionally dressed children, both ethnic Lao and upland minorities, emerged from the house to witness a rare visit by Westerners. After we climbed the ladder into the house, we noticed they had been watching a television powered by a car battery. On the TV were current popular music videos being broadcast from Khon Kaen, Thailand, hundreds of miles to the south. In this village seemingly three miles from the end

A traditional house in the remote provincial capital of Salavane, Laos, with television antenna but no regular electricity

of the earth, the young generation was fully aware of modern entertainments emanating from Southeast Asian cities.

Throughout history, distinctive musics have resulted not from isolation but through contact. It is the unique mixing of peoples, events, and responses that generates the energy that leads to new and hybrid musical styles and instruments—and sometimes even to completely new genres. The United States offers many examples of this: jazz, blues, and gospel are three results of the energy produced when Europeans and Africans reacted to each other during the late nineteenth and early twentieth centuries

Many places in the world could be used as case studies, and indeed later chapters will highlight this issue. Some of the most obvious include

Japan, where indigenous culture was profoundly influenced by the cultures of China and to some extent Korea (especially as a filter through which Chinese culture passed). Southeast Asian culture came about from indigenous civilization becoming infused with new elements from India to the West, China to the north, and later Europe and the United States as well. Caribbean musics have to be defined in these terms, for all of this area's distinctive musics—including calypso, steel pan, reggae, salsa, and rhyming spiritual—result from the mixing of peoples and cultures.

A Case Study of Istanbul, Turkey: A Lesson in Geography, History, Religions, and Musical Exchange

We have chosen the modern city of Istanbul, Turkey, as a case study of cultural exchange. Its strategic location straddling the Bosphorus (a broad river connecting the Black Sea to the Mediterranean) marks the boundary between Europe and Asia. A remarkable amount of history and culture passed through here, profoundly affecting vast areas from Europe to Central Asia and North Africa. Indeed, travelers to Istanbul will encounter the remains and monuments of each historical layer. Although now seen as an Islamic city—albeit in a secular Turkish state—Istanbul was once a major center of European civilization. How Istanbul's status changed, and its musical implications, is the subject of this case study.

The story begins with the conquests of Greek Macedonian, Alexander the Great (356–323 B.C.), son of Philip of Macedonia (382–336 B.C.). Soon after being crowned in 336 B.C., Alexander set off to conquer a vast territory that eventually included northern Greece, much of modern Egypt, and vast lands across Western Asia into Central and South Asia, an expansion that continued until his death in 323 B.C. These conquests brought Macedonian Greek (also called Hellenistic) civilization, including aspects of architecture, language, sculpture, art, and most likely music as well, to the conquered peoples, although there is no clear evidence of *their* influence on Macedonia. The area of the Bosphorus was well within the Greek world, and the small city founded on the European side was called Byzantium.

The Roman Empire expanded as Alexander's declined, and by the death of Emperor Trajan in A.D. 117, the Romans occupied much of western, central, and southeastern Europe, northern Africa, and most of the territory conquered by Alexander. Within a few hundred years, Rome's unity would crumble, and the humble village of Byzantium would become one of the world's greatest cities. In 330 Roman Emperor Constantine I made Byzantium the capital of the eastern portion and (humbly) renamed it Constantinople. His successor, Theodosius I, in 395 divided the empire into Western and Eastern halves, giving each

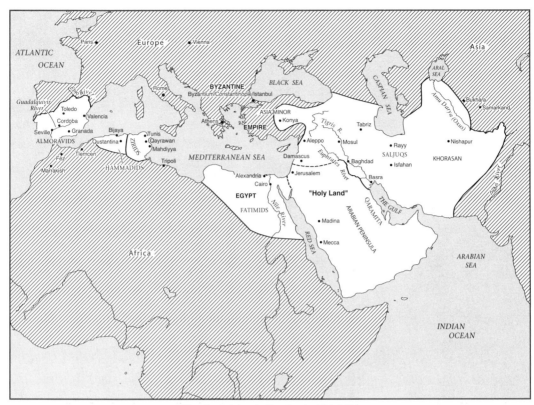

The Early Islamic Empire (c. 800 A.D.)

of his sons dominion over them, but with the decline of the Western Roman Empire the eastern half rose to greater prominence.

Whereas Rome was the center of what came to be called Roman Catholic Christianity, Constantinople was the center of the Eastern Rite, also called Byzantine Rite, the origin of a plethora of "Orthodox" faiths, each headed, not by a Pope, but a Patriarch. With the fall of Rome to the Ostrogoths in 476, Constantinople assumed its place as capital of what remained of the Roman Empire (the Eastern Empire) and center of the Eastern Church. The blending of Greek and Middle Eastern civilizations brought about a culture, religious and otherwise, that was distinct from that of Rome. Emperor Justinian I (reigned 527–565) attempted to reform the Church, strengthened the Empire, and built one of the city's noblest churches, the Hagia [Saint] Sophia cathedral.

The birth in 570 of an obscure man named Muhammed in Mecca on the Arabian Peninsula was to change everything. By the death of Muhammed, the Prophet and founder of Islam in 632, Arabia had been converted to Islam, and by 656 parts of North Africa and most of the eastern expanses of the Eastern Roman Empire had been conquered as well. By 814 Islam had spread entirely across north Africa and throughout Spain. At the same time the Catholic and Byzantine Churches engaged in disputes with each other while each was torn internally by disputes.

The great church of St. Sophia in Istanbul, Turkey, built in the sixth century, became an Islamic mosque, with added minarets, after the conquest of Constantinople by the Ottoman Turks in 1453

By 1054 a formal schism between East and West completed the separation.

As Islam conquered the "Holy Lands," a succession of events led to the Crusades, organized by various European emperors and kings to reclaim Jerusalem from what were termed the "Infidels." There were seven crusades organized at various points in Europe between 1096 and 1270. These great armies spent months, if not years, marching across vast lands, rivers, and mountains in fighting to regain Jerusalem and the Holy Land. Those that traversed the land had to fend for themselves, often raiding and destroying the cities and killing the unlucky residents. Some sailed through the Mediterranean, but storms often reduced such navies to bands of survivors. The ill-fated Fourth Crusade, organized in Venice in 1202, only reached Constantinople in 1204. Although all involved were Christian, the Crusaders plundered the capital of the Eastern Church, even establishing a line of Latin emperors, but failed to reach their goal, the Holy Land. Although there was a restoration of Eastern Emperors and a flourishing of the Church in the eleventh century, Constantinople remained under pressure, not just from Islam, but also from the Muslim Seljuq Turks expanding from the east.

The siege of Constantinople, begun in 1395, ended in 1453 when the city fell to the Ottoman Turks, and the city's name was changed to its present form, Istanbul. The Turkish ruler, Mehmed II, repopulated the city with people brought from elsewhere in the rapidly expanding

Ottoman Empire and converted the city's great churches into mosques. Not only were the great mosaics of these buildings covered in plaster, but towers, called *minarets*, were added around the building, these both indicating the importance of the mosque and providing a tower from which a Muslim *muezzin* called the faithful to prayer five times daily. Under Mehmed II and especially Süleyman the Magnificent (1520–1566), great mosques were constructed following the same basic cruciform (cross-like) pattern of the earlier eastern churches.

The Ottoman Empire continued to expand, especially into southeastern and central Europe, reaching its point of greatest expansion at the gates of Vienna in 1680, after which the empire began to recede and crumble. The Ottoman emperors, called Caliphs, ruled from magnificent Topkap Saray Palace overlooking the Bosphorus from the west, accumulating great wealth expressed in the arts, architecture, and music by bleeding the subjugated areas dry of resources. Because the Ottoman Turks were so brutal, many rebellions arose, leading to great battles that make absorbing a full history of the Empire and southeastern Europe daunting.

Of importance, because of its musical implications, is the *Janizary* [spelled *Yeniceri* in Turkish and *Janissary* is some Western writings], a corps of elite troops commanded by the Ottoman Caliphs from the late fourteenth century until their destruction in 1826. Consisting of Christian youths brought from the conquered Balkan provinces, these celibate (until the late sixteenth century) soldiers included bands of musicians who played martial music in parades. What made them distinctive was their use of double reed aerophones (called *zurna*), trumpets, and a battery of percussion including bass drums, triangles, cymbals, and other percussion, including a pole with jingles, later called a "jingling johnny" in Europe. To Europeans these "exotic" instruments were quite attractive.

After 1680, as the Empire retreated from Europe, replaced by the now-growing Hapsburg or Austro-Hungarian Empire, the government became increasingly corrupt and experienced various coups. After joining Germany as part of the Axis in World War I and being defeated, the Ottoman Empire was ripe for total reform. This came in the form of Mustafa Kemal (later given the title *Atatürk* [Father of the Turks]), who disbanded the Empire in 1922 and reformed Turkey into a modern, European-oriented secular republic. He also changed the writing system from Arabic to the Latin alphabet in the process. At this writing, Turkey is a member of NATO and aspires to membership in the European Union.

The modern traveler visiting Istanbul will be struck by the many layers of its history to be seen, all within walking distance. There are Greek style ruins, an Egyptian obelisk covered with hieroglyphics brought to Byzantium by conquering Romans, the incredible Roman cisterns—football field–sized chambers beneath Istanbul supported by stone columns from dismantled government buildings designed to store water for a city notoriously short of it—great Christian churches with their magni-

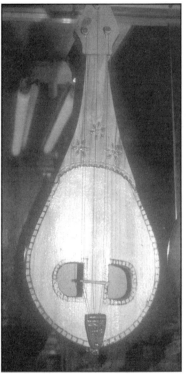

Turkish *kemence* (left) and Greek *lyra* (right). Note the similarities to the medieval instruments played by angels depicted in a cathedral carving shown below.

ficent mosaics, and mosques that rival the great cathedrals of Europe.
The musical results are many:

- Greek and Arabic music theory were closely related. They in turn
  became the basis for Medieval European music theory, the foundation for the system used today.
- Certain procedures and melodic styles from Turkey became fundamental in southeastern Europe. Likewise, various Arabic styles
  penetrated Spain, Portugal, and certain Mediterranean islands.
- When Islam expanded into Europe, it became a permanent part
  of many countries, including Albania, Bosnia-Herzegovina,
  Kosovo, Bulgaria, and Macedonia. The mosques throughout these
  lands practice typical Islamic forms of chant, including the Call to
  Prayer and the reading of the Koran, Islam's holy book.
- Although the Byzantine Church once headquartered in
  Constantinople (now Istanbul) has long since disappeared, its
  direct descendant, the Greek Orthodox Church, even today
  retains many of its musical practices.
- The Rom (often called gypsies) came from India and migrated
  over a long period of time into northern Africa and Europe. They
  brought with them much musical culture from Western Asia. In
  some places the public music of the Rom became, or at least
  blended with, local traditional musics, making conceptual separation nearly impossible.

Musical interchange occurred for many reasons:
1. The flow of culture from the Greek west to the conquered lands
   of the east thanks to Alexander the Great, and the return flow of
   culture from these lands to the west as it was conquered by the
   Ottoman Turks.
2. The Crusaders, who no doubt brought aspects of European culture to the lands they crossed and the souvenirs, mental and physical, they carried back if they were lucky enough to return home.
3. Intellectual, cultural, and material interchange within each of the
   great empires that successively occupied these lands. Because
   the Ottoman Turks were so hated in Europe, many people
   are still reluctant to admit the degree to which Turkish culture
   influenced the architecture, cuisine, dress, languages, life styles,
   and music of the conquered lands, but they are often quite obvious to an outsider lacking these age-old grudges.

Even a casual comparison of Turkish instruments with many found
in Greece, Albania, Romania, Bulgaria, and the former Yugoslav states
will reveal obvious relationships. While the patterns of diffusion into
both Asia and Europe are complex, we note some of the more obvious
examples here:

The Turkish *ney* (Terry Miller and Bob Snider)

1. Fiddles or Bowed Lutes. The distinctive shape of the Turkish *kemence* seen in the photo below appears in several southeastern European countries, including Greece *(lyra)* and Bulgaria *(gadulka)*, among others. We can only speculate on whether these instruments are also related to such instruments as the medieval German *Scheitholt* and the French *rebec.* In some cases the route of entry could have included Moorish Spain during the Muslim Arabic occupation.

2. End-Blown Flutes. The Turkish end-blown flute called *ney,* shown in the photo at left, also appears in southeastern Europe.

3. Dulcimer or Hammered Zither. Among the most widespread of instrumental types is the hammered zither (organologically called a dulcimer), which nearly always has a box resonator in trapezoid shape. The origin is thought to be the Persian *santur.* The instrument traveled west throughout Europe, transforming into, for example, the Greek *sandouri,* the Rom *cimbalom*, the German *Hackbrett,* and

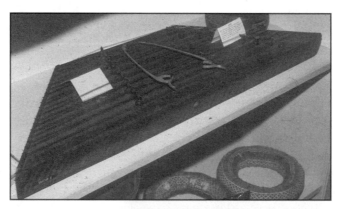

The Persian (Iranian) *santur* (above) and American "hammered dulcimer" (right)

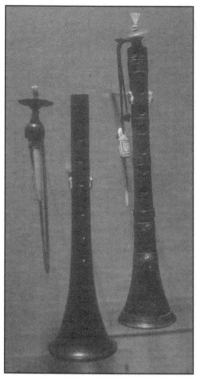

Turkish *zurna* (left) and Malaysian *serunai* (right)

Turkish lute *ud* (left) and Greek *lauto* (right)

 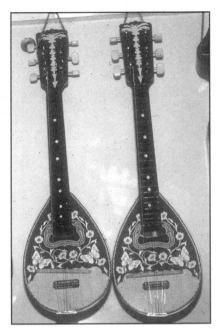

Turkish *baglama* (left) and Greek *bouzouki* (right)

SANTUR

A hammered zither from the Persian classical tradition. Often cited as the origin of hammered zithers found throughout Asia, Northern Africa, Europe, and the Western hemisphere.

ZURNA

(Also, ZOURNA)
A double-reed aerophone from Turkey, North Africa and Greece.

BAGLAMA

A round-bodied lute from Turkey.

the French *doulcemelle*. It also traveled east to Asia, and west to North America, where it is called the "hammered dulcimer."

4. Double Reeds. Like the dulcimer, double-reed instruments have traveled east and west, though it does not seem probable that all are related to those from Western Asia. The Turkish/Arabic *zurna* instruments are the likely predecessors of the Greek *zournas,* in a chain of instruments leading all the way to the French *bombarde* and even perhaps to the capped reeds such as the medieval and renaissance *shawm* or *Schalmei*. It is also possible that all of these instruments descended from the ancient Greek *aulos*, first developed in Western Asia, then transmitted back to Europe.

5. Pear-Shaped Lute. The name for a pear-shaped lute in Arabic and Turkish is *al-'ud,* the root of the English word "lute." As the *al-'ud* traveled west it evolved into folk instruments such as the Greek *lauto* and Romanian *cobza*, as well as the highly refined instrument of the Renaissance simply called "lute." The Renaissance lute played in France, Germany, and England most likely entered from Arabic (Moorish) Spain. The *al-'ud* also traveled east, where it became the Chinese *pipa*, the Japanese *biwa*, and the Vietnamese *dan tyba.*

6. Round-Bodied Lute. Round-bodied lutes abound in Western Asia and Southeastern Europe under a variety of names, but they also occur in Europe outside the areas occupied by the Ottoman Turks. The Turkish *baglama* (also called *saz*) is made in various sizes with movable frets, and similar instruments, usually called *tambura* or a variant of this term, are found in, for example, Bulgaria, Croatia, and Serbia. Possibly even the Italian *mandolin*

derives from these prototypes. Ironically, the best-known Greek instrument, the *bouzouki,* descends from the Turkish *buzuq,* and as a result some nationalistic Greeks refuse to listen to *bouzouki* music, since they consider it a survival of their hated Turkish oppressors.

Our study of Turkish music shows how culture ebbs and flows between and among sometimes strikingly different civilizations over time and place. These processes are always complicated and can never be sorted out precisely, but it is clear that today's world results from a series of events that have been taking place over a long period of time. Without an awareness of these interactions, it is impossible to understand why things are the way they are today.

Questions to Consider

1. How might an "insider" to a musical tradition hear it differently from an "outsider"? Why are both perspectives necessary for a complete picture?

2. What music best expresses your individual identity?

3. What distinguishes "modern" from "postmodern" scholarship in music?

4. What role does music play in your spiritual life?

5. How has technology changed the kinds of music we listen to and how we hear them?

6. Why is history important to the study of world music?

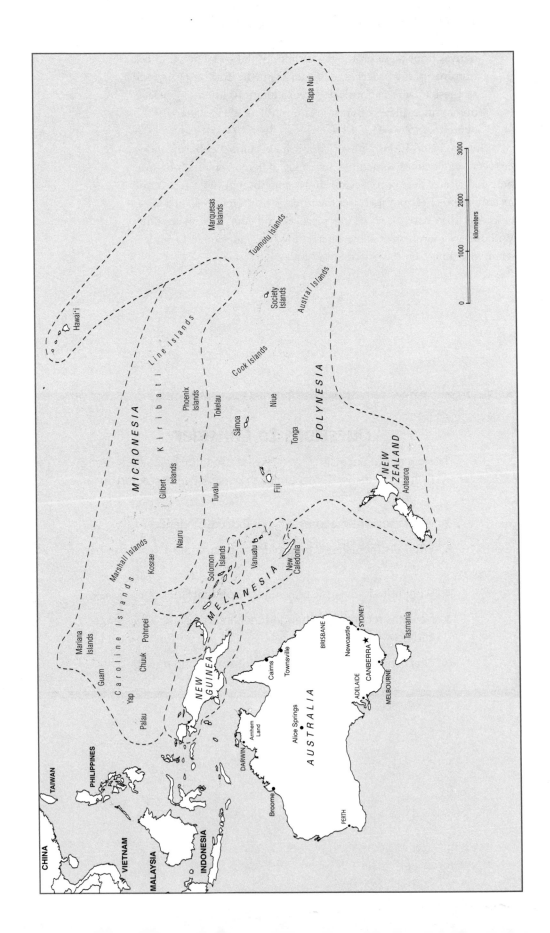

Ayers Rock on the central Australian plain southwest of Alice Springs (Max T. Miller)

CHAPTER 4

Oceania:
Voices of Land and Sea

Background Preparation

*T*he area known as Oceania includes Australia and numerous island groups spread across thousands of square miles in the Pacific Ocean. Whereas the land area of Australia is nearly three million square miles, the total land area of the Pacific Islands is less than 500,000 square miles, smaller than the state of Alaska. The islands of New Zealand, Papua New Guinea, and Hawaii comprise over 90 percent of this land area, while the remaining islands, numbering almost 25,000, account for fewer square miles of land area than the state of Indiana. The Pacific Islands are divided into three subregions: Melanesia (meaning "dark islands," a name referring to the dark skin pigment of many of the island's inhabitants), Micronesia (meaning "small islands"), and Polynesia (meaning "many islands").

Most of Oceania is considered tropical or subtropical. The Pacific Islands straddle the equator, with Micronesia in the northern hemisphere and most of Melanesia and Polynesia, as well as Australia, being part of the southern hemisphere. While Australia and larger islands such as New Zealand and Hawaii are accessible by plane, many of the smaller islands and atolls of the Pacific are still quite isolated, with ships arriving on only a weekly or monthly basis. Tourism is a primary economic resource in the Pacific, but most indigenous groups continue to survive on subsistence farming or hunting and gathering. Australian aboriginal communities continue to keep their traditional practices fairly secluded, though many have adopted an urban lifestyle or rely on government support.

While extensive European cultural influence is found throughout Oceania due to colonization of the region, primarily by the British, the indigenous populations of Australia and the Pacific Islands maintain traditional cultural practices. These are widely varied and considered in many cases to be among the most ancient customs on the planet. A common denominator for all groups is a close relationship with nature. Complex animistic and totemistic spiritual systems have evolved throughout Oceania, in which practitioners call on animals and natural elements for guidance, protection, and subsistence. Rituals involving musical activity are most often associated with these beliefs, and many songs are believed to derive from ancestral spirits who are inevitably linked with spiritual forces of nature.

Along with these traditional beliefs one finds much Christian influence, introduced by European missionaries throughout the nineteenth and twentieth centuries. Missionaries, along with colonial governments, drastically changed the cultural customs and social systems of many populations throughout Oceania. English or French are considered the "official" languages of most nations, though indigenous dialects continue to be spoken. Home to roughly 1,200 languages, Australia and the islands of the Pacific provide some of the most fertile soil for linguistic and anthropological studies. Because vocal traditions predominate, effective research on music traditions from Oceania often requires specialized linguistic study.

The music of Oceania is primarily vocal. With few exceptions, instruments tend to be small and portable. Most are idiophones or membranophones. Slit drums are common, especially in Melanesia. The few aerophones that are found are primarily flutes, though the most famous instrument from the region is likely the Australian *didjeridu*, classified as a trumpet. Chordophones—namely the guitar or derivatives of it—are largely European in origin.

Myths and belief systems, along with practical knowledge and oral histories, are passed from generation to generation through song and dance. Music is often considered a link to the spiritual plane, and specialists in ritual-associated music traditions are common. Subtle distinctions in vocal performance are considered vital to the identity of individual social groups; thus, music and dance are regarded as highly valued cultural property.

Planning the Itinerary

Our review of music traditions from Oceania begins with the mysterious sound of the didjeridu—an instrument found among the aborigines of northern Australia, who maintain some of the planet's most intriguing and ancient cultural practices. Next we introduce an example of one of the world's most common instrument types, the mouth harp (also referred to as *Jew's Harp*), as we travel to Papua New Guinea, which has been of major anthropological interest for several decades. While ethnomusicologists have studied this region extensively, many music traditions remain largely unexplored due to the great cultural diversity found among its indigenous populations. We then arrive on more familiar ground—Hawaii—to examine indigenous vocal practices associated with the precolonial period of Polynesia. Finally, we introduce the choral traditions of the Pacific through an example of Kiribati vocal performance, which reveals the influence of European musical creation over the last two hundred years.

Arrival: Australia

The Australian wilderness is home to some of the most unique species of animals on the planet. The koala, kangaroo, and platypus, just to name a few, have intrigued animal lovers worldwide for decades. While many of the coastal areas have moderate vegetation that support such species, the interior of the continent, known as the Outback or Bush, mainly consists of vast plains and large desert regions. The major cities—Sydney, Melbourne, and Perth—are located along the coast, while the few inhabitants of the interior are mostly members of Australia's well-known indigenous population, who are referred to as Aborigines.

While most Aborigines live in urban settings today, a government reserve in the Northern Territory, known as Arnhem Land, is home to more than 30,000 Aborigines who maintain cultural practices that have existed for roughly 40,000 years. Though some of these aborigines live in government-sponsored housing, many continue to follow a semi-nomadic lifestyle. These Aborigines acquire few material possessions, and these mostly relate either to hunting (such as spears or boomerangs), or spiritual practices (musical instruments).

ABORIGINES

A generic term for an indigenous population, often used to describe native peoples of Australia.

DIDJERIDU

A long trumpet made from a hollowed tree branch and played by aborigines from Australia. The sound is characterized by a low, rumbling drone.

AUSTRALIA

The koala bear, one example of Australia's unique wildlife (Max T. Miller)

The close affinity Australian Aborigines have with their environment is revealed in their totemistic belief system. Totemism centers on the relationship of an individual or group with animals or natural objects or elements, such as specific mountains or the ocean. Animism—the belief that all living things as well as more general phenomena, such as the wind or fire, have a spirit—also plays an important role in the Aboriginal cosmology. Known as *The Dreaming* or *Dreamtime*, this cosmology is the focus of much artistic activity within the Aboriginal communities of Australia.

DREAMTIME

A term describing the Australian aboriginal spiritual belief system and concept of creation.

Site 1: Australian Aborigine Song with Didjeridu

Track 1

First Impressions. The vocal exclamations in this example are accompanied by the steady pulse of wooden clapsticks and the low rumble of

An Inside Look
Amy Kuʻuleialoha Stillman

Hawaiian music is my ancestors' tradition. My mother took me to hula lessons when I was five years old, and I had an ʻukulele in my hands by the time I was seven. After an adolescence hooked on Elvis and the Beatles, I returned to

Amy Kuʻuleialoha Stillman, Music researcher and scholar

Hawaiian music in my high school years and have embraced it as my passion since. As an undergraduate at the University of Hawaiʻi in the 1970s, I read anthropological scholarship on Hawaiians and had an uneasy feeling that my parents' and my traditions of "modern" Hawaiian music were being devalued as inauthentic because of their westernized character. That's when I realized that I needed to get a Ph.D in order to join the scholarly conversation at a level where I would be taken seriously and could have an impact. I've consciously chosen to focus on research and writing and decline requests to teach performance because there are many talented performers who do teach excellently, but as yet few scholars with the training and patience necessary to engage in laborious archival research. My work has been devoted to exploring how contemporary Hawaiian performance retains critical Hawaiian performance and conceptual parameters even as Hawaiian people embraced westernization and conversion to Christianity. I've reached back into archival resources and uncovered hundreds (if not thousands) of pieces, a musical repertoire, only a fraction of which had been passed to the present in continuous performance. The 1970s cultural revival of Hawaiian culture has created a demand for this repertoire. Yet hundreds of pieces have remained unrecognized because of the circumstances of their being institutionalized in archives that for many decades were not hospitable to Hawaiians seeking their heritage. My aspiration is to bring the archival repertoire back to life by reuniting it with the performers who have maintained the skills of singing and dancing. E ola!

An Aboriginal dance accompanied by clapsticks and *didjeridu* (Axel Poignant)

the *didjeridu,* an end-blown trumpet that is the most distinctive feature of traditional music from Arnhem Land. The vocalist is like a storyteller shouting his words to all who would listen, including ancestral spirits, while the constant drone of the *didjeridu* may suggest a cloud of hornets swirling overhead or the rumbling sound of a large waterfall.

Aural Analysis. The *didjeridu* is traditionally made from a tree branch, typically eucalyptus, hollowed out by termites. Some *didjeridu* are made of bamboo, while modern instruments used in nontraditional contexts are sometimes made of plastic or even metal. Most *didjeridu* are between three and half and seven feet long, with a diameter of one to three inches. The ring of the blowing end is covered with beeswax to protect the performer's mouth from the wood's ragged edge and to shape the blowing end to a preferred size, in order to create a solid seal around the player's mouth.

The guttural sound of the *didjeridu* is made by relaxing the lips and blowing air through the mouth to make the lips flap or buzz. This vibration echoes through the instrument producing a deep fundamental drone with a multitude of overtones. An adept performer can create different timbres and a rhythmically patterned drone by altering the airflow with his mouth and tongue. He may also force sudden bursts of air through the instrument to increase the volume or alter the pitch and timbre. Performers often make vocalizations, such as humming or growling, to change the sound of the instrument. This latter technique is especially important when performers attempt to imitate the sounds of birds or other animals.

Fundamental to playing the *didjeridu* is utilization of the circular breathing technique, which creates a continuous airflow, making it possible to produce a steady drone. Air is expelled through the lips by tongue and cheek muscles. As the performer exhales, he simultaneously inhales through his nose to replenish the air reserve stored in the cheeks. An easy way to try this technique is with a cup of water and a straw; a continuous airflow will maintain a steady stream of bubbles. While a beginner can soon do this with a small tube, the larger didjeridu is more difficult to master, because it requires much more air and pressure to produce a consistent and correct tone.

The clapsticks that are used to accompany *didjeridu* are generally made of hard woods, and tend to be roughly a foot and a half in length and about an inch in diameter. Some Aboriginal groups use boomerangs as clapsticks, especially in ceremonies that prepare hunting parties for expeditions. The clapsticks provide a steady pulse, which the vocalist uses to frame his vocal phrases. The *didjeridu* performer may also correlate his rhythmic drone to the clapsticks by adding overtone bursts in conjunction with the pulse of the clapsticks. These bursts alter the pitch of the drone. In our example, this pitch alteration, which raises the initial pitch by a half tone, occurs on roughly every other pulse shortly after the clapsticks enter. Oftentimes the clapsticks are played only during the *didjeridu* interludes, and not during sung sections—though they do sound throughout both sung and instrumental sections of our example.

This performance consists of two parts: a presentation of the main text and a secondary vocables section in which nonlexical (meaningless) formulaic phrases are used. Though some overlapping of pitches occurs, the main text is generally sung in a higher range than the vocables section, which concludes in a comparatively lower range. Throughout the piece, the melodic contour of the vocal line is typically descending. Here is a transcription of the words heard before the clapsticks enters (the main text is in boldface):

CIRCULAR BREATHING

A technique used to maintain a continuous airflow in aerophone performance.

Village elders chant with accompaniment by *didjeridu* and clapsticks
(Mark Crocombe)

Dijan old jong, dijan iya—bushfire
[This one's an old song—bushfire]
[Didjeridu enters]
ga **andegarrana andegarran(a)**
andegarrana andegarran(a)
andegarrana andegarrana *ya*
a ga na ya ya ga ga
[Clapsticks enter]
(*Bunggridj-bunggridj: Wangga Songs by Alan Maralung; Northern Australia.* SF 40430. Washington DC: Smithsonian-Folkways, 1993, p. 30.)

The vocal timbre is nasal and there is only one singer, which is typical among the Aborigines—though group vocal performances do occur. There is only one *didjeridu* player, as is almost always the case, because the fundamental pitches of different *didjeridu* are not generally the same. The instrumental dynamic level remains consistent throughout, while the secondary vocables section is at a slightly lower volume than the main text.

Cultural Considerations. The title of this example, "Bushfire," with its animistic reference to a natural phenomenon, is indicative of the strong association between musical performance and spiritual belief that is characteristic of Australian Aborigines. Most traditional Aboriginal performances, whether in ritual contexts or for entertainment, have a sacred element that relates to *The Dreaming,* the Aboriginal cosmology. *The Dreaming* tells of an ancient mythological past when the earth was merely a featureless swirl of creative energy. At that time, ancestral spirits *(wondjina)* roamed the planet creating life and shaping the topographical features of the earth. The spirits also created songs, known as history songs, that provided the framework with which the Aborigines were able to maintain their society, the land, and totemistic relationships. Through the correct performance of these songs, the Aborigines are able to tap into this ancient and creative power left behind by the ancestral spirits. Aborigines believe that these history songs have remained unchanged since the beginning of time.

While history songs are regarded as the most important, songs related to totems or social activities also exist. New songs in the latter two categories are sometimes composed, though they usually are considered to have been inspired by an ancestral spirit or taught to an individual in a dream. Women do not usually perform songs along with men and are prohibited from playing the *didjeridu.* The sound of the *didjeridu* is considered the most sacred of all sounds and is regarded not only as symbolic of the creative powers of the ancestral spirits, but as an actual aural manifestation of their creative energy. Female performance of the didjeridu is taboo primarily because aborigines believe that exposure to the instrument's spiritual power would make a woman more fertile, causing her to birth too many children for the community to support.

A nighttime *corroboree* ritual performed by Aborigines from Arnhem Land, Australia (Axel Poignant)

The most common contexts for traditional Aboriginal music performances are mortuary rites and boys' circumcision ceremonies. Songs are also performed on more informal occasions, most frequently during a *corroboree*, or nighttime ritual. Most of these events are considered sacred and are closed to the uninitiated; thus, there is little documentation of them. Dance plays an important role in ritual contexts. White paint is applied to the dancer's dark-skinned body according to prescribed patterns associated with a clan's totems and the specific ritual. At the nighttime *corroboree*, this paint shines in the firelight. During these events, which are believed to connect participants with ancestral spirits, the hypnotic sound of the *didjeridu* helps create a feeling of disorientation from time and place.

Arrival: *Papua New Guinea*

While Papua New Guinea has a population of fewer than five million inhabitants, there are more than seven hundred languages spoken among its diverse cultural groups. Comprising the eastern half of the island of New Guinea, the region is the largest in Melanesia. Its precolonial history dates to roughly 50,000 years ago and is believed to be linked with the Aboriginal populations of Australia, due to several cultural and genetic similarities.

The major cities are found along the coast while the highland interior is home to much of the population. Most indigenous groups practice subsistence farming—that is, they grow food and raise livestock for personal use rather than for commerce. While English is the official language due to years of British colonial influence, only a small portion of the population speaks it fluently. Indigenous languages predominate, along with Tok Pisin, a pidgin English combined with Melanesian.

Christian missionaries, primarily from Europe, have had some influence on indigenous spiritual beliefs found in Papua New Guinea. Local traditions that were considered pagan or erotic in nature were prohibited by many missionaries, in particular traditional dancing that was targeted as an immoral activity that promoted sexual promiscuity. As a result, many local customs, especially in lowland areas where missionaries have had the most influence, have been lost or modified.

Nevertheless, a wide array of traditional music and dance is still found in Papua New Guinea, and many customs have been

PAPUA NEW GUINEA

MELANESIA
A collection of islands in the Pacific Ocean. The term is derived from Greek, and means "black islands," a reference to the darker skin pigmentation of the majority population.

Enga men play the *kundu* goblet drum in Papua New Guinea (Don Niles)

reestablished since the country achieved independence in 1975. Tourists are visiting the island in increasing numbers, drawn by the elaborate dress and varied cultural activities of the many different ethnic groups. Probably the most visible of instruments found among the Papuans are the large slit drums called *garamut* and the hourglass-shaped drums known as *kundu*. These are used in many ceremonial contexts and have become a staple of tourist shows and government-sponsored festivals. Less popular at these events, but perhaps the most widespread instrument in the country, is the *susap*, a bamboo mouth harp commonly played for self-entertainment.

Track 2

Site 2: Susap from Papua New Guinea

First Impressions. The *susap* has a distinctive metallic "twangy" timbre, as if the performer were talking through an electronic voice modulator. A first-time listener not seeing the instrument might imagine the performer is striking a metal spring or cable with a small wrench or screwdriver, creating a wavering "boing" effect. This unique tone quality makes our example memorable even in the absence of a singable melody or repeatable rhythm.

A Baruya man plays the *susap* mouth harp from the Eastern Highlands province of Ⓒ Papua New Guinea (Don Niles)

Aural Analysis. Mouth harps, such as the *susap*, are one of the most common instruments found throughout the world. Most are made of either wood or bamboo, while some are made from metal. They are not technically classified as harps but belong, rather, to a subcategory of idiophone known as *lamellophones*. Lamellophones in general have a flexible tongue that is typically plucked to produce sound. Mouth resonated lamellophones usually have a flexible tongue set or cut into a frame. The performer plucks the tongue *(lamella)* so that it vibrates within the frame, producing a distinctive "twangy" timbre. The tongue must pass very close to the frame to produce the desired effect. A small piece of wax is sometimes fixed to the end of the tongue to encourage the tongue's vibration or to change the instrument's timbre.

To play the *susap*, the performer holds its frame tightly within the lips, holding one end to maintain the proper angle while plucking an extension that is attached either to the frame or to the tongue. Oftentimes a small string is attached and is pulled to vibrate the tongue. The mouth acts as a resonator, amplifying the sound of this extremely quiet instrument. The performer alters the sound by changing the size and shape of his oral cavity and vocal tract. While the fundamental pitch of the mouth harp does not generally change, the manipulation of overtones resonating in the mouth can produce recognizable melodic features, usually more closely related to speech than song.

In our example, the performer maintains a steady plucking pattern, but varies the rhythmic content through timbral changes. While the performance is likely improvised, the example can be segmented into four sections. The opening section includes twenty pulses without much timbral variation. This is followed by a more rhythmically active section in which the player begins to "speak" with the instrument, producing an accented low tone echoed by a faint overtone. The rhythmic emphasis shifts frequently: sometimes the fundamental tone is played twice before the echo is sounded, other times the player alternates evenly between the two timbres, producing one overtone for every low tone. This section is also marked by the frequent use of a dotted rhythm created by the performer using his tongue to silence the resonation just before plucking the instrument to produce the accented tone. One might express this rhythm as a short/long pattern, such as "du-duu, du-duu."

The third section occurs approximately ninety pulses into the performance and is characterized by a less-prominent role for the lower, accented tone and a new emphasis on varying the timbre of the higher overtones. Variations in timbre are produced through manipulations of the size of the mouth cavity and by changes in the position of the player's tongue. This section is the most "speech-like" of the four sections. The final section commences at approximately 150 pulses and is marked by the "boing" effect already mentioned, which is created by flickering the tongue inside the mouth cavity to produce a wavering, "wobbly" sound. This is perhaps the most unique timbral effect of the performance.

Cultural Considerations. In Papua New Guinea, as elsewhere, the mouth harp often acts as a "speech surrogate." Performers use it to imitate speech patterns and phonemes in order to create the illusion of speech in a musical context. The sounds of the mouth harp are often considered to be speech that is "disguised," in order that it not be understood by eavesdroppers.

While mouth harps are commonly used for self-entertainment, they are also frequently found in traditional courting rituals. In Papua New Guinea the *susap* is considered to possess love-controlling magic that men can use to attract a woman's affections. By using the instrument as a speech surrogate, the man is able to "say" things to the woman that might otherwise be considered inappropriate. The instrument also provides impunity from rejection. If the woman is attracted to her suitor, then the magic has worked; if not, the magic was either ineffective or not correctly utilized by the performer. An ignored suitor either has to improve his technique or use a different instrument to put the woman in the desired mood.

Arrival: Hawaii

HAWAII

The fiftieth state of the United States of America is geographically considered a part of Polynesia, a region including many well-known islands, such as Tahiti, Samoa, Easter Island, the Cook Islands, and even New Zealand. The first inhabitants of Hawaii most likely arrived from the Marquesas Islands and Tahiti, the largest of the Society Islands, sometime between the seventh and thirteenth centuries. These early settlers subsisted primarily on fish and *poi*, a pasty food made from taro plants. Their social organization was essentially feudal and incorporated strict taboo systems, called *kapus*.

POLYNESIA

A collection of islands in the Pacific Ocean. The term is derived from Greek, and means "many islands."

The first European visitor to Hawaii was the Englishman Captain James Cook, one of the most famous explorers of the late 1700s. Arriving in 1778, Cook was initially welcomed by the islanders, but relations between the British and Hawaiians soon turned sour, and in 1779 Cook was killed in a skirmish. Within only a few years, however, the islands became an important port for European and North American trade. Increasing contact with outsiders brought many changes to indigenous ways of life. The islands were politically unified in 1810 by King Kamehameha I, who encouraged foreign trade and successfully maintained Hawaii's independence from colonial control. He also supported native cultural customs and the indigenous religion until his death in 1819.

Support for Hawaiian culture was, however, abandoned by Kamehameha's son and successor, Kamehameha II, who in less than a year destroyed the old system of *kapus* and abolished the ancient ritual practices. The temples and idols of the old religion, a complex form of animism, were ordered destroyed and the king welcomed the arrival of Christian missionaries soon afterward. These events brought drastic changes to secular life as well, and the 1800s saw rapid changes in social organization, political power, and economic patterns. Sugar cane became a major export, and wealthy American businessmen began to acquire much power and land throughout the islands. The political power of the Hawaiian monarchy evaporated in the 1890s, and the country was eventually annexed by the United States.

The early 1900s saw an increased influx of immigrants from the United States, the Philippines, China, and Japan. Most came as laborers to work for the burgeoning pineapple industry and sugar cane plantations. The Japanese attack on Pearl Harbor on December 7, 1941, precipitated U.S. entry into World War II and made the islands of vital strategic interest to the United States. Initially, Japanese-Americans in Hawaii were distrusted, but their bravery in the ensuing war—they comprised some of the most decorated regimental military units in American history—diminished racial prejudice against them in the postwar years. Hawaii acquired statehood in 1959 and quickly became one of the most popular tourist destinations in the United States.

PORTAMENTO
A smooth, uninterrupted glide from one pitch to another.

Site 3: Hawaiian Drum-Dance Chant

First Impressions. While chanting in most traditions is strongly speech-like, Hawaiian drum-dance chant is often more song-like. Each phrase rolls off the vocalist's tongue like the gentle lap of ocean waves on a white-sand beach or the graceful flowing arm movements of Hawaii's famous *hula* dancers. The drums add a solid, but not overbearing, undertone that gives the performance an earthy feel, suggestive of a spiritual connection to nature.

Track 3

Aural Analysis. Hawaiian drum-dance chant consists simply of a voice, one or two drums, and accompanying dance. The preferred vocal timbre is usually full with a deep, resonant tone quality. Vocal ornamentation is important as with all styles of Polynesian chant. A prominent feature of Hawaiian vocal performance is the use of *vibrato* (a wavering of a tone). While vibrato is commonly used in many traditions, it is generally applied to sustained pitches. Hawaiian vocalists, however, frequently apply vibrato to shorter tones as well. The text setting is primarily syllabic—that is, it employs only one pitch per syllable, utilizing only two tones at an interval of a minor third. The vocalist emphasizes the upper pitch, but "falls" or "slides" to the lower pitch on sustained tones. This "sliding" technique is referred to as *porta-*

A Hawaiian musician plays the *kilu* (left) and *pahu* (right) drums
(George Bacon)

mento, and involves a continuous movement from one pitch to another, usually from high to low, with all of the frequencies between the two pitches being sounded. The singer in our example uses portamento occasionally at the beginning of the performance.

Another distinctive feature of Hawaiian vocal performance is

Near the edge of Hale Ma'uma'u Crater, dancers perform a *hula* in honor of Pele, the volcano goddess
(Adrienne L. Kaeppler)

PAHU
A single-headed
cylindrical membrano-
phone from Hawaii that
stands vertically on
a carved footed base.

KILU
A small drum from
Hawaii, usually made from
a coconut shell with a
fish skin face.

inherent in the language itself. Most words end with open vowel sounds, such as *ah, oh, oo, ai,* and so on, rather than closed hard consonants, such as *k, t,* or *p.* While hard consonants are found at the beginning of some words, they tend to be de-emphasized. As such, the singing flows from one phrase to the next with smooth transitions, as in our example, which begins with the vocalist speaking the phrase *"(Ai) Kaulilua i ke anu Waì alé ale"* before singing it. The open vowel sounds facilitate the use of portamento, as well as vibrato, and give the music its "flowing" feel.

The accompanying drums are known as the *pahu* and the *kilu* (also *pūniu*). The *pahu* is a single-headed cylindrical membranophone that stands vertically on a carved footed base. The base and drum are typically a single unit made from either a breadfruit or the wood of a coconut tree. The *pahu* can be as short as around nine inches or as tall as almost four feet. Its face is usually made from sharkskin, or sometimes from manta ray skin, and is attached with twine made from the outer fibers of coconuts. The *kilu* is a smaller drum usually made from a coconut shell and has a face made of fish skin. The *kilu* is sometimes attached to the performer's leg with a strap. It is played with a narrow strip of braided coconut fibers, creating a higher "slapping" sound relative to the *pahu,* which is played with the hand. The *pahu* is considered the more important of the two instruments, and its irregular rhythmic patterns correspond to important points in the song text and associated dance movements.

Cultural Considerations. The best-known examples of Hawaiian music today are heavily influenced by European musical traditions. Because Christian missionaries were often strict with regard to the vocal practices of converted islanders, much of the vocal music is based on European hymnody, and utilizes conceptions of harmony that presumably did not exist prior to contact with Europeans. Popular instruments such as the Hawaiian steel guitar, which uses a steel slide to stop the strings, or the *ukulele*, a small chordophone modeled after the guitar, only appeared in Hawaiian music after the colonial period began. Thus, "traditional" ensembles that tourists see accompanying hula dancers or hear on popular recordings reveal much Western influence.

Hawaiian drum-dance chant, however, is considered free from outside influence and remains a vital aspect of Hawaiian musical identity. The songs play an important role in the maintenance of indigenous language, spiritual beliefs, history, and social customs. While the poetic text of these songs or chants is the primary focus, the musical delivery is important too, as it enhances the efficacy of the words. Poetry used in drum-dance chant is generally referred to as *mele*. There are several categories of *mele*, the most sacred of which, *mele pule*, consists of prayers dedicated to traditional gods, performed by ritual specialists known as *kahuna*. Lesser categories of *mele* trace genealogical histories, name and honor people, or signify specific ritual contexts, such as weddings or funerals.

Mele hula are songs specifically associated with dance. Some are purely vocal, while those called *hula pahu* are those accompanied by the *pahu* drum. *Pahu* are highly valued ritual objects that hold much spiritual power (or *mana*). The sound produced is considered a voice and traditionally was believed to "speak" to the gods. Drums were typically the property of chiefs or priests and were symbolic of their authority and sacred power. As such, they were treasured items sought after by rival kingdoms. The *pahu* was used in many ritual contexts, such as important births or memorial services, but today is primarily found accompanying dances and rituals promoting Hawaiian ethnic identity.

Arrival: Kiribati

Kiribati is a collection of islands in Micronesia situated about 2,500 miles southwest of Hawaii. Its thirty-three coral islands, all but one of which are atolls (circular islands with a central lagoon), are divided into three groups: the Line Islands (east), the Phoenix Islands (central), and the Gilbert Islands (west), the latter being where most of the population resides. Kiritimati, also known as Christmas Island, is the largest coral atoll in the world and was among the many islands of the Pacific explored by Captain James Cook in 1777. Throughout the 1800s, British and American sailors visited the islands while hunting sperm whales and expanding trade routes. The British eventually claimed most of the islands of Kiribati as British protectorates; thus, English is widely spoken

HULA PAHU
Hawaiian dance songs using drum accompaniment.

MICRONESIA
A collection of islands in the Pacific Ocean. The term is derived from Greek, and means "tiny islands."

KIRIBATI

Kiribati women dance to the singing of a choir seated behind them
(Adrienne L. Kaeppler)

along with the native tongue, Gilbertese, an Austronesian language.

The first Protestant missionaries arrived in 1857, while the earliest Roman Catholics came in 1888. Much of modern social life revolves around church activities. International sports, such as soccer and volleyball, are popular along with traditional competitive activities, such as canoe-racing. Many I-Kiribati, as the islanders are known, rely on fishing and subsistence farming for survival and live in traditional houses made of wood and coconut palms, though there are also urban areas where inhabitants live in modern houses and import much of their food and other necessities.

Track 4

Site 4: Kiribati Group Song

First Impressions. Vocal performance among Pacific islanders is often a communal activity. The choir in our example is comprised of both men and women and has a distinctive "childlike" tonal quality. The recording evokes images of flower garland–adorned dancers in grass skirts surrounded by enthusiastic islanders singing in celebration. One feels that even tourists could join in by clapping along with the group.

Aural Analysis. Vocal choirs are common throughout Micronesia and Polynesia. Because most traditional performances are sung in unison, the use of harmony in our example reflects European musical influences, primarily introduced by Christian missionaries. Indigenous songs tend to use fewer pitches than those associated with the church—normally no more than five. The "youthful" vocal timbre is difficult to describe: it is a bit nasal and somewhat strained, even though many of the male voices are forceful and full.

In the Kiribati islands, vocal performances influenced by the church frequently start with a freely rhythmic section that is closer to indigenous traditions. This is followed by a metered section marked by the steady pulse of handclaps. During the metered section, the voices follow a call-and-response pattern, though the call is primarily just a shout that establishes pitch and signals the choir's entrance. The text setting is mostly syllabic. A whistle is used to signal the choir to close the performance with a brief series of handclaps.

Cultural Considerations. Choral traditions in Oceania predate the arrival of European colonialism. In Kiribati, music and dance were important symbols of social identity. All members of a performance group were of the same descent group. Participation in performance was essential to community cohesion and musical skills were regarded as valuable clan property. Song was considered a vital link to ancestral spirits and supernatural powers associated with natural elements, such as the wind or the ocean. Communities would sing in communal meetinghouses called *maneaba* the night before a battle, in order to help protect warriors or weaken enemies.

In lieu of physical combat, battles between rival clans frequently took the form of music and dance contests. Contests could involve the whole community or consist of matches between individuals. Competitors drew upon their knowledge of song to empower themselves with offensive and defensive magic. A dancer might call on the wind to "knock over" his enemy or conjure up a wall of dark thunderclouds to hide himself from his opponent. Through song, powerful deities were called on for strength and disparaging insults were traded, wrapped in metaphorical phrases, intended to antagonize the rivals. For example, a deity may be called on to strike the "distant rocks" (i.e., the rival group), so that they would crumble into the ocean and be eaten by baby sharks—a request that obliquely insulted the strength of the competitors, because baby sharks were viewed as weak and harmless. Competitions could put the dancers into an ecstatic state in which the power of the spirits would seem to work through the performers. These states were marked by labored breathing, trembling, and occasional screaming, and performers generally fainted after the spiritual power had left them.

The colonial government and Christian missionaries found the dances and their associated spiritual beliefs to be irreligious, unhealthy, and unproductive. As a result, restrictions were placed on dance activity to subdue the potential for ecstatic physical states. At the same time, church-related groups and social clubs without lineal affiliation began participating in the competitions, which undermined their function as surrogate battles between lineages. The focus of the competitions shift-

MANEABA
Term for a communal meeting house in Kiribati.

ed from an emphasis on descent groups and the supernatural powers of the participants to the artistic skills of the dancers and musicians.

Along with this shift in focus came changes in musical values. European musical practices, namely the use of harmony, became markers of superior musical performance and thus a common feature of song in Kiribati. Since achieving independence in 1979, however, Kiribati has experienced a revival of interest in traditional culture that has encouraged the performance of unison singing.

Questions to Consider

1. Why would vocal traditions predominate in Australia and Oceania?

2. How do you circular-breathe? Why is this technique useful when playing certain musical instruments?

3. How do Hawaiians use music to express their unique identity within American culture?

4. Why is music important to the Australian Aborigine's cosmology, *The Dreaming?*

5. How might musical instruments be used in courting practices? Does your culture have any courting rituals? If so, does music play a role in them?

6. Name some ways in which Christian missionaries have influenced traditional music in Oceania.

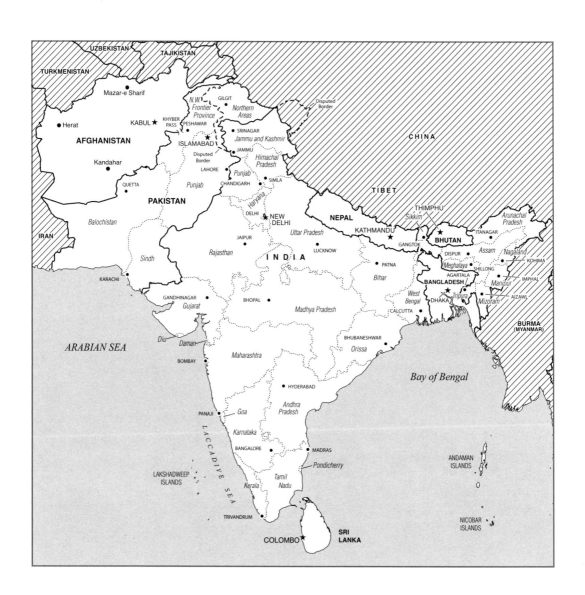

One of many great temples on the sacred Ganges River in Varanasi (Benares), India (Max T. Miller)

CHAPTER 5

South Asia:
Music With a Spiritual Dimension

Background Preparation

There are two areas of the world that can easily overwhelm someone wishing to explore their musics. The first is East Asia, where approximately one quarter of the world's people live. The second is South Asia, an area with 1.4 billion people, again nearly a quarter of the world's people. One nation—India—dominates South Asia demographically and in terms of landmass, but the region also includes Bangladesh, Nepal, Bhutan, Pakistan, Sri Lanka, and even Afghanistan (in some groupings). India, Pakistan, and Bangladesh all have extensive coastlines stretching to the Arabian Sea and the Bay of Bengal, leaving the other countries landlocked—except for Sri Lanka, which is an island off the south coast of India. In addition, a few island groups, though insignificant in the larger picture, are also considered part of South Asia, including the Andaman

Village in the hills near Kathmandu, Nepal, from which could be seen the tops of the Himalaya Mountains

and Nicobar Islands, the Maldives, and the Seychelles. Parts of Afghanistan and Pakistan and most of Nepal and Bhutan are mountainous, but unlucky Bangladesh is not only flat but also only a little above sea level, leaving it open to numerous typhoons and the resultant flooding.

Much of the region experiences fairly harsh climates, varying from the intense heat of India to the tropical moisture of Bangladesh and Sri Lanka to the arid winters of the northern and upland areas. Temperatures in India can range as high as 127° Fahrenheit, making life extremely difficult. Conversely, temperatures in India's snowy northern mountains are frigid in winter. Numerous great rivers drain the Himalayas through India and Bangladesh, including the well-known and sacred Ganges (or Ganga), along with the Indus and Brahmaputra. Parts of Pakistan and Afghanistan, however, are desert. Populations tend to be the greatest and most concentrated where water is most plentiful; most great civilizations began and flourished along rivers, and this principle holds true for South Asia.

In South Asia, India is obviously the 500 pound gorilla that no one can ignore. It is a nation of striking contrasts. India has riches in the form of palaces, treasures, and temples that are beyond imagination, but it also has great poverty. Many in the West are familiar with the misery of many in places like Calcutta and the good work of Mother Theresa doing what she could to alleviate suffering. India is the world's largest democracy, but is always near the precipice of ethnic Armageddon. India is a nation with hundreds of millions of farmers working in the pre-industrial age alongside the world's largest computer programming industry. India is home to several of the world's great religions, all having the common goal of peace, but it is also a place where inter-ethnic carnage quickly happens when the wrong leaders stimulate old rivalries and hatreds.

Most South Asian music known in the West is associated with cities. This is especially the case for India, where wealth and learning are concentrated in urban areas. While three quarters of India's population live in small towns and villages, the country has a number of immense cities. The best known of these include the country's economic capital, Mumbai (formerly Bombay); the political capital, New Delhi; Calcutta; and Madras (formerly Chennai). Cities elsewhere in South Asia are not as overwhelming, and include Dhaka (Bangladesh), Karachi and Lahore (Pakistan), and Colombo (Sri Lanka), as well as the even more

CASTE SYSTEM
A system of social organization based on hereditary status found in India.

modest cities of Katmandu (Nepal) and Kabul (Afghanistan).

South Asia primarily consists of a small number of large countries, but these monolithic political groupings belie the diversity of the region's populations. During the colonial era prior to the formation of both India and Pakistan in 1947, the British collected together some 562 states into the Indian Raj, which originally included Pakistan and Bangladesh. While modern-day India uses only two main languages—Hindi and English—the constitution recognizes sixteen official languages. In reality there are some 1,652 dialects spoken in India today. In addition to India's many languages, Persian (Farsi) and Turkic languages are spoken in Afghanistan, Urdu in Pakistan, and Nepali in Nepal. Most are part of the vast family of Indo-European languages.

Built between 1640 and 1648 by Shah Jahan, a ruler of the Islamic Mughal period, Delhi's Red Fort (Lal Qila) was actually a palace

Many different religions can be found throughout South Asia. Hinduism is the major religion of India and of Bali, an island that makes up part of Indonesia. Islam is also found within India, principally in the north, and is the dominant religion of Bangladesh, Pakistan, and Afghanistan. (Pakistan was formed in 1947 as a separate Muslim state and originally consisted of eastern and western portions separated by India. In 1971 Pakistan's Eastern Province seceded to become Bangladesh.) Theravada Buddhism is the primary religion of Sri Lanka, though the country has a Hindu minority as well. Mahayana Buddhism predominates in Nepal and Bhutan, but some Hinduism is also found in both countries. Finally, Jainism, Sikhism, and Christianity, not to mention a small community of Jews, can all be found in India.

Traditionally, social organization in South Asia was hierarchical. This was especially true in India, where the population was organized into castes or groupings—ranging from

A Mountainside village in Afghanistan (Courtesy Afghan Assistance)

the highest or priestly class to the lowest or "untouchable" class—to which an individual was assigned based on their status at birth. This system, which is tenuously related to Hinduism, has now been abolished in India, though many older people still think in caste terms.

An Inside Look

Shanti Raghavan

As a child growing up in India, I displayed an innate talent for music. My passion was playing the *veena,* a traditional South Indian instrument. It looks like a North Indian *sitar* but has four strings to play on and three more strings on the side on which to keep the beat. Its sound resembles the human voice, and if it is played well it makes listeners feel that they are listening to someone singing.

Shanti Raghavan, teacher of South Indian Music

I often spent hours listening to our neighbor, an excellent musician, playing this instrument. Listening to a musician of that caliber, music must have rubbed off on me. I turned out to be a very good student; my guru was elated as I flew from one level to the next. My mother wanted me to become a music professional, but I wanted to get bachelors and masters degrees in the arts or sciences just like everybody else. When I was a student, music turned into just a hobby. When I got married and came to the United States, I had two daughters who displayed a lot of talent for singing. When people noticed that they were singing so well, they approached me to teach their children. I was reluctant at first, unsure whether this would all work out. But once I started I have never looked back. It has been a wonderful experience.

Teaching in the United States is a challenge. To teach children growing up in a culture entirely different from India requires some understanding and wisdom. A teacher cannot turn away a student on the basis of lack of talent. In India, teachers do refuse to teach children if they find they do not have an affinity for music. Abroad, however, it is the teacher's job to create this talent and affinity in every child who comes to learn, as this is one of the ways to introduce Indian culture to children. Everybody has to be given this opportunity, and lack of talent is not reason enough to refuse a child. Though it has been an uphill and arduous task, it has also been very rewarding. To hear the children finally sing well is very pleasing. To have an opportunity to explain the spiritual concepts and themes of these songs is satisfying: South Indian classical music, more commonly known as Carnatic music, is necessarily spiritual in nature. The technicalities of Carnatic music are complex. Mastering the various rhythms, beats, and ragas undoubtedly sharpens the brain. Therefore, besides raising the level of thinking from the mundane to high spiritual awareness, Carnatic music helps children be better students of everything. Children are able to participate in many Indian events, both religious and cultural. Music study gives them an identity as an Indian and knowledge about Indian culture. My own children sing very well. My younger daughter, Akhila, is very talented and participates in various Indian functions. My older daughter, Shruti, has studied music in India and now teaches and gives concerts. I hope I have made a positive difference in all the children's lives.

Aashish Khan

I was initiated into North Indian classical music at the age of five by my grandfather, the legendary Acharya Baba Allauddin Khan Sahib, exponent of the Senia Beenkar and Senia Rababiya Gharana founded in the 16th century by Mian Tansen, court musician to Emperor Akbar. I also learned music from my father, Ustad Ali Akbar Khan, and aunt, Smt. Annapurna Devi, both leading musicians in India.

Aashish Khan, concert artist, composer, and teacher of North Indian Classical Music

In 1953, I gave my first public performance at age thirteen with my grandfather on the All India Radio National Program in New Delhi. In 1961, I accompanied my father as a representative of the Government of India to the East-West Music Encounter in Tokyo, Japan. By 1967, I was performing the sarod internationally at such places as the Hollywood Bowl in Los Angeles (for an audience of over 20,000 people) as well as throughout India. In 1978, my brother, Pranesh Khan, and I founded the "Allauddin Academy of Music and Performing Arts" in Calgary, Alberta, Canada.

In 1989, I was appointed to the prestigious post of Composer and Conductor for the National Orchestra, Vadya Vrinda of All India Radio, New Delhi, succeeding such musical stalwarts as Pandit Ravi Shankar and Pandit Pannalal Ghosh. A few years later, I traveled to South Africa on a concert tour organized by the governments of India and South Africa. I was the first Indian musician to represent India as an ambassador of Indian culture and classical music.

My work can be heard in numerous films, such as Sir Richard Attenborough's *Gandhi,* John Houston's *The Man Who Would Be King,* Clint Eastwood's *Breezy,* and David Lean's *A Passage to India,* as well as Tapan Sinha's *Aadmi aur Aurat* and *Joturgriha,* for which I received the "Best Film Score Award" from the Bengal Film Journalist's Association.

I have collaborated with such diverse Western musicians as John Barham, George Harrison, Ringo Starr, Eric Clapton, Charles Lloyd, John Handy, Alice Coltrane, George Brooks, Emil Richards, Dallas Smith, Don Pope, Jorge Strunz, Ardeshir Farah, and the Philadelphia String Quartet.

I have been a music guru (teacher) for many years and have been on the faculties of the Ali Akbar College of Music; Ravi Shankar's Kinnara School of Indian Classical Music; The University of Washington, and The University of Alberta. I teach students throughout the United States, Canada, Europe, South Africa, and India while pursuing a busy career as a concert artist and composer.

I am a true believer and follower of the "Guru Shishya Parampara," one of the oldest methods of teaching Indian classical music in an oral, practical, theoretical, and traditional manner. My true belief and objective is to pass on for generations to come the 16th century traditions and culture from which I descend.

South Asia exhibits striking contrasts in terms of level of development. Afghanistan, a thinly populated and mountainous country with little internal unity, remains the least developed, while the urban areas of Pakistan and India are highly developed. Indeed, India and Pakistan have produced many of the world's greatest scientists and thinkers, and today India is a leader in the high-tech world. With its crushing population statistics, however, India must struggle mightily to keep its population fed, clothed, and employed. As in many other developing countries, there are great contrasts between the wealth of the few and the poverty of the many. In Afghanistan and Sri Lanka, and sometimes in Pakistan as well, political instability has made modernization and development difficult to maintain.

HINDUSTANI
A term referring to the cultural traditions of North India.

CARNATIC
(Also, KARNATAK) A term referring to the cultural traditions of South India.

Planning the Itinerary

Each of the nations that comprise South Asia offers exciting and distinctive musics, but it is the "classical" music of India that has gained virtually all the attention of outsiders. A visit to any large record store offering "international" releases will demonstrate this clearly. Culturally, India is divided into a northern region and a southern region, with the former comprising two thirds and the latter one third of the country. Northern culture is called Hindustani and southern culture is called Carnatic (also spelled Karnatak). The north of India was deeply influenced by Indo-European invaders who brought the Aryan civilization from the northwest between 2000 and 1500 B.C. No one religion dominates the north, a situation not only giving rise to many coexisting faiths (Hinduism, Jainism, Sikhism, Islam), but also resulting in a more secular society. Hindustani music reflects this diversity, with far fewer relationships to religion than Carnatic music. Most northern languages are related to Hindi, while southern languages are mainly Dravidian, having been derived from layers of people who preceded the Aryans. The South in general has experienced less outside influence, and as a consequence Hinduism predominates—leading to a society that makes little distinction between the sacred and secular.

Not surprisingly, Carnatic music is closely tied to Hinduism, though it has little to do with temple activities per se. Classical music in both traditions can be vocal or instrumental. The North Indian classical music that Western audiences are much more familiar with is primarily instrumental. Carnatic music, on the other hand, is primarily vocal. Indeed, even the instrumental music of South India consists primarily of transcriptions of vocal compositions.

Indian classical music, unlike the communal music of Africa or the ensemble music of Southeast Asia, is individual, soloistic, and often virtuosic. One attends a concert to hear a particular artist—often a star—rather than specific compositions, because most Indian classical music is composed on the spot during performance, through a process called improvisation. These improvisations usually unfold at a very leisurely pace: a full performance of a single improvisation can last anywhere from thirty minutes to two hours, and Indian classical concerts can easily last four or more hours.

In spite of the fact that Indian classical music is widely disseminated both in and outside India, the majority of the Indian population sings or listens to other kinds of music. Hindu lay people often sing devotional songs called *bhajans*, which can be semi-popular in style. Music written for and transmitted by the movies is widely popular; in fact the term for pop music is *filmi*. And because India's film industry produces more films per year than that of any other country, the number of *filmi* songs is understandably vast.

FILMI
(Also, FILMI GIT)
Popular music taken
from films in India.

North Indian (Hindustani) music played by Buddadev das Gupta, *sarod* lute, Zakir Hussain, *tabla* (drums), and Elizabeth Howard, *tambura* (drone lute)

Our musical tour of South Asia also takes us to eastern India—known as Bengal—and to Bangladesh and Pakistan. Most striking in Bengal and Bangladesh are the Bauls, free spirits who comment in their songs on topics as diverse as society, philosophy, and the joys and pains of daily life—and who can perhaps be thought of as the equivalent of America's "singer-songwriters." Although Pakistan is an independent nation with a Muslim majority, it has no single type of music that epitomizes its culture. Depending on the region, its music alternately reveals relationships with Afghanistan, Iran, and India. The only kind of Pakistani music to have attracted a following outside of Pakistan, however, is Sufi Muslim devotional song, called *qawwali* (sometimes spelled *kawwali*). In our short survey of the music of Southeast Asia, we will pass over the traditions of Afghanistan, Nepal, and Bhutan, as fascinating as these cultures are. Afghanistan, while nominally a nation, is really a collection of diverse cultures with little overall cohesion: no single musical example could possibly represent such a "nation." As for Nepal and Bhutan, two Buddhist countries nestled against the Himalayas to the north of India, their musical traditions are too diverse and too little known.

QAWWALI
(Also, KAWWALI) Sufi
Muslim devotional songs.

Arrival: North India

NORTH INDIA

India's northern cities—such as Mumbai, Pune, Delhi, Varanasi (Benares), and Lucknow—reflect the diversity of the peoples who together created modern Hindustani culture. In them one finds great mosques, Sikh and Jain temples, the palaces of the Mughal emperors, and the many governmental and celebratory edifices left by the English colonials. These vast cities are also the home of North India's complex and sophisticated classical music tradition.

Track 5

Site 1: Hindustani Raga

First Impressions. Hindustani instrumental improvisations, called *ragas*, are normally quite long. Because a piece of an hour or more would not be practical to study, we have chosen an example that lasts less than five minutes—but that is nonetheless a "complete" raga performance. If you listen carefully to the very beginning, you will hear several sounds from an instrument with plucked strings—though its timbre has a buzz, too. Almost immediately, a more prominent and commanding stringed instrument asserts itself, while the first instrument continues in a slowly repetitious manner. After an extended period of rather dreamy music that lacks a steady beat and gradually grows more excited, there is a sudden deceleration—followed by the entry of drums and the return of the other instruments. This new phase continues to the end.

Indian street musician "charms" two cobra snakes with his *punji* double clarinet consisting of gourd windchest, drone pipe, and melody pipe with finger holes (Max T. Miller)

Several elements stand out: the twangy sound of the first instrument, the constant ornamentation and pitch-bending of the main melodic instrument, and the regularity of the drums, one of which seems to match pitch with the melodic instrument. Neither of the drums sounds like they are played with hard sticks; in fact, their mellower sound stems from the use of fingers. Perhaps you also notice changes in your level of relaxation and an increase in tension as the performance proceeds.

Aural Analysis. Few other areas of the world's music require as much technical explanation as does Indian classical music. That is because an appreciation of this fascinating blend of fixed and improvised elements involves an understanding of several important musical aspects. Even as it employs a highly systematic compositional process, Indian classical music also allows for endless variation, and the genius of a performer is not in how well he or she follows established conven-

MODE
A set of rules or guidelines used to compose or improvise music in a particular tradition.

tions, but in how those conventions are manipulated for the purposes of individual expression.

The word *raga* (or *rag*, meaning "color" or "atmosphere") denotes a total system for the simultaneous composition and performance of music in both North and South India. Because the English word *improvisation* suggests a near total degree of spontaneity, it fails to capture the control, predictability, and bounded nature of raga. The creation of a raga is a highly controlled compositional process, with established constructional boundaries—even if it allows for nearly unlimited individual variations within these boundaries. Western ethnomusicologists use the term *mode* to describe these systems. Think of them as *composition kits*. Whereas most Western music is written down by "composers" before its performance, Indian classical music is never written, even though ragas unfold in highly predictable ways. The length of a performance can vary from a few minutes to a couple of hours, depending on time constraints and the interest of the audience.

Raga is comprised of several elements, one being tonal material (what might be called a "scale"). These "scales" consist of a hierarchy of strong and weak notes, a set of typical melodic figures, and a set of extra-musical associations with such things as moods, times of the day, and magical powers. Ragas are sometimes represented pictorially as individual human beings in miniature paintings called *ragamalas*.

The pitches of a raga are expressed in solfège syllables, the Indian equivalent to the West's *do-re-mi-fa-sol-la-ti-do;* they are *sa-re-ga-ma-pa-dha-ni-sa*, and students of Indian raga can sing melody using them. As in the West, there are actually more pitches in the total tuning system than these seven because some pitches can be flatted or sharped; in India the total is usually said to be 22, whereas only 12 pitches are used in the West. More than one raga may use the same set of pitches, but identical pitch sets vary in practice from raga to raga, due to differences in pitch hierarchy, typical melodic units, and extramusical aspects. The two most important pitches, usually *sa* and *pa*, are continuously reinforced by the strumming of the *tambura*, a stringed instrument whose background buzz could be likened to aural incense permeating a room.

Those "buzzing" pitches briefly heard alone at the beginning of the piece are played on the *tambura,* a four-stringed, long-necked lute with a large gourd body. The person who plays this instrument, often a young

The *tambura* lute has an unfretted neck, four strings, and is played throughout a raga to produce two drone pitches (Andrew Shahriari)

The late Indian musician Vasant Rai plays the *sarod* (lute)

SAROD
A fretless plucked
lute from India.

ALAP
Opening period of
exploration of a
raga performance.

disciple or a spouse of the lead instrumentalist, simply plucks the four strings in order throughout the raga. The four pitches reinforce the two most important pitches of the raga, usually the fundamental or "home" pitch (I) and another an interval of a fifth above (V), and are generally played as I, V (upper), V (upper), V (lower).

The main melodic instrument in our example is the *sarod,* also a long-necked lute. The sarod is generally around forty inches long and has a large wooden body covered with calfskin. Its neck is tapering and hollow. The sarod has six main strings of metal running over a fretless metal fingerboard to large tuning pegs, but there are also eleven to fifteen "sympathetic" metal strings running from within the neck (out through small, ivory-lined holes) to a series of smaller pegs on the side of the neck. These latter strings are tuned to vibrate "sympathetically" with the main strings, and provide a background of ethereal ringing. Sometimes the player will strum them briefly, mostly at the beginning of the piece. Using a triangular wooden pick held in the right hand, the player holds the instrument horizontally (similarly to the way a guitar is held) and can simply pluck the string or pull it to the side with the left hand to create the tone-bending and ornaments that practically define Indian raga.

The first portion of a raga is called the *alap* and could be described as a period of exploration of the raga and its characteristics. The principal melodic player begins with the lower pitches, approaching them in a leisurely and experimental manner; there is no regular beat because the melody is played in free rhythm. An *alap* can last for a mere minute or so or be extended to an hour or more, depending on the taste of the performer and the interest of the audience. As the *alap* progresses, the player explores more pitches and melodic units, moving from the lowest note, which represents relaxation or repose, into the higher ranges, which increases tension. Gradually the rhythms become somewhat steadier, though they never become totally metered; the term *jor* refers to this tenuous regularizing of beat. As the tempo and excitement increase (along with the tension), the player begins a regular alternation between melodic pitches and a set of drone strings called the *jhala*. Just

JHALA
Refers to a set of drone strings on Indian chordophones. Also, a reference to the climactic end of the *alap* section of raga performance in India.

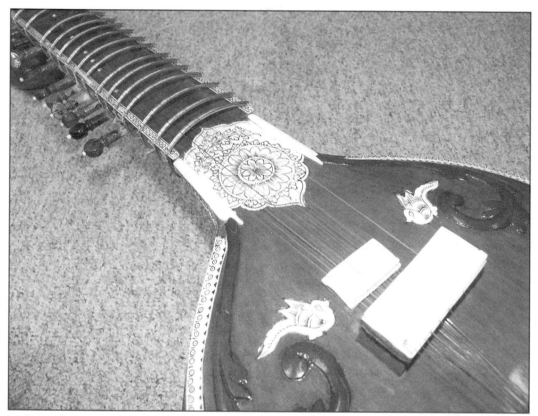

Below the main strings of the sitar, and passing beneath the curved metal frets, are a large number of "sympathetic" strings that vibrate involuntarily when the main strings are played

as the playing reaches a feverish level of excitement, the "drive" suddenly slows as the player quickly descends through the scale back to the point of relaxation.

At this point the drums enter. These consist of a small cylindrical wooden drum with a single head called *tabla* and a larger, round metal drum with single head called *baya*; together, the pair is also called *tabla*. Most players strike the smaller drum with the right hand and the larger with the left. The *tabla* (that is, the smaller of the pair) is tuned to a fundamental pitch by tightening or loosening leather straps; their tension is controlled by cylindrically shaped pieces of wood wedged

TABLA
A pair of drums found in Hindustani music from India.

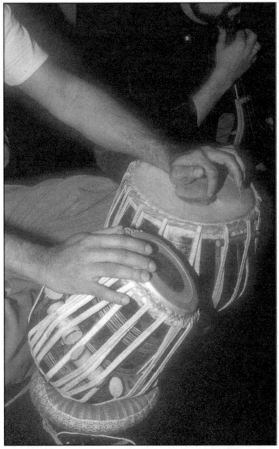

Tabla refers to both the pair of Hindustani drums and to the cylindrical drum (below) in particular, while the kettle drum (above) is called *baya*

between the straps and the body of the drum. Each drum stroke has a name, and drummers memorize the stroke names as part of the learning process. Indeed, most drummers can *speak* the strokes, in a kind of "verbal drumming"—and many listeners are able to keep track of the cycle of strokes through patterns of handclaps and waves.

The drummer plays a cycle of strokes called the *tala*. A tala is considered a closed cycle, because it has a fixed number of beats; these are subdivided into three or four sections. There are literally dozens of possible talas, each with its own name and specific number of beats, theoretically ranging from 3 to 128. In practice far fewer are used, and talas using 7 to 16 beats are the most common. Of these, the best known and most often encountered is *tintal*, a tala having 16 beats divided into four groupings of 4 pulses each. While talas are played beginning on beat 1, they do not end on the last beat, i.e., 16, but rather end on beat 1 of what would have been the next cycle. The audience can hear where they are in the cycle by listening for the deep tones of the *baya* drum; the *baya* either drops out or is played quietly during the third group (beats 9–12), allowing listeners to prepare for the restatement of beat one.

Each drum stroke—whether played on a single drum or by a combination of drums—has a name, such as *dha*. Drum stroke names are called *bols*. The entire pattern or set of words for a given tala is called the *theka*. The most basic *theka* for *tintal* is: dha, dhin, dhin, dha, dha,

TALA

Rhythmic framework found in raga performance in India.

BOLS

Mnemonic syllables corresponding to drum strokes in Indian drumming traditions.

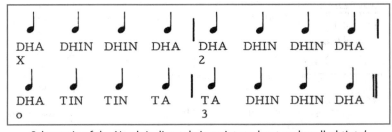

♩	♩	♩	♩	♩	♩	♩	♩
DHA X	DHIN	DHIN	DHA	DHA 2	DHIN	DHIN	DHA
♩	♩	♩	♩	♩	♩	♩	♩
DHA o	TIN	TIN	TA	TA 3	DHIN	DHIN	DHA

Schematic of the North Indian tala in a sixteen beat cycle called *tintal*

dhin, dhin, dha, dha, tin, tin, ta, ta, dhin, dhin, dha. Talas can be recited in syllables as well. Skilled drummers play patterns that go far beyond this basic set, including a great many elaborate "compositions," each based on the tala's cycle of beats.

When the drum enters, it actually starts in the middle of the tala cycle (beats 9–16). The sitar or sarod, now playing more calmly, plays a short composition—a kind of tune—called the *gat* (in vocal music this is called *chiz*). The *gat* is the skeletal melody around which the player will improvise. When improvising, the player may fragment the *gat,* restate it in whole, or depart from it entirely. Some longer raga performances have more than one *gat,* perhaps a slow *gat* first, then a fast *gat.* The name of the raga remains the same regardless of the *gat* chosen, and although the *gat* is a composition, it does not usually have a "title" and the identity of its composer is not generally of significance.

The length of the *gat* matches the length of the tala; therefore, the use of *tintal* requires a 16-beat *gat.* In a sense, anything can happen during the *gat* section, which can last anywhere from a few minutes to an hour. The length depends on the audience's reaction, the performers' skill level and ability to cooperate or challenge each other in positive ways, and the context of the performance.

The instruments of India are numerous, and quite a few of them can be used as the lead melodic instrument in ragas. In the West, the instrument that has become most famous is the *sitar,* which for Westerners is virtually synonymous with Indian music. The *sitar* is a long-necked plucked lute, with a body made from a gourd and with seventeen arched metal frets running along the fingerboard. Over these frets pass seven main strings and beneath them pass around twelve sympathetic strings. Ragas can also be performed on many other stringed instruments, such as the *sarod,* the *santur* (hammered zither)*,* or the *sarangi* (bowed lute), as well as on the *bansri (*flute) and several reed instruments. Among the most curious of instruments used in ragas is the *jaltarang,* a series of small china bowls each filled/tuned with a different level of water and struck with a small beater. Ragas can also be vocal. Vocal ragas are structured according to one of two patterns, both of which are different from patterns used with instrumental raga. These patterns, called *Dhrupad* and *Khyal,* both require great endurance on the part of performers. Full appreciation of vocal ragas naturally requires knowledge of Indic languages, and this may be why vocal ragas remain little known in the West.

Now that we have run through some of the basic principles and characteristics of the raga, we will return to our musical example. It is *Raga ahir bhairav,* a type of raga appropriately performed at daybreak. The ascending and descending scale used in this performance consists of the pitches C, Db, E, F, G, A, Bb, c—though in the ascending form the G is often avoided. The tala used is a fast *tintal* (16 beats).

Cultural Considerations. If you were to attend a raga performance, you would probably be amazed at the musicians' dexterity, creativity, and stage presence, and at the way that their music can involve an audience. These are some of the aspects that have long made Indian raga attractive to Western audiences and to a number of Western popular performers, including George Harrison and John McLaughlin.

GAT

The skeletal melody used for improvisation in a raga performance of classical Indian instrumental music.

RASA

A mood or sentiment associated with artistic activity in India.

While a raga performance may be relatively easy to follow on an aural and visual level, there is, however, much more involved than mere sound and sight. Important extramusical cultural and philosophical matters come into play as well, encompassing the raga's relationship to and effect on the smooth working of the universe.

The extramusical aspects of raga, which may seem merely curious to outsiders, are essential to Indians. Each raga has an articulated mood, called *rasa,* which creates in performer and listener alike a state of mind, such as love, heroism, or anger. The *rasa* can become so pervasive that listeners begin to conceive of the *rasa* as a person. Personified ragas are often depicted in miniature paintings called *ragamala,* usually showing humans performing music. Some ragas are believed to have magical powers. A raga performed correctly can heal, influence personality, and even bring the divine into both performer and listener. *Raga Dipak* was said to create fire when performed well, and the *Mallar* ragas can create rain. *Kedar* ragas will cure diseases and melt stones. Indian jailers, always ready to earn some extra money, are said to have taught *Raga Kedar* to prisoners

An Indian miniature painting, or *ragamala,* entitled "Krishna and Radha watching rain clouds," from India's Punjab Hills, c. 1790 (Cleveland Museum of Art)

who hoped to melt the stones of the prison and escape.

Each raga is to be performed at a proper time, and consequently there are ragas appropriate for all times of the day, from before dawn to after sunset. For Indians this is important because they believe there is a reciprocal relationship between the sound of music and a smoothly functioning universe. Walter Kaufmann, who researched ragas in India prior to World War II, reported that one great musician predicted the coming of that terrible war, which he claimed would result from the Western habit of playing music at the wrong times (as when funeral music is played when there is no funeral). He shouted to Kaufmann, "How long will the universe tolerate this abuse of music, music, mind you, a most sacred thing?" As a result a great calamity would befall the West he said—and indeed it did.

During the 1960s, many Westerners turned to the East—India in

GURU
A teacher or spiritual guide, primarily associated with Hindu traditions from India.

particular—in search of spiritual enlightenment. Because Indian music is especially spiritual, it soon became popular with Western audiences. Ravi Shankar, the Hindustani sitar specialist, who has also composed many film scores, toured the United States as early as 1964 and soon he became a cultural icon. George Harrison of The Beatles studied sitar with Shankar, and Harrison's use of the sitar in several Beatles' songs, including "Love You Too" from *Revolver* (1966) and "Within You Without You" from *Sgt. Pepper's Lonely Hearts Club Band* (1967), brought about a rising interest in Indian music. England's John McLaughlin, leader of both Shakti and the Mahavishnu Orchestra, also invoked Indian sounds and spirituality. These groups, and many others, added Indian drummers and sitarists, making the distinctive dry sound of the tabla and the twangy sitar familiar to many Westerners. Today the sounds of the tabla and sitar can be easily imitated on synthesizers and have become part of mainstream Western popular music, as heard, for example, in Ricky Martin's "She's All I Ever Had," a bolero-tempo song on his album *Ricky Martin* (1999).

Ravi Shankar, India's most famous musician, plays the sitar, Ⓒ a long-necked lute with sympathetic strings
(© Jack Vartoogian/FrontRowPhotos)

Because Indian music is played by soloists, one finds both virtuosos and a "star" system. Ironically, Indian musicians can make more money touring in Europe and North America than in India. Ravi Shankar made a great success for himself doing this and his daughter, Anoushka Shankar, has followed in his footsteps. A few Americans, such as Ken Zuckerman, have completely mastered Indian instruments and styles and have become professional Indian musicians, touring both here and in India. Even though Indian music no longer holds Western popular culture in its thrall, Indian concerts in the West continue to attract large audiences of both Indian expatriates and Westerners.

Track 6

Site 2: Bhajan Devotional Song

First Impressions. Over the continuous sound of a reedy instrument and a pair of drums, a male vocalist sings a short line, which is answered by a group of singers, both male and female. The melody is rather simple and easy to imitate. A metallic instrument joins the group, adding a measure of excitement. The singers do not sound like professionals, but more like ordinary people meeting communally, as for worship.

Aural Analysis. The reedy sound first heard is a *harmonium*, a free-reed pump organ originally from the West. Harmoniums became popular parlor instruments in "better" American and European homes during the nineteenth century, and many families today still preserve one as an antique for the living room. These domestic instruments were fairly large, had a keyboard, a bank of pull stops, and were pumped by two pedals. The instrument heard here, however, is quite compact; it has a small keyboard and its bellows are hand-pumped at the rear of the case. This type of harmonium was originally designed for missionaries and other traveling religious leaders, who used it to accompany hymns. Many English missionaries went to India, bringing the harmonium with them— though they certainly did not anticipate that Indians would embrace the instrument so enthusiastically and blend it into their traditional music. In *bhajans* today the harmonium player can either provide a drone or lead the melody.

A man sings while playing a hand-pumped harmonium pump organ in Kathmandu, Nepal

In addition to a harmonium, our example features a drum (or, more properly, two drums), with a sound that should seem familiar: it is a tabla, an instrument heard earlier in our example of Hindustani raga. Unlike the tala patterns heard in most ragas, the one heard here is simple and regular: it alternates between a 4- and an 8-beat cycle. The metallic instrument that is also heard is called a *kartal* and consists of a steel rod struck from within a horseshoe-shaped beater. In this example, it plays a short/short/long pattern throughout.

Bhajan singing typically follows a call-and-response format in which a leader (in this case male) sings a phrase that is then sung by the group. This pattern differs from call-and-response performance in most traditions, because normally a group completes a vocal line sung by its leader, rather than simply repeating it. Therefore, *bhajan* practice is closer

BHAJAN
Devotional songs
from India.

to antiphonal singing, in which leader and group alternate. Practically speaking, the leader in *bhajan* performances is also prompting the singers, who might not know the words otherwise. The vocal lines are very simple melodically and are repeated. In our example, there are basically two phrases, both of which use a pentatonic scale. The five tones could be described as 5, 6, 1, 2, 3, with 5 and 1 as the most important and 1 as the fundamental pitch.

Bhajan texts are sung in Hindi, and sometimes even in Sanskrit, the sacred language of Hinduism. The text of our example was written for the Sai Baba sect, and begins (in translation) with these exhortations: "Worship the savior and the Lord of the Universe, Lord Sai Nanda Gopal. Glory to the son of Nanda, the cowherd boy. Worship the Lord of Mathura, Lord Krishna, who sings enchanting melodies" (from *Sai Devotional Songs,* n.d., p. 129).

Cultural Considerations. *Bhajans* are devotional Hindu songs sung by lay people for many occasions, both formal and informal, at home or in a temple, accompanied or unaccompanied. They can be traditional songs, homemade ones, or a blend of traditional and popular music styles. In a sense they are the Hindu equivalent of the Protestant Christian hymn. Indeed, some Indian Christians have adopted *bhajans* to their own faith. *Bhajan* meetings are often held during the week, and anyone in the congregation can lead a song. Services usually begin with the chanting of *om,* the fundamental sacred sound of Hinduism.

Worshippers sing *bhajan* devotional songs during a Sunday morning service at a Sai Baba Hindu temple near Chaguanas, Trinidad

Bhajan texts can be sung in any language and may consist of nothing more than a repetition of the names of God, because God has many incarnations. Other texts express the devotees' love for God, and offer praise and devotion.

Bhajans can be heard throughout India, Nepal, the Tamil parts of Sri Lanka, and anywhere else where there are Hindu communities, such as South America and the Caribbean, particularly Guyana and Trinidad and Tobago. Among the Hindu spiritual teachers who have attracted followings outside India is Sai Baba, originally from the Indian states of Andhra Pradesh and Karnataka. *Bhajan* singing typically takes place in Sai Baba temples on Thursday or Sunday. The *bhajan* selected for inclusion here was recorded in a temple in Chaguanas, a town in central Trinidad, where there is a concentration of Hindus. (Around 40 per cent of Trinidadians are descendents of Indians brought to the country as indentured workers.) *Bhajan* singing is a major aspect of Sai Baba worship, but is also found among Hare Krishna devotees, who have also established congregations and temples worldwide.

SOUTH INDIA

Arrival: South India

For some, southern India is the *real* India, because it shows less influence from the foreign cultures that invaded northern India. Primarily Hindu, southern India is thought to preserve what remains of India's earliest civilization, that of the Dravidians. The sophisticated music of south India, called Carnatic music, is closely associated with Hinduism, though not with temple rituals.

1

Track 7

Site 3: Carnatic (South Indian) Classical Singing (Kriti)

First Impressions. Our example begins with a few notes played on a plucked chordophone, after which a rich-toned male vocalist begins to sing in free rhythm. Following this short introductory section, a drum joins the singer and the music becomes metrical. As the singer presents the song phrase by phrase, another instrument—a bowed stringed instrument—seems to be shadowing him. The drumbeats are distinct and accented, giving the music an almost square and march-like feel. Though the metrical aspect of the piece seems a bit more obvious than that of our Hindustani example, there is a great deal of ornamentation on the part of the singer (and his bowed shadow). Additionally, some lines of text are repeated, so that a fairly short text is extended into a long performance.

KRITI
A genre of devotional songs using Hindu poetry from South India.

Aural Analysis. The most important difference between the classical music of North and South India is that, whereas Hindustani music is mostly improvised, Carnatic music is essentially composed. Carnatic music's most common compositional form is a type of religious song called the *kriti*, which is based on a genre of devotional Hindu poetry of the same name. The composer of a *kriti* normally writes both the poetry and the melody, the former being written in one of several South Indian scripts (e.g., Telugu, Sanskrit, Tamil). Pitches are written in one of the many local notational systems; though only the main pitches are indicated, ornamentation is determined by oral tradition and is not freely improvised. Vocalists may, however, sometimes perform a brief improvised introduction (called *alapana*) before launching into the kriti itself.

The example, "Sarasa sama dana," is a kriti by Tyagaraja (1767–1847), south India's most famous composer. Kriti texts are typically in three sections. The first, called *pallavi*, consists of one or two lines. This kriti's text begins with the words "You are the artful expert of the ruler's strategies: timely, friendly persuasion, wise gifting, dividing to conquer, and, lastly, use of force—." (The text translation cited here is by William J Jackson, *Tyagaraja: Life and Lyrics* [Madras: Oxford, 1991]),

A Carnatic (South Indian) classical singer performs a *kriti* devotional song, flanked by a violinist (right) and a *mridangam* drummer (left), at a St. Tyagaraja Festival

The pallavi is followed by a second section, called *anupallavi*, which begins "Ravana, known as great Lord Siva's major devotee, ..." The final section of text, called *caranam*, is longer than the others, and may be completed with part of the *pallavi* text, giving it a "rounded form."

South Indian ragas, whether they are *kritis* or other musical forms, mostly operate on the same principles as the ragas of North India—but the specifics are quite different. The Carnatic system is, at least on the surface, unusually extensive, because there are so many theoretically possible scales. If you allow for all possible arrangements of the seven pitches (some available in three forms), there are 72 possible scale forms. When you factor in other variables, there are theoretically some 36,000 possible ragas. Practically, only a small number are commonly used. Our example is a *Raga Behag* (also called *Byag* or *Byagu*), the twelfth raga of the twenty-nine used most often in the Carnatic system. If the pitch "sa," the "fundamental," is written as C, the pitches of this raga are C, E, F, G, A, B, c, though sometimes the syllable "ma" (F) is sung as F#. Tonally this is one of the simpler raga scales available, and to Westerners it might sound somewhat "major" in feeling.

South Indian drum cycles are called *tala* just as in the North, but follow a different set of principles. As with the Carnatic raga system, the tala system also allows for far more cycles than are actually used. In practice, the system is actually fairly simple, but like so much of Indian music it seems confusing to beginners because of its extensive terminology.

A Carnatic tala consists of three variable elements, called *anudrutam, drutam*, and *laghu*. As in the North, South Indian music uses a system of hand gestures to symbolize tala patterns. The *anudrutam* is signed as a one-beat clap; the *drutam* is a clap followed by a wave of the right hand; the *laghu*, which consists of a variable number of beats, is signed as a clap followed by right hand finger counts. South Indian audience members

South Indian *mridangam* drummer,
plays during a St. Tyagaraja Festival

A South Indian violinist plays during
a St. Tyagaraja Festival.
Note how he holds the instrument between
his chest and right foot, making it easier to play
the ornamentation required in this music.

often "keep the tala" on their hands during a performance, and sometimes a singer will also use the gestures as he or she performs. Each tala has a name that combines two elements: a tala name and a *jati* name, with the latter representing a variable number of beats in the *laghu*.

The most commonly used *tala* is properly called *triputa* (*tala* name) *catu-rasra* (*jati* name), and consists of a four-beat *laghu* (clap and three counts) and two *drutams* (each a clap and wave). The full cycle of eight beats, then, is "clap, count, count, count, clap, wave, clap, wave." To Westerners, this sounds like common time, but it is indeed a closed cycle of eight beats. Because the name *triputa catu-rasra* does not roll off the tongue so easily, the nickname *adi tala* is commonly used. The drum usually used is called *mridangam*; it is a two-headed barrel drum with leather strap lacing, and heads that are weighted (tuned) with a mixture of burnt rice and ash. Players use their hands to strike each head. Many players also wrap the body of the drum in cloth.

The first sounds heard in our example are those of the *tambura*, the same drone chordophone found in Hindustani music. As in the North, the tambura is used in South Indian music both to provide a ringing background drone and to reinforce the basic pitches of the raga. The bowed instrument that shadows the singer is a violin—but one that is held in a way that no Western violinist would ever use: it is placed between the chest and right foot of a player seated on the floor. The violin, like the harmonium, was introduced into India by British colonialists. Its function in Carnatic music is to closely follow and imitate the singer. Thanks to the way that the instrument is held, players can easily slide their left hand along the neck to create any of the twenty-three named ornaments found in both the instrumental and vocal music of South India.

Cultural Considerations. Whereas Hindustani music is primarily improvised, albeit with a pre-composed *gat* or *chiz* serving as a skeletal framework in the metrical portion of the raga, Carnatic music is primarily composed in song form, though with the expectation that the performer will add typical (and codified) ornaments to the main notes. Consequently, South India has, like Europe, a small pantheon of saint-like composers, of whom Tyagaraja is the most famous. Other renowned composers include Muttusvami

Diksitar (1776–1835), Syama Sastri (1762–1827), and Svati Tirunal (1813–46), all contemporaries of Beethoven, Schubert, Chopin, and others from early-nineteenth-century Europe. Tyagaraja, a man who prophesied his own death and is therefore called "Saint" in English, is celebrated in an annual *aradhana (*festival), originally held in Tamil Nadu state but now observed in many parts of the world, including the United States. Since 1907 the festival has included, in addition to *puja* (worship), performances of Tyagaraja's compositions by both amateurs and professionals. We are personally familiar with an increasingly extensive festival held each year in Cleveland, Ohio.

While they predominate, *kriti* are not the only form found in South Indian classical music. Vocalists sometimes improvise extensive *alapana*, together with a violinist who imitates entire phrases following the main performer's rendition. Carnatic repertory also includes other song genres, including the *varnam, ragam-tanam-pallavi,* and *tillana.* Some are secular, even erotic, and may include extended passages of melisma in which the performer shows off his or her mastery of improvisatory technique.

St. Tyagaraja (1767-1847) is South India's most famous composer, whose music is still celebrated in festivals throughout the world (Aradhana Committee, Cleveland, Ohio)

The instruments of South India are fewer than those of North India, but several are worth mentioning. The most important is a plucked lute called Sarasvati *vina* (or *veena*). Held horizontally or even placed on the floor, this instrument has up to nine strings for playing melody and rhythm, but generally no sympathetic strings. Players may use plectra or their bare fingertips. The most memorable South Indian instrument is a long, black double-reed called *nagasvaram,* usually played in pairs and accompanied by a pair of loud drums called *tavil.* One may also encounter performers using the *venu* (flute) or the *dilruba* (bowed lute). In recent years, several new Western instruments have been adapted into Carnatic music, most prominently the mandolin, made famous by one player, the youthful U. Srinivas. Other Western imports include the cello, the viola, and the clarinet; the latter's reeds and mouthpiece have been altered to allow for greater ornamentation and tone-bending. In South India, instrumental music consists primarily of vocal compositions performed without words, though the original melody is generally elaborated on through improvised passages requiring great virtuosity.

ARADHANA
A South Indian festival.

VINA
A plucked lute from South India, often associated with the Hindu goddess Sarasvati.

NAGASVARAM
A double-reed aerophone from South India.

TAVIL
A pair of drums from South India, often used to accompany the *nagasvaram.*

The *sarasvati vina* (lute) of South India ⊡

BANGLADESH

Arrival: Bangladesh

When the British granted independence to its Indian colony in 1947, what might have been a unified India divided itself into two countries, India and Pakistan. India was primarily Hindu and Pakistan was primarily Muslim. In addition, Pakistan was itself a divided country, having eastern and western parts divided by thousands of miles of India. In 1971 the eastern part gained independence, calling itself Bangladesh, with its capital at Dacca. Culturally it is Bengali and therefore closely related to eastern India. One of the rainiest areas of the world, Bangladesh is both blessed and cursed by three great rivers that reach the sea through its territory, the Ganges, Brahmaputra, and Meghna rivers. While these rivers bring plentiful supplies of water and rich silt, they also flood much of the nation, little of which is more than 300 feet above sea level. During times of flooding, as much as half of the country might be under water. Many islands in the Bay of Bengal have been known to disappear, leading to a regular loss of life.

①

Track 8

Site 4: Baul Song from Bangladesh

First Impressions. This song has an earnest, earthy feel, and features a full-throated male vocalist, accompanied by a rather strange-sounding stringed instrument and some jingly percussion. The melody is passionate and full of changes of mood, and exhibits much syncopation, which adds to its excitement. Clearly, this is not a "classical" raga, but something much more raw and direct, seemingly expressing the feelings of the down-and-out.

Aural Analysis. The song, entitled "Bhana ghare," speaks to the misery and poverty of India's rural population. "How long," the singer asks, "will you stay in a ruined house [by patching it up]? That day the rain comes, it will clean up and leave no trace of you at all." The concluding lines leave the listener with a sense of hopelessness: "The house measuring fourteen quarters [hands]—within it reside those sixteen people. It is difficult to live in such houses" (Charles Capwell, *The Music of the Bauls of Bengal*. Kent, Ohio: Kent State University Press, 1986, 182–3).

The instruments heard are characteristic of the "folk" or village music of eastern India and Bangladesh, an area known culturally as Bengal. Our recording features the *gopiyantro*, a single-stringed instrument also called *ektara* ("one-string"), which combines characteristics of both membranophones and chordophones. The base is like a small single-headed drum with a string attached to the "head" at the bottom.

Above the base is a flexible split-bamboo frame with a triangular shape (similar to the Eiffel Tower), the top of which supports the other end of the string on a tuning peg. The player can squeeze the flexible bamboo frame to change the tension (and therefore pitch) of a string while plucking the string with the first finger. The instrument is capable of both discrete pitches and gliding tones created when plucking and squeezing occur simultaneously. In

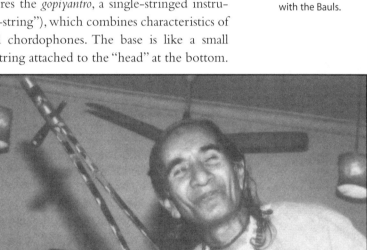

A Baul musician playing a *gopiyantro*, a single-stringed squeeze chordophone, Calcutta (Charles Capwell)

addition, the singer wears on his ankle a bracelet called *ghunur*, consisting of small metal bells similar to Western sleigh bells.

Cultural Considerations. India is home to hundreds, if not thousands, of local music traditions, both in its villages and in larger towns. Among these traditions, which are mostly little known to outsiders, one has received special attention: the songs of the Bauls, which influenced India's greatest modern poet, Rabindranath Tagore (1861–1941), and have become known in the West through live performances, recordings, and scholarly studies. The Bauls, who constitute a cultural group rather

BAULS
A group of itinerant musicians from India, especially noted for their poetry.

GOPIYANTRA
(Also, EKTARA)
A single-stringed chordophone with a membrane base found in India and often associated with the Bauls.

GHUNUR
A string of bells worn around the ankle, commonly associated with the Bauls of South Asia.

than an "ethnic" group, are itinerant singers and instrumentalists who once wandered among the villages and towns of India's Bengal and in neighboring areas of Bangladesh, but who today are more likely to be heard in festivals and through the media. Although their songs are usually about universal themes, such as love and brotherhood, they are also expressive of a loosely organized, nonmainstream religious tradition in which nature, mysticism, and spirituality play major roles.

The poet Tagore was not a Baul, but he was deeply influenced by them. Born in Calcutta to a Brahman-class family, Tagore was a playwright, songwriter, poet, philosopher, and educator. His works, many expressing thoughts similar to those of the Bauls, remained little known in India until his emigration to England in 1912. In England, Tagore was "discovered" through translations of his works; he received the Nobel Prize for Literature in 1913, and was knighted in 1915—though he renounced his title in 1919 following the Amritsar Massacre, in which English colonialists killed hundreds of his fellow Indians. Through Tagore, Bauls and their philosophy became better known outside India, and these rough-and-tumble artists are forever linked to his work.

It is tempting to draw comparisons between the Bauls and somewhat similar groups in the West. We used the term "singer-songwriter" earlier because Baul singers comment on the life around them through songs that they themselves perform. Their free and nonmaterialistic lifestyle makes them in some ways resemble the hippies of the 1960s (and perhaps even more so the Beatniks of the 1950s). Because of their vague, nonmainstream religious views emphasizing spirituality, Bauls also resemble members of various Western New Age movements. Some writers have spoken of them as "Bohemians"—thus linking them with the intellectual milieu of late-nineteenth-century Europe, and specifically of Paris's Montmartre area. In a way, they are similar to all of these types but like none of them. They are as "traditional" as traditional musicians can be, and yet they celebrate freedom from tradition, from orthodoxy, and from social norms.

Indian Filmi Git (Film Song)

Even though Indian film songs reveal the clear influence of Western pop songs, you will probably hear them as more "Indian" than "Western," in spite of the presence of Western instruments. While Indian film songs, or *filmi,* are clearly not part of the classical raga tradition, many film directors and performers were trained in Indian classical music, and as a result *filmi* retains some classical characteristics.

Modern Western audiences may find Indian films incredibly escapist and contrived, and hopelessly bogged down by the songs that interrupt rather than move the action along. But historical film buffs will recall that many American films from the 1930s and

1960s also included numerous songs. While the song-film format fell out of favor in the West long ago, it has not in India, a country where millions toil every day in the heat for little reward. No matter how seemingly "silly" it is for jaded Western moviegoers, a film that transports people from the grinding poverty of their own lives into fantasies of love, adventure, or exceptional religious devotion is clearly of some value. The Indian film industry, somewhat jokingly referred to as "Bollywood" (a combination of the words *Bombay* and *Hollywood)*, has become the world's number-one producer of films, releasing roughly 700 to 1,000 films per year. The film industry was traditionally dominated by Hindustani artists, and as a result for many years mainstream *filmi git* were also generally Hindustani. Eventually, the South developed its own style of film songs, and in recent years these have gained popularity throughout India and abroad.

The first Indian "talkie" was released in 1931. Early films required the actors themselves to sing songs derived from "light classical" Indian music into a "single-system" camera. By the 1940s, however, when sound and image could be recorded separately, producers began using "playback singers," individuals who recorded the songs in a studio; the songs were then played back to the actors who lip-synched the words on the film set. Because of India's diverse population and languages, songs might be recorded in more than one of India's major languages.

Film producers hired music directors who, with a team of writers and musicians, created, performed, and recorded all the music for a given film. To this end, studios had to retain a great many musicians playing primarily Western orchestral instruments plus a few Indian instruments, especially for "traditional" scenes. Today's film music, however, makes greater use of synthesizer. Certain of the film music producers became major figures in their own right, and most of them were musicians themselves.

The "playback" singers who have performed most songs since the late 1930s are far fewer in number than the actors and actresses they sing for, meaning that audiences hear the same voices doing the songs in film after film, regardless of who is being seen. Two figures have tended to dominate the scene, either personally or by setting the style. Male actor-singer Kundan Lal Saigal set the standard early on with his warm voice, which recorded well with the early microphones. But a single female singer, Lata Mangeshkar, has dominated the industry for six decades, since 1942; her light, "little girl" voice is virtually the signature sound of Indian *filmi*. Cited by the *Guinness Book of World Records* as having produced more recordings than any other singer, she has recorded thousands of film songs in numerous languages.

BOLLYWOOD
An informal name for India's film industry, combining "Bombay" and "Hollywood."

Questions to Consider

1. Why does the Indian classical tradition dominate the musical image of South Asia in the West?

2. Discuss the following terms important to a Hindustani classical music performance: *Raga, Alap, Gat, Tala, Rasa*.

3. Compare and contrast Hindustani and Carnatic music traditions.

4. How do *filmi* songs differ from Baul songs?

5. In what ways is Indian music spiritual?

6. What made India and Indian music attractive to the "world traveler" or "hippy" generation of the 1960s and 1970s?

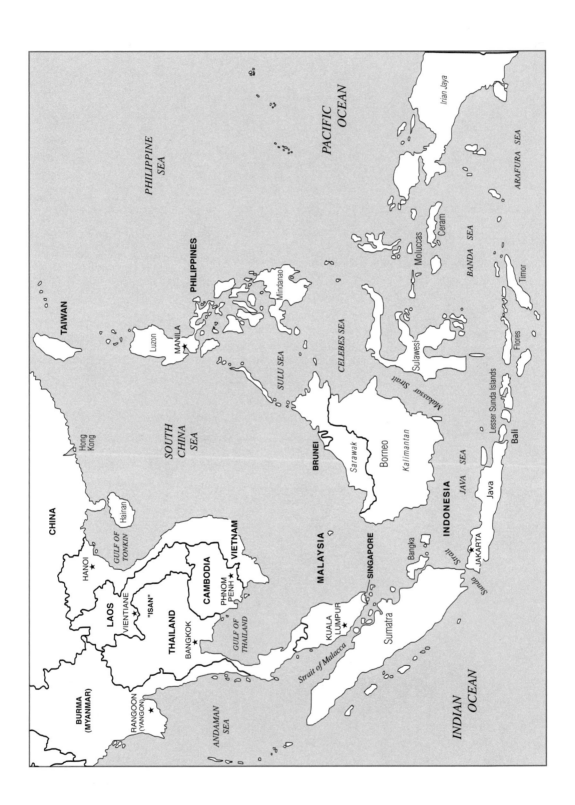

Bangkok's Wat Arun (Temple of Dawn), a Buddhist complex next to the Chao Phraya River, attracts thousands of visitors each month drawn to its architectural design and brilliant colors

CHAPTER 6

Southeast Asia: A Land of Bamboo and Bronze

Background Preparation

I t is difficult to imagine a more colorful region of the world than Southeast Asia, a vast area consisting both of the Asian mainland and of some of the largest islands in the world. It is now divided into eleven independent states, seven on the mainland and four among the islands, of which all but Thailand were colonialized by European powers before each gained independence during the twentieth century. Prior to the colonial period, Southeast Asia consisted of both large and small kingdoms whose borders constantly expanded or retreated depending on a given power center's projection of influence. The names of some countries may be familiar, but others are understandably little known, including that of the region's newest nation, East Timor, which only gained independence from Indonesia in 1999. The nations on the mainland include Myanmar

Typical of modern Southeast Asian cities, Bangkok's endless traffic and general congestion can be both exhilarating and exhausting

A typically timeless village near the banks of the mighty Maekhong River in southern Laos near the Khong waterfalls

(formerly Burma), Cambodia, Laos, Malaysia, Singapore, Thailand, and Vietnam, while the island nations are Brunei, Indonesia, the Philippines, and East Timor.

There are many more ethnic groups than there are states, however—mainland Southeast Asia alone is home to more than 140 named ethnic groups. Population densities throughout the region vary widely: both Vietnam and Indonesia (especially the main island, Java) have high-density and rapidly growing populations, while the populations of Burma and especially Laos are scattered and sparse. The largest urban areas grew rapidly during the last half of the twentieth century, especially as rural populations migrated to the cities seeking safety (during periods of war) or economic opportunities. The region's largest cities include Jakarta in Indonesia, Bangkok in Thailand, Ho Chi Minh City in Vietnam; Manila in the Philippines, and the city-state of Singapore at the tip of the Malaysian Peninsula. Some capital cities, however, remain relatively small and undeveloped; these include Vientiane in Laos, Rangoon (Yangon) in Burma, and Phnom Penh in Cambodia. Because Southeast Asian cities exhibit the most modern aspects of life in each country, it is in the small towns and villages, where rice-growing and animal husbandry are often the chief occupations, that "traditional" culture thrives.

Many aspects of Southeast Asian life—agricultural, ritual, and festive—are shaped by broad weather patterns called *monsoons* (winds). Life on the mainland is governed by alternating wet and dry monsoons; the former comes from the sea and brings on the rainy season, and the latter comes from the Asian continent and brings dry weather, either cool or hot. During a given season, the weather tends to vary little. Island climates are generally more even throughout the year, however, because the humidity that produces rain is nearly always present. Overall, Southeast Asia is tropical and rather humid, but upland areas, especially on the mainland, can become quite cold during the cool, dry monsoon. Temperatures in northern Thailand and upland Laos can fall to freezing, and snow has been known to fall in the highlands of central Laos. Because most rice is grown in flooded paddy fields, rice agriculture is restricted to

The terraced rice paddies of Bali, Indonesia, effectively utilize every inch of available space (Amy Unruh)

the rainy season. Countries experiencing a dry monsoon period have only one harvest, while those with rain year-round may have two or more.

Poverty remains a major issue in many Southeast Asian countries. Economically, most of Southeast Asia is considered "Third World," though Malaysia, Thailand, and Singapore have achieved rapid growth and modernization in recent decades. In developed countries such as these, one finds fully developed communication, and sanitation infrastructures, but in the less developed areas, such as Laos, there are still few paved roads, no railroads, and little modern communication.

Planning the Itinerary

Because around two hundred distinct, named ethnic groups are found throughout Southeast Asia, an exploration of the region's cornucopia of musics is as exciting as it is daunting. Each of the larger nations, with the exception of the Philippines, has or had aristocratic courts that were the longtime patrons of the arts. Wherever these court systems thrived, highly sophisticated "classical" music developed, performed by relatively large instrumental ensembles in a variety of contexts, including dance and theater. In one case, that of Bali in Indonesia, these ensembles were primarily associated with Hindu temples rather than with the royal court. Outside of courts and temples, music was largely found in the rural areas, primarily in villages, because Southeast Asian farmers prefer to live in clusters. In these areas, music-making is necessarily simpler because few musicians are able to devote themselves to it full-time. Many nations also have large minority groups, usually living in remote uplands. Their music is often unrelated to that of the dominant lowland cultures. Throughout Southeast Asia, though especially in urban areas, there is also a great variety of modernized popular music. In countries with developed media, this type of music reaches into the most remote areas, even if the televisions have to be powered by car batteries.

An Inside Look

Priwan Nanongkham

Although I am now a doctoral candidate in Ethnomusicology in the United States, I grew up in a rice-farming village in northeast Thailand, a region that is culturally Lao and known locally as Isan. When I was in the seventh grade at

the local secondary school, I joined a Thai music club because people told me that playing music was not just for enjoyment but it also made people into good human beings. There I studied the *ranat thum* (lower xylophone) and *saw u* (two-stringed fiddle). Because of this experience, I decided to switch schools, and restarted seventh grade in Roi-et city at the local Natasin, a kind of high school for the arts that includes the first two years of college. There I majored in central Thai *piphat* ensemble.

*Mr. Priwan Nanongkham,
Thai musician and teacher*

Because I was from Isan, I decided that I should learn to play the music of my home region. My school offered such courses to help preserve our tradition, which is feeling the effects of modernization and globalization. This included studying the Lao free-reed mouth organ called *khaen* as well as the instruments of a fairly new ensemble that emphasizes its lead instrument, a vertical xylophone called *pong lang*. Our school troupe was invited to perform throughout Thailand and even went to Germany and the Netherlands in 1988.

After spending six years in Roi-et, I decided to expand my work in music through the study of pedagogy so that I could teach others to make music too. This I did at Chulalongkorn University in Bangkok, where I earned a Bachelor of Music Education degree in 1991. Because of my growing interest in the musics of other countries in Asia, such as Japan, China, and Korea, I entered the masters program in Cultural Studies at Mahidol University near Bangkok, but unfortunately I did not finish this degree because I pursued an opportunity to come to the United States to teach Thai music to a family in Denver, Colorado, in 1994. After moving to New York where I taught Thai music in a Thai Buddhist temple, I entered the graduate program in Musicology-Ethnomusicology at Kent State University and wrote an MA thesis on *pong lang* music from Isan.

My dream is to become a music professor, field researcher, scholar, and musician in Thailand where I can devote my life to the study of the music of my own regional culture, Thailand as a whole, and of the rest of Southeast Asia, if not the world.

If Southeast Asia is known for anything, it is bronze, an alloy of the naturally occurring metals copper and tin. Bronze metallurgy is extremely old, going back to around 2000 B.C. For this reason, a great variety of bronze instruments are found throughout the region. Because of their great rigidity and weight, bronze instruments are invariably idiophones. Many ensembles that feature bronze instruments also include non-idiophones, especially drums. A second key

The famous triple *chedi* in fourteenth-century Wat Sri Samphet in Siam's (Thailand's) former capital, Ayuthaya, which was destroyed in 1767 by Burmese armies

feature of this region's music is the widespread use of bamboo, although bamboo instruments are also found in East Asia. In Southeast Asia's tropical climate, bamboo grows rapidly and easily, providing material not just for musical instruments, but also for numerous every-day objects.

Demographics must be considered when categorizing the music of the region. One basic division is between lowland and upland peoples. Most lowlanders live in villages and are generally rice farmers, though the people of the great lowland cities, who vary from wealthy businessmen and high-ranking government officials to unskilled laborers, live quite differently. Uplanders everywhere remain rural, with some practicing what is called swidden agriculture, in which nomadic communities clear hillsides or mountaintops for temporary agricultural use by burning the trees and planting dry crops such as rice or maize. Besides its indigenous peoples, Southeast Asia also hosts great numbers of Chinese immigrants, most of whom came to the cities to engage in commerce during the nineteenth and twentieth centuries, often retaining their distinct temple traditions, instrumental music, and opera. On a smaller scale, the same is true of immigrants from India.

Southeast Asia is a subcontinent known more for instrumental ensembles than for soloists. Vocal music also plays a strong role, because many traditional forms articulate narratives of great warriors, royalty, and religious men, as well as great women, comic characters, and super-human heroes. Theater is exceptionally important as well, and virtually all Southeast Asian theater types require instrumental music, song, and dance. Additionally, theater employing puppets of various sorts—especially flat, leather shadow puppets—is a major art form throughout the region. Vietnam's unique water-puppet theater, which takes place in a pond with the manipulators behind a screen standing waist-deep in water, features amazingly agile wooden puppets placed at the ends of long mechanical arms.

All musics, whether traditional or modern, require a system of patronage in order to survive. While the courts and royal families of Vietnam, Laos, and Burma have long since disappeared, royal arts in those countries continue to a degree thanks to modest state support. Even in Thailand, Malaysia, and Cambodia, which retain kings and royal families, patronage has also been taken over by the state, which supports the arts in various ways, especially through the education system. Only in Indonesia, where various Javanese sultans still hold court, does royalty actually support the traditional arts. But even there, government-supported music conservatories can be found. Traditional music, theater, and dance at the local and regional levels, however, are mostly left to their own devices, and with increased modernization and the spread of popular culture through globalization, have had a tough time surviving. Some forms have retained widespread support by modernizing, but many have simply become rare or extinct as people turn increasingly to various popular musics, both of local origin and foreign. All Southeast Asian countries now have their own popular music, much of it originally stimulated by the importation of Anglo-British ballroom dance music from the 1930s on.

VIETNAM

Arrival: Vietnam

Vietnam stretches dragon-like along the South China Sea for at least 1,500 miles. Two major rivers create vast sandy deltas before they empty into the sea: the Red River in the north, which flows past the capital city, Hanoi, and the Mekong River, which splits into nine branches—the "Nine Dragons" (*Cuu Long* in Vietnamese)—and flows through the endless rice fields of the south. Vietnam's backbone is a chain of mountains that runs from south to north, spilling into neighboring Cambodia, Laos, and China. Vietnam's vast population of more than 84 million people (as of 2004) is predominantly Viet (or Kinh), a wet rice–growing people who live in the lowland plains between the mountains and the sea. In central Vietnam, the coastal plains are sometimes no more than a few miles or even a few hundred feet wide. Indeed, north of the old imperial capital of Hue, "Sea and Cloud Pass" brings the mountains into the sea itself. The majority of Vietnam's people live in the lowlands, while some fifty-four minority groups, most unrelated to the Viet, live in the hills and mountains that border Cambodia and Laos to the west.

Culturally speaking, Vietnam has three distinct regions, the north, the center, and the south. Each has a different history, a distinct accent, and different preferences for instruments and genres of music or theater. The north includes Hanoi, the country's ancient capital and the locale for several important kinds of music, including the music of the distinctive water-puppet theater. The center's heart is the old imperial city of Hue, seat of the Nguyen dynasty until 1945, when Vietnam's last emperor, Bao Dai, abdicated. The south, centered on Ho Chi Minh City (formerly Saigon) and several major cities in the delta, has the youngest culture and is also the most easy-going.

The people who live in the mountains are mostly different from the Viet, and speak a variety of Austroasiatic and Malayo-Polynesian languages. Living in tiny isolated villages and often practicing "slash-and-burn" or "swidden" agriculture on the mountainsides, they relocate from time to time when the fields are depleted. Their musical cultures encompass both songs and instrumental music. Most instruments in the uplands are made of bamboo and other organic materials, but they are nonetheless incredibly varied. Perhaps the most surprising are the large bronze gong sets played during numerous rituals and festivals.

An upland Bahnar village near Kontum, Vietnam. Note the lightly framed houses with stucco walls and the steps carved into a log

For many in the West, "Vietnam" is a war, but, of course, it is actually a country—and *one* country, not two as during that war. Our arrival is in the capital, Hanoi, formerly only known as a forbidding Communist city and the prime target of American bombers in "North Vietnam." Located along the broad Red River, whose delta forms a vast plain in the north, Hanoi's architecture reflects three eras: fascinating temples dating back to the eleventh century, much of the French colonial architecture created during the later nineteenth and twentieth centuries, and finally the modern buildings of a capitalist-leaning Vietnam reborn in the 1990s.

Our visit to Vietnam must necessarily be brief, and many exciting and colorful kinds of music will have to be ignored. First we will visit the Central Highlands to experience a bronze gong ensemble. Afterward, we will go to Ho Chi Minh City and the Mekong Delta to hear a typical expression of the Viet, a refined string ensemble with the characteristic tone-bending and extensive ornamentation that make Vietnamese music so sensuous.

Site 1: Upland Bronze Gong Ensemble

Track 9

First Impressions. Listeners may be struck by this music's apparent hypnotic effect. The music sounds fairly simple. The metal gongs with somewhat "fuzzy" pitches and the seemingly slightly off-kilter rhythm instruments are intriguing. The struck instruments are clearly idiophones and the drums are membranophones. Listening more carefully, you might note that the mix of sounds changes because the musicians are walking in a circle past a stationary microphone. Unfortunately, the audio recording cannot capture the graceful female dancers who lead the group of male players.

Similar to the Jarai gong ensemble, but using fists instead of beaters, members of the Stieng minority perform on a set of flat bronze gongs in Vietnam's Central Highlands (Phong Nguyen)

Aural Analysis. The ensemble heard in our example consists of approximately thirty members, all from the Jarai ethnic group, and was recorded in Pleiku in Vietnam's Central Highlands. Led by young female dancers, the male musicians walk in a circle, each holding a single bronze gong. These vary in diameter from about twenty-four inches to around twelve inches. Some have bosses (raised knobs), and others are flat; all are struck by padded beaters. In addition, the ensemble includes drums and cymbals. If one listens carefully one can count six pitches in the octave, expressed as 1, 2, 3, 4, 5, and 7—but because the Jarai do not theorize about their music, this scale has no name. The range of the melody is relatively narrow, and the intervals between adjacent notes are no more than a fifth.

Because each musician has only one gong, capable of producing only a single pitch, the sounds of the different gongs are strung together to produce melody. This is an example of *interlocking construction*, in which a succession of individual pitches played by different people creates the effect of a continuous melody. Considering that each musician only strikes one gong, it is not surprising that there is no ornamentation. Clearly in duple meter (countable in multiples of two beats), the rhythm sounds fairly simple except for a certain freedom displayed in the pitches' nonsimultaneity. One senses that these performers cooperate but do not feel obligated to play in lockstep. Upon closer examination, one notices that the melodic units are relatively short, have a narrow range, and fall to the lowest pitch (1), which acts as the "home" note and creates a feeling of rest and resolution. Although the music consists primarily of a single melodic line, making it monophonic, accompanying gong-players sound the "pillar" pitches of 1 and 5 from time to time, giving the music a strong tonal framework. Its form is iterative in that the melody is repeated for as long as necessary. There are no apparent dynamic shadings.

Cultural Considerations. Ensembles of gongs are relatively common among upland Vietnam's ethnic groups. They are associated with both festivals and religious rituals, including funerals and the annual buffalo sacrifice. Because they require a large number of musicians, none of whom dominates any other, these ensembles reflect the communal nature of upland village life. In this music, as in the society, each person has a specific role to play in order for it to function: some reiterate the pillar-like pitches, some play melody, and some dance; overall, there is no apparent distinction between "musician" and "nonmusician."

Gong ensembles typically play for funerals, and thus have a strong association with the afterlife. But visitors are more likely to encounter them during public upland festivals now promoted by the government. Perhaps the most difficult event to accept is the buffalo sacrifice, during which several young men seem to become nearly hypnotized as they begin piercing the hide of a buffalo tied to a tree. Accompanied by the gongs, whose music lends itself to this hypnotic state, they continue stabbing the buffalo until it finally dies. For most Westerners, this is not a pleasant experience—but here the sacrifice is an important ritual that honors the spirits in order to assure the continuity of human life and successful harvests.

Many unanswered questions remain about the relationships between upland and lowland cultures. While bronze metallurgy has been dated to around 2000 B.C., it is unclear which culture developed it first. Are the upland peoples the remnants of the original inhabitants of Southeast Asia, whose ancestors were pushed from their lowland homes by advancing peoples (early ancestors of the Viet) coming from the north? Because the lowland Viet make little use of bronze and play instruments that reflect Chinese influence, it is tempting to conclude that the upland peoples reflect the earliest layer of musical culture in Vietnam. Others argue, however, that upland cultures have always been at the margins of Vietnamese society and have absorbed aspects of lowland culture no longer prominent. That would suggest that upland cultures reflect what is called "marginal survival," in which aspects of mainstream culture now lost are preserved in outlying areas, where culture changes more slowly. At present, however, there is no way to prove either theory.

Site 2: Tai Tu Amateur Chamber Music

Track 10

First Impressions. A southern instrumental chamber genre, *tai tu,* is a gathering of amateur instrumentalists who play more for their own enjoyment than for others. In this way it is similar to the Chinese *sizhu* "silk and bamboo" chamber music from Shanghai (see Chapter 7). On closer hearing you will note that the melodic and rhythmic coordination among the musicians seems quite free and improvisatory. There is much tone-bending and a flexible feeling that perhaps goes along with the hot, humid climate of the Mekong river delta.

Aural Analysis. While many Vietnamese instruments were derived from Chinese instruments, they nearly always have been modified to

A southern Vietnamese *nhac tai thu* group performs at a culture club in Ho Chi Minh City. From left to right: singer, *dan nhi* (fiddle), *dan gi-ta* (guitar), *dan nguyet* (lute), and *dan tranh* (zither)

SONG LANG

A clapper idiophone from Vietnam.

TAI THU

(pronounced tai tuh) A type of chamber music ensemble from Vietnam.

allow for the tone-bending typical of Vietnamese music. Thus, Vietnamese string instruments have higher frets and looser strings than their Chinese equivalents. The decoration on Vietnamese instruments also tends to be unlike that found on Chinese instruments—generally, it features lots of intricately cut, mother-of-pearl inlay. These refined decorations are in some ways analogous to the ornamentation that is so crucial in Vietnamese music.

The recording that we have selected uses three melodic instruments—the *dan kim* lute, the *dan tranh* zither, and the *dan co* fiddle, plus the *song lang* "slit-drum" clapper—but while this is a typical ensemble for this type of music, on other occasions other instruments may join in as well, such as the Vietnamized guitar, a type of flute, or the pear-shaped lute.

Vietnamese music is generated from a complex modal system. Each mode has its own set of pitches (basically five), hierarchy of strong and weak tones, required ornamentation, and associated extramusical meanings. In this way, the Vietnamese system resembles the *raga* system of South Asia more than anything found in East Asia, even though East Asia is the source of Vietnamese instruments. Another aspect of Vietnamese music that points to India is the use of a closed cycle of beats similar to the Indian *tala;* in Vietnam, the clicks of the *song lang* clapper articulate points in these cycles. Certain pitches in each of the Vietnamese modes are outside the Western tuning system, giving Vietnamese music a piquant feeling due to its apparent "out-of-tuneness." Another distinctive feature of Vietnamese music is its tendency toward rhythmic syncopation (that is, toward shifting the accent to a weak beat in a measure).

The musicians in a *tai tu* ensemble play the same fundamental melody but add ornamentation typical of their instrument, resulting in the phonic structure called *heterophony*. It is customary for each musician, in succession, to improvise a short introduction in free rhythm before the group begins playing the tune. Improvisation of this sort is atypical of the rest of Southeast or East Asia, lending further credence to the view that Vietnamese culture, while deeply influenced by East Asia, sometimes exhibits traits more typical of South Asia.

Cultural Considerations. Vietnam is, musically, an extremely complex country. The example used here, *tai tu*, is but one of many kinds of music played by small instrumental ensembles. Some types of music are associated with rituals, some were formerly used at the court in Hue, and some, like *tai tu*, are still used simply for entertainment. It is difficult to divide Vietnamese music into categories like "classical" and "folk," because the same repertory of tunes can be played in many different ways. A learned musician will most likely approach a given piece differently than a farmer would—but in fact many farmers are highly refined and skilled musicians. Within the span of a few days, the same musicians might be hired to play for a religious rite and a theater performance—and might also perform together for their own enjoyment. In fact, *tai tu* music was the basis for the music that accompanied the *cai luong* theater, a genre created and cultivated in the south from around 1917 until its gradual decline in the 1990s.

Arrival: Thailand

THAILAND

Thailand has long been one of Southeast Asia's favorite destinations. For many years travelers entered the country through Bangkok's Don Muong Airport, but with the development of southern Thailand's beaches and island resorts, quite a few fly directly to Phuket Island and skip Bangkok altogether. As beautiful as these islands are, they provide visitors with little of the country's musical and artistic culture. Although going to Bangkok is obligatory for anyone wishing to experience Thai music, many visitors also travel to the northern region and its principal city, Chiangmai, where many tourist-oriented regional musical performances can be heard. Few travelers, however, make it to the northeast region called Isan. Isan maintains a vibrant traditional culture, which, if somewhat modernized at times, remains an integral part of society and is not geared toward outsiders.

Bangkok is a busy, sprawling city famous for its gorgeous Buddhist temples, palaces, shopping, and, alas, world-class traffic jams. Tourists are still enticed to Thailand by colorful posters of small boats laden with produce and crafts on the *khlong* (canals), but if you want to see this "floating market" phenomenon, you must now travel far to the southwest where it is maintained as much for tourists as for the Thai. While old neighborhood markets can still be found in many areas, the outlying and newer parts of Bangkok are covered with gigantic malls and

Old-fashioned *khlong* (canal) at Bang Khen east of Bangkok in 1972. The same area now is fully developed with high rises and the small boats and waterside houses have been driven away by fast, modern boats

shopping plazas, where megastores that dwarf most Walmarts attract throngs of shoppers.

Traditionally, Thailand (or Siam, as it used to be called) was an absolute monarchy. Following a revolution in 1932, the monarchy lost political power, though it retains tremendous moral authority to this day. Thailand is now a constitutional monarchy with a revered royal family headed by King Bhumibol Adulyadej, Rama IX—who, incidentally, once aspired to become a jazz musician. Prior to 1932, the court maintained an elaborate system of music, theater, and dance; following the revolution, the government created the Fine Arts Department to oversee these arts. For many years, instruction in the "classical" arts was provided by only a few public institutions; since the 1980s, however, there has been a tremendous growth in their study, particularly in undergraduate and graduate programs at virtually all of the country's institutions of higher learning.

Track 11

METALLOPHONE
An idiophone consisting of several metal bars graduated in length to produce different pitches.

PIPHAT
(pronounced *bee-paht*)
A type of classical ensemble from Thailand characterized by the use of melodic and rhythmic percussion and a double-reed aerophone.

Site 3: Classical Piphat Music

First Impressions. For first-time listeners, the music of Thai classical court ensembles can be difficult to follow. Like Bangkok's sometimes patternless traffic, the music seems to be a jumble of notes, produced mostly by tuned idiophones but also by some kind of reedy sounding aerophone. After an initial listen, some elements will perhaps stand out: the somewhat regular clacks of a pair of small, bright-sounding cymbals; a pattern of beats played by one or more drums; the predominance of a very active high-pitched xylophone, the Thai version having a "keyboard" of twenty-one hardwood or bamboo pieces suspended over a boat-shaped resonator; and the seemingly meandering reed instrument, which seems to operate in a rhythmic world all its own.

Aural Analysis. Called *piphat mai khaeng* in Thai—a name referring to the musicians' use of hard mallets—these ensembles create what is perhaps the most characteristic sound of Thai traditional music. Our example belongs to a category of *piphat* ensemble pieces known as *phleng naphat*. Central Thai instruments are quite varied. They include wooden-keyed instruments (xylophones), metal-keyed instruments (metallophones), circular frames of tuned metal gongs, bowed and plucked strings, flutes, double reeds, drums, and small rhythmic percussion. Although some can be used as solo voices, Central Thai instruments are usually found in ensembles. Three ensemble types predominate: (1) the *piphat*, made up of tuned and untuned percussion and the double reed; (2) the *mahori*, consisting of tuned percussion, strings, and flute;

A *piphat* ensemble performs for guests at the Siam Society in Bangkok. From left to right: *khawng wong yai* (large gong circle), *daphon* (drum), *ranat ek* (higher xylophone), *pi* (double reed), and *ranat thum* (lower xylophone)

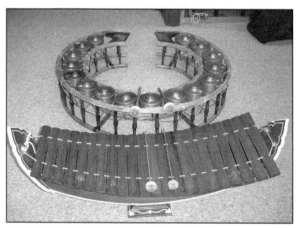

khawng wong yai (large circle gong) and *ranat ek* (higher xylophone)

Instruments of the Thai classical ensemble.

L to R, rear: *thon* (goblet drum), *rammana* (frame drum). L to R, front: *chap lek* (larger cymbals), *ching* (small cymbals), and *krap sepha* (wood clappers)

L to R: two sizes of *pi* double reeds, three sizes of *khlui* vertical flutes

and (3) the *khruang sai,* consisting of strings and flute alone. Whereas the *piphat* primarily plays theater and ritual music, the other ensembles primarily play lighter, more entertaining and tuneful music.

Piphat ensembles require at least three melodic instruments and two rhythmic instruments, but usually add to these. Although the high xylophone (*ranat ek*) is the most active and leading instrument, the lower circle of tuned gongs (*khawng wong yai*)—whose player sits in the middle of a round rattan frame—plays the most fundamental form of the composition. In addition there is a lower-pitched xylophone (*ranat thum*) that plays a highly syncopated, even playful, version of the composition, plus a higher gong circle (*khawng wong lek*) that plays a highly active version. The aerophone heard in our example is a quadruple-reed oboe called *pi,* and its duty is to play a somewhat free form of the melody.

Because the Thai tuning system—at least with instruments of fixed pitch—has seven equidistant tones in an octave, in contrast to the European system of twelve equidistant pitches, some of its pitches do not match any pitches of the European tuning system and therefore sound "out of tune" to the Western ear. Within a given passage, however, the melody will mostly employ a pentatonic scale of only five tones, in the form of 1, 2, 3, 5, 6. Because this kind of music sometimes shifts from one "key" center to another, however, it is usual to find a total of six or even seven pitches in use.

Virtually all Thai music is in duple meter, which means it operates with patterns of two, four, or eight beats. Certain strong beats are articulated by a pair of small bronze cymbals that have the onomatopoetic name *ching,* though they actually can play two strokes, the undamped "ching" and the damped (stopped) "chap." Thai meter is organized cyclically, somewhat like an analog clock. The cycles of much of the repertory have four *ching* strokes ("ching-chap-ching-chap"), with the final stroke ("chap") being accented. This means that Thai music is actually *end*-accented, making it the opposite of Western music generally, which accents beat one.

The lower gong circle is key to the organization of *piphat* music. This group of gongs plays the simplest form of a given composition; that is, its part has fewer notes—a lower rhythmic density—than the other instruments. Although it can be hard to hear, all of the melodic instruments play idiomatic variants of the part played by the lower gong circle. Thus, the phonic structure of Thai *piphat* music is best described as a kind of layered heterophony, known as "polyphonic stratification," that is, a layering of simultaneous variants of the same melody.

Thai classical compositions are often quite regular and predictable. "Sathukan," which is our example, differs from that principle, however, because it is constructed of many short musical motives rather than long, regular tuneful phrases. And because these motives do not have clear-cut cadences that articulate sections, the music is continuous and sounds both very busy and seemingly directionless. Even when a composition is built out of set phrases, it may be difficult to tell, because Thai

PI
(pronounced bee):
A double-reed aerophone found in the piphat classical ensemble of Thailand.

CHING
A pair of cup-shaped cymbals from Thailand.

musicians rarely play a section the same way twice. Indeed, what makes this music interesting for performers and connoisseurs alike is the ingenuity of the performers as they draw upon a vast "bag of tricks" to vary the main melody in appropriate—that is, idiomatic—ways.

Cultural Considerations. During the heyday of the Thai monarchy in the nineteenth and early twentieth centuries, classical music was generously patronized and played a major role in court ceremonies, both secular and Buddhist-related. As a consequence, Thai classical music is closely associated with the society's most important state occasions, festivals, and sacred rites of passage, such as ceremonies to honor teachers, ordinations, funerals, and certain Buddhist rituals. Perhaps we can say that Thai classical music as a sonic structure is mainly of interest to musicians; for others, it serves to engender positive feelings and to reaffirm Thai cultural identity. Although relatively few Thai choose classical music for general listening, there is a broad consensus that classical music best represents the country and its traditional culture.

"Sathukan" is essentially a Thai gerund, because it translates as "greeting." When Thai *sathu* each other, they put their hands together as in prayer position and bow slightly to the person they are greeting. The musical composition alludes to the "teacher greeting ceremony" or *phithi wai khru*, the last word being the Thai pronunciation of the well known Indian term *guru*, and *wai* is another word for *sathu*. "Sathukan" is the first composition played at the ceremony that honors teachers, be they of music, dance, the fine arts, or even teachers in

KHRU
A Thai teacher; the term is linguistically associated with the word guru found in Hinduism.

A teacher initiates new students of Thai music at the annual *wai khru* "teacher greeting" ceremony at Bangkok's Chulalongkorn University
(Andrew Shahriari)

general. In Thai society, the act of teaching, of passing on knowledge, is considered near sacred, and one honors not just the present, living teacher but that person's entire lineage leading back to the ultimate sources of knowledge, the pantheon of gods drawn from animism, Hinduism, and Buddhism. Simple *wai khru* ceremonies are performed at schools in which students simply reaffirm their allegiance to all their teachers, but for classical musicians and other such artists the teacher-greeting ceremony is one of the most important rituals of their life.

A *wai khru* ceremony requires an elaborate altar area containing tables covered with many kinds of food, finely crafted objects, the theatrical masks of the deities, and a full set of musical instruments. A male ritualist intones sacred words in a mix of Thai and Pali, the latter being the sacred language of Thai Buddhism. In addition to "Sathukan," the *piphat* ensemble performs other pieces throughout the ceremony—which concludes when the ritualist marks the forehead of each student and musician with ashes and places a small cone made of banana leaf behind one of their ears. If a student has not studied before, they are given a ritual first lesson on the large gong circle or, for young children, a lesson on playing the small *ching* cymbals.

RAMAYANA

An Indian mythological epic about the Hindu god Rama found throughout South and Southeast Asia.

KHON

A classical masked drama based on the Thai version of the Ramayana.

The Ramayana

One of the great epics of world literature is The *Ramayana*, a story based on Hindu mythology and believed to be more than 3,000 years old. Originating in India, this tale spread throughout much of South and Southeast Asia and is a fundamental key to understanding many elements of the cultures of the region. The *Ramayana*'s influence has been profound. For centuries, social and moral codes drew on the stories and characters of the *Ramayana*. Political structures, city planning, marriage customs, and basic human interaction have all been shaped by the epic. Indeed, the present king of Thailand is known as Rama IX, after the *Ramayana*'s main character.

Much artistic activity in the visual arts, dance, and music is inspired by scenes found in the *Ramayana*. In Thailand, where the story is called *Ramakien*, the most important classical genre of entertainment, known as *Khon*, is based on this work. Performed monthly at the National Theater in Bangkok, *Khon* features masked dancers who enact a different scene from the epic, each performance to the accompaniment of a *piphat* ensemble. The dancers do not speak while onstage; rather, a vocalist sings the story as the actors mime the epic's best-known scenes. *Khon* has become symbolic of the arts in Thailand; it is performed by students and professional performers in tourist shows, school plays, and television broadcasts, and in festivals and other cultural programs overseas.

Although countless variations exist, the basic storyline of the *Ramayana* is: The prince Rama, an incarnation of the Hindu god Vishnu, retreats to the forest at his father's request for several years accompanied by his wife, Sita, and brother, Lakshmana. During his exile, Sita is kidnapped by the evil demon, Ravana, after the two brothers are lured from her protection by a golden deer. Ravana takes Sita to his island fortress, Lanka, where he tries to persuade her to marry him, but she refuses as she is loyal to her husband and confident in her rescue.

During her capture, Sita dropped a clue to a watching band of monkeys who aid Rama in rescuing his wife. Key among these characters is Hanuman, the white monkey god who has many supernatural powers. Hanuman's adventures are numerous as he searches for Sita. He eventually discovers where Sita is imprisoned and returns to Rama to aid in a great battle with Ravana's demons. Allied with the monkeys and bears of the forest, Rama defeats Ravana's demon army, kills Ravana, and rescues the princess.

The conclusion of the story varies depending on the region. In the Indian version, Rama and Sita return to his kingdom together, but rumors doubting Sita's fidelity while imprisoned force her to undergo a trial by fire to prove her loyalty. Although she passes the test, Rama still exiles her lest his rule be tainted by the rumors undermining his authority. In the Thai version, Rama and Sita are reunited after the trial by fire and live happily ever after.

A *khon* masked dance performance of the *Ramakian,* Thailand's version of the Indian epic *Ramayana.*

Mural scene of performances at the funeral of Totsakan, the demon king of Lanka. The performance includes a *piphat* ensemble and the large shadow puppets that actually perform the *Ramakian* story

Arrival: Laos and Northeast Thailand

ISAN

(pronounced ee-sahn)
A term referring to
Northeast Thailand and
its regional culture,
including music.

KHAEN

A bamboo free reed
mouth organ from
Northeast Thailand
and Laos.

Track 12

Various historical events, including the colonization of much of Southeast Asia, led to the Lao people being separated into two areas. Currently, only about four million live in sparsely populated Laos north and east of the mighty Mekong River, while approximately twelve million live in the northeast quarter of Thailand. In both countries, they share a common language, cuisine, literature, and traditional way of life, but the two populations are also now quite different due to their political separation. Until the 1970s both areas where Lao people are concentrated were equally undeveloped: Laos was a former French colony with no modern infrastructure, while the northeast of Thailand was that country's most neglected region. After 1975, when the royal Lao government fell to the communist Pathet Lao, Laos went backward economically and it still has not recovered to a great extent, whereas Northeast Thailand's level of development was raised dramatically by Thailand's booming economy and the government's new attention to the region.

For this book, we have chosen to focus on Lao music from Northeast Thailand, or Isan, as it is usually called. Music in Isan includes both old-fashioned forms and many newer ones—including pop songs featuring dancing girls and bright lights. Even modern forms often appear in a traditional context, however, such as a Buddhist or New Year's festival. The piece we have selected is an example of an older form of singing that was popular until the 1990s, when it was eclipsed by more modern styles.

Site 4: Northeast Thai Lam Klawn

First Impressions. Upon first hearing the instrument that accompanies the vocalists in this recording, many people will be reminded of music from America's Appalachian region. There is nothing odd about the tuning, and the scale is pentatonic. The instrument's timbre sounds familiar, perhaps like a harmonica. Two singers, one male, one female, alternate. Their tone is slightly nasal but certainly not unusual. Once the music gets going, it has a comfortable, steady pulse.

Aural Analysis. There is a saying about the Lao people: If a man lives in a house on stilts, eats sticky rice, and plays the *khaen*, he is a Lao. Traditionally, the Thai, Lao, Khmer, Burmese, and even Malay lived in houses built on stilts, partly for protection, partly to provide a shelter for their animals. Sticky, or glutinous, rice, however, is peculiar to the Lao; the rest of Asia eats non-glutinous rice. Musically, what defines a Lao is playing the *khaen,* the culture's most significant instrument. The *khaen* is a free-reed bamboo mouth-organ ranging in length from about twenty-three inches to more than three feet. It has sixteen thin bamboo tubes that are fitted into a carved, hardwood windchest and wrapped with a kind of wide grass at the top and bottom.

Left: Mr. Ken Somjindah plays the Northeastern Thai *khaen paet* with sixteen pipes in Ban See-Kaeo, Roi-et province

Below: the *khaen paet* shown in side view and front view with parts labeled

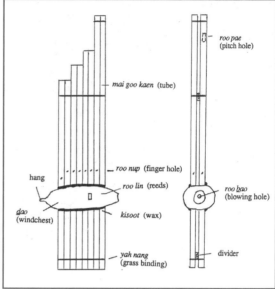

Each bamboo tube has a hole in its wall fitted with a thin plate of copper-silver alloy into which is cut a three-sided tongue. With the reed section sealed inside the windchest by a black insect wax, the tongue vibrates up and down when the player blows into the windchest. Each tube has a finger hole, and the reed only sounds when the finger hole is covered. Since many finger holes can be covered at once, the *khaen* is capable of clusters of pitches which form sounds analogous to Western chords.

Isan singers perform *lam*, a kind of singing in which the melody is generated according to a basic pattern that is coordinated with the lexical tones of the words (Lao and Thai being tonal languages). The language is the Lao spoken in Northeast Thailand, also called Isan. The term *maw* denotes someone with a skill, and thus a singer is a *mawlam* and a *khaen* player is a *maw khaen*. There are numerous genres of *lam* among the Lao; the one heard here is performed by a pair of singers, one male and one female, and is called *lam klawn* (poetry singing) or *lam khu* (pair singing). Although *lam klawn* has lost much of its popularity in the last fifteen years, as several modernized genres of *lam* have become the rage among the younger generation, it is still performed for special events and embodies Lao traditions better than any other form.

A night of *lam* begins around 9:00 P.M. and continues to nearly 6:00 A.M. The performance takes place on a temporary stage, and the singers and *khaen*-players stand to perform. When the male is singing, the female usually performs a simple but graceful dance, and vice versa. The performance proceeds in three sections, the first lasting most of the

LAM KLAWN
(pronounced lum glawn)
Vocal repartee with *khaen* accompaniment from Northeast Thailand.

139

A female *mawlam* singer, accompanied by *khaen*, performs on a small temporary stage at a Northeast Thai Buddhist temple with her male counterpart dancing next to her in Mahasarakham, Thailand

night. Called *lam thang san* (literally "short-way singing"), this first section consists of the male and female vocalists singing in alternation, each beginning a section with an unmeasured introduction followed by the main poem in meter. The scale is pentatonic, and could be described as C, D, F, G, A, with C as the "home" pitch. The meter is always duple. Singers memorize vast amounts of poetry, all written in four-line stanzas with a rhyme scheme peculiar to Lao poetry. The example here represents the beginning of *lam thang san* for both male and female singers.

Cultural Considerations. *Lam klawn* is not merely entertainment, even though it can be highly entertaining. While a performance often takes the form of an imaginary courtship between the singers, and can involve earthy double-entendres, it also addresses many essential aspects of Lao life. The vocalists often "discuss" or debate (in sung verse) matters of history, religion, literature, politics, geography, and etiquette, offering listeners a model of approved thinking and behavior. Here is a typical example of love poetry, sung by a female:

> *O la naw* [introductory words without meaning]
> You are a handsome one.
> Please divorce your wife and then marry me.
> I will also divorce my husband and we will marry each other; can you?
> *O la naw*, you are a handsome man.
> One day I looked at the stars in the clear night,
> And found the moon and many stars.
> But for myself, I could find no one. . . .

Translation by Jarernchai Chonpairot.

Not surprisingly, then, the governments of the United States and Laos used *mawlam* singers to perform anti-communist poems in Laos preceding the overthrow of the Lao monarchy in 1975.

As recently as the 1980s, *lam* was enjoyed by people of all ages throughout Northeast Thailand. Before Northeast Thai villages were electrified, entertainment was scarce, and everyone availed themselves of the chance to hear live music. In Laos, the old days remain, because there has been less development; the situation there is much as it was in Isan thirty years ago. In Northeast Thailand, *lam* was most often heard during the cool or warm dry seasons (November to April), in conjunction with various events including monk ordinations, Buddhist festivals, the New Year (Western, Chinese, and Thai), an annual temple fair, and even funerals. People gathered and sat on the ground around the stage, which was open on four sides and flanked by vendors selling snacks. As the *lam* performance progressed without breaks, the audience ate, slept, wandered off, flirted, or gossiped.

The three most common musical instruments of Northeast Thailand, L to R: *saw bip* (fiddle), *phin* (lute), and *khaen* (free-reed mouth organ)

This form of *lam* lost popularity in the later 1980s as electricity—and thus radio and television—became widespread, and as a type of popular song called *luk thung* (see below) became the rage. *Lam* singers fought back, creating a new fast-paced, popularized, brightly lit genre called *lam sing* ("sing" meaning "racing" or anything that is fast). *Lam sing* and other modernized genres have since swept Northeast Thailand, although they have barely penetrated impoverished Laos. Because there are so many Isan people living and working in Bangkok, *lam sing* and its related genres have become well known there and throughout Thailand. As a result Isan music in particular and Isan culture (and food) in general have become popular. Even McDonalds serves the now famous Isan green papaya salad.

LAM SING
(pronounced *lum sing*)
A popular music form
from Northeast Thailand.

Site 5: Phleng Luk Thung from Northeast Thailand

Track 13

First Impressions. As the song starts, it does not sound very different from the *lam* we listened to previously. But after a few seconds, the music changes into what is apparently some kind of popular song, featuring a drum set, harmony, and an attractive, danceable beat. If you are accustomed to current forms of American popular music, this will probably strike you as very old-fashioned and not too sophisticated.

One of the instruments is a keyboard synthesizer that sounds like it came from a low-end discount store, and the singer's voice is quite even.

Aural Analysis. Regardless of how outsiders might view them, songs of this type are all the rage in Thailand today. Called *luk thung* (literally "child of the fields"), this genre is rural Thailand's answer to the pseudo-sophisticated *luk krung* (literally, "child of the city") songs that used to be popular among city dwellers, particularly those in and around Bangkok. If it sounds like our previous example, the *lam klawn,* that is because *luk thung* were derived from *lam,* and the singer in this recording likely learned *lam* before crossing over to *luk thung.*

The combo that accompanies the vocalist includes the *khaen,* but also other instruments: a central Thai classical *saw u* fiddle, which has a coconut body, a calfskin resonator, and two melodic strings with the hairs of the bow passing between; a *phin* plucked lute from the northeast; a drum set and other percussion; and an electronic keyboard. The scale form heard is pentatonic but unlike that of the *lam* that we have discussed. Here it sounds minor, having the pitches A, C, D, E, and G, with A as the "home" pitch. At the beginning of the piece, the rhythms are rather free and not in meter, but when the singer enters a clearly marked duple meter commences, articulated by the drum set.

While the poetry is strophic, this is not quite clear from the melodic style, because there is no rigid repeated tune. The language is Isan, which is essentially the same as Lao. Because it is a freestanding song and not part of an extended *lam* performance, it has a title: *Fan rak fan rai,* literally "love dream, bad dream." The cassette album from which it comes is entitled "Tears Drop on the Bed," and the female singer's name is only given as Sri-Isan, which means "a good person from Isan [the northeast]." Cassettes like this one are issued by the hundreds from companies both great and small and are sold in small stores, outdoor markets, and on the street, and sometimes in Thai or Lao groceries in the United States.

Cultural Considerations. Some Western writers have referred to *luk thung* as "country songs." This allusion to Nashville has its merits. Both American and Thai "country songs" speak for people who have traditionally been looked down on, are generally poor, have often had to migrate to distant cities in search of low-paying work, whose lives have more than their share of challenges, and who—stereotypically—prefer a pickup truck if they can afford one.

Luk thung songs originated without much notice during the later 1960s and early 1970s, as singers took traditional regional styles from the north, south, and northeast and created pop versions that included—besides the traditional instruments—drums, electric guitar, and, later, keyboard. Most *luk thung* singers had a background in traditional genres and crossed over when it became apparent there was money to be made. *Luk thung* from the north and south, however, disappeared, while those from the northeast became increasingly popular, eventually coming to dominate Thai media in the 1980s. This process was accelerated

PHIN
(pronounced pin)
A fretted, plucked lute
from Northeast Thailand.

as tens of thousands of northeasterners migrated to Bangkok as Thailand developed into an "Asian Tiger" economy. These now relatively prosperous transplants became a natural market for all manner of *luk thung*–related media products and events. These included *luk thung* movies, live *luk thung* shows, and, of course, *luk thung* cassettes. Get into most any taxi in Bangkok and you will hear *luk thung* songs on the radio or cassette, because most taxi drivers come from the northeast. Go into the servant's quarters of an upper class house or into factories and you will encounter them as well.

Luk thung has given rise to star singers who, in spite of the poverty they grew up in, have become quite wealthy singing songs that express the feelings and lives of their compatriots. Early favorites who solidified the style

Dancers at the Akademi Seni Tari Indonesia (College of Indonesian Dance) in Yogyakarta, Java, Indonesia, perform the highly refined Bedhaya court dance (R. Anderson Sutton)

include the late female singer Pompuang Duangjan and the late male singer Suraphon Sombatjalern. Today there are too many *luk thung* singers to mention, some making recordings and being heard throughout the land, others singing their songs in local restaurants and clubs in gritty upcountry towns. *Luk thung* shows nearly killed traditional *mawlam* by the late 1980s, and traditional performers, because they receive no government support as "cultural carriers," had to change in order to stay in business. Isan theater adopted *luk thung's* songs into their format, as did the *lam klawn* form, with its alternating male and female singers. Because Isan was producing the most popular type of music in Thailand, it stopped being thought of as a backwater full of poor rice farmers, and came to be seen instead as a hotbed of stylish young musicians.

Arrival: Indonesia (Java and Bali)

INDONESIA (JAVA & BALI)

Indonesia, the largest archipelago in the world, consists of more than 13,000 islands created by centuries of volcanic activity. Though many of these islands are uninhabited, the larger islands, especially Sumatra and Java, are densely populated. The first-time visitor will be struck immediately by the extreme heat and humidity due to Indonesia's position on the equator and its sea-level elevation. Tropical rainforests are found on many of the islands, along with mist-shrouded mountains and volcanoes, white-sand beaches with spectacular offshore underwater reefs, colorful flowers, and unique wildlife, such as orangutans. The heavy annual rainfall helps support an agricultural system largely based on rice cultivation, which together with sea-faring activity provides the mainstays of Indonesian cuisine.

Though the official religion of Indonesia is Islam, Hinduism,

Danced by two males, the *barong* is a Hindu-derived
mythological beast that represents "good" in Balinese theater
(Amy Unruh)

Buddhism, and a variety of animistic traditions are also present, and give rise to varied cultural activities. Though there are over 300 languages spoken throughout the islands, the national language is Bahasa Indonesian. English and Dutch are widely spoken as well.

The music of Indonesia, which is dominated by ensembles of bronze instruments, is perhaps the most studied and best known of all world music traditions. Many early ethnomusicologists, such as Jaap Kunst, Colin McPhee, and Ki Mantle Hood, took an interest in the music of Indonesia and spread knowledge of it through writings, teaching, and their own musical compositions. Various well-known composers, such as Claude Debussy, Benjamin Britten, Francis Poulenc, Philip Glass, and Steve Reich, have also acknowledged the influence of Indonesian music on their works. This music has greatly affected the development of modern music in Europe and America, and its influence can be seen in everything from orchestral music to television commercials. The ethereal sound of bronze gongs and metallophones is hypnotic, as is the music's repeating cyclical structure.

GAMELAN
An ensemble from
Indonesia comprised
primarily of
metallophones.

Although there are hundreds of distinct musical traditions found throughout the numerous islands of Indonesia, the most recognized music is that of the gamelan. We will focus on two traditions, Javanese court gamelan and Balinese *gamelan gong kebyar*, in order to introduce this intricate and entrancing music.

Site 6: Javanese Court Gamelan

①

Track 14

First Impressions. A gamelan is an ensemble comprised primarily of idiophones made of either bronze or iron, including a variety of hanging gongs, rack gongs, and metallophones. Other instruments, such as flutes, zithers, various drums, and a fiddle called the *rebab*, may also be present along with vocalists, both male and female. The music of the Javanese Court Gamelan is mellow and tranquil, and is divided into two basic styles, *soft* and *strong*. The soft style has a "misty" quality reminiscent of an early morning fog lifting as the sun rises from the ocean. In contrast, the strong style has a bold, direct character laced with wispy embellishment like a rice field on a breezy day in the midday sun.

Aural Analysis. Javanese court gamelan is based on a *colotomic structure*, meaning that it is music organized into cycles defined by periodic punctuation played by a specific instrument—in its case, hanging gongs. The principal melody is typically provided by either voices and/or melodic instruments, such as the rack gongs, metal-keyed instruments called metallophones, or wooden-keyed instruments called xylophones, or non-idiophones such as the fiddle or bamboo flute. Other rack gongs, metallophones, and xylophones embellish this melody by filling in the aural space, giving the music its "misty" quality.

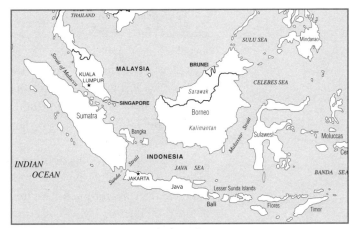

Indonesia

A full gamelan ensemble from Northern Illinois University, DeKalb, Illinois

Two photos of the University of Michigan's bronze Javanese gamelan.

(Left) A student musician plays the *gender,* a series of bronze keys over tube resonators.

(Right) A series of large, hanging bronze gongs, part of the *kempul* set

Our example includes styles of Javanese court gamelan performance, described as *strong* and *soft*. Strong-style gamelan emphasizes the metallophones and bossed rack gongs, which carry the principal melody at a faster tempo. Though the soft-style gamelan often includes a female vocal soloist and a male choir, this example does not include them. The non-idiophone instruments, namely the fiddle, zither, and bamboo flute, support the principle melody, and the tempo is slower than in the strong style.

After a brief introduction by a *bonang* (rack gong), the principle melody is loudly proclaimed. This melody can be simply notated using numbers to represent pitch. The full ensemble enters on the last pitch of the introduction, which is also the start/stop point of the cycle marked by the largest and deepest pitched hanging gong (*gong ageng*).

Principal Melody of Javanese Gamelan Audio Example

Introduction	- 1 1 1	5 6 1 2	2 1 6 5	6 1 6 5
A	6 5 3 2	6 5 3 2	2 3 5 3	6 5 3 2 (repeat)
punctuation	- - - -	- ★ - -	- ★ - -	- ★ - +
B	1 5 6 1	5 6 1 2	2 1 6 5	6 1 6 5 (repeat)
punctuation	- - - -	- ★ - -	- ★ - -	- ★ - +

★ = upper gong + = lower gong

Each melodic line is repeated once before the entire melody is repeated (AA-BB-AA-BB-AA, etc.). Notice that the phrasing of the melody is symmetrical (there are two groups of four phrases with four beats each), exemplifying an emphasis on balance typical of Javanese music. Underlying this melody is the periodic punctuation provided by the hanging gongs (marked by 0 and +). These instruments punctuate specific points in the cycle to articulate the underlying aural framework of the piece. Falling between the pitches of the principal melody at twice the rhythmic density are the quiet embellishments of other metallophones and rack gongs. These three parts are most easily heard in the strong-style gamelan performance.

The soft-style section is signaled by the drums. The tempo slows and the quieter instruments provide the principal melody along with the subdued sounds of the gongs. The colotomic structure and embellishing instruments are still present, but the shift in mood gives the music a haunting quality. The dynamic level diminishes with the slowed tempo and both increase again when the strong-style gamelan returns.

Cultural Considerations. See below (combined with Bali).

Site 7: Balinese Gamelan Gong Kebyar

First Impressions. Whereas the music of Java conveys a sense of tranquility, the music of Bali is filled with dynamic energy. Similar

Track 15

instruments are used, including bronze gongs, metallophones, flutes, and drums, but the character of the music continually shifts, with sudden bursts of brilliant virtuosity contrasting with airy melodic phrases. A feeling of continual agitation pervades the music as it accelerates, slows, crescendos, and relaxes. Then just when you think you have it figured out, the music again turns in an unanticipated direction.

Aural Analysis. Balinese Gamelan Gong Kebyar is also organized according to a colotomic structure. However, this structure is not always as evident as with Javanese Court Gamelan. Many compositions are through-composed, meaning that the melody does not repeat in a series of continuous cycles. Also, Gamelan Gong Kebyar frequently uses sectional solos in which different instruments, such as the drums and cymbals, flutes, metallophones, or rack gongs, are highlighted. This shifting orchestration, along with dynamic variation and sudden tempo changes, contributes to the sudden shifts of mood that characterize the Balinese gamelan style.

GAMELAN GONG KEBYAR

An ensemble type from Bali, Indonesia, comprised primarily of metallophones and characterized by rhythmically dense performance technique.

The high rhythmic density of Balinese Gamelan Gong Kebyar is also a distinguishing characteristic. In many sections of a performance the musicians interlock their parts, so that more than one musician is required to produce a given melodic line. For example, if Player X plays the odd-numbered pitches (1, 3, 5, 7, 9) and Player Y plays the even-numbered pitches (2, 4, 6, 8, 10), the players must interlock their pitches to play them in consecutive order from one to ten. This interlocking of melodic pitches enables the performers to create a high rhythmic density, so that the music sounds as if the melody is being played

A Balinese *Gamelan Gong Kebyar* ensemble performs for visitors at a Hindu temple
(Jerrold Moore)

A pair of *gender wayang* (bronze-keyed idiophones with tube resonators), with an identical pair tuned slightly differently to produce shimmering sounds

at a "superhuman speed"; indeed it is often faster than a single player could perform.

Another noticeable distinction of the Balinese Gamelan Gong Kebyar is what might be described as the "shimmer effect." This shimmering sound is most evident in the wavering tones of the small metallophones on long sustained pitches. The effect is produced by the use of pairs of identical instruments tuned slightly apart. When the instruments are played simultaneously, the slight tuning difference produces perceptible cycles of "beats" due to the slight increase in volume as the pitch frequencies overlap.

Cultural Considerations. Although the gamelan music of both Java and Bali uses similar instrumentation based on colotomic musical organization, the sharp contrast of musical characteristics between Javanese Court Gamelan and Balinese Gamelan Gong Kebyar reveals strong differences in musical values. These values are in large part due to differences in the function and contextual associations of the two musics.

The population of Java is predominantly Islamic. Gamelan music is frequently associated with court ritual functions, usually presided over by a Sultan. The slow, stately sound of the gamelan reflects the regal atmosphere of these occasions, and the music is characteristically calm, to avoid distracting attention from the ceremony or the Sultan. To that end, soft mallets are used on the idiophones. When dancers are present, they too reflect the serene scene with slow-moving choreography and subtle gestures. Tranquility and balance are the key cultural values reflected in the music of the Javanese Court Gamelan.

The island of Bali, however, is predominantly Hindu. Temples are found throughout the island, each devoted to a particular Hindu deity. Most temples have a gamelan ensemble, which is expected to perform for festivals or other events associated with the temple's deity or the Hindu faith. Frequently performances function as a musical offering, and the music is therefore intended to attract and entertain the deity as well as participants. The dynamic character and bright timbre of the Balinese Gamelan Gong Kebyar, with its "superhuman speed" and use of hard mallets on the metallophones, becomes the center of attention. Dances are often vigorous and characteristically "angular," with quick movements of the head, arms, and legs.

There are some contexts in which both Javanese and Balinese music are found, such as shadow puppet plays and live theater, but in sound the two styles still remain clearly distinct. Indeed, the contrast between the entrancing serenity of the Javanese Court Gamelan and the hypnotic dynamism of the Balinese Gamelan Gong Kebyar is a testament to the creative power of Indonesian

Dancers at the Sultan's Kraton (palace) in Yogyakarta perform Bedhaya, considered the "crown jewel" of Javanese court dances
(© Jack Vartoogian/FrontRowPhotos)

musicians, who have managed to create two very different musics out of similar resources.

A young boy in traditional costume dances to the accompaniment of a Balinese gamelan (Amy Unruh)

A Balinese puppeteer brings the story of the *Ramayana* to life through his skillful manipulations of leather shadow puppets
(Amy Unruh)

KECAK

A Balinese theatrical performance of *The Ramayana.*

Kecak: The Balinese "Monkey Chant."

The "Monkey Chant" has become one of the most popular tourist attractions on the island of Bali. Its performers, who are considered a kind of "human gamelan," act out scenes from the Indian epic *The Ramayana* (see page 136), without the use of stage props or costumes. The name of the genre, *kecak,* is derived from the interlocking "cak" sounds of the performers as they imitate armies of monkey soldiers in a mythological battle of good versus evil. Other performers sound out the colotomic structure by imitating gongs of the gamelan ensemble. In addition to the monkey armies, there are costumed dancers who portray the major figures of the story. The performances were originally intended as musical offerings to the Hindu deity Rama, a major character in the epic. This association, however, as well as the storyline, is typically unfamiliar to Bali's many visitors.

A *kecak* or "monkey chant" performance derived from the Indian epic, *Ramayana* (Jerrold Moore)

Questions to Consider

1. To what extent are the terms "classical," "folk, " and "popular" appropriate labels for describing Southeast Asian musics?

2. What are some factors that help maintain traditional Southeast Asian music in the face of modernization?

3. Metrical cycles are characteristic of many Southeast Asian musics. How does this work in the sites reviewed?

4. How do the types of "heterophony" found in Vietnamese Tai Thu, Thai Piphat, and Javanese Gamelan differ?

5. Though Thailand and Vietnam are both part of Southeast Asia, what historical and cultural factors have determined the present musical differences?

6. Compare function and use for both Javanese and Balinese Gamelan. How do these differing functions affect the musical styles of each?

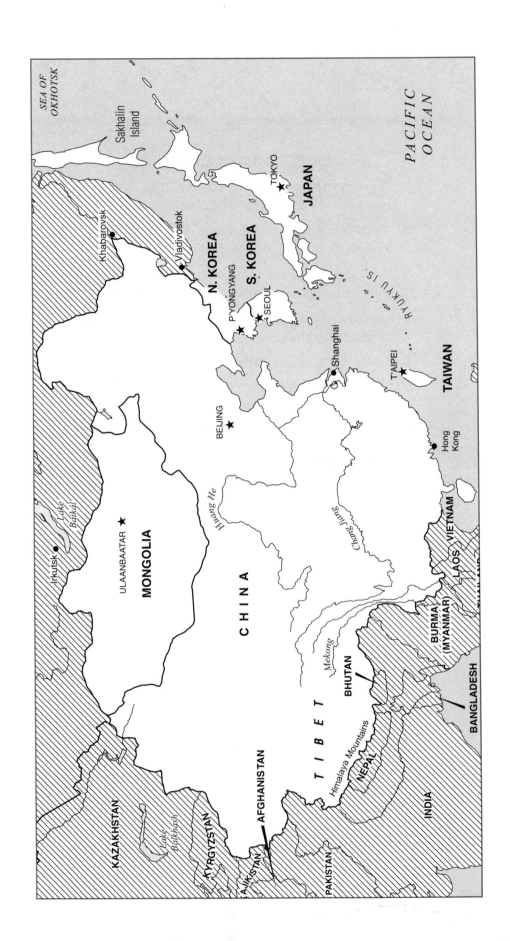

The Great Wall of China
north of Beijing
(Max T. Miller)

CHAPTER 7

East Asia:
Ancient Echoes in the Modern World

Background Preparation

No other region of the world matches East Asia in terms of size, population, and cultural diversity. Culturally, East Asia incorporates not just the immense nation of China, but also Korea, Japan, and Mongolia. Geographically it also encompasses the eastern half of Russia, including Siberia, which constitutes Northeast Asia. East Asia is home to roughly one quarter of the earth's population: China has 1.28 billion people, the Koreas 70.5 million, and Japan 127 million, for a total of 1.47 billion. The other areas, including Mongolia and eastern Russia, have very slight populations spread over a vast territory.

The term *Chinese*, broadly speaking, can be applied to cultural activity found not only in the People's Republic of China and the Republic of China (Taiwan), but also in the self-governing

153

city of Hong Kong and in other places where "Overseas Chinese" comprise important segments of the population. These places include Malaysia, where one third of the population is of Chinese ancestry, the city-state of Singapore, and other cities with large Chinese populations, such as Bangkok, Thailand; Manila in the Philippines; Jakarta, Indonesia; and Ho Chi Minh City, Vietnam. Roughly 90 million people out of China's total population belong to some fifty-five non-Chinese minority groups as diverse as the Hmong and Dai of the southwest and the Koreans of the northeast.

In spite of its immense size, East Asia is unified in certain ways. Foremost among the factors that bind East Asian cultures together is an ideographic writing system developed by the Chinese millennia ago, in which "characters" have meaning rather than phonetic sound. At various times in history, each East Asian culture has adopted the Chinese writing system, allowing literate people in all areas to communicate even though the spoken languages (e.g., Japanese, Korean, Vietnamese, or Mongolian) were otherwise unrelated and mutually unintelligible. Over time, however, distinctive writing systems developed in Japan, Korea, and Mongolia, while Vietnam romanized its language while under French colonial control.

Geography has played a major role in the development of East Asian culture. The original Chinese civilization, that of the "Han" Chinese, arose along the Yellow River in northern China forty centuries ago (ca. 2000 B.C.) and over time spread through the vast territory of East Asia, even into Southeast Asia. At the same time, the Chinese civilization was profoundly influenced by outside cultures, especially those coming from Western and Central Asia along the "silk

IDEOGRAPH

The Chinese unit of writing, a written symbol or "character" that is associated primarily with meaning rather than sound.

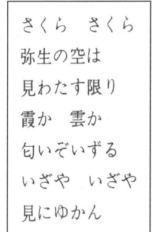

From left to top right and bottom right, the scripts of Japan, China and Korea

road." Many foreign elements, such as Buddhism, came to the Chinese first, were transformed into a Chinese form (a process called "Sinicization"), and then absorbed by neighboring cultures. Chinese civilization spread mostly to the south and southeast, because eastern China is relatively flat, while the rest of the country consists of mountains, deserts, and high plateaus. Even today, in fact, the vast majority of China's 1.28 billion people live in the eastern third of the country.

The Korean civilization developed on a peninsula to the northeast

	CHINA		KOREA		JAPAN	
	ANTIQUITY					
	Xia	21st to 16th century				
B.C.E. 1200	Shang	c. 1600–1045				
1100	Zhou	1045–256				
1000						
900						
800					**ANTIQUITY**	
700	Spring and Autumn	770–476			Zyômon	to c. 200
600						
500						
400	Warring States	475–221				
300	**DYNASTIES OF IMPERIAL CHINA**					
200	Qin	221–206			Yayoi	c. 200 B.C.E.–250 C.E.
100	Han	202 B.C.E.–220 C.E.				
C.E. 0						
100						
200	Three Kingdoms	220–280				
300	Jin	265–420	**THREE KINGDOMS**		Kohun Culture	c. 300–400
400	Northern and Southern Dynasties	420–589	Koguryŏ	?–668		
			Paekche	?–660		
500			Silla	?–668	**IMPERIAL PERIOD**	
	Sui	581–618			Asuka	c. 550–710
600	Tang	618–907	**DYNASTIES OF ROYAL KOREA**			
			Unified Silla	668–935		
700					Nara	710–794
800					Heian	794–1192
900	Five Dynasties and Ten Kingdoms	902–979	Koryŏ	918–1392		
	Liao (Qidan [Khitan])	916–1125				
1000	Song	960–1279				
	Northern Song	960–1127				
1100	Southern Song	1127–1279			**MEDIEVAL PERIOD**	
1200	Jin (Nüzhen [Jurchen])	1115–1234			Kamakura	1192–1333
	Yuan (Mongol)	1279–1368				
1300						
	Ming	1368–1644			Muromati	1334–1573
1400			Chosŏn	1392–1910		
1500					**PREMODERN PERIOD**	
1600					Azuti–Momoyama	1573–1610
	Qing (Manchu)	1644–1911			Edo	1600–1867
1700						
1800					**MODERN JAPAN**	
	MODERN CHINA		**MODERN KOREA**		Meizi	1868–1912
1900	Republic of China	1911–	Japanese colonial period 1910–1945		Taisyô	1912–1926
	People's Republic of China	1949–	Republic of Korea (South)	1948–	Syôwa	1926–1989
2000			Democratic People's Republic		Heisei	1989–
			of Korea (North)	1948–		

of China, and although Korea was profoundly influenced by China, its culture is otherwise distinct. Because the Korean peninsula is rather mountainous, Korea has limited arable land and harsh winters, and the Korean people have often struggled to survive. After the division of Korea into South and North Korea, the south has prospered and developed its own form of democracy, while the north has suffered immense ecological damage from industrialization and deforestation, which has brought cycles of droughts and floods. In addition, the development of an autocratic government has isolated North Korea. The result is that many people in the North are starving, while their culture has been completely politicized.

Japan's culture is also deeply affected by its geography. Japan is a chain of islands, stretching from cold and bleak Hokkaido in the north

An Inside Look

Luo Qin

As a professional violinist (concert-master), amateur composer, and occasional conductor, I had learned how to lead an orchestra and to create musical works for an ensemble. I was basically a Western-centered person at this time, although

Dr. Luo Qin, Professor of Musicology, Shanghai Conservatory of Music; president and editor-in-chief of Shanghai Conservatory Press

I was familiar with Chinese music and instruments as well. However, the graduate program at the Shanghai Conservatory of Music, where I majored in the history of Chinese music, changed my thoughts. After teaching at the Conservatory for several years, in 1991, as a young scholar and graduate student, I entered the Ethnomusicology program at the University of Washington and then went on for doctoral study in ethnomusicology at Kent State University. During my time in the States, I not only learned various musics from around the world but also came to understand the peoples, societies, and cultures related to these musics. Through the study of the theories and practices of Ethnomusicology, I feel I became a true musician, scholar, and person who loves music, culture, people, and their lives.

I specialize in two fields: the history of Chinese music and the urban ethno-orientated study of Shanghai City and its people. I have done much fieldwork and published several works, such as *History of Chinese Musical Instruments; Kunju, a Chinese Classical Theater and Its Revival in Social, Economic, Political and Cultural Contexts; Street Music: An Epitome of American Society and Culture; Heart & Music.com: World Music and Its Narration*, and others. I also love to create music for people who intend to communicate with each other by playing music. For example, while directing Kent State's Chinese Ensemble, I revised a violin concerto called *The Butterfly Lovers* into a work combining violin solo and Chinese ensemble.

After receiving my Ph.D degree I came back to China. At the present, I am a Professor of Musicology at the Shanghai Conservatory of Music, one of China's premier music institutions. In addition I am in charge of the Research Department. Through several years' teaching, I have learned that I could and should do more if I want people to understand more musics and their cultures. Therefore, I entered the publishing business. Right now, I am the President and Editor-in-Chief of the Shanghai Conservatory Press. Nonetheless, I still teach. I hope to continue making contributions to the society in which I live and work and help more and more people to love music.

to the warm and lush Ryukyu Islands trailing southwest from Kyushu, Japan's southernmost large island. Although influenced by Chinese civilization, Japan was relatively isolated, which allowed it to develop a distinct culture. With most of Japan's population, which is nearly half that of the United States, crowded into the main islands of Honshu, Shikoku, and Kyushu—together smaller than the state of California— efficient land use is critical. Because of their historical isolation, the Japanese have developed an amazingly homogenous culture, to the extent that Japanese joke that they need not speak to each other because each knows what the other is thinking.

Whereas Western histories are conceived in terms of centuries, Chinese history—and by extension Korean and Japanese history—are conceived in terms of dynasties, a dynasty being a succession of related rulers, such as the Sung or the Ming. The Chinese dynastic chart reveals a fairly consistent pattern of change. First, an energetic new Chinese dynasty forms and quickly unifies the country under newly effective rule; then, over time the dynasty's effectiveness erodes, enemies begin nibbling at China's borders, and public services and safety break down; finally, the dynasty crumbles. Between China's greatest, most stable, and longest-lasting dynasties were periods of disunity and chaos, such as the "Warring States" period (403–221 B.C.) and the "Six Dynasties" (222–581 A.D.). During certain dynasties, such as the Yuan (1260–1370) and Qing (1636–1911), for-

The statue of China's greatest philosopher and teacher, Kong Fuzi (Confucius), in the ancient Kong temple of Quanzhou, China

eign invaders—in these examples, the Mongols and Manchurians respectively—dominated China. Even though the rulers were foreigners, the vast Chinese bureaucracy maintained a control over Chinese institutions that insulated them from foreign cultural influence. Indeed, some foreign conquerors ended up being Sinicized to the extent that their own cultural distinctiveness eroded or disappeared.

The arts have long been elements of the political process in China. Seeing the arts as far more than mere entertainment, the government has often harnessed music and theater for their ability to influence the thinking and behavior of the general population. There also was a belief that music could have an influence on a person's ethical character. In ancient China—and by extension elsewhere in East Asia—the views of

DYNASTY

A ruling family, like the Ming, and the era characterized by that family's dominance.

philosopher Kong Fuzi (romanized as Confucius, 551–479 B.C.) had a profound influence on the role of music in the lives of the scholar class. In more recent times, Chairman Mao Zedong, China's communist leader from 1949 to 1976, not only believed that music and theater influenced people, but insisted they be harnessed by the state to create correct political thinking.

Planning the Itinerary

Our musical tour will encompass China, Mongolia, Korea, and Japan. The music of each country is extremely different in overall sound, timbre, character, and process. Yet all share certain traits that bind them together, making the concept of "East Asian" music a reasonable one. One way to explain this is through an analogy with food. If you've had opportunities to visit Chinese and Japanese restaurants, even in North America, you probably know there are striking differences. Those differences in the way food is prepared and presented and in overall atmosphere are analogous to some differences between the various countries' musics. Consider the décor: Chinese restaurants are usually highly decorated with colorful lanterns, dragons, and phoenixes in strong shades of red, gold, blue, and green, whereas Japanese restaurants tend more to plain white walls and natural wood, especially light-colored varieties. Whereas Chinese dishes, which feature colorful mixtures of many ingredients, are randomly placed on the table and shared by everyone, Japanese meals are usually served individually on lacquered trays with many compartments for well-separated delicacies. The space separating the food in Japanese restaurants is analogous to the silence separating sounds in Japanese music. Whereas the behavior of both patrons and staff in a Chinese restaurant—especially in Chinese cities— is informal, enthusiastically loud, and busy, behavior encountered in a Japanese restaurant is much more formal, quiet, and subtle. Once again, many of these distinctions also apply to Chinese and Japanese music.

The second analogy we will use to help explain some of the major differences between different kinds of East Asian music has to do with attitudes toward "tradition," preservation, and change. Consider the following metaphor: A wonderful, ancient bridge (akin to traditional music) occupies a key position in the city. Because it is no longer adequate to handle modern traffic, the government calls for engineers to study the situation, one Chinese, one Korean, and one Japanese. After a thorough consideration, the Chinese engineer announces that the bridge will be preserved as best as can be but also brought up to modern standards. Workers will replace and widen the deck, put on new railings, add modern lampposts, rebuild the support system, and level the approaches. Thus, they claim, the old bridge will remain, but it will have been "improved" and "modernized." The Korean and Japanese engineers, however, conclude that the bridge is wonderful in its present form and should be preserved as is. Recognizing the demands of modern travel, however, the engineers recommend both keeping the old bridge open for those who prefer to use it and building a new one nearby for those who need it.

Thus, in China most "traditional" music struggles to survive as best it can, while newly arranged and orchestrated music, considered "improved" and "modernized" by the Chinese, is used to represent Chinese music to the outside world. In Korea and Japan, however, institutions both public and private preserve all surviving forms of traditional music and theater as living anachronisms in an otherwise modern world. As a result there is little difficulty in defining "tradition" in Korea and Japan, whereas in China there are differing views of what is traditional and what music should represent China, while foreign researchers may have their own views that contradict those of the Chinese. The state of traditional music in Mongolia resembles the Chinese situation, whereas traditional Tibetan music survives intact, primarily in exile in countries such as Nepal and Bhutan.

Arrival: China

CHINA

As with all major civilizations, the Chinese developed their great cities and agricultural centers along rivers and around great lakes. Indeed, the names of many Chinese provinces reflect geographical features. For example, the name of Shandong province means "east of the mountains," while Shanxi means "west of the mountains." Similarly, Hubei is "north of the lake" and Hunan is "south of the lake." China's greatest threats in earlier times have come from the northern border areas where non-Chinese invaders, including the Jürched, the Mongols (of Chinggis [also spelled Genghis] Khan fame), and the Manchu originated. China's Great Wall, stretching 1,400 miles over the northern mountains, was built to keep out the northern "barbarians."

Being a vast land, China has more than one gateway city. These include Beijing (the capital), Shanghai (China's largest city), and Guangzhou (its most internationalized city). Beijing, a sprawling city of 13 million built around the spacious Forbidden City (the former palace of the emperors), is the center of government and culture, whereas Shanghai and Guangzhou are centers of industry. The majority of the Chinese population lives in eastern China, an area with a remarkable number of large cities unknown to most foreigners. Though little known to outsiders, Shandong province in central China nonetheless produces products that are much appreciated. Owing to Shandong's earlier colonialization by Germany, it is the center of Chinese beer-making, with Qingdao being the home of "Tsingtao" beer. But to the Chinese Shandong is more important as the province of the ancestral home of Kong Fuzi (Confucius) in the small city of Qufu near the sacred mountain called Tai Shan.

On arrival in China, do not expect to see the romanticized scenes and buildings of the recent martial arts film *Crouching Tiger, Hidden*

Dragon. China has undergone an extreme makeover since the 1990s, and the construction crane is far more prominent than temples or red-tiled roofs. Skyscrapers, department stores, vast restaurants, and wide roads represent China today, and one cannot go far without stumbling on a McDonalds, Pizza Hut, KFC, or Wal-Mart. In this din of modernity, traditional music is only one small voice.

In terms of culture, it is customary to make a distinction between northern and southern China. One essential difference is that the northern Chinese eat wheat (in the form of breads and noodles), because wheat grows more readily in the relatively dry and temperate north, while in southern China, which is subtropical, rice is the fundamental carbohydrate. Distinctions between northern and southern are also made in music and theater.

CULTURAL REVOLUTION

A ten-year period in China's history, from 1966-1976, marked by severe social and political upheaval.

Even within northern or southern China, there are numerous regional distinctions, often identified with specific provinces. There are regional styles of Chinese cuisine, such as Sichuan, Hunan, Guangdong (Canton), Shanghai, Beijing, and so forth. Language is also regional, because Chinese civilization developed in relatively isolated pockets. While all Chinese languages are related (as all the European Romance languages are), they are also mutually unintelligible, even though the writing system is the same for all. Even within a single province, for example, Guangdong, there are several languages, including Cantonese, Hakka, and Chaozhou. Today's national language, called "Mandarin" in English, was originally from the north. Regional distinctions are also extremely important in Chinese music, especially in the narrative and theatrical genres.

Until the latter part of the twentieth century, most writing on Chinese music focused on ancient instruments, rituals, and aesthetic principles. The great Chinese music documents often included the living music of the time, but when Westerners began writing about Chinese music, they tended to omit living music. Older scholars often viewed the latter as unsophisticated remnants of the glorious past. Ethnomusicological research into Chinese music increased dramatically during the last three decades of the twentieth century, because, in earlier years, China had been off limits to most researchers because of near continuous war from the 1920s until 1949 and its subsequent political convulsions. This was particularly so during the Cultural Revolution (1966–76), a top-down upheaval initiated by Chairman Mao Zedong and his influential wife, Jiang Qing, a former actress. After the end of the Cultural Revolution, a few foreign researchers came to China, while most Chinese scholars were still collecting "folk music" for use in compositions by conservatory-trained professionals. Much of the new research, however, was confined to urban phenomena because the government for some time rarely permitted research in actual villages and favored sending conservatory ensembles on foreign tours. Today the government has little interest in either urban or village music, and all non-commercial music is struggling to be heard. The question of what music best represents Chinese culture remains a topic for discussion even today.

China has an incredibly diverse array of instruments, many of which had origins outside China, but were Sinicized over time. Traditionally, the Chinese classified musical instruments into eight categories, known collectively as the *bayin* (or "eight materials")—namely, wood, bamboo, metal, stone, clay, skin, silk, and gourd. For the Chinese, the number "8" had a philosophical and aesthetic significance, and philosophically complete ensemble would necessarily include instruments in all eight categories. Many ensemble types have names that refer to these material categories, including one studied here, the "silk and bamboo" ensemble (*sizhu*).

Chinese music is fundamentally vocal music. Besides endless regional folk songs, there are many regional forms of narrative song and theater, the latter always having music. Because of the language problem, however, Western recording companies have preferred to release instrumental music over vocal, giving a skewed impression of the reality in China. Chinese music is primarily based on melodies that can exist in any number of guises and contexts, be they vocal or instrumental, solo or ensemble. Most have programmatic titles that allude to nature (e.g., "Autumn Moon and Lake Scenery"), literature or myth (e.g., "Su Wu the Shepherd"), a mood (e.g., "Joyous Feelings"), or even musical structure (e.g., "Old Six Beats"). Whether a composer's name is known or not—most are anonymous—the tune exists at an almost conceptual level, ready to be performed as an unaccompanied or accompanied instrumental solo, an ensemble piece, a song with or without accompaniment, an orchestral piece arranged for modern ensemble, or even as an operatic aria or modern popular song.

Besides this vast body of instrumental and vocal music, there is also the now rarely heard but once vibrant narrative

BAYIN
The Chinese organological system.

SIZHU
A "silk and bamboo" music ensemble comprised of Chinese stringed ("silk") instruments and flutes ("bamboo").

Inner court of the Kong or Confucian temple in Quanzhou, China

tradition in which singers combined speaking and singing to tell long tales, accompanied by one or more instruments. More prevalent today are the nearly countless regional forms of theater, all of which have music and singing as integral parts. Beyond these one could also explore a variety of forms of instrumental and vocal music associated with

QIN/GUQIN
A bridgeless,
plucked zither.

Track 16

Daoism and Buddhism, as well as the now revived music of Confucian ritual. The twentieth century has also seen the development of many new forms of Chinese music reflecting "international" (read, "Western") influence, from violin-inspired *erhu* fiddle playing, to fully orchestrated arrangements of Chinese traditional melodies played by Western-style orchestras using "traditional" instruments, to all manner of Western-style classical music and popular song. Now mostly abandoned but not forgotten is the politically influenced music, the Revolutionary Operas and Revolutionary Ballets, created during the Cultural Revolution.

Site 1: The Qin Seven-String Zither

First Impressions. While the music of the *qin* represents Chinese culture at its most historical and refined, its sound can be hard for Westerners to appreciate on first hearing. Many students are struck by its sparseness, its lack of a clear beat, and its variety of odd timbres, including scraping sounds. If you were to experience it live, you would also wonder how an audience could possibly hear such music, because it is extremely quiet.

Aural Analysis. The *qin* (also spelled *ch'in* and pronounced "chin") is one of the most ancient instruments in the world to have remained in continuous use. Known also as *guqin* (meaning "ancient zither"), it is a roughly 51-inch-long rectangular board zither made of paulonia wood painted black, and has seven strings, traditionally of twisted silk, running lengthwise from end to end, without frets or bridges. There is also a series of eleven inlaid mother-of-pearl circles

The Chinese *qin* or *guqin* (seven-string bridgeless zither), one of China's most ancient instruments, played by Lai Wah-Chiu

along one side marking the acoustical nodes or vibration points in each string. To the player's left, the strings pass over the end and are tied underneath to two small peg-like feet attached to the instrument's lower board. At the right end the strings run over a slight ridge that acts as a bridge, then pass through holes to the underside where they are tied to small wooden pegs. The instrument is tuned by twisting these pegs to loosen or tighten the string's tension. The player, seated on a chair with the instrument on a table or frame, plucks the strings with the fingers of the right hand and stops the strings with the fingers of the left hand.

The characteristic timbres of the *qin* are many, as a typical *qin* performance includes plucked sounds produced either by the nail or the flesh of the finger, tone-bending created by the sliding movements of the left hand, and the use of harmonics (clear, hollow sounds produced by gently touching the string at a node). Because the strings have a rough texture, when the player slides the left hand along them, scraping sounds are produced. Sometimes these sliding movements continue even after the string has stopped vibrating, expressing the view that music does not have to be heard to exist. Each string is tuned differently, but the same pitches can be produced at various nodes on different strings. Sometimes a pitch is repeated not on one string, but on different strings or stopping points, which creates a series of slightly different timbres. While *qin* music is fundamentally pentatonic (built on five tones), other pitches may come into play, but all sound familiar enough to ears accustomed to the Western tuning system, because the Chinese system is similarly constructed.

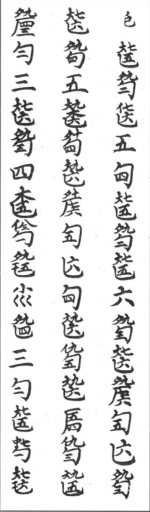

Qin Tablature notation.

Rhythmically, *qin* music sounds fluid, improvisational, alternately halting or rushing, especially because often there is no clear beat to define a steady meter. *Qin* notation is in a form called *tablature;* more precisely, it consists of a chart that indicates how to pluck, stop, or touch each string, with minimal indications of pitch or rhythm. Thus, it is left up to each individual performer to express the meaning of a piece through their own somewhat idiosyncratic rendition.

Qin music, like most traditional Chinese music, is basically monophonic, but is more often built of short motives rather than extended melodic lines. For this reason, *qin* compositions may sound inconsistent at times, because they can suddenly change style or digress. Perhaps this explains why the *qin* is a connoisseur's instrument, and something of an acquired taste.

Our example, entitled *"Yangguan Sandie"* (Parting at Yangguan), illustrates the most common *qin* traits: a contemplative atmosphere, a rather changeable form, and a great variety of subtly different timbres. Much of the beginning is played with stopped tones, but there are brief passages of harmonics at 1:30. During some of the higher-range passages you can clearly hear the scraping sounds, produced as a finger or thumb of the left hand slides up or down to reach the next pitch.

Cultural Considerations. From ancient times and continuing at least into the nineteenth century, the *qin* was closely associated with the *literati* or scholar class, from which the Chinese government chose its officials. Scholars were required to be knowledgeable about Confucian Chinese literature, poetry, calligraphy, divination, history, philosophy, and music. Music, rather than being a pleasurable or sensuous art, was a way of inculcating and expressing the ethical values of Confucianism,

TABLATURE
Notation that indicates how to pluck, stop, or touch each string.

which included restraint, order, balance, subtlety, and hierarchy. Nonetheless, much qin music is indeed quite sensuous. When scholars played a *qin* composition, they had to flesh out and interpret the score by taking into account the meaning of the piece, its mood, and their own feelings in relation to it. In short, *qin* music was a form of personal expression that aided in self-development and brought the player closer to China's highest ideals through a kind of sonic meditation.

Because *qin*-playing was part of a scholar's general cultivation of learning and of sensitivity to the arts, it is not surprising that "Parting at Yangguan" was inspired by a poem—specifically, a Tang Dynasty poem by Wang Wei (701–61) entitled "Seeing Yuan Er Off to Anxi." Sometimes performers will sing this poem as they play "Parting at Yangguan" on the *qin*, because the form of the composition closely parallels the poem's verse structure. The earliest tablature notation of "Parting at Yangguan" appeared in 1491 in the *Zhiyin Shizi Qinpu*, although the version performed here is from an 1864 publication.

Qin playing, because it was cultivated by a small elite, was probably always rare and little known to the general public. Today it is similarly rare, and the scholar class of bureaucrats who once practiced *qin*-playing along with their calligraphy and poetry has long been replaced by Communist party functionaries. Nonetheless, *qin* players of many nationalities are still found throughout the world in small numbers, and in recent years, these scattered groups of musicians have been linked together by the Internet.

Site 2: The "Silk and Bamboo" Sizhu Ensemble

Track 17

First Impressions. Most listeners find China's "silk and bamboo" ensemble music readily accessible. Compared to *qin* music, one can more easily hear a tune, clear phrases, and repetitions of certain musical ideas. The music is quite busy, as each instrument plays continuously throughout and makes frequent use of ornamentation. Also, because most instruments play in a high range, the overall sound is "thinner" than in Western music, in which higher-pitched lead instruments are supported by bass instruments and harmony.

Aural Analysis. Why the name *silk and bamboo*? Recall that in China the classification of instruments is based on a set of eight materials. "Silk" instruments are those with strings, both plucked and bowed, because the original material used for strings was twisted silk. "Bamboo" instruments are flutes, both vertical and horizontal. Thus a "silk and bamboo" ensemble consists of fiddles, lutes, and flutes, with or without a few small percussion instruments. Although classified as a "gourd" instrument because its windchest was a gourd rather than a metal bowl 2,000 years ago, the *sheng*, a free-reed mouth organ with seventeen pipes, sometimes joins the ensemble, as it does on this track. These ensembles play named compositions or tunes.

A gathering of amateur musicians at a teahouse in Shanghai's historical district plays *Jiangnan sizhu* (silk and bamboo) chamber music

Our example's title, *"Zhonghua Liuban,"* literally, "middle flowers, six beats," does not allude to nature or literature but describes technical aspects of the music's organization. This piece is an embellished and extended version of an earlier piece called *"Lao Liuban"* (Old Six Beats). The Chinese term *fangman jiahua* means "adding flowers" (i.e., ornaments), and thus *zhonghua* refers to a "middle" degree of ornamentation. The adding of "flowers" is traditionally improvised according to the idiomatic characteristics of each instrument. The word *Liuban*, although meaning literally "six beats," is unclear in meaning, some saying it refers to the notation of the music in six vertical columns (read from right to left, top to bottom), some saying it means in fact "six beats."

The "silk" category includes a wide variety of bowed and plucked string instruments, including certain lower-range versions introduced during the twentieth century as part of China's drive to modernize. Four instruments, however, are essential: the *erhu* (fiddle), *yangqin* (hammered zither), *pipa* (lute), and *dizi* (horizontal flute).

The *erhu* fiddle consists of a round or hexagonal resonator with python skin covering one face. A long stick serving as the neck pierces

The Chinese *erhu* two-stringed fiddle
(Andrew Shahriari)

the body and has two rear tuning pegs at the top. Two silk strings run the length of the instrument, although their acoustic length is limited to the section between the string loop along the neck and the

bridge in the middle of the resonator. The horsehairs of the bow pass between the two strings, and the player pulls or pushes the bow against the appropriate string while touching the strings with the left hand to create specific pitches; unlike the violin, the strings are not pulled so to touch the neck.

The Chinese *yangqin* (hammered zither)

The *yangqin* dulcimer, formerly a small trapezoidal-shaped instrument with two rows of bridges, was modified during the twentieth century to increase its range and power, first to three bridge sets, then four, and most recently to five or six. Each "string" is actually a course of two or three strings, which are struck by two small bamboo beaters. The *yangqin* is often used as an accompanying instrument, much like the piano in Western music.

The *pipa* is one of China's quintessential instruments, as it has an extensive solo repertory in addition to appearing in ensembles. It is a pear-shaped lute with four strings that pass over raised bamboo frets that allow for chromatic playing (that is, playing using twelve tones). Earlier instruments had fewer frets because older Chinese music used only seven tones. The player, using fingernails or plectra covering the nails of the right hand, plucks the strings in an outward fashion. The use of all five fingers in rapid-fire delivery during some passages is a particularly distinctive stylistic feature of *pipa* performance.

The *dizi* is a bamboo tube ranging in length from about six-

The Chinese *pipa* (pear-shaped lute)
played by Lai Wah-Chiu

teen inches to two feet, with a blowing hole at the left end, a membrane hole, and six finger holes. The membrane hole must be covered with a thin piece of skin taken from the inside of a piece of bamboo. When properly tightened, this skin vibrates to create a buzz that gives the *dizi* its particular timbre.

The Chinese *dizi* (bamboo flute)

While some regional styles of Chinese music make use of pitches that sound out-of-tune to Western ears, "silk and bamboo" styles originating in the Shanghai region, such as our example, uses pitches that should sound quite familiar. Players need only instruments capable of playing the seven regular pitches of the D Major scale (seven pitches are required even though the music is essentially pentatonic, because the melodies expand to more than five pitches through shifts in tonal center or conjunct passages). The two most common keys—called *diao* in Chinese—are D and G, especially in the Shanghai area. Unlike *qin* music, the meter of which is often vague, "silk and bamboo" music has a clear duple meter, with obvious downbeats and upbeats. Rhythms tend to be relatively simple, with nothing more complex being found than a few syncopations and many dotted values.

What might strike you about our example, though, is that all the musicians are playing the same tune differently, resulting in heterophony. Also, virtually all instruments have a high range, giving the music a bright, busy quality. If you listen carefully, you can hear the timbres of individual instruments and differences in the way each plays a phrase. The *erhu* "slides" into some notes, the *dizi* "flutters," the *pipa* utilizes its tone-bending and "rapid-fire" plucking techniques, while the *yangqin* "bounces" along adding occasional ornamentations, primarily at the octave. Also notice that the instruments play all the time and that there is little shading of dynamics. This type of music is quite tuneful, however, and if you listen to it often enough you may find yourself humming the catchier melodies, some of which are quite well known and are part of the foundational repertory of Chinese music.

Even though such compositions are tuneful, the more advanced repertory—which *Zhonghua Liuban* is an example of—tends to be through-composed or continuously unfolding. What binds a piece together is the use of a number of short musical motives that reappear often, as well as the use of a single key and a consistent heterophonic structure. For the most part, this music is played at one dynamic level and with little more subtlety as far as tempo is concerned than a slowing down at the end. What makes the music fascinating, however, is the ever-evolving interplay of the different instruments, which makes each performance unique in its details.

Cultural Considerations. As with Chinese cuisine, "silk and - bamboo" music is regional, and there are at least four distinct traditions. Our example, as we've already noted, represents the tradition found in and around Shanghai. Because the mile-wide Yangtze River, the more southern of China's two major rivers, reaches the ocean at Shanghai, it forms a major geographical marker for the region. For this reason, the region is known as *Jiangnan* ("south of the river"), and the "silk and bamboo" music from the area is called *Jiangnan sizhu* or the "silk and bamboo music south of the river." The other distinct regional types are Cantonese (from Guangdong province in the south), *Chaozhou* (from eastern Guangdong province), and *Nanguan* (from Xiamen in Fujian province).

A *Jiangnan sizhu* (silk and bamboo) ensemble playing informally in its meeting room, Shanghai, China (Phong Nguyen)

"Silk and bamboo" music is best described as an amateur music, because it is played by nonprofessionals in a casual, clubhouse setting for their own pleasure, rather than on a stage for an audience. Originally, however, Jiangnan music was more widely heard in other settings, including weddings, and also accompanies one of the operatic genres of Shanghai. As in many Asian cultures, professional musicians in China traditionally had a low social status, especially those who played for opera performances, weddings, and above all funerals. "Silk and bamboo" ensembles allowed ordinary working people the opportunity to be artistic without damaging their reputations. While all regional styles are typically played in a private clubhouse or meeting room situations, the *Jiangnan* style is most often heard by visitors in the Mid-Lake Pavilion teahouse in Shanghai's historical district, where the sounds of the music mingle with the chatter of patrons and the clatter of dishes. In addition, music conservatories now teach students to play this music but in refined, fully written-out arrangements.

Site 3: Beijing Opera (Jingju)

Track 18

First Impressions. On listening to our recorded example, you probably cannot help but notice the clangor of the percussion, particularly the "rising" and "falling" sound of the gongs. The prominent fiddle is quite nasal-sounding and some of the pitches it plays probably strike you as out of tune. The vocal quality is quite shrill compared to Western singers. The music of the Beijing Opera is not easy for first-time listeners to appreciate, although everyone would enjoy the visual spectacle that accompanies it: the vivid costumes, the striking painted faces of some of the performers, and the stage action—especially the acrobatics.

Aural Analysis. With many musics from around the world, timbre is the aspect that most challenges the first-time listener. This is certainly true of Beijing Opera, called *jingju* (meaning "capital city opera") in

Jingju (Beijing Opera) performance: a red-faced general is flanked by a painted face *(jing)* to his right and a young man *(xiao sheng)* to his left

Chinese. For most listeners, even in China, the vocal quality of *jingju* is decidedly different from what is normally encountered. All roles are sung with little or no vibrato, and many sound rather nasal and quite high in range. Female impersonators—males playing women's roles—use the falsetto (or "head") voice. The *jing* (painted-face characters) tend to sing in a rough, declamatory style.

The instrumental accompaniment is a combination of melodic and percussion instruments. The melodic group is divided into "civil" and "military" sections, the former led by the genre's distinctive short,

JINGJU

Literally "capital city opera," known as "Beijing" or "Peking" Opera.

bamboo fiddle, called *jinghu,* the latter by the loud double-reed called *suona.* Listeners are often struck by the unusual tuning of the *jinghu,* because some of the pitches it plays sound quite flat to Western ears. Other melodic instruments include a *jing erhu* fiddle and the moon-shaped *yue qin* lute, and possibly other lutes. The percussion, or military, section is led by a "conductor," who plays a clapper held in the left hand and uses a stick held in the right hand to beat on a distinctive small drum. He is accompanied by musicians playing both large and small gongs and cymbals. The conductor's drum has a dry, hollow timbre, while the tone of the large gong decays downward (i.e., its pitch drops as its volume falls), and that of the small gong decays upward (its pitch rises as the volume falls). Besides marking beats, these percussion instruments also provide sound effects that symbolize actions, emotions, or objects.

Singers have to work closely with both the "conductor" and the *jinghu* player, because singing is

The *jinghu* fiddle, the main instrument of *jingju* opera.

Student musicians accompany a rehearsal performance of *jingju* (Beijing Opera) at the Shandong Opera School, Jinan, China

improvised according to a host of variables, which comprise what is called a "modal system." This practice is quite unlike that of many other regional opera traditions, which feature lyricists who simply write poetry to fit preexisting, named tunes. Simply put, the "modal system" that governs the creation of melody consists of several variables that allow for a kind of composition simultaneous with performance. Among these are: (1) role type; (2) melodic mode; (3) metrical/rhythmic pattern; and (4) linguistic tone.

Our example features an aria from the opera *Mu Kezhai* (named after the main character), which is sung by a female warrior, Mu Guiying, the daughter of an infamous outlaw from the Song Dynasty. After an introductory section performed by the percussion, during which she performs militaristic stage actions, the female warrior begins singing in speech-like rhythms, accompanied by the melodic instruments. After another percussion interlude, she begins a section in a regular duple meter during which the conductor's clapper is clearly heard.

Cultural Considerations. While most Asian theater traditions strive for symbolic rather than realistic action, depict individual characters as universal types, make music an integral part of the performance, and generally stylize all aspects of performance, *jingju* perhaps develops these tendencies to a greater degree than any of the other local theater traditions found throughout China. Most use realistic, if stylized scenery, but *jingju* does not. The props are minimal, normally only a table and two chairs. As with most Chinese theater traditions, actors use a special stage language, but in *jingju* the comedians speak in Beijing dialect to indicate their low class status. Although many of the local theaters were—and continue to be—performed in a ritual context on a temporary stage before the main god's altar at a temple, *jingju* is mostly performed in formal theaters, the other context for Chinese opera. Most non-*jingju* players receive informal training within a troupe, but *jingju* can be studied formally in government-supported schools. Indeed, *jingju* has come to be the preferred way to represent traditional Chinese culture to the outside world; other kinds of theater are rarely encountered outside overseas Chinese communities.

A performance of a military style play in Taipei's Military Theater as seen from the lighting booth

The typical *jingju* performance places the music ensemble on stage left (the audience's right). Actors and actresses enter and exit to the left or right, using the minimal props to represent everything from a throne to a mountain. An actor holding a stick with a simulated mane is understood to be riding a horse, and an official flanked by young actors holding cloth flags with wheels painted on them is understood to be riding in a chariot. Because women were often banned from the stage-- because theater was seen as morally corrupting—men had to play women's roles, singing in falsetto (head) voice. Today, although such bans are long gone, women not only play female roles but sometimes play men's roles as well, while some men continue to impersonate women. Regardless of his or her gender, each performer specializes in a role type. There are four major role types with numerous subdivisons: (1) *sheng* (male roles), subdivided into young man, old man, and military male; (2) *dan* (female roles), which are similarly subdivided; (3) *jing* (painted face roles), which feature a facial pattern that symbolizes the person's character; and (4) *chou* (comedians), who are easily identified by the white patches in the middle of their faces.

If you see a performance given in North America by a visiting troupe, chances are the singing portions will be shortened and the acrobatic sections lengthened, because it is commonly believed that Western audiences cannot tolerate the musical aspects of *jingju* well. But within North America there are also *jingju* clubs that give performances for connoisseurs who do not need rapid stage action to maintain their interest.

YANG BAN XI

Literally, "model revolutionary Beijing Opera," the Chinese term for Beijing Operas, which were infused with communist and nationalist political messages during the Cultural Revolution (1966–1876).

Site 4: Revolutionary Beijing Opera

First Impressions. Were you able to see a live performance of

Track 19

what is translated as "Revolutionary Peking (Beijing) Opera," called *yangbanxi* in Chinese, you would be struck by a host of differences between this form and traditional *jingju* (Beijing Opera). First, in *yangbanxi* the actors and actresses wear modern costumes, including

Four images of *jingju* (Beijing Opera)

Military *jing* painted face character

Imprisoned *dan* female character with *chou* (comedian) keeper

Dan female preparing makeup in dressing room

Military scene with numerous generals

military uniforms. Second, the stage is much more realistic looking, because it features props and backgrounds. Third, frequently some or even all of the instruments used are Western, and even when the instruments are all Chinese, the music is arranged and often uses Western harmony. Some of the elements of *yangbanxi* may be reminiscent of *jingju*, especially the use of percussion and the sound of most voices, but unlike the fanciful stories

Scene from the Revolutionary Beijing Opera *Taking Tiger Mountain by Strategy* (Peking: Foreign Languages Press)

found in *jingju,* in *yangbanxi* the story clearly has political ramifications. Indeed, even without knowing Chinese you can easily differentiate the "good guys" from the "bad guys": the former stand nobly tall, have determined looks, and are well lighted with healthy-looking skin, while the latter are often hunched, even cowering, have unhealthy greenish-looking skin, and are dimly lit. Invariably, the "good guys" are the followers of Chairman Mao, while the "bad guys" are variously the Nationalist Chinese of Chiang Kai-Shek, the Japanese, evil Chinese landowners, or even American soldiers.

Aural Analysis. During the ten years of the Cultural Revolution (1966–76), a number of "modernized" Peking Operas were made into political (that is, "revolutionary") works. Some of them, including our example, the 1967 work *On the Docks,* were held up as models to represent Communist ideals. Although *On the Docks* was not the most satisfactory revolutionary opera in terms of its dramatic effectiveness, it was considered the most politically progressive of all. Mao's wife insisted on a revision of the work in 1972, and this revised version is heard on the recording we have selected. Originally recorded by the "On the Docks" Group of the Peking Opera Troupe of Shanghai, the opera combines Western orchestral instruments with certain traditional Chinese instruments, including the *jinghu* fiddle and the percussion section.

The music of revolutionary opera may preserve many or just a few sounds of traditional *jingju* depending on the version; whatever the case, it is played from a completely written-out score. More like film music than old-style Chinese music, it creates dramatic shifts of mood. Those versions that were most modernized also use many Western orchestral instruments, and the scores include other Western features such as harmony, counterpoint, and orchestration,

Excerpts from the one-page English synopsis included with the Chinese-language libretto give an idea of the opera's political goals.

"On the Docks" depicts the spirit of patriotism and internationalism of the Chinese working class.

The time is early summer in 1963. The place, a dock in Shanghai. FH, secretary of the Communist Party branch of a dockers' brigade, and KC, are Communist team leaders, who are leading the dockers in a rush job before the coming of a typhoon. They have to finish the loading of a big batch of rice seeds for shipment to Africa so as to support the anti-imperialist struggle of the Asian, African and Latin American peoples. [Wheat sacks left out must also be moved.]

During the rush young docker HH, who looks down on his work and is absent-minded, accidentally spills a sack of wheat. ... Pretending to help sweep up the spilled wheat, C seizes the chance to pour the fiberglass in his dustbin into the wheat sack [and mixes it with the other sacks meant for export.]

FH, working closely with her mates, discovers the incident of the spilled sack. What happened? With this problem in mind, she re-reads the Commuique of the Tenth Plenary Session of the Eighth Central Committee of the Chinese Communist Party. [Eventually] H awakens to his mistake and exposes C's criminal activities. The enemy is completely revealed and the dockers fulfill their aid mission with flying colors.

Red flags fly over the rippling waters and in the morning sun the Shanghai dockers march on with revolutionary militancy toward the great goal of communism.

Cultural Considerations. Music and politics have long been intertwined in China as they have been in the West as well. From the time of Kong Fuzi (Confucius), music was viewed as having ethical power, the ability to influence people and thinking. Right music led to right thinking and right behavior. Confucianism has

The hero character in the Revolutionary Beijing Opera
Taking Tiger Mountain by Strategy challenges his oppressor
(Peking: Foreign Languages Press)

continued to underlie much of Chinese culture to the present, requiring restraint, balance, and non-individuality. But China underwent severe disruption to its traditional society in the twentieth century. In the 1920s a civil war broke out between the Communists under Mao

Zedong and the Nationalists under Chiang Kai-Shek, which led, after the defeat of Chiang in 1949, to the founding of the People's Republic of China, while the Nationalists fled to Taiwan where they continued the Republic of China.

Chairman Mao Zedong, leader of China's Communist Party from 1920 to 1976, understood the power of music and theater, and used them as his most potent weapons both to fight his enemies and to influence and control his subjects. It was actually one of Mao's wives, former actress Jiang Qing, who supervised the politicization of *jingju*, primarily during the Cultural Revolution (1966–1976), a period of top-down revolution and chaos in China when "traditional" culture, including Beijing Opera was prohibited.

During these years the Chinese people were subjected to non-stop propaganda, much of it in the form of artistic productions (including music, dance, spoken theater, opera, art, and literature). Jiang Qing oversaw the creation of the "Eight Model Works": five Revolutionary Beijing Operas, two Revolutionary Ballets, and one Revolutionary Symphony. When President Richard Nixon surprised the world with his visit to China in 1972 at the height of the Cultural Revolution, he witnessed a performance of *The Red Detachment of Women*, one of the Revolutionary Ballets.

Besides the Revolutionary stage works, there was an abundance of new music written with socialist themes, mostly played by new sorts of ensembles (with or without vocalists), which used full orchestrations and harmony. These works varied from settings of Chairman Mao's words to music (e.g., the song "A Revolution Is Not a Dinner Party"), to music praising Chairman Mao (e.g., "Chairman Mao's Love for Us Is Deeper Than the Ocean"), to music calling for revolutionary action (e.g., "The People in Taiwan Long for Liberation") or extolling the Communist work ethic (e.g., "Driving Tractors in Dazhai-Type Fields").

Because people were forced to hear so much revolutionary music and opera during the Cultural Revolution, you might expect that this is the last thing they'd like to hear now. Ironically, because people still have nostalgic feelings for that period in their lives, record companies have released karaoke versions of the opera, and new VCD (video compact disc) versions of the films have been reissued. The younger generation of Chinese, however, were nearly all born after the Cultural Revolution and only know the economically liberalized nation of today. For them, popular music is virtually the only music that they are exposed to, and as the government released its grip on culture, there is more and more of it. Twenty years ago Chinese artists were struggling against government controls to be heard, but now they struggle against the near dominance of imported popular music from the West as well as nearby countries.

Arrival: Mongolia

MONGOLIA

Mongolia, in spite of its tiny population, is a country of great diversity, of numerous if little-known ethnic groups, and of religious complexity. Many Mongolians still live a traditional nomadic life on the grasslands herding livestock, while others live in Soviet-influenced cities. Originally, much of Mongolia's music had spiritual and religious significance, because music was often considered a form of communication between the worlds of humans and spirits. Under Communism, however, most musical traditions were secularized and put on the stage. Music that had been—and continues to be—passed down orally has also been harnessed by formal conservatories. While it is overtone singing that has brought Mongolian music to world attention, the country's most typical form of music is actually the *urtyn duu,* the "long songs" accompanied by Mongolia's most interesting instrument, a trapezoid-bodied, long-necked bowed lute called the *morin huur.*

A first-time visitor will be struck by Mongolia's apparent emptiness. Although the capital city, Ulaanbaatar, appears large, its population is only slightly more than half a million—nonetheless, the city is home to fully one quarter of the country's population. With a land area nearly four times that of California, Mongolia has a mere 2.7 million people. Traditionally, the Mongols have been nomadic herders, riding their small but sleek horses over the country's vast grasslands. Mongolia's neighbors include Chinese Turks to the southwest, Russia to the northeast, and the Republic of Tuva (properly, Tyva) to the northwest; the latter, a member of the Russian Federation, is home to thriving musical traditions that are similar to those found in Mongolia. Despite Mongolia's historically small population, in the twelfth century the Mongol civilization became extremely powerful, and the armies of the Khans, particularly Chinggis (Genghis) Khan (d. 1227), subdued not only China during the Yuan Dynasty (1260–1370), but a vast area stretching from Korea to the

A Mongolian horseman herds sheep on the barren grasslands (Unknown)

Tseyen Tserendorj playing the Mongolian *morinhuur* (two-stringed, "horse-head" fiddle), New York City
(© Jack Vartoogian/FrontRowPhotos)

Black Sea and including parts of Southeast Asia. When Marco Polo visited China in the late thirteenth century, his host was the Mongol emperor Khubilai Khan, grandson of Chinggis.

The capital city of Mongolia is hardly a haven for traditional culture; instead, it reflects the Soviet influence Mongolia came under after achieving independence from China in 1921. The city's architecture looks far more Soviet than Mongolian, and because of the influence of "socialist realism" and the development of "folkoric troupes" to represent Mongolian culture to the outside world, most musical performances seen by visitors to Ulaanbaatar are by ensembles that are not at all traditional.

Site 5: Mongolian Throat-Singing

First Impressions. First-time listeners may wonder how these unearthly sounds, which somewhat resemble whistling, are produced. Most students will assume this singing is performed by two people, because there are clearly two sets of pitches, a low, held drone and an upper melody. In fact, surprising as it may seem, a single person is producing both vocal lines simultaneously.

Aural Analysis. The Mongolian term for this type of singing is *khöömei* (also romanized as *höömii*), while in English it is called *throat-singing* (a somewhat odd term, because all singing takes place in the throat). What makes this form of singing so distinctive is the way in which it manipulates what are called *overtones*—a term that requires some explanation. Any tone or pitch, except perhaps one generated electronically, consists of a fundamental and a series of harmonics, called *overtones* or *partials*. The timbre of a given tone is determined by which overtones are emphasized—a function of how the fundamental was produced (e.g., by a double reed, a vibrating string, buzzing lips, etc.)—and by the relative weakness or strength of the various overtones. A tone in which the lower overtones are emphasized will likely sound "warm," whereas one in which the upper overtones are emphasized will probably sound "bright" or "hollow."

In overtone singing, the performer—formerly only male, now female as well—produces, usually with significant pressure, a fundamental and by shaping the mouth cavity brings out different overtones. A series of well-controlled, changing overtones produces an actual melody over a drone. The example we have chosen demonstrates five different ways of producing these overtones; in fact, the recordings are part of a demonstration rather than performances of actual songs.

OVERTONE
One of the ascending group of tones that form the harmonic series derived from the fundamental pitch.

KHÖÖMEI
Throat-singing tradition from Mongolia.

Track 20

Mongolian "throat" singer, Ts. Sengedorj, performs in full costume
(© Jack Vartoogian/FrontRowPhotos)

177

Cultural Considerations. Among "world music" enthusiasts nothing has attracted as much attention in recent years as "throat-singing," also called "overtone singing." While it is the similar singing in the Republic of Tuva that has attracted a great following in the West in recent years, Mongolian throat-singing is certainly as striking. Few outsiders will ever have the chance to hear Mongolian throat-singing in its original context—that is, performed in a *yurt* (round tent), with singers surrounded by family and friends. Nonetheless, many recordings of throat-singing exist, some combining throat-singing with various forms of Western music.

This unique style of singing is closely tied to the animistic beliefs still held by many Mongolians. The sound is meant to imitate the sounds of nature, attempting to duplicate the rich timbres of natural phenomena, such as the swirling wind or rushing water. Mountains, rivers, even animals are believed to hold a spiritual energy tht is manifested not only physically, but sonically as well. Echoes off a cliff, for example, are infused with a spiritual power. Throat singers believe they can assimilate such power by recreating such sounds.

KOREA

Arrival: Korea

Although the Korean language is unrelated to the languages of its closest neighbors, China and Japan, the fact that it is partially written in Chinese characters shows that early in its history Korea absorbed many aspects of China's civilization. Korea also accepted the teachings and philosophy of Kong Fuzi, the emperor system, Chinese Buddhism and Taoism, and many of China's instruments and musical types.

Sandwiched between China and Japan, Korea has suffered repeatedly as each of these kingdoms expanded. From 1910 to 1945 Korea was a colony of Japan. Following World War II, Korea found itself as the battleground in a struggle between China and the West; this led to a kind of internationalized civil war, which ended with an armistice in 1952. Today, the Korean peninsula remains divided into two countries, North Korea and South Korea.

Altogether, the Korean peninsula is only the size of Idaho. While North Korea is the larger of the two countries, it has less than half of South Korea's population. The two nations are unequal in many other ways as well: the South is a modern, developed nation that manufactures goods for the entire world, while in the North, currently under the strict control of the despotic ruler Kim Jong-Il, malnutrition and outright starvation are common. Culturally speaking, both countries have departed from the old Korean traditions, the North because of its peculiar form of communism, the South because of modernization. Nonetheless, in some major cities, such as Seoul, the capital of South Korea, "traditional" culture continues to flourish in certain government-sponsored institutions.

Just as Korean cuisine has attained little presence in the West, Korean music has also struggled to be appreciated, even within Korea;

for Westerners both the food and music can be described as "acquired tastes." From the first century onward Korea absorbed much Chinese musical culture, especially court and ritual musics, much of which was essentially preserved through the centuries, even as music in China continued to change. As a consequence, Korea preserves what is likely the oldest continuously living music in the world, the Confucian ritual music called *a-ak*. These hymns to the ancient Chinese philosopher, Kong Fuzi (Confucius), still sung once a year on his birthday (September 27), have nonetheless undergone change, to accommodate Korean tastes. Similarly, Korean court music, preserved today by several government-supported cultural institutions, remains extremely archaic but was long ago remodeled to suit Korean sensibilities.

With the politically induced stresses of the last century, particularly the Japanese occupation (1910–45), World War II, the Korean War, and the Korean Peninsula's division into north and south, traditional forms of music have struggled to survive. South Korea has preserved some forms in educational and cultural institutions where they are still taught and performed as museum pieces, while North Korea has discarded most vestiges of tradition in favor of newly created and highly politicized forms of music inspired by Soviet "Socialist Realism."

South Korea nonetheless retains a rich repertory consisting of solo, semi-improvised instrumental music (called *sanjo*), ensemble music, narrative and lyrical song, theatrical music, "farmer's band music," and the now widely known folk-derived percussion music called *samul-nori*. But Korean music takes some getting used to. Although there are exceptions, China's instrumental timbres tend to be bright and clear, while those of Korea may sound rough, fuzzy, and wavering because of the strong use of vibrato. While China's music is clearly based on tunes, Korea's does not sound tuneful to foreign ears; indeed, when Korean ensembles play together, some listener's have trouble hearing the instrumental parts as related to each other. Finally, ornamentation in Korean music tends to come unevenly in sudden spurts.

P'ANSORI
Korean narrative vocal performance style, featuring epic-length stories.

Site 6: P'ansori

First Impressions. Just as Korean food has neither become popular in the West nor lent itself to adaptation, Korean music has remained little known outside small circles of enthusiasts. Just as many Korean dishes have exceptionally strong tastes—for example, Korea's signature food, *kim chi* (spicy, pickled cabbage)—Korean music has strong timbres. It will not be surprising if many of you find that this track, an example of *p'ansori* narrative, takes some getting used to. Accompanied by seemingly random drumbeats, a vocalist with a strong voice employs a great variety of techniques, from near whispers to speaking to singing and even raspy shouting, sometimes employing extreme vibrato. The way the words are delivered suggests that whatever else *p'ansori* is, it is highly evocative, emotional, and dramatic.

Track 21

Aural Analysis. *P'ansori* is one of Asia's greatest narrative forms and certainly its most dramatic. Although considered a kind of "folk" music, *p'ansori* requires extensive training, a prodigious memory, and – incredible physical strength and vocal endurance. Today singers perform only five stories, each lasting several hours, but in the distant past there

were as many as twelve. This example provides an excerpt from one of the five, *Ch'un-Hyang-Ka*, the story of a young woman whose name means "Spring Fragrance." As with many classical stories from East Asia, the plot revolves around a young student and his lover; in this case, the student is named Li Mongnyong and his lover is called Ch'un-Hyang. Ch'un-Hyang's mother is a *kisaeng*—that is, a professional singer/entertainer—but does not want

Korean *p'ansori* (narrative) performers, the singer on the left, the *puk* barrel drummer on the right (courtesy Embassy of Korea)

her daughter to follow in her footsteps. The two lovers are secretly married before Li Mongnyong departs to Seoul to begin the classical studies that will hopefully lead to a position of authority in the government. After many years as an official, he returns to his hometown disguised as a beggar to check on his wife, and discovers that she and her mother have suffered greatly during his absence. He then reveals his true identity. Some have interpreted the story as a critique of feudalism and its abuses.

The story is realized by two performers, a vocalist—in this case a respected and elderly female master—and a drummer. The drum used is the *puk*, a shallow barrel drum with two tacked heads, held vertically by the drummer, who strikes the right head with a stick and the left head with his hand, and occasionally calls out praise or encouragement to the singer. Both performers have a kind of freedom to improvise within strict conventions. The vocalist's performance is governed by a modal system that provides an appropriate scale, melodic motives, and conventional ways to express emotions. The drummer's part is based on fixed cyclic patterns of drumbeats, but because the cycle is rather long in duration and the drumbeats are not continuous, the cycle may have a random feel to it.

The range of vocal timbres is exceptionally rich, as the vocalist varies from speaking to declamation to song, to raspy, tense bursts of sound. The vocal range is unusually wide. Different pitches (depending

Thai Buddhist monks chant in an afternoon service, Roi-et, Thailand

Gypsy musicians perform for visitors to the Great Plain near Bugac, Hungary

The *ntahera* ivory horn ensemble of the Asantehene, Kumase, Ghana (Joseph S. Kaminski)

Japanese tourists watch a Thai Cultural Show at a Bangkok restaurant that caters strictly to tourists

Spiritual Baptists in the tiny Caribbean nation of St. Vincent and the Grenadines sing a hymn in a trance state called "doption" (from the "adoption of the Holy Spirit")

A street performance of Chinese Chaozhou regional opera with percussion accompaniment in Shantou, Guangdong province, People's Republic of China

The altar for a Thai *wai khru* (teacher greeting ceremony) is extremely elaborate

The great church of St. Sophia in Istanbul, Turkey, built in the sixth century, became an Islamic mosque, with added minarets, after the conquest of Constantinople by the Ottoman Turks in 1453

A Baruya man plays the *susap* mouth harp from the Eastern Highlands province of Papua New Guinea (Don Niles)

Indian street musician "charms" two cobra snakes with his *punji* double clarinet consisting of gourd windchest, drone pipe, and melody pipe with finger holes (Max T. Miller)

Ravi Shankar, India's most famous musician, plays the sitar, a long-necked lute with sympathetic strings
(© Jack Vartoogian/FrontRowPhotos)

St. Tyagaraja (1767-1847) is South India's most famous
composer, whose music is still celebrated in festivals
throughout the world (Aradhana Committee, Cleveland, Ohio)

The *sarasvati vina* (lute) of South India

Luk thung pop songs are part of the performance of *lam sing,* a modernized form of the traditional *lam klawn* repartee. This performance took place on a temporary village stage on New Year's Eve southwest of Mahasarakham, Thailand

Danced by two males, the *barong* is a Hindu-derived mythological beast that represents "good" in Balinese theater (Amy Unruh)

Dancers at the Akademi
Seni Tari Indonesia (College of
Indonesian Dance) in Yogyakarta,
Java, Indonesia, perform the highly
refined Bedhaya court dance
(R. Anderson Sutton)

A young boy in traditional costume
dances to the accompaniment of a
Balinese gamelan (Amy Unruh)

on the particular scale/mode) have different degrees and kinds of vibrato, a distinctive feature of *p'ansori* performance. Throughout, the intensity of expression parallels the emotional intensity of the story. Indeed, emotional intensity is characteristic of *p'ansori* and of Korean music in general, despite the restraint and balance seemingly demanded by Confucian aesthetics.

Cultural Considerations. Before 1910, when Korea was still a kingdom, certain music traditions were maintained by the court, while others were practiced by the ordinary people of the villages. A tremendous variety of instrumental and vocal music existed, performed in ritual contexts, on official occasions, and for entertainment. During the twentieth century, because of the Japanese occupation and especially because of the Korean War and the following division of Korea, many traditions were prohibited or lost. After 1952, as South Korea modernized into one of the "Asian Tigers" and North Korea slid into despair under Kim Il-Sung's "cult of personality" style of rule, traditional music struggled to survive. In the North music was harnessed for state purposes under the banner of "socialist realism," and was both "modernized" and turned into propaganda. In the South, the government made the decision to preserve rapidly dying cultural traditions by museumizing them. Traditional ways of life were "preserved"—really reconstructed—in designated "ethnographic" villages where time stands still both politically and technologically. Music, dance, and theater are similarly preserved in rather rigid forms within certain government-sponsored cultural institutions and the educational system.

P'ansori is one of the types of music that have been "preserved" through government support. These storytellers were once found amidst festival events, where their voices had to compete with other activities. Wandering bards, they traveled the countryside telling their tales. Some found favor with aristocratic audiences, who continually debated over the artistic value of these talented, but lower-class performers. By the middle years of the twentieth century, *p'ansori* performers were an "endangered species," until 1964, when the Ministry of Culture and Information designated several performers as "holders of artistry of intangible cultural assets." Since that time, *p'ansori* has been found primarily on concert stages in an "institutionalized" setting along with other traditional Korean arts, such as *sanjo*.

A visitor to South Korea can still hear and see the most formal of ritual musics, the most refined of vocal and instrumental genres, and even "folk song," all alive but now unchanging. These are studied in many cases with designated masters—"living national treasures"—the nation's most valued culture-bearers. Odd as this practice of keeping archaic forms of music alive "artificially" may seem, it reflects a decision that traditional Korean music is worth preserving as an expression of what is most essential and defining in the Korean soul.

While much of Korean musical culture came originally from China, most of this imported Chinese culture was modified to suit the nature and personality of Korea. For example, the Chinese zither (*zheng*), formerly having sixteen strings but now expanded to twenty-one, is played with plectra (originally finger nails), giving it a crisp, clean timbre. The Korean equivalent, the *kayagum*, has only twelve strings, but they are thicker and played with the fleshy part of the fingers, giving the music a more diffused timbre. There are also, however, aspects of Korean musical practice that are not derived from China, such as a preference for 6/8 and 9/8 meters, which are exceptional not just in East Asia but in all of Asia. These give Korean music a lilting rhythmic quality not heard elsewhere.

Korean musicians have built new kinds of music while keeping the old alive. Today one finds orchestras of traditional instruments, the mixing of Korean and Western instruments, and various kinds of popular music that sound more or less Korean. Most striking of all, however, is a new genre that has received worldwide attention, *samul-nori*. Derived from the old-time or "farmer's band music," *samul-nori*, which means "four instruments playing," was created in 1978 by four musicians who played large and small gongs, an hourglass-shaped drum, and a barrel drum, performing mostly fixed compositions with amazing agility and passion. During the 1980s and especially the 1990s, other groups expanded *samul-nori* to include more and larger drums, creating one of the most dramatic, energetic, and appealing new genres in the world. Because *samul-nori* has grabbed the attention of foreigners as no other Korean music had before, even the government has promoted it as an expression of Korean identity in spite of the music's newness.

JAPAN

Arrival: Japan

Because Japan is an island nation, consisting of four main islands (from north to south, Hokkaido, Honshu, Shikoku, and Kyushu, plus the Ryukyu chain), land and resources are severely limited. Consequently, the Japanese have been forced to use their land efficiently. Because they live crowded together in a country slightly smaller than California, but with a population nearly four times as large, the Japanese also have to be tolerant of each other. Although profoundly influenced by Chinese civilization, Japan (like Korea) modified the imported culture to suit their own needs and to express their individualism. Also like Korea, Japan has tended to preserve its traditional music, theater, and dance separately from new developments, offering visitors the opportunity to experience archaic forms much as they were hundreds of years ago.

SANKYOKU

A Japanese chamber ensemble, consisting of voice, *koto* (zither), *shakuhachi* (flute), and *shamisen* (lute).

Just as Japan itself is compact, its traditional arts are few and well defined. Japan's court music and court dance, called *gagaku* and *bugaku* respectively, are among the oldest genres on the earth; to be appreciated properly, both must be experienced live and in their original context. Three forms of traditional theater are particularly striking: the ancient *noh*, the more recent *kabuki*, and the incredible puppet theater known as *bunraku*. Three instruments—the *koto* zither, the *shakuhachi* flute, and *shamisen* lute—are essential in Japanese music. When they play together with a vocalist, they comprise Japan's chamber music, called *sankyoku*, meaning "three instruments." Other essential types of traditional music include folksong, festival and dance music, and Buddhist chant.

The Japanese *koto* (left) and the *shakuhachi* (right)

Japan's music, like its arts generally, is best understood in terms of Japanese specialist William Malm's well-known aphorism, "maximum effect from minimum means." Whereas Chinese and Korean musics can sound continuously "busy," Japanese music makes silence an integral part of the soundscape. This spareness, together with the use of strongly articulated notes, requires calm and attentive listening on the listener's part. In Japan musical instruments are treated as extremely refined, artistic objects and remain unusually expensive, even student models. Indeed, most kinds of Japanese performance, including performances of folksongs or music for *bon* (festive) dancing, are quite formal, even ritualized.

Whereas Chinese tunes are continually rearranged and are embellished freely, Japanese music tends to be played with greater consistency. Musical spontaneity is not characteristic; in fact, some Japanese instrumental music is notated exactly, even down to the ornamentation. In short, whereas flexibility and casualness are characteristic of Chinese music, Japanese music is characterized more by consistency and close attention to detail.

GAGAKU
A Confucian derived ritual court ensemble from Japan, literally "elegant music."

Site 7: *Gagaku*

Track 22

First Impressions. If any music embodies the idea of timelessness or suspended time, it would be *gagaku* (or "elegant music"). What makes an immediate impression is the way the piece seems to be constructed of clearly differentiated elements, with each instrumental timbre apparently having a separate function: melody, punctuation, background. As with much Japanese art—and music in particular—where sparseness is preferred, there is relatively little activity, with much aural space separating the musical elements. If you were to witness a *gagaku* performance at a temple or palace, you might notice that the architecture and its decoration have elements that echo the character of this music: patches of empty white space, stark contrasts of colors and material, and

A Japanese *gagaku* court ensemble performs on stage, Taipei   C

Japanese *gagaku* court musicians

Hichiriki double reed

Kakko two-headed drum

Sho free-reed mouth organ

a rugged, almost four-square quality created by massive wood beams and large pieces of cut stone. "Entenraku" sounds massive and timeless and seemingly transports us into another plane of existence.

Aural Analysis. The first sound heard in our example is that of the *ryuteki*, a small horizontal bamboo flute (called the "dragon flute") that plays an unadorned melody; some of the pitches it plays are outside the Western tuning system, and thus may strike you as "out of tune." A drum accompanies the flute, but its patterns do not create an obvious metrical structure. Suddenly a pungent-sounding double reed called the *hichiriki* joins the flute; both now play over a foundation of dense tone clusters created by a group of *sho*, small free-reed mouth organs with seventeen pipes. As the melody unfolds in its own time-stretched world, certain sustained pitches are punctuated by alternating instruments playing a brief, rising three-note motive; the first one heard is the *koto*, a long board zither with thirteen strings, and the second is the *biwa*, a pear-shaped four-stringed lute derived from the Chinese *pipa*.

The tension rises as the flute (later, joined by the double

reed) rises to ever-higher pitches. The music seems to ebb and flow between states of tension and relaxation even without the use of harmony—the West's way of creating these effects. Even though the meter may not be easily heard, it does underlie the music; some sense of beat is created through the punctuation of drums and the three-note motives played by the *koto* and *biwa*.

Not only the music's sound is stately: *Gagaku* is performed with extreme formality by expressionless musicians who hold and play their instruments in ritualistic ways. It should come as no surprise, then, that the title of this piece translates as "music of divinity." What does surprise, though, is the fact that its melody is said to have been a "popular" song during the Heian period (794–1185).

Cultural Considerations. Originally a specific kind of court music imported from China in the sixth century, *gagaku* grew into a complex of ensembles and functions that have come to symbolize both the imperial court and certain non-court ritual functions. Our example, "Entenraku," is just one composition out of many, but perhaps the best-known. It comes as no surprise that the title translates as "music of divinity." What does surprise though, is the thought that its melody is said to have been a "popular" song during the Heian period (794–1184).

Gagaku is one of the products of Japanese culture that has fascinated the West the most, along with *haiku* (Japan's extraordinarily succinct poetry), *bonsai* trees, *origami* paper folding, the tea ceremony, and *sumo* wrestling. There have been at least a few attempts to capture the sound world of *gagaku* in a Western context, such as French composer Olivier Messiaen's 1962 piece for chamber orchestra, *Sept Haïkaï;* Movement IV, entitled "Gagaku," reproduces the sound of the Japanese ensemble by using trumpet, oboe, and English horn for the melody and eight violins for the *sho* clusters.

Site 8: Kabuki Theater

Track 23

First Impressions. When listening to an audio recording of a music theater work, it can be difficult to make sense of the music because one cannot see how it relates to the dramatic action. *Kabuki,* a theater type developed in Japan during the late seventeenth and early eighteenth centuries as a newly rising middle class of business people coalesced in the city of Edo (now called Tokyo), has considerably more action and visual interest than Japan's earlier and more classic theater, *noh.* Noh features slow-moving actors behind masks playing eternal human types to the minimalist accompaniment of three drums and a horizontal flute. *Kabuki* kept the instruments used in *noh,* but added plucked lutes, sound-effects instruments, and a greater variety of vocal sounds. Both *noh* and *kabuki,* however, include one kind of sound not heard elsewhere: the "yo" and "ho" calls of the drummers.

Aural Analysis. Our example features various forms of theatrical speech, and several types of instruments. First among the instruments

KABUKI
Popular music theater form developed by Japan's middle class in the eighteenth century.

Japanese
kabuki actors
(Unknown)

heard is a group of long-necked plucked lutes called *shamisen*. The *shamisen*'s square resonator body is covered with catskin that supports a bridge carrying three strings from the bottom up the fretless neck to the top end. Because players use a large ivory (or plastic) pick, the resonator skin is reinforced with an additional patch for its protection. These picks give the instrument its strongly percussive timbre. Three drums then begin to punctuate the *shamisens'* sound: an hourglass-shaped drum called *o-tuzumi,* which is held at the hip; a smaller version of the same drum, called *ko-tuzumi* and held on the shoulder; and a small barrel-shaped drum called *taiko*, which is played with two sticks. Next, a horizontal bamboo flute called *nokan* joins the ensemble. Lastly, one of the sound–effects instruments, a small metal gong, joins in. The total effect is one of diverse, unblended sounds that together make *kabuki* a unique sonic world.

As with much Japanese music, tonal subtleties abound, especially because of the frequent tone-bending. Although each part seems to operate in its own world, all work together to achieve a constantly changing flow of tension, relaxation, movement, and meaning. Underpinning this are the standard drum patterns, but their minimal number of beats make perception of a regular downbeat challenging.

Cultural Considerations. Kabuki theater, like Japan's other "classic" arts, is preserved in a living, but museum-like setting. In the heart of Tokyo's fashionable shopping district, the Ginza, sits a major theater, the Kabuki-za, which is dedicated entirely to twice-daily performances of *kabuki*. Inside this otherwise modern building is a wide proscenium stage. Two aspects are exceptional, however. First, there is a long walkway leading from the front of the stage through the audience area, over which actors enter and exit when

Kabuki musicians: (back row) singers, *shamisen* players; (front row) *taiko* drum, *o-tsuzumi* side-held drum, *ko-tsuzumi* shoulder-held drum
(© Jack Vartoogian/FrontRowPhotos)

Chobo narrators (left) and *shamisen* lute players accompany the story in a Japanese *kabuki* performance (© Jack Vartoogian/FrontRowPhotos)

required. Second, most of the musicians are plainly visible on stage (positioned at stage left). Most of the singing and all of the narration are performed by a single vocalist accompanied by a *shamisen*-player; this pair is known as *chobo*. Unlike the *noh* stage, which has no props and only a painted pine tree as a backdrop, the *kabuki* stage has realistic scenery and props, including buildings.

Performances begin in the morning and continue in the afternoon following a lunch break, which may be taken within the theater itself. Because of this schedule, there tend to be more women, some drawn to their favorite actors, than men in attendance, because most men work during the day. Women actresses have been banned from the stage for centuries, and some of *kabuki*'s most famous actors actually play women's roles. The stories depict the lives of imaginary people from Japan's feudal age, the age of the *samurai* warrior. As with virtually all Asian theater traditions, the goal is not realism but a highly stylized depiction of archetypical human scenarios, characters, and emotions.

TIBET

Arrival: Tibet

Tibet is often referred to as "The Rooftop of the World" because it has the highest elevation of any inhabited region on the planet. The southern border of this region is formed by the Himalayas, which includes Mount Everest, the tallest mountain in the world at over 29,000 feet. The northern and western borders are also surrounded by mountains, making the Tibetan plateau one of the world's most isolated areas.

Most Tibetans live between 4 and 17 thousand feet above sea level. Generally, they live in rural areas practicing subsistence farming or raising small herds of Tibetan yaks, which provide milk and meat for nourishment as well as fur and leather for clothing and shelter. While nights in Tibet are typically bitter cold, daily temperatures vary widely. Early morning hours are often below freezing, while by midday the temperature can rise to more than 80 degrees Fahrenheit.

Sudden storms are common, and travelers must always be prepared to find shelter should a sudden dust or snow storm occur. The high elevation and lack of vegetation results in low oxygen levels. While outsiders visiting Tibet may find it difficult to breathe, several centuries of living in the region have enabled Tibetans to develop an increased lung capacity. Still, Tibetans are cautious not to sleep at high elevations while traveling for fear of death from lack of oxygen. Tibetans cope with such difficulties in survival through a strong spiritual life.

Tibetan Buddhism is practiced by the majority of the population, despite the region being considered a part of the People's Republic of China. While Tibet's relationship with China has ebbed and flowed for many centuries, Tibetans lived with relative autonomy under a theocratic government until 1959, when the Communist Chinese government asserted their authority over the region. The Chinese placed severe restrictions on religious practice, and in general attempted to Sinicize the region. The Dalai Lama, considered by most Tibetans to be their secular and spiritual leader, fled to India to escape capture. Many monasteries were pillaged and numerous monks and other Tibetans were killed defending sacred sites and the Tibetan way of life.

DUNG-CHEN

A long metal trumpet with low tones blown during Tibetan ritual.

Relations are still strained between Tibetans and the Chinese authorities. The Dalai Lama remains in exile, but has helped to establish many Tibetan communities in India, Nepal, Bhutan, and elsewhere. While restrictions against religious practices in Tibet have eased, many of the monasteries are today considered museums and are more frequented by visiting tourists than occupied by monks. Tibetan secular culture continues to survive, but the centuries-old spiritual practices of the Tibetans are best examined in monasteries and Tibetan communities outside of the region.

Track 24

Site 9: Tibetan Buddhist Ritual

First Impressions. Tibetan ritual music has a mysterious and eerie sound. Alternately blaring and foghorn-like sounds produced by trumpets come in slow waves, supported by the rumble of drums and punctuated by the sound of a single cymbal. The guttural chants seem fitter for ghosts and goblins than Buddhist priests.

Aural Analysis. The music of Tibetan Buddhist ritual involves a limited number of instruments. The *kang-dung* trumpet, traditionally made from a human thighbone, but today made of metal, is most prominent with its widely wavering blare. *Dung-kar,* conch shell trumpets, are played with a similar technique and are difficult to distinguish from the *kang-dung* based on timbre alone. The *kang-dung* and *dung-kar* are played in pairs, with one performer overlapping his sound with the other, so that a continuous sound is produced. In our example the *kang-dung* sounds first with a slightly brighter timbre and a higher pitch, while the *dung-kar* echoes at almost a semitone lower. The other distinctive trumpet is the *dung-chen*, a long metal aerophone that is usually between five and twelve feet long. The longer instruments are usually played outdoors. *Dung-chen* produce very low pitches and are also frequently played in pairs.

The percussion instruments found in Tibetan Buddhist rituals usually include drums and cymbals. The most common drums, *nga-bom*, are double-faced frame membranophones that hang vertically in a stand and are struck by a hook-shaped stick. They have a

Tibetan Buddhist monks of the Gyuto sect performing the   ⓒ *dung-chen* (long trumpets) (© Jack Vartoogian/FrontRowPhotos)

Tibetan Buddhist monk plays the *gyaling* (double reed aerophone)

Tibetan Buddhist monks play a *rom* (pair of large cymbals)

189

deep timbre and are struck with slow, solitary pulses that usually correspond to either the trumpets or chanting. Large cymbals, called *rom*, are common as well, and are most often played to accompany chant. While our example includes only one cymbal, which is struck lightly with a wooden stick, the *rom* are usually quite loud and are used to punctuate the ends of chanted phrases.

Throughout our example, the upper trumpets waiver on their respective pitches a mere semitone apart, creating a very dissonant, unsettling sound. The *dung-chen* begins with a low straight tone before rising to the pitch produced by the *kang-dung*, which is a tritone, or flatted fifth, above—an interval Westerners generally consider "uncomfortable." The percussion instruments are heard as well, seemingly in free rhythm, but actually following a long metric cycle articulated primarily by the drum.

After the opening instrumental section, the drum provides a steady pulsation that accompanies the chanting monks, who dwell on a single low pitch. The instruments then interrupt before the *dung-chen* sounds with percussion accompaniment.

Bodhnath Stupa, a temple frequented by Tibetans living in exile near Kathmandu, Nepal. A man chants on the left while a man turns a prayer wheel on the right

Cultural Considerations. In Tibet, the chants and instrumental performances used that appear in Buddhist ritual are regarded more as spiritual sounds than as music. The primary intended audience for such performances are various deities and spirits associated with Tibetan Buddhism.

Buddhism is thought to have come to Tibet during the mid-eighth century with the arrival of Padmasambhava (717–62 A.D.), a legendary monk who was believed to have great magical powers that could drive away demons. Padmasambhava practiced a unique form of Buddhism known as Tantrism, which emphasized the use of symbols, ritual objects, and yoga practices in the quest for enlightenment. A primary goal of Tantric Buddhism, as Tibetan Buddhism is often called, is to overcome the fear of death, and thus make death powerless to prevent a person from attaining enlightenment.

Tibetans have long been preoccupied with death. The fragility of life in the harsh environment of the Tibetan plateau led, before the arrival of Buddhism, to the development of a spiritual belief system known as *Bonism*, which was centered on a group of dangerous and fearful demons. Because these demons could control the elements and take life unexpectedly, Bonist priests performed rituals and gave offerings in order to appease them. Many of these priests were feared, as human sacrifices were among the methods used to win the demons' favor. When Padmasambhava arrived with the assurance that Buddhism could overcome death and drive away such demons, most Tibetans embraced the new religion and its nonsacrificial rites.

One of the more interesting customs found in Tibetan Buddhism is the use of prayer wheels. While the ultimate goal of all Buddhists is to attain enlightenment, most accept that attaining a higher rebirth in the next life is a more practical spiritual goal. Chanting prayers is considered a way to earn spiritual merit, which in turn helps boost one's chances of a higher rebirth. Prayer wheels can help with this accumulation of merit. Each wheel has a prayer written on the outside, as well as a prayer written on parchment inside. Tibetan Buddhists believe that each time the wheel is spun, the words are "written on the wind."

Musical performances are most important to rituals involving groups, rather than individuals. The blaring sounds of the trumpets are meant either to drive away evil deities or to call benevolent ones. The deep sound of the *dung-chen* is said to imitate the trumpeting of the elephant, which is considered a powerful animal. The *dung-kar,* which are highly valued instruments because conch shells are rarely found so far from the sea, can call spirits as well, but are also frequently used to make announcements or to sound warnings. The *kang-dung* is ideally made from a human thighbone, to remind believers that physical life is impermanent. These trumpets often play a prominent role in calling the faithful, be they living or ancestral spirits. The percussion instruments function primarily to emphasize structural points, by marking the ends of both instrumental and chanted phrases.

Chanting the *sutras*, or Buddhist prayers, is a primary activity among Tibetan Buddhist monks. The deep guttural utterances are said to represent the fundamental sound of the human body when all else is in complete silence. Complete awareness of one's physical self is an important aspect of preparing for the body's eventual demise. The body is, however, merely the cup that holds the spiritual nectar. When the body dies, the spirit is released and is housed in a new form. This consciousness of the impermanence of all things is fundamental to Tibetan theology.

Certain Tibetan Buddhist sects practice a unique form of chant in which they sound two tones at once, a low fundamental tone and a high frequency overtone. This technique is believed to enable a monk's spirit to travel to the spiritual plane. By visiting the spiritual plane, the monk is able to achieve "death without dying," and he thereby gains knowledge of the afterlife, thus robbing death of some of its fearful sting. During this chanting, a monk's heartbeat can slow dramatically and his breathing may become almost imperceptible. While only Tibetan monks perform these spiritual practices, the spiritual life of all Tibetan Buddhists is focused on overcoming death.

Questions to Consider

1. How do attitudes towards traditionality and modernization affect music differently in China on the one hand and Japan and South Korea on the other.

2. In China, how did the Cultural Revolution affect the development of music and theater?

3. How are the aesthetics of music in Japan shaped by both Confucianism and Buddhism?

4. How are the types of East Asian theater different from theater and opera in the West?

5. What spiritual role does music play in Tibetan Buddhist ritual?

6. Discuss East Asian attitudes towards professional musicians and actors and explain why amateur music making was held in such high esteem.

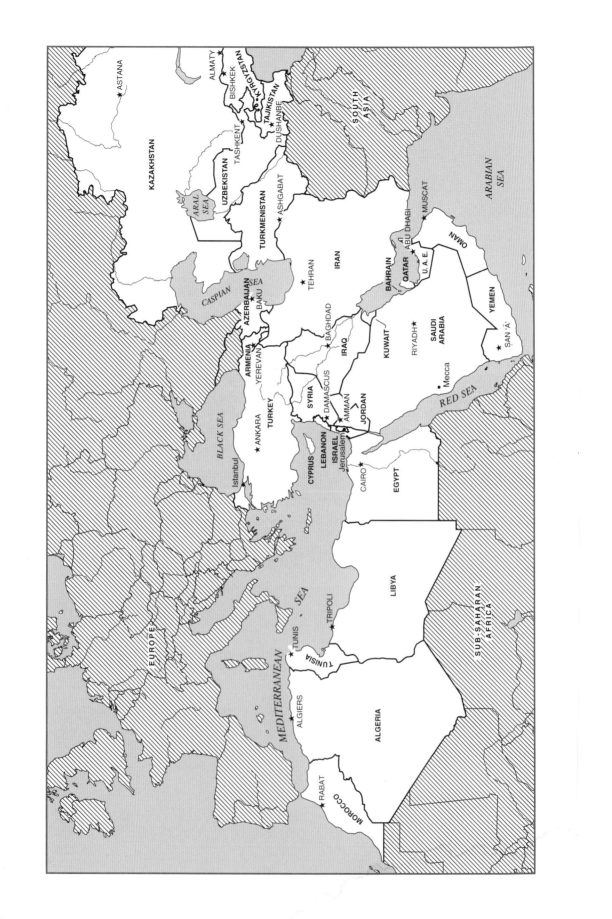

Egypt's great temple of Ramses II at Abu Simbel moved to its present location when the Aswan High Dam was built in 1970 (Max T. Miller)

CHAPTER 8

The Middle East:
Music in the Cradle of Great Religions

Background Preparation

Geographically, the area covered in this chapter is difficult to describe. The designation *Middle East* is conventional and convenient—but it is also ethnocentric, as are *Near East* and *Far East*. After all, the regions these terms describe are only "near" or "far" from the perspective of the West. On the other hand, referring to the "Middle East" as "West Asia and North Africa" is clumsy. For this reason, we will simply adhere to conventional terminology, whatever its drawbacks may be.

A second problem is that the boundaries of this region are less clearcut than those of most other areas: potentially, they encompass everything from Morocco in the west (directly south of Europe) to China's westernmost province, Xinjiang. The nations that can be said to comprise this

MAGHRIB
Literally, "the time or
place of the sunset."
The Arabic name
designating the region
from present-day
Libya west
through Morocco.

MASHRIQ
Literally, "the time or
place of sunrise–the east."
The Arabic name
designating the parts
of Asia (and Egypt)
conquered and
populated by the Arabs.

ARABIC
A Semitic language
originating with the Arab
ethnic group, also the
holy language of Islam,
and a musical tradition
whose history is
intricately linked with
the spread of
the language.

area straddle three continents: part of Turkey is in Europe; five of the Middle Eastern nations are in Africa; and the rest are in Asia. However, some consider the former republics of the Soviet Union, such as Turkmenistan, Uzbekistan, and Kazakhstan, to be part of "Central Asia" rather than of the Middle East.

It has been customary to subdivide the Middle East into sectors. The major units are: (1) the *Maghrib* or North Africa, consisting of Morocco, Algeria, Tunisia, and Libya; (2) the *Mashriq*, consisting of Egypt, Israel, Jordan, Lebanon, Syria, and Iraq; and (3) the Arabian Peninsula, consisting of Saudi Arabia, Yemen, Oman, and the various smaller nations on the Persian Gulf. Turkey, Iran, and Central Asia are usually treated as separate areas, and culturally speaking Israel and Armenia are treated as special cases.

It is tempting to describe this vast region as the "world of Islam" because its nations and peoples are predominantly Muslim, but there are important exceptions such as Christian Armenia and Georgia and Jewish Israel. Islam, while certainly the predominant faith, is no more a unified monolith than, say, Christianity is in Europe, or Buddhism is in Asia. Linguistically, while several mutually unintelligible language families are present, a certain unity has been created through the use of classical written Arabic, allowing learned people over a vast area to communicate, much as Latin once unified Europe and Sanskrit (or Pali) parts of Asia. Arabic belongs to the Afro-Asiatic family of languages, which includes all Semitic languages, Hebrew and Egyptian among them. The Indo-European languages are represented in the region by the Indo-Iranian subfamily, which includes Persian and Kurdish. Armenian is a stand-alone language, while Turkic languages, which stretch from Turkey to China's Xinjiang, are part of the Altaic family and are related both to Mongolian in the east and Hungarian in the west. While language similarity might be expected to create greater unity, clearly it does not; as only one example, Arabs and Hebrew-speaking Jews have related languages, and have been warring for decades. Similarly, while Islam would seem to unify the region, it also is the basis for division, because Islam has numerous sects that can be as different from one another as Christianity's multitude of sects.

When the Middle East is mentioned, many of us in the West likely envision deserts, camels, nomads, pyramids, and dirt-poor villages where people are surviving at a subsistence level. While it is true that much of the Middle East is desert, other parts are quite lush, especially along the Nile, Tigris, and Euphrates Rivers. Outside the main areas most associated with the Middle East (i.e., Libya, Saudi Arabia, and so on), there are even regions filled with green fields, forests, and mountain streams. Parts of the Middle East get quite cold in the winter as well. While some Middle Eastern nations have world-class oil deposits, others have none and must import all the oil they use.

The Middle East is home to some of the world's earliest and most important civilizations. Indeed, the valley of the Tigris and Euphrates

The exquisite Patio de los Leones (Courtyard of the Lions) is the most famous place in Granada,
Spain's fourteenth-century Moorish palace, the Alhambra

Rivers, once called Mesopotamia and now largely within Iraq, is known as the "Cradle of Civilization." The ancient Egyptians developed a great civilization along the Nile, leaving the world with incredible monuments, the pyramids among them. And Alexander the Great conquered much of the Middle East, leaving a strong imprint of Greek civilization throughout much of the region. The Middle East is dotted with extensive Greek and Roman ruins, testaments to the early spread of Greek learning and culture and the development of sophisticated urban areas.

During Europe's Middle Ages following the dissolution of the Western Roman Empire and the splintering of Europe into small, disorganized entities, classical learning continued to flourish among the Arabs. Alexandria, Egypt, was home to what was perhaps the world's greatest library until 642, when its contents were burned on the orders of the city's conqueror, Omar, Caliph of Baghdad. Arabic scholars, such as al-Kindi (ca. 790–874) and al-Farabi (872–950), preserved and developed Ancient Greek music theory, which later influenced European theory. Whatever we may think of the Middle East and its many political and social problems today, the region was once synonymous with civilization and culture. In fact, today's Middle East continues to produce highly sophisticated music, often in combination with some of the world's most fluid and sensuous poetry. In the midst of seemingly endless wars and internecine violence, the Middle East remains home to

An Inside Look

George Dimitri Sawa

I was born in Alexandria, Egypt. For socio-economic and political reasons, my music career began with Western rather than Arabic music. Before European colonization, an *ud* (lute) was often part of an Egyptian bridal dowry, but afterwards middle class wealth combined with the Arab inferiority complex towards the West caused us to replace it with the more expensive and "technologically advanced" piano. My father, who provided for his yet unmarried sister, and who always planned ahead, bought a piano as part of her dowry. My aunt never married, and lived with us, so the piano became part of our household.

George Dimitri Sawa, Egyptian musician and historian

I began my musical career by playing Egyptian popular songs by ear on the piano. My father, eager for me to develop good technical habits, took me at the age of ten to a private teacher, the eccentric and highly talented violinist and pianist Madame Irene Drakides. She had been a student of Alfred Cortot and had many stories to tell about her acquaintances with famous French composers Maurice Ravel and Gabriel Fauré, some of whose works she had premiered. She trained me well, and I later contemplated a career as a concert pianist. However, when I was in Sweden as an exchange student in electrical engineering, and played both Arabic and Western music on the piano to my hosts, they asked me the obvious question that I had never asked myself: "Why don't you play an Arabic instrument?" So I resolved to learn the *qanun* (zither), an instrument that had fascinated me from early childhood. At the Higher Institute for Arabic Music in Alexandria, the teachers were all touched that an Egyptian skilled at the piano would turn to the *qanun!* I had a lot to learn, such as oral learning and the art of improvisation, but more to unlearn, because Arabic pre-composed pieces were not frozen entities, but instead improvised ornaments, tastefully executed, that made every performance unique.

After completing degrees in piano, *qanun,* and yes, electrical engineering, I emigrated to Canada to study musicology and ethnomusicology. Arabic music was to be my career, and there was no turning away from it. I was most interested in its performance history, which led me to research the medieval sources on theory and ethnography. No music program in North America could provide the training for this type of work, so I created my own program by doing a Ph.D in two departments, Music and Middle Eastern studies. The latter gave me the necessary training in socio-cultural history and the bibliographical tools to research my subject. The medieval Arabic world that unravelled before my eyes was stunning. There was a fusion of musical styles, Arabic, Persian, and Byzantine; court patronage that generously maintained practitioners and scholars; a scholarship that combined the writings of the practitioners with Greek music theory and Middle Eastern humanities. In short, it was a discipline that predates modern ethnomusicology by a thousand years. I was hooked for life.

unusually attractive music in spite of Islam's traditional abhorrence for such a sensuous art.

Arabic influence on Europe goes far beyond the ancient Greco-Arabic music theory that formed the theoretical systems of Europe's first millennium. The city known consecutively as Byzantium, Constantinople, and Istanbul served an historic role as a bridge between Asia and Europe through which culture passed in both directions. The vast Ottoman Turkish Empire that incorporated much of Southeast Europe for hundreds of years—in places into the early twentieth century—left those areas with many Turkish musical instruments and other musical influences. In fact, most of Europe's instruments can be traced to Arab sources. These instruments entered Europe both through Turkey and from North Africa, especially via Spain. For a thousand years or more before the expulsion of the Moors and Jews from Spain in 1492, both North Africa and Southern Europe were part of a unified Mediterranean culture. Europe—and European music in particular—would be unthinkable without Arab influence.

Planning the Itinerary

Unfortunately, our survey of the music of the Middle East can only embrace the major traditions. We simply lack the space to explore the innumerable local traditions of each country. This means, alas, that we must skip over the Central Asian nations, whose music has been little studied. We will also have to ignore distant Xinjiang, the westernmost province of China, where Turkic peoples create music with close ties to the music of Turkey itself. At the other end of the Middle East, Morocco, where the remnants of Moorish-Andalusian music survive from Europe's Middle Ages, will also have to be passed over.

While three major language groups are found in the Middle East—Arabic, Turkic, and Persian—Turkic and Arabic musical traditions are close enough that we can combine them and reduce our discussion of Middle Eastern music to two broad traditions: Arabic and Persian music. Three of the recorded examples chosen to illustrate broad trends in the Arabic tradition are performed by Turkish musicians, while the fourth was recorded in Egypt. Our example of Persian music was, naturally, recorded in Iran.

Because Islam is of central importance throughout the entire region, we must of necessity give some consideration to the relationship between music and mosque. And because Israel is the world center of Judaism, we must also consider the role of music in the synagogue. In fact, because of the significance of religion in the region, we have departed somewhat from the structure of the book's other chapters: our last two "Arrivals" are not centered on countries per se, but on religious faiths, namely Sufism and Judaism.

OTTOMAN EMPIRE
A powerful Turkish dynasty that ruled over various parts of West Asia, Eastern Europe, and Northern Africa from the thirteenth through twentieth centuries.

Arrival: Turkey

TURKEY

Turkey bridges East and West, culturally as well as geographically. Slightly larger than Texas, it has a temperate climate unlike most other Middle Eastern nations, and areas of lush forest and green fields reminiscent of Europe. Throughout history parts of its territory have been incorporated into successive empires, from that of the Greek Macedonian, Alexander the Great (382–36 B.C.), to the Eastern Roman Empire, to the Ottoman Empire. Its capital city, Istanbul, straddles the Bosporus, a broad channel connecting the Black Sea to the Mediterranean, and has traditionally marked the boundary between Europe and Asia. The city was founded by Alexander under the name Byzantium, and was at first an outpost of Hellenistic civilization. Renamed Constantinople, it later became the center of the Eastern branch of Christianity. In 1453 the Turks, who had expanded into the Eastern Roman Empire from what is now eastern Turkey, conquered Constantinople, which they renamed Istanbul. The city then became the center of one of the world's most aggressive and expansive empires, the Ottoman Empire. A succession of ambitious sultans or caliphs based in Istanbul acquired incredible wealth and power, largely by

In Istanbul, Turkey, shops surround the Lateli Cami (Mosque), originally built in 1790

bleeding conquered territories dry. This wealth and power found expression in the creation of elaborate gardens and beautiful mosaic art, along with endless quantities of furniture, jeweled teapots, thrones, and the like. But the sultans also expressed their wealth by building vast stone mosques that could accommodate hundreds or thousands of Muslim worshippers. (For more on the history of this city, see the Case Study in Chapter 3.)

Track 25

Site 1: Islamic "Call to Prayer"

First Impressions. In our example, which features a man calling the faithful to prayer, the vocalist performs a single melodic line, adding fairly extensive and technically demanding ornamentation. This performance seems to meet most definitions of "music," as it has definite pitch, rhythm, and contour. Yet, in an Islamic context, this would not be considered to be "singing"; it would be thought of, rather, as heightened speech, delivered in a style requiring both declamation and the spinning out of syllables. For this fact to be understood, further discussion of Islamic attitudes toward music is required.

Aural Analysis. Anyone who has visited a Muslim nation has likely heard the "call to prayer"—in Arabic, the *adhān*—which is uttered five times daily. In most places today, considering the size of modern cities and the amount of noise from traffic, *adhān* are transmitted through loudspeakers mounted on a tower at a local mosque. Because the purpose of the call is to communicate a specific message and because Islam discourages the use of the sensual arts, the call is essentially spoken words, but the manner of delivery takes on characteristics of melody. Indeed, some versions of the *adhān* are highly virtuosic and melismatic. The set of pitches used is normally characteristic of a musical *mode*, a term denoting not just a scale but typical melodic patterns as well. *Adhhān* are melodically improvised to a certain degree and are also in free rhythm, being a series of declaimed phrases each separated by a pause. The words used are declaimed in classical Arabic and are virtually the same throughout Islam—the only exceptions being that the line "Prayer is better than sleep" is only chanted during the predawn call, and that Shiah Muslims add the line "Ali is his successor" after affirming that Muhammad is the prophet of God:

SHIAH
The fundamentalist branch of Islam.

SUNNI
The mainstream branch of Islam.

SUFI
The mystical branch of Islam.

Allāhu akbar, Allāhu akbar	God is great, God is great,
Ashhadu an lā ilāha illa llāh	I testify that there is no god but God.
Ashhadu anna Muhammadan rasūl Allāh	I testify that Muhammad is the prophet of God
Hayya ʿalā ʾl-salāt	Come to prayer.
Hayya ʿalā ʾl-falāh	Come to salvation.
Al-Salāt khayr min al-nawn	Prayer is better than sleep.
Allāhu akbar, Allāhu akbar	God is great, God is great.
Lā ilāha illa llāh	There is no god but God.

Cultural Considerations. Islam has a great deal in common with Judaism and Christianity, despite the misunderstandings and conflicts that have arisen between adherents of these three religions. All three are monotheistic—in fact, they worship the same god, who is called Allah by Muslims, Yahweh or Jehovah (also known as Adonai, meaning "Lord") by Jews, and God by (English-speaking) Christians. All trace their lineage to Abraham and recognize the biblical prophets, including Jesus of Nazareth—although they disagree on whether Jesus was the Messiah.

The Beyazit Camii, built in 1504, is Istanbul's oldest standing mosque

Judaism rejects Jesus' divinity and still awaits the coming of the Messiah. Islam sees Jesus as just one historical prophet in a series that continues up to Muhammad (570–632), who was born in the Arabian Peninsula, lived in Mecca and Medina, and founded Islam. While all Muslims accept the teachings of Muhammad, divisions arose after Muhammad's death. As a consequence there are "denominational" differences in Islam, especially between the more mainstream Sunni and the more emotional Shiah. In addition, there are smaller sects including the Sufi, who seek union with God through trance, often induced through a whirling dance.

Muhammad designated Mecca as the holy city, and built a great mosque there, containing Islam's holiest shrine, the *Ka'ba*. Since that time, every Muslim capable of doing so is expected to make a pilgrimage (*hajj*) to Mecca; pilgrims become *hajji* upon their return home. Muslims are also expected to pray five times a day, facing in the direction of Mecca. The call to prayer developed as a reminder to the faithful to fulfill this obligation.

In English the term *mosque* denotes any building used for Islamic worship. In fact the proper and more specific terms are *jamaca* (for a main mosque) and *masjid* (for a local mosque). There is no typical architectural form associated with mosques; indeed, many early mosques were converted Christian churches. In Istanbul the oldest mosques, those built in the sixteenth century, follow the same basic design as the city's much older Byzantine churches: both feature a central dome surrounded by smaller half-domes. Each mosque, however, has a *mihrab*, a niche in a wall that helps orient worshippers toward Mecca. Mosques are relatively empty compared to churches, because worshippers pray on the (usually carpeted) floor. While Friday is the day for hearing sermons in the mosque, Muslims pray seven days a week.

Two minarets of Istanbul's famous Sultanahmet Camii, better known as the "Blue Mosque," built in 1616. From the minaret, fives times a day a *muezzin* calls the faithful to prayer

One architectural feature that distinguishes all but the earliest mosques from churches is the presence of one or more tall, thin towers called *minarets*. An essential function of the *minaret* is to provide a place from which to sound the call to prayer. The person who gives the call is commonly called a *muezzin* (properly a *mu'adhdhin* in Arabic). When people hear the call, they are expected to stop what they are doing and either pray or be still and silent. This applies to traffic as well as to television programs in many countries, although this occurs more frequently in Islam-dominated states, such as Yemen, than in secular states such as Turkey.

Although Islam is primarily associated with the Middle East, it is a major religion in other areas as well, including much of the central third of Africa, northern India, parts of southeastern Europe (especially Albania and Bosnia), and parts of Southeast Asia, especially Malaysia, Indonesia, and the southern Philippines. Consequently, one hears the call to prayer in somewhat unexpected places, such as Singapore; Bangkok, Thailand; Manila, Phillippines; New Delhi, India; and Lagos, Nigeria, not to mention the United States. For overseas Muslims out of hearing range of a mosque, two substitute methods have been devised. Some believers tune into a radio station that broadcasts the call to prayer, while others purchase a plastic, miniature mosque clock that is programmed to emit a recorded call to prayer five times a day.

As with Christian denominations influenced by the sixteenth-century Swiss theologian John Calvin (1509–64), most branches of Islam are suspicious of music, which they view as overly sensual. In Islamic aesthetic theory, expressions that combine pitch and rhythm—all of which would usually be classified as "music" in Western culture—are divided into a higher-level category called *non-musiqa* (non-music) and a lower-level category called *musiqa* (music). All categories of *non-musiqa*, including the call to prayer, are considered "legitimate." These include readings from Islam's holy book, the *Qu'ran* (or *Koran*), which are delivered in heightened speech, as well as chanted poetry. Some *musiqa* is also legitimate, including familial and celebratory songs, occupational music, and military band music, but the classical genres of *musiqa* as well as local types of "folk music" are considered "controversial," meaning that more fundamentalist Muslims generally discourage these traditions. At the bottom of this hierarchical scale is "sensuous music," such as American popular music, which is branded "illegitimate." However melodic, musical, or sensuous you may find the call to prayer, it is considered by Muslims to be "non-music" and unsensuous, and therefore legitimate. These views clearly illustrate that definitions of "music" are culture-based and not universal.

Site 2: Arabic Modal Improvisation

First Impressions. This example may remind you of belly dance music, though it is dreamier. It lacks a regular beat and sounds as

ADHAN
The Islamic call to prayer.

MUHAMMED
Muslim prophet and Arab leader who during his lifetime (571 A.D.–632 A.D.) spread the religion of Islam and unified a great deal of the Arabian peninsula.

Track 26

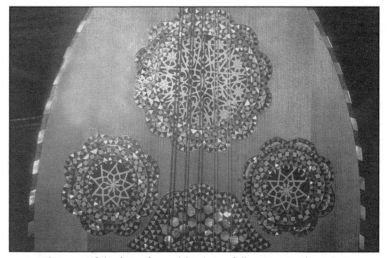

Close-up of the face of an *ud* (lute). See full picture in Chapter 3

if it might be improvised. Two stringed instruments, both gently plucked, alternate lead and supporting roles. It is difficult to know where we are, for this kind of music is heard throughout the Arab world, including Turkey. We could be in Beirut (Lebanon), Damascus (Syria), Baghdad (Iraq), Cairo (Egypt), Tripoli (Libya), Amman (Jordan), or any number of other places.

Aural Analysis. The first instrument heard is the *ud,* a large pear-shaped lute with a short fretless neck, which is found throughout much of the Middle East and is associated mostly with the "classical" tradition rather than village styles. With a history going back to the eighth cen-

Ali Jihad Racy, originally from Lebanon and now of the United States, plays the Arab *buzuq* (lute) (© Linda Vartoogian/FrontRowPhotos)

tury A.D., the *ud* has undergone numerous changes over time in terms of size and number of strings. Today the instrument most typically has five "courses" of strings, a course being a pair tuned in unison, but *ud* with four, six, or even seven courses exist. Because there are no frets, the musician can stop the strings anywhere, allowing for fine gradations of intonation. The player uses a plectrum, or sometimes the fingers or fingernails of the right hand, to pluck the strings over the middle of the instrument's body. The Middle Eastern *ud* is considered the original form of an instrument that traveled to Asia—where it became the Chinese *pipa*, the Japanese *biwa* (see Chapter 7), and the Vietnamese *tyba* (see Chapter 6)—and to Europe, where it became the European *lute*, which reached its popularity during the Renaissance, then gradually disappeared during the eighteenth century. Indeed, the word lute derives from the word *ud*.

The second instrument heard in our example is called the *buzuq*, and is different in many ways from the *ud*. It is used in both classical and nonclassical music and has a rounded body, nylon frets wrapped around its neck, and three double courses of strings played with a plectrum. One of the three double courses plays the melody, while the other two are primarily strummed to create intermittent drones. The *buzuq* probably derives from a similar instrument that the Turks call *saz*, and a form of it is found in Greece, where it is known as the *bouzouki*. The Greek version of the instrument is rejected by some Greeks as a remnant of the Turkish occupation.

Because it is unmetered, the music in our example may sound improvised. In a sense it is improvised, but as with the Indian *raga*, Middle Eastern "improvisation" should not be understood as a license for the player to do whatever they want. Rather, it provides an opportunity for the performer to compose, within strict boundaries, while playing. The usual Arabic term for the system within which improvisation occurs is *maqam* (*makam* in Turkish), a word loosely translated as "mode." As with modes in a European context, each *maqam* (pl., *maqamat*) consists not only of a scale but of much more; they are perhaps best viewed as "composition kits." In fact, many fully written ensemble compositions have been created that include no improvisation but nonetheless follow the conventions of *maqam*.

Because the theory that underlies is quite complex, we can offer only a simplified explanation here. Each *maqam* has a name and is characterized by a specific starting and ending note—as well as a set of specific pitches organized into two groups of four pitches, each called a *tetrachord* in English. Describing these pitches is difficult, however, because many differ from all twelve pitches found in the Western equal-tempered chromatic scale. Theorists have devised a system—which may vary slightly in actual practice—of twenty-four pitches in an octave, with each measuring fifty cents (that is, a half semitone, or quartertone). The basic seven steps of individual scales consist of combinations of two, three, four, or six quartertones. Two of these quartertones equal one Western semitone and four equal a Western whole tone, but three comprise an interval that is between a Western semitone and whole tone and six form an augmented (raised) second interval. A given

UD (AL 'UD)
A fretless, plucked, pear-shaped lute found in Arabic music traditions as well as the origin of certain lutes of Africa, Asia, and Europe.

MAQAM
(Also, MAKAM)
Arabic mode or system of rules and expectations for composition and improvisation.

performance may shift from one *maqam* to another. The complete track from which our exerpt comes begins in *maqam kurd*, with the pitches C, Db, Eb, F, G, Ab, Bb and octave c, but then shifts to *maqam rast* (F, G, A [half b], Bb, C, D, E [half b], to *maqam 'ajam* (F, G, A, Bb, C, D, E), to *maqam nahawand* (F, G, Ab, Bb, C, Db, Eb), and, finally, to *maqam bayyati* (C, D [half b], Eb, F, G, Ab, Bb). Theorists disagree on the number of *maqamat*: some claim there are up to seventy or more. There is also disagreement on the categorization of *maqamat*, which are divided into three families by some theorists.

Though not considered to be artwork, the intense decoration of a mosque is analogous to the ornamentation of Arabic music. The niche in the center is the *mihrab* of Istanbul's Beyazit Camii built in 1504

In our excerpted example, two musicians realize the *maqam* through improvisation—that is, they explore the characteristic intervals and melodic fragments gradually and spontaneously, alternating between *ud* and *buzuq*. When one musician is prominent, the other strums lightly, playing drone effects or modestly mimicking the phrases of the other. Any resulting simultaneity of notes is incidental and does not constitute harmony of any sort because the music is conceived monophonically. These improvisations may occur alone or as a part of a longer suite that includes fixed compositions in meter. An unmetered movement featuring improvisation is called a *taqasim* (or *taqsim*) when performed by instrumentalists, and *layali* or *mawwal* when performed by vocalists. Whereas musicians of nearly any skill level can play metered compositions, only the most skilled can play *taqasim* with any authority.

Cultural Considerations. In addition to being suspicious of the sensual aspects of music, Islamic aesthetics frowns on realistic representation in art, especially of the human form to avoid the temptation towards idol worship. But as with sound, it may not always be obvious to outsiders what is considered art and what is not. Important mosques boast interiors covered with beautiful ceramic tiles, which certainly appear "artistic" to the Western eye, even if their designs are nonrepresentational. Indeed, even Arabic calligraphy lends itself to incorporation into decorative design and is considered to be art.

Within various cultures, an apparent correlation often exists between the degree of decoration found in art and architecture on the one hand and music on the other. In the case of Arabic music, this correlation is fairly compelling. Mosques characteristically have little undecorated space within them, and this is paralleled by the busy character of much Arabic music, in which the distinction between main notes and ornamentation is frequently blurred. Interestingly, whereas the ornamentation of classical *musiqa* is clearly categorized as "controversial," the same thing in a call to prayer is "legitimate" because the call to prayer is *non-musiqa*.

As previously mentioned, Arab decoration made a strong impression on Europeans in the eighteenth century and onward. The French term *arabesque* came to be used to refer to European architectural embellishments featuring floral or curlicue patterns. In music the term denotes elaborately embellished melodies or countermelodies, such as Claude Debussy's *Deux arabesques* for piano. Few of these compositions, however, have any further relationship to Arabic music per se. Some composers and musicians, particularly pianists, at Middle Eastern conservatories, though devoted to European music alone, sought to assert something of their roots by composing or improvising their own "arabesques" as well.

Arrival: Iran

IRAN

Little known to Western travelers, Iran, a country the size of Alaska, is home to over 64 million people. Because much of the country is mountainous and rainfall is scanty except along the coast of the Gulf of Oman, Iran's large population must work quite hard to survive. Earthquakes are a constant concern in many areas, and when one occurs, typically large numbers of people die.

While sitting in the heart of the Middle East, Iran, known as Persia until the 20th century, is different from most of its neighbors on several accounts. The vast majority of its inhabitants share a non-Arab origin and speak Farsi, an Indo-European language related to that of the Kurds

Dome of mosque and two minarets in Isfahan, Iran, one of the country's centers of Islam (Rex Shahriari)

living at the juncture of Iran, Turkey, and Iraq. Most of Iran's population is Shiah Muslim, Shiah being the division of Islam that has traditionally attracted the lower classes and that expresses itself more emotionally and militantly than Sunni Islam, which has become the mainstream form of Islam in most Middle Eastern countries. Shiah Islam has a more developed clergy, in which the lower-ranking members are called *mullahs* and the higher-ranking ones *ayatollahs*. At various times, its more radical manifestations have posed a problem not only for the West, but for non-Shiah Muslims as well.

Persia has a long history, from its first flourishing in the sixth century B.C. under Cyrus the Great, through its periods of subjugation by Alexander the Great, the Parthians, the Turks, and the Mongols, to independence in the eighteenth century. Some consider its greatest period to have been during the rule of the Sasanian dynasty (third to seventh centuries A.D.). Modern Iran was created in the early twentieth century, along with a hereditary line of rulers called *shahs*, the last of whom was Shah Muhammad Reza Pahlevi, who ruled until deposed by revolutionaries in 1979. Since 1979 Iran has been a theocracy, ruled by an uneasy union of semi-official *ayatollahs* and official secular leaders.

Track 27

Site 3: Dastgah for Santur and Voice

First Impressions. On first hearing, this Iranian example may sound rather similar to the Arabic example heard earlier. It begins with a stringed instrument that plays a rhythmically free melody in an impro-

A musician plays the Persian *santur* (dulcimer) in a classroom demonstration

visatory manner. This section then gives way to a section featuring an unaccompanied female singer, who continues the rhythmically free approach. Despite the apparent similarities between Arabic and Iranian music (or, more properly, Persian music), however, the two systems are conceptually quite different.

Aural Analysis. Although the instrument that introduces our example is obviously a chordophone, if you listen carefully you will detect a certain percussiveness that distinguishes it from the plucked instruments heard earlier. Indeed, the player is using two small wooden hammers to strike the strings. Organologically, such an instrument is called a "dulcimer" or a "hammered zither," because the strings are parallel to a soundboard without a neck and struck by mallets. What we are hearing is the Persian *santur*, Iran's most distinctive and basic instrument, and the great-grandfather of the rest of the world's dulcimers, which are distributed as far as China and Korea in the east and the United States in the west. Indeed, some scholars even consider the European piano to be a descendant of the *santur*, because it works on the same principle, except that keys flip the hammers against the strings.

The *santur* is constructed of hardwood in a trapezoidal shape, with a lower side around three feet wide and an upper only around fourteen inches wide. Courses—groups—of four strings stretch from tuning pins on the right over two rows of moveable bridges, in rows of thirteen and twelve respectively, to anchor pins on the left. Players hammer the strings near the bridges on either side of the left row and on the left side only of the right row. If plain wooden hammers are used, the tone is more percussive than when players cover the mallet ends with felt or cloth, as is the case in our example. The *santur*, in slightly different forms, is also played in other Middle Eastern countries, though elsewhere it is not the centrally important instrument it is in Iran. Iconographical evidence dates the *santur* at least to the Babylonian period (1600–911 B.C.).

The vocal soloist who enters following the introductory section sings verses from the *Masnavi*, a book of mystical poetry written by the thirteenth century poet Jalal al-Din Muhammad Rumi, who also founded the Mevlevi order of Sufi Islam, famed for its "whirling dervishes" (see Site 5). Written in rhythmically free verse, the sung text begins with the following lines: "The grieving of the heart announces the state of love / And there is no illness like that of the heart." Persian music, like Arabic music, is based on an elaborate modal system (recall that the term *mode* refers to a "composition kit" used in improvisation), which in Persian music is called *dastgah* (plural *dastgah-ha*). Officially there are twelve *dastgah*, each based on seven pitches, plus a number of submodes called *avaz*. The track heard here is in *Dastgah shur* (also spelled *shour*), which uses the pitches C, Db (flat one quarter step), Eb, F, G, Ab, Bb, and c.

There are, however, essential differences between the Arabic *maqam* and Persian *dastgah* systems. Unlike Arab musicians, who rely on an oral tradition of melodic phrases appropriate to a specific mode, Persian musicians have created a vast body of "composed" melodic phrases that amount to short compositions; these are called *gusheh*. Each *dastgah*, then, is learned by memorizing a variable number of these short *gusheh* compositions that can then be strung together to create a longer and

SANTUR
A hammered zither from the Persian classical tradition.

DASTGAH
Persian mode or system of rules and expectations for composition and improvisation.

RADIF
A collection of *gusheh* for each *dastgah* in Persian classical music.

more complete performance/composition. The *gusheh* are organized around specific pitches of the *dastgah,* allowing the player to progress from the lowest (or home) note, called the *ist,* to higher pitches, where the musical tension becomes greater. The number of *gusheh* employed in any particular performance depends on the performer's knowledge and needs, while the specifics of the *gusheh* used vary according to the player's "school" (or tradition). For pedagogical purposes, as well as to set a kind of national standard, scholars have collected and printed all the *gusheh* for all the *dastgah* in a book called the *radif.* Therefore, a student can memorize as many *gusheh* as might be needed for performance within a particular "school."

A complete performance of a *dastgah* typically unfolds in several sections, and requires a substantial amount of time. Because the sections can be quite different from each other, these performances resemble a suite. A typical performance's opening movement, called the *daramad,* is rhythmically free and emphasizes the lower-pitched *gusheh*. Following this is the *tahrir,* another section in free rhythm emphasizing melismatic melodic work. Then follow two metered pieces called *kereshmeh* and *chahar-mezrab* respectively, which are followed in turn by a repetition of the rhythmically free *daramad*. The track included here features only the first two of these sections.

Cultural Considerations. The classical *dastgah-ha* of Iran form a vast and flexible system, which allows musicians to create both fixed compositions and improvisations by stringing together numerous short compositional blocks. Naturally, this system also calls for an element of individual creativity, because Persian music-making is about far more than building Lego-like performances. The art comes in how the *gusheh* are joined to each other, and in how they are subtly changed and elaborated on. Because musicians belong to various "schools" and consequently have learned different approaches to the *dastgah,* specific *gusheh* generally sound different from one performance to another. The use of measured rhythm in metrical cycles

A musician plays the Persian *tar,* a distinctively shaped lute with four strings

is no longer as significant in Persian music as it once was, and the metered pieces found in suites, such as the *chahar-mezrab,* employ fairly simple rhythmic patterns. While foreign audiences generally prefer the metered compositions because of their use of one or more drums and their steady beat, Persian musicians value rhythmically free improvisations most highly, for the display of refined musicianship that they allow.

Although the *santur* is probably Iran's most distinctive instrument, other kinds of instruments are important as well. These include two plucked lutes, the *sehtar* and the *tar*. The latter's skin-covered body has a distinctive shape, resembling the number 8. Also important is the round-bodied bowed lute called *kemancheh*. One aerophone, the *ney,* an end-blown notch flute found throughout the Middle East, is commonly heard. The main percussion instrument is a goblet-shaped, single-headed drum called the *dombak* or *zarb*, which resembles the Arabic *darabuka*.

Arrival: Egypt

EGYPT

If any nation typifies the Middle East, it is Egypt. Her ancient civilization, nearly as old as civilization itself, seems to live on through incredible relics—the pyramids, the sphinx, great temples, hieroglyphics, wall paintings, and mummies—and is symbolized by the River Nile, which flows thousands of miles northward out of Africa to the Mediterranean Sea. This nation, which constitutes the northeast corner of Africa, is smaller than Canada's Ontario province, but has a population of nearly 70 million. That the land can support so many is surprising considering how much of Egypt is desert. Most of the fertile land is found along the Nile, where many crops, including great quantities of exported cotton, are grown. The Suez Canal, opened in 1869, connects the Red Sea to the Mediterranean Sea and separates the main part of Egypt from the Sinai Peninsula.

Egypt's Sphinx, with its nose allegedly damaged by Napoleon's soldiers, along with the pyramids is a symbol of ancient Egypt
(Denise A. Seachrist)

Although ancient paintings depict musicians playing harps, lyres, lutes, flutes, double reeds, and other kinds of instruments, little is known about the sound of Egyptian music before contact with Islam, or even long after. However, coastal Egypt, particularly Alexandria, was part of the ancient Mediterranean civilization, where post-Islam Arab music theory was brought to an intellectual zenith during the first millennium of the Christian era. Music in modern-day Egypt reflects a welter of more recent influences, including from European art music, which has made Egypt—at least urban Egypt—an extension of European musical culture. Recall, for example, that Italian composer Giuseppi Verdi's opera *Aida* was commissioned by Khedive Ismail in 1869 for the opening of the Cairo Opera House.

Site 4: Islamic Song with *Takht* Instrumental Accompaniment

Track 28

First Impressions. With its catchy beat and sinuous melody, this piece may bring to mind the image of a veiled belly dancer swaying gracefully before an audience. Some of the instruments might seem familiar, including one that sounds like a tambourine, but a number of the intervals heard sound "off," in particular one of them.

A small *takht* ensemble (front row) and two belly dancers (back row).
Front row, L to R: *ud* (lute), *kanun* (zither), *darabukka* (drum) (George Sawa)

TAKHT

An Arabic music ensemble, including zithers, bowed and plucked lutes, drums, aerophones, and often other non-traditional instruments.

Aural Analysis. Songs accompanied by instrumental ensembles pervade Egyptian musical life. They run the gamut from religious songs—as heard in this case—to folk songs, wedding songs, and love songs. Egyptian instrumental ensembles may also, however, perform on their own, without a vocalist. The musical systems found among Egyptians generally contrast slower-paced and unmetered music played by a single musician with clearly metered music played by a group, with or without a vocal part. In contrast to the improvisatory approach that is such an important part of solo performance, instrumental groups play fixed compositions. In Egypt the typical ensemble is called a *takht* and consists of three to five players, though more are possible. In modern times these ensembles have often been enlarged through the addition of new instruments, some borrowed from the "Near North" (i.e., Europe).

Most of the melodic instruments found in takht ensembles are chordophones, in the bowed lute, plucked lute, and zither categories, but at least one aerophone, the end-blown cane flute (*ney*), is nearly always present as well. Among the most prominent of the plucked lutes is a pear-shaped lute known as the *ud*. Of the bowed lutes, the *kemanja*, an unfretted spike fiddle, is most prevalent, but today *takht* ensembles may also incorporate violins, cellos, and even string basses. The most important zither is the *kanun*, an oddly shaped, four-sided instrument resembling an autoharp that has an amazing number of tuning mechanisms to allow for various tunings (see photo on page 38). Our recorded example features

Middle Eastern frame drums come in many sizes and shapes, some with metal discs in the frame. The preferred material for the heads is fish skin

a *ney* flute, three *ud* lutes, ten violins, a cello, a bass, two *qanun* zithers, and a *riqq* frame drum. The melodic instruments perform the same melody but with slight variations, resulting in a slightly heterophonic texture.

Three types of drums are found in *takht* ensembles: the *duff*, the *riqq*, and the *tabla*. The *duff* is a small, single-headed drum sometimes having snares; the *riqq* is similar, but has pairs of small cymbals inserted into the frame that jingle when the head is struck (i.e., a tambourine). The *tabla* is a small, goblet-shaped single-headed drum similar to others with different names found throughout the Middle East and is not related to the Indian pair of drums of the same name.

Arab drumming is highly organized, and much of it is conceived as being in closed cycles of beats. The standard, named patterns realized by drummers are known in Arabic as *iqa* (plural *iqa-at*) and are sometimes called *rhythmic modes* in English. Using named drum strokes, drummers continuously play a given mode or cycle, with greater or lesser degrees of elaboration and ornamentation, to reinforce the metrical organization of a composition's melodic parts.

Even when composers create fixed pieces, they work within the Arab modal system called *maqam*, which governs the choice of pitches and intervals and offers standard melodic patterns as well. Compositions are also divided into certain well-known set forms with names like *dulāb, tahmīla,* and *bashraf*. Our recording is an example of the last form, which is derived from the Turkish Ottoman Empire, and features the alternation of a recurring theme (*taslīm*)—called a "rondo" or "ritornello" in European music—and new melodic material. This form is often used, as in this case, for light music. In a *bashraf* composition, the change from one section to the next is sometimes signaled by a change in the mode

KANUN
(Also, QANUN)
A plucked zither used in Turkish and Arabic music traditions, prominent in *takht* ensembles.

being used. The main mode used in this *bashraf* has a prominent augmented second interval right above the home pitch and could be expressed as C, D, E, F, <u>G</u>, Ab, B, C. Certain of the pitches, especially the F, sound out of tune to Western ears, as their intonation differs from the Western equal-tempered scale. A second scale could be expressed as C, D, E, F, G, A, B, C and sounds more familiar as far as tuning goes.

During the mid-twentieth century, an orchestra-sized variant of the *takht* ensemble appeared. Known as *firqa*, these larger ensembles sometimes include a chorus in addition to the principal vocalist. As with the smaller ensembles, the instruments used are mostly chordophones and aerophones, the former including most Arab possibilities plus members of the Western violin family, and the latter being mostly end blown flutes of the *ney* variety. While traditional ensembles play heterophonically, performances by modernized *firqa* ensembles are usually highly arranged, with varied orchestration and even harmony.

Cultural Considerations. In addition to accompanying singers, *takht* ensembles also accompany dance. From the perspective of most Westerners, Middle Eastern dance is synonymous with "belly dance," which is assumed to be erotic because of the undulating pelvic movements that are so stereotypical. In fact, this dancing is a highly skilled activity that is often appreciated for its technical merits. Traditionally, the dancers who mastered the most rapid hips movements were called *ghawazi*, a term derived from the name of the Ottoman coins that

RAQS SHARQI

The Arabic name for what is commonly referred to by outsiders as "belly dance."

Belly dance performance accompanied by violin and darabukka (behind dancer) (Andrew Shahriari)

adorned their costumes. The nearest equivalent to the Western conception of belly dance is the *raqs sharqi*, which varies from performances by fully clothed artistic dancers to stripteases. The latter were historically performed by foreigners rather than Arab women, because Arab women could never hope to be married if they became associated with erotic displays. Another distinctive form is the *sham'idan* (candelabrum dance), so called because the dancer performs with a large, heavy candelabrum with lighted candles balanced on her head. Some theorize that these dances once symbolize fertility for Egyptians, but others claim that they came from the Halab and the Ghajar, two Rom tribes from India, who entered Egypt most likely with the Ottoman Turkish armies in 1517.

Dance in Egypt is also closely associated with religious expression, particularly among members of the more mystically inclined sects. Dance in a religious context can bring participants to great spiritual heights, including states of ecstasy and even possession.

Ali Jihad Racy, a noted scholar and performer of Arabic music, asserts that the essential difference between European music and Middle Eastern music is that the former strives for the representation of images and concepts (including structural patterns), and the latter strives to evoke intense emotions in both the performers and listeners. These emotions can affect people in both positive and negative ways, a concept known as *ethos* to the Greeks and *ta'thir* to the Arabs. Indeed, for Arabs, music has the power to heal and to bring people closer to union with God. As Ali Jihad Racy remarks in his book *Making Music in the Arab World,* "In Arab culture, the merger between music and emotional transformation is epitomized by the Arab concept of *tarab*" (p. 5). Although much Arabic music can be described in purely technical terms (e.g., the modal system), the goal of Arab music-making is not to create clever structures but to bring listeners toward a state of ecstasy. Although this ecstasy can have a religious dimension—by bringing the hearer into spiritually heightened states—music's sensual aspect is still viewed as suspicious by Islamic theologians, and consequently, as we have read, *musiqa* is proscribed from the mosque.

Arrival: *Sufism*

SUFISM

Sufism is frequently described as the "mystical" branch of Islam. While Sufis regard themselves as being part of the Sunni tradition, and as having the same core religious values as all branches of Islam—namely, belief in Muhammad as the last prophet of Allah—their interpretation of the Koran allows for activities, especially with regards to music, that are discouraged or prohibited by other Muslims. A fundamental philosophy of Sufism is that a person can become one with Allah through the elimination of the ego, a belief rejected by orthodox Islam. This controversial belief results in varied opinions of Sufi practices. Many Muslims consider Sufis devoted followers of Allah, while others view them as heretics whose ritual practices are sacrilegious. In Turkey, Sufis have been held in high esteem for centuries. The Mevlevi sect, one of the best-known Sufi orders, was founded there in the thirteenth century and exerted great influence on rulers of the region for several centuries.

TARAB
Arabic word for a state of emotional transformation or ecstasy achieved through music.

The term *"Sufi"* is derived from the Arabic word *"suf"* meaning "wool," in reference to the woolen robes worn by devotees. Sufi brotherhoods are numerous, each having their own rules and rituals. Many Sufis seclude themselves in monasteries, called *tekke* or *khanegah,* in order to focus exclusively on their spiritual quest to know Allah. Others practice trades in the secular world, and perform the sacred rites of their brotherhood only on specific occasions. Still others commit themselves to an itinerant existence. This latter lifestyle earned Sufis a secondary title, *dervish,* which loosely translates as "beggar," as the wandering monks rely on alms from the general public for their survival. *Dervish* is the term most frequently used in the Western world for those Sufi orders that present public performances of sacred music and dance as a means of disseminating knowledge about their religion.

Track 29

Site 5: *Sufi Dhikr Ceremony*

First Impressions. Unlike most Islamic worship, with its solemn mood, Sufi music is often cheerful, though with an undertone of seriousness. This performance, a hymn recorded in Turkey, is almost like a spinning top: it seems repeatedly to slip and then straighten itself, until it finally slows and comes to rest. Accompanied by several instruments, the voices swirl round and round and up and down. This exuberant celebration of love for Allah then gives way to a more solemn mood as a single voice cries out over the hearty chant of fellow worshippers.

Aural Analysis. Sufi hymns, known as *ilahi,* vary in mood and instrumentation. The *ud, qanun, kamance* (a spiked bowed fiddle), *ney,* and *bandir* (a frame drum) are the most common instruments, although the *tanbur* (a fretted plucked lute), *riqq* (tambourine), and occasionally the *kudum* (a kettle drum) and *halile* (cymbals) are sometimes included as well. The *ney* is particularly important in Sufi ceremonies, and often is used for extended solos.

DHIKR (Also, ZIKR)
A Sufi ritual in which believers chant the name of God with the goal of entering an ecstatic state.

Vocal performance in Sufi music belongs to one of three categories. The most prominent type is associated with the male vocal specialists known as *zakirler,* who perform metered passages in unison. This type of singing is heard in the first section of our selection. The melodic contour of this vocal performance continually rises and falls, supported by the melodic instruments, while the *bandir* provides a steady duple-metered pulse. The tonal center shifts frequently, keeping the music always slightly off-balance. While the text setting is primarily syllabic, melismatic descents occur at the peaks of concluding phrases.

After this "swirling" singing, the tempo slows and the other two vocal categories are heard simultaneously. In the foreground, the vocal soloist chants rhythmically free melismatic passages akin to the *muezzin*'s call to prayer. This style of singing is known as *kaside.* Some instruments accompany the voice, providing key melodic pitches for the vocalist's reference rather than complete melodic passages. This allows the vocalist to improvise his melodic phrases without being bound to a specific melody or rhythm. Other instruments do, however, follow a pulse, which is articulated by the remaining *dervishes,* whose performance is an example of the third vocal category. The chorus sings a deep, raspy chant, consisting of repetitions of the phrase "*Hū, hū,*" meaning "It is He" ("He" being Allah).

Cultural Considerations. For Sufis, chants provide the believer the opportunity to attain union with Allah. Indeed, they believe that music is a primary way of reaching this ultimate goal. Sound is thought to be a vital link between the spiritual and physical realms. Whereas orthodox Islam, as we have seen, generally discourages musical performance, especially in the context of worship, Sufis emphasize its use as a means of heightening spirituality. Rather than believing that music tempts the soul away from Allah, Sufis assert that music merely strengthens a person's inclinations and temperament. Thus, music performed in religious contexts with the intention of uplifting the soul is acceptable and often necessary, whereas music played in the context of sensual indulgence only reinforces the sinful nature of the flesh.

One of the most important contexts for Sufi musical performances is the ritual known as *dhikr (zikr)*, a name that translates as "remembrance." The practice of *dhikr* differs between Sufi orders, but the best-known form of the ceremony is associated with the Mevlevi sect founded by Jalal al-Din Muhammad Rumi (1207–73

Sufi Muslims of the Mevlevi ('Whirling') sect from Turkey perform the *Sema* ritual on stage in New York City (© Jack Vartoogian/FrontRowPhotos)

A.D.). In this version of the ceremony—which is particularly associated with the December 17th memorial celebrations held in Rumi's honor in Konya, Turkey—music and dance often are performed for the public. The Western notion of Sufis as "Whirling Dervishes" is derived from this and similar ceremonies, because the dances require performers to spin in a circle on one foot for an extended period at varying speeds. When a dancer is spinning at his fastest, his white robes become a blur, much like an ice skater doing a final spin at the Olympics.

A Sufi devotee uses music and dance in these ceremonies to progress through the evolutionary stages of the soul toward the ultimate goal of experiencing the absolute reality of Allah. By chanting the names for the ninety-nine divine attributes of Allah while performing specific ritualistic movements, Sufis enter a trance-like state in which they become spiritually ecstatic. Sufis describe this feeling as "soaring." Many Sufi ritual performances are hidden from the public and involve such amazing feats as piercing the body with swords, chewing on glass, or walking on hot coals to demonstrate the power of Allah working through the individual believer. Our recorded example is typical of the music found in private ceremonies.

The "whirling" dances of the Mevlevi sect are also intended to help believers achieve a spiritually ecstatic state. As the musicians play, the dancer rises and removes his black outer garment, which symbolizes the darkness of the secular world. Beneath this outer garment are inner

JALAL AL-DIN MUHAMMED RUMI

Sufi saint of Islamic mysticism known for his poems and as the founder of the Mevlevi religious order.

Jerusalem's Dome of the Rock, a part of the Temple Mount called Qubbat As-Sakhrah in Arabic and built between 687 and 691, is a revered shrine *(mashhad)* for both Muslims and Jews.

white robes that symbolize the purity of Allah. As the dancer spins, he raises his right hand toward the sky and lowers his left hand toward the earth. This action represents Allah handing down his divine grace to all humanity. The spinning motion symbolizes the movement of the heavenly bodies—i.e., the earth and moon—and helps the dancer to detach himself from the material plane and achieve a heightened sense of spiritual awareness.

JUDAISM

Arrival: Judaism

While Judaism is practiced by more than 15 million adherents throughout North Africa, Western Asia, Europe, and the Americas, its "homeland," the state of Israel, is in the Middle East. A nation slightly smaller than Massachusetts, Israel was created on May 14, 1948, out of an area formerly known as Palestine. Sometimes called "The Holy Land," Israel is of great religious significance for Jews, Christians, and Muslims, as it contains what are perhaps the most revered historical sites or monuments for each group: the Wailing Wall for the Jews, the Church of the Nativity for Christians, and the Dome of the Rock Mosque for Muslims and Jews. As a result this land has been fought over for more than one thousand years, going back to the time of the medieval Crusades. Traditionally, people of all three religions lived together in the region—and they still do—but since 1948 there has been continuous tension over land, water, and religious and political rights and privileges.

Israel is a nation with both "traditional" (i.e., Asian/North African) and immigrant populations (European, American, Asian, African). Historically, most Jews lived in the "Diaspora"—that is, the countries outside of the Middle East to which they spread—often suffering discrimination and marginalization. In Europe, Jews were long kept at arm's length from the mainstream populations but allowed to establish themselves in certain occupations, music being one of them. Over the centuries, in many times and places, Jews were used as scapegoats for Europe's problems. During the 1930s, the genocidal policies of Nazi Germany led to the deaths of some six million Jews. In reaction to this history of oppression, Zionism, a Jewish political movement begun in central Europe in 1897, advocated the founding of a Jewish state that would be a refuge for Jews worldwide. The establishment of Israel in 1948 realized that goal, though European Jews had already been migrating to Palestine for many years.

KLEZMER
A European-derived dance music commonly associated with Jewish celebrations, influenced by jazz and other non-Jewish styles.

Jews in the Diaspora belong to several distinct communities. The term *Sephardic* originally referred to Jews forced out of Spain by King Ferdinand and Queen Isabella at the end of the fifteenth century, but has come to be applied to any Jew of North African or Asian origin. Jews from Europe are called Ashkenazi Jews, and because they were the primary advocates for the establishment of Israel, they tend to dominate modern Israeli politics. The musical traditions of the two communities are quite different, and among Sephardic Jews there are many distinct local traditions, such as that of Jews from Yemen.

The terms *Jewish music* and *Israeli music* are difficult to define. The former refers not only to music (both chanting and singing) heard in tabernacle rituals, but also to nonliturgical songs of many sorts having Jewish content. Israeli music can only be defined as the sum of its parts, because Israeli society is partially secular and is comprised of people from all over the world. Perhaps the best-known representative of "Israeli music" is *klezmer,* a kind of European-derived dance music mostly developed in the United States influenced by jazz and other non-Jewish styles. We have chosen to represent the religious side of Jewish identity through a genre from the synagogue, liturgical cantillation.

Site 6: Jewish Liturgical Cantillation

First Impressions. This unaccompanied male singing seems rather random and hardly tuneful, suggesting that the text itself might be more important than the performance's musical qualities,. Not being able to understand the words is a serious obstacle in this case. There is one scale interval in particular that sounds Middle Eastern.

Aural Analysis. The musical elements present in our example are mostly functional; that is, they serve primarily to give the text prominence. If you listen carefully, you'll detect eight pitches spanning slight-

Track 30

Toledo, Spain, once the home for a large Jewish community, preserves the Synagogue of Santa Maria la Blanca, a 12th century building with Moorish arches, later converted into a church in 1411 when the Jews were driven from Toledo

ly more than one octave. In notation, from low to high, they are D, E, F, G#, A, B, C, E. Two of them seem more important than the others, the A and lower E. These are the reciting pitches, with E being the resting point that gives a feeling of finality. The G# is what gives the chant its Middle Eastern flavor, because G# down to F natural is an augmented second. Descending from G# to F also produces an incomplete feeling only relieved by hitting the lower E. There is no regular meter; rather, the words are delivered in "speech rhythm." While the text setting is generally syllabic, there is also some melisma present.

Jewish cantillation, called *nusach,* is an oral tradition, though some scholars have attempted to notate the chants of particular singers. We say "attempted" because notating a freely sung text is an inexact science. The version performed here is attributed to a European singer named Zev Weinman and has been notated in a collection of service music in transcription. Tabernacle singers (called *cantors*) construct melodies from a body of traditional modes and melodic formulas which can be freely interpreted. The text chanted in the audio example is "L'dor vodor" and is sung in Hebrew, the sacred language of Judaism as well as the national language of Israel. The words, taken from a Sabbath morning service, translate as "From generation to generation we will declare Thy greatness, and to all eternity we will proclaim Thy holiness. They praise, O our God, shall never depart from our mouths; for Thou, O God, art a great and holy King."

Cultural Considerations. The term *cantillation* is used to denote a kind of heightened speech that is between speaking and singing. Most religions of the world employ some kind of cantillation, because full-fledged singing is often forbidden or discouraged for various reasons, its sensuality being the common objection. In some cases, religious ritualists are forbidden to sing; thus, even if the cantillation they perform is quite melodic, it is still not referred to as "singing." It appears to be true throughout the world that sacred texts or holy words are thought to have more authority and mystery, and to be more clearly understood, if delivered in some form of heightened speech. The human relationship with the spirit or spiritual world requires an extraordinary form of dialogue, one that takes it outside the realm of ordinary speech or singing.

Judaism worships the same god as Christianity and Islam, but Jews have had continuous communication with that god during their more than four-thousand-year history through a line of prophets beginning with Abraham. Judaism is especially distinguished by its careful attention to sacred law, which requires Jews to observe greater or lesser numbers of specific requirements depending on their position in the continuum from Ultra-Orthodox to Reformed. The audio example comes from the Orthodox tradition, though Conservative and Reformed Jews may also chant in this style.

The sacred texts of Judaism, written in Hebrew, constitute what is called the Old Testament by Christians. Of these books, the first five, called the *Torah* or *Pentateuch,* are most important. Sacred writings, both biblical and non-biblical (as in the present example) are read in heightened speech, or cantillation. Such readings may occur either in a synagogue or in a private home. The term *service* describes liturgical rituals that can be held several times each day, though those held on the eve of the Sabbath (Friday evening after sundown) and on the Sabbath itself (Saturday, before sundown) are most important. Jews also celebrate their religion through an annual cycle of festivals, as well as through more private rites of passage such as circumcision, *bar mitzvah* or *bat mitzvah* (held when, respectively, a

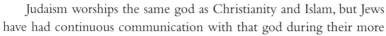

A Jewish ram's horn trumpet or *shofar* (Joseph S. Kaminski)

TORAH
In Judaism the first five books *(pentateuch)* of the Bible or more generally, all sacred literature.

SHOFAR
A ram's horn trumpet frequently mentioned in *Torah* and used in Jewish ritual.

young man or woman comes of age), and marriage. In Orthodox Judaism only males may recite the scriptures and liturgy. The use of musical instruments is generally avoided, but there are exceptions. Jews traditionally have used a ram's horn, called a *shofar,* as a ritual trumpet blown to mark divisions in a service.

After a revolt against their Roman conquerors failed in 70 A.D., the great temple at Jerusalem was destroyed, leaving only the Wailing Wall, and the Jews were dispersed to many parts of the world. Jewish congregations today tend to be either Sephardic or Ashkenazi, though mixed tabernacles exist. Sephardic congregations preserve musical practices derived from the *maqamat* tradition of Arabic modal music. Ashkenazi congregations practice what is called the "Jerusalem-Lithuanian" style characteristic of Eastern European Jews. The audio example represents the tradition common to Eastern Europe, especially Poland, German, and Hungary. In Ashkenazi tabernacles the main ritualist who intones the sacred texts—the cantor—sings in a European style and may be accompanied by an organ in contexts where instruments are permitted, especially in Reformed congregations. While cantors in both traditions are not considered singers per se because what they do is technically "cantillation," many cantors are in fact fine singers and have turned their cantillation into a performance art rather than merely a way to declaim texts. Indeed, some, such as Robert Merrill, have become renowned opera virtuosi.

Questions to Consider

1. How has Islam shaped conceptions of music for the peoples of the Middle East?

2. What is modal improvisation? Is it primarily a compositional or freely expressive form of performance?

3. Because the Islamic Call to Prayer and Jewish Biblical cantillation clearly have musical characteristics, why are they not considered "music" or "singing"?

4. What are the key factors that make Persian classical music different from Arabic music?

5. How do Sufi attitudes toward music differ from attitudes found in the other branches of Islam?

6. Taking into consideration Chapters 3 and 10, what are some of the musical relationships between the Middle East and Europe, especially in terms of instruments and musical styles?

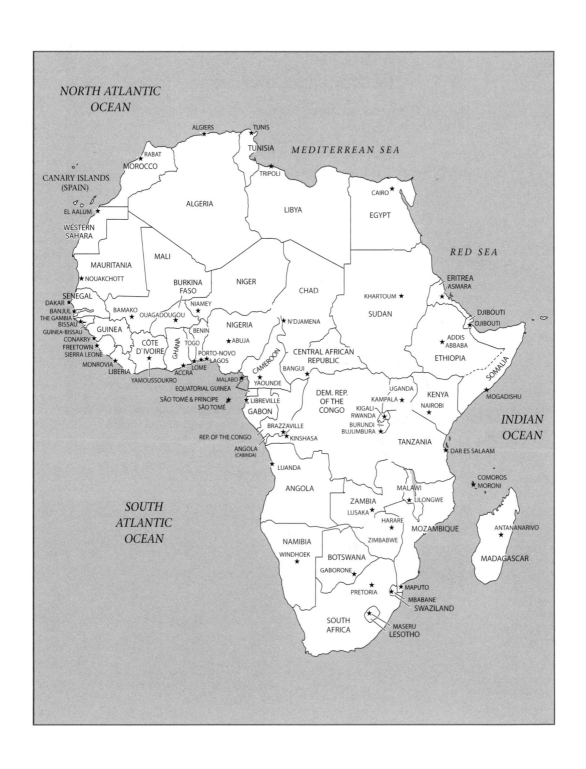

Kete drummers in a funeral procession at the court of the Asantehene (chief or king), Kumase, Ghana (Joseph S. Kaminski)

CHAPTER 9

Sub-Saharan Africa: The Rhythms of Community

Background Preparation

Africa, the world's second-largest continent, is home to nearly three thousand separate ethnic groups spread across 11.7 million square miles. While Africa boasts many densely populated urban areas, most areas are still rural and have limited infrastructure. Farming is the primary occupation of most Africans, although many people living in areas rich in natural resources, such as diamonds and coal, are employed by large mining companies and related industries.

The continent is customarily divided into three cultural zones: the pan-Arabic zone, including the countries bordering the Mediterranean Sea; the Sahel Zone, including those areas dominated by the vast Sahara desert; and sub-Saharan Africa, the rest of the continent south of the

Zebras in a South African game reserve, a visual icon for Africa (Max T. Miller)

Sahara desert; the latter is the focus of this chapter. Western, Eastern, and Central Africa are equatorial and therefore quite hot and humid. Rainforests dominate the central interior, whereas the red-soiled Kalahari Desert typifies the arid landscape of southern Africa. Few mountain ranges exist, though several dormant volcanoes, the most famous being snow-capped Mount Kilimanjaro in northeastern Tanzania, provide a contrast to the vast rolling plains seen throughout most of sub-Saharan Africa. Wildlife safaris are commonplace throughout much of the continent, which is home to such well-known animals as the African elephant, lion, zebra, giraffe, and rhinoceros.

While the ancient Egyptian pharaohs ruled the most famous kingdoms of North Africa, the kings of sub-Saharan Africa also held dominion over vast territories for numerous generations. In western Africa, the earliest known kingdom was the Kingdom of Ghana, which controlled the trade routes of West Africa from roughly the fifth to the eleventh century A.D., when it was overtaken by Muslim militants from present-day Mauritania. Other important empires prior to the colonial era included the Mali kingdom (mid-thirteenth to late fourteenth century), and the Songhai kingdom (fifteenth to late sixteenth century), both of which were Islamic. In southern Africa, the Zulu king Shaka (1787–1828) is best known, having organized a powerful military machine that conquered many peoples throughout South Africa and as far north as Tanzania. Historical warriors and royal lineages continue to play a vital role in the cultural identity of modern Africa.

The political borders of present-day Africa are the result of European colonial occupation. Throughout much of the nineteenth century and during the early years of the twentieth century, vast regions of Africa were claimed as colonies by several European powers. The 1884–85 Berlin Conference is often cited as a decisive moment in Africa's political history, particularly for the Congo region. At this meeting, German, Belgian, French, British, and Portuguese officials, along with representatives of governments that had no colonial stake in the region, such as the United States, divided the territorial rights to most of central and southern Africa without the presence or participation of a single African. New African nations were formed with little regard for the cultural differences of the various peoples contained within their borders. Consequently, even today many different ethnic populations, with diverse cultural traditions, often exist in close proximity within a single country.

Decades of European presence left a strong mark on African religions, governmental forms, and languages. Travelers to Africa will encounter multilingual speakers who know a number of indigenous dialects (of which there are nearly 800 in sub-Saharan Africa alone), as well as one or two European languages, the most common of which are English, French, and Portuguese. Though colonialism affected many of the cultural activities of African peoples, often oppressively, traditional practices still thrive throughout the continent, especially in rural areas. Islam and Christianity have long existed in sub-Saharan Africa, but the influence of earlier animistic traditions remains visible in the ritual activity of many believers of the mainstream institutionalized religions.

An emphasis on the collective community is an overarching principle essential to the social organization and cultural identity of many African populations. Social identity is valued over individual identity, as expressed by the common proverb, "I am because we are." Each person serves a function within the overall group. In smaller villages, everyone is considered part of the same family, whether or not they are related by blood. A person's possessions are frequently "shared" with other members of the community, as if everyone lived in the same house.

Boy *kete* dancer at an Asante funeral in Kumase, Ghana (Joseph S. Kaminski)

Furthermore, these "extended families" comprise not only living members of the community, but the spirits of ancestors as well. Even when a person is physically "alone," he is accompanied by one or more ancestor spirits who act as guardians and confidants.

Music is a vital aspect of the daily lives of people throughout sub-Saharan Africa. Even the most mundane tasks, such as canceling stamps at the post office, pounding millet, or walking are made enjoyable by putting them into a musical context. Dance and singing are equally essential; indeed, music, dance, and singing, conceptualized as distinct from one another in the West, are described in many places with the same terminology, because they are considered inseparable. The emphasis on the collective community that characterizes traditional African life is reflected in three main activities associated with music: communal

An Inside Look

Adesanya Adeyeye

My name is Adesanya Adeyeye, and I play the traditional instruments and sing the songs of my native Nigeria. I was born in Ilesa, Osun State, Nigeria, in 1952. My early education included study at St. Mary's Catholic Primary School in

Adesanya Adeyeye, professional musician

Ilesa, Ilesa Grammar School, the Federal School of Science in Onikan, Lagos, and later at Yaba College of Technology where I studied Mechanical Engineering and obtained an ordinary National Diploma. My music study began rather late in my life, starting at the now defunct Chris Ajilo's Nigeria Institute of Music in 1978 and 1979. I also studied composition privately with Mr. Taiwo Ogunade, theory and guitar with Baba Falana at Baba Oloosa in Mushin, Lagos, and piano with Baba Theo Fayemi. Later, I had intensive guitar lessons with a Highlife musician, Amingo Egin in Idi Oro, in Mushin, Lagos.

After performing with Demos Deniran's Dynamo Luko Funk group at the Western Hotel in Idi Oro, Mushin, Lagos for nine months, I decided to enter Kent State University (USA) in 1981. With support from an Oyo State Government scholarship to study music composition, I graduated with a Bachelor of Music degree in 1985. Thereafter I earned a postgraduate Diploma in Theatre Arts from the University of Ibadan, Nigeria, in 1991. I also earned a Master of Arts degree in African Studies (Music) from the University of Ibadan in 1999.

As a professional musician, I have performed widely in both the USA and Nigeria with my group playing a variety of African traditional instruments. In the United States, I have played at the National Museum of African Arts and the Smithsonian Institution (Washington, D.C.), the American Museum of Natural History (New York City), the Cleveland Museum of Natural History, and the Virginia Museum of Fine Arts (Richmond). I have also performed widely at various American universities including Kent State University; University of Akron; University of California, Los Angeles; Oberlin College; and the University of Rochester as well as at clubs, such as the Sound of Brazil and the Pyramid Cocktail Club in New York City.

After returning to Nigeria in 1987, having established a successful reputation in the United States, I accepted a position as Music Lecturer at the Polytechnic School of Ibadan. For twelve years (1988-2000), I lectured, performed, and conducted research there, but in 2000 I established my own Institute of Arts Technology here in Ibadan. The institute emphasizes the use of Nigerian local raw material as a medium for the construction of musical instruments. It also sponsors research and publications in the fine arts, textiles, music, and music technology. The institute welcomes researchers from within Nigeria and also from overseas, especially from the USA. During my career I have also made numerous audio and video recordings. I am always open to invitations to lecture or perform anywhere in the world.

Habib Iddrisu

I was born into the Dagomba/Dagbamba family of court historians and musicians in Gukpegu/Tamale in northern Ghana. There I was brought up under the tutelage of my grandfather, Manguli-Lana Adam Alhassan, chief drummer in Tamale, and was inspired by my great uncles, many of whom were famous Dagbon musicians, especially Jabling (Fuseini Alhassan).

Habib Iddrisu, Dagbon drummer and dancer

Like many of my cousins, I started playing both the *lung-a* (talking drum) and *gungong* (supporting drum) at age six. By age eight, I was renowned throughout the region for my dancing and drumming in styles such as Takai, Bamaya, and Atikatika. As a young man I studied traditional Dagbamba music and dance as well as other genres from across Ghana and West Africa. The wealth of expressive styles that I encountered sparked my interest in sharing and teaching this material to as broad an audience as possible. Soon I was coaching in Ghana's largest cities, especially in Accra where I taught and performed with some of the city's finest cultural groups. Then I traveled extensively around the world to perform, and I won Ghana's Best Dancer Award in 1992. Between 1999 and 2004, I studied at Bowling Green State University where I received undergraduate and graduate degrees in African Studies and History respectively. I also coached a variety of African music and dance classes. In 2002, my choreography was selected and presented at the National American Dance College Festival at the Kennedy Center in Washington D.C. My studies have significantly enriched and broadened my artistic and analytical thinking.

The music of Dagbamba *Lung-si* (drummers) is completely filled with language. Its rhythmic nature may lead an outsider to think the music is entirely impro-vised, but the reality is that almost every drum phrase represents Dagbamba spoken language (Dagbanli). The music of my tradition is very intricate, yet easy to understand. It's intricate in that performance depends entirely on a person's ability to listen and memorize all the drum language that accompanies each occasion. Because drummers are story-tellers, they must be able to talk (on their drums, of course) about the history, politics, and economic lives of the people. The drum language dictates the mood of not only the listeners but the musician as well. When we drum in weddings, naming ceremonies, for the enskinment of a new chief, or just for a commoner in the marketplace, the atmosphere at the time is quickly absorbed by the *lung-si*. For instance, when we drum during funerals, we react to the mood around, not like actors or actresses taking roles but as those whose heartbeats are attached to the messages the *lung-a* is sending at the time. The *Lung-si* role is quite versatile within the context of the community's needs. At any occasion when we drum, someone may fall into trance. When this happens, we assume the role of the "healer" who controls the mediums responsible for trance, thereby subduing the spirits and leading the person out of the trance at the appropriate time. Our main role in the community is to keep the history of our people alive and exciting, and this is what makes us *Lung-si*.

dance; call-and-response singing; and the use of polyrhythm in instrumental performance. Informal dance activity often takes place when large groups of people are gathered. An individual may spontaneously step out from the crowd to dance in conjunction with a musical performance. The crowd may respond with cheers, and others may be inspired to dance as well. Spontaneous dance participation, however, is generally brief, and the dancer will fall back into the group to make way for others. The individual thereby demonstrates deference to the community, by only briefly asserting an individual identity within the context of a larger social scheme. Formal dance activity also tends to emphasize group participation, though dance in ritual contexts, such as trance dancing, often involves only a few specialized performers. In these instances, the performance requires a specific knowledge of tradition or that the individual dancers are of a specific social status, such as performers with royal patronage. The set choreography of these dances differs from dancing in informal contexts and may not include opportunities for individual expression. Formal dance activities are performed with some social function in mind, i.e., honoring royalty or inviting ancestral spirits to participate in community events.

POLYRHYTHM

A term meaning "multiple rhythms"; the organizational basis for most sub-Saharan African music traditions.

Vocal performance can occur as part of religious ceremonies or other ritual activities, in the context of storytelling, dance, or royal functions, or merely as entertainment. Though many solo vocal traditions can be found, the majority of vocal performances involve group singing, generally with a call-and response organization. In call and response, an individual will sing a "call" and the group will "respond" appropriately. (A familiar American example: *Call*: Give me a G…, *Response:* G!; *Call*: Give me an 'O…', *Response:* 'O!'; *Call*: What's that spell?!, *Response*: Go!!!) This organization may also be thought of as a "question" by the caller and an "answer" by the group.

Polyrhythm is the predominant structure for organizing instrumental (as well as some vocal) musical performance. For centuries, the polyrhythmic music traditions of sub-Saharan Africa were largely incomprehensible to outsiders. The rhythmically dense drumming traditions of Western Africa were often characterized as "chaotic" by missionaries and foreign explorers. Colonial governments suppressed these musical practices and often labeled the "wild" playing associated with "pagan" rituals as evil music that corrupted the soul. Ignorance of how the complex polyrhythmic music organization worked was a primary factor behind these negative attitudes. Fortunately, modern ethnomusicologists, both foreign and African, have developed a better understanding of the inner musical workings of these traditions, which are some of the most complex on the planet.

While drumming is considered by many Westerners to be the primary musical activity of Africans, much other musical activity occurs that involves the use of aerophones and chordophones, as well as idiophones and membranophones. Unique vocal traditions are quite common, and storytelling is of particular importance, as the histories of many of Africa's ethnic groups are passed from generation to generation via oral tradition.

Planning the Itinerary

Our survey of musical performance in sub-Saharan Africa will of necessity be brief and highly selective, but will seek to illuminate some of the key elements of African music-making. An examination of drumming traditions from Ghana, the type of African music perhaps most familiar to the outside world, begins our tour. Before leaving Ghana, we will take a look at the popular genre known as palm-wine "highlife" guitar. Our visit to Senegal-Gambia will introduce the renowned poet-praise singers/oral historians of the Mandinka, called *jali*. We will then consider the music of the Pygmies of Central Africa, xylophone traditions from Uganda, and lamellophone performance in Zimbabwe. Finally, we will focus on a Zulu choral tradition from South Africa known as *mbube*, which somewhat differs in its musical organization from much music found in the rest of sub-Saharan Africa.

Arrival: Ghana

GHANA

The Western world is perhaps most familiar with the cultural activities of African populations found in West Africa because this region is geographically closer to both Europe and the Western hemisphere than any other area of sub-Saharan Africa. The bulk of Africans forced into slavery by Europeans and Americans during the colonial period (roughly the 1500s to the late 1800s) were taken from this region, and as a result the cultural traditions of West Africa were disseminated throughout the Caribbean and the Americas. The spiritual traditions of the Dahomey people from Benin and of the Yoruba from Nigeria, for example, are found throughout the "New World" in various permutations, namely as *vodou* (voodoo) in Haiti, *candomblé* in Brazil, and *santeria* in the United

The Nsuase *kete* drum group performing at an Asante funeral in Kumase, Ghana (Joseph S. Kaminski)

States and Cuba. Textiles and clothing used by African Americans to represent their African heritage frequently draw on the stylistic features of West African formal attire, and characteristics particular to music traditions from Western Africa, especially the prominent use of drumming, are often incorrectly associated with all music from the sub-Saharan region. The Euro-American characterization of African music as "drumming," while not accurate for the continent as a whole, is thus understandable because drumming is the predominant musical practice found throughout West Africa.

Track 31

Site 1: Polyrhythmic Ensemble

First Impressions. Polyrhythmic music can seem bewildering on first listening. The music does not follow "a beat" in the Western sense of the term; that is, there is not a consistent pulsation that can be grouped into an easily identifiable meter. The complexity of the interwoven rhythmic patterns creates a dense sound that is agitating for some listeners, hypnotic for others. High-pitched and low-pitched drums, rattles, bells, and voices all combine to create a multifaceted kaleidoscope of sound that continuously spins the same musical elements into an energetic torrent of "rhythmic melody." While these polyrhythms are difficult to grasp analytically, their effect can be powerful and immediate. Even many novice listeners will be inspired to dance along with this vibrant music.

Aural Analysis. Polyrhythm is a system of musical organization that may be hard to fully grasp for those steeped in European harmonic musical creation, where rhythm tends to be quite simple by comparison. There is no conductor who articulates the basic beat that everyone follows, and there is no notation that the musician reads to play their part correctly. Each participant plays a rhythmic pattern that in and of itself is generally not difficult. Each pattern follows its own time—or what some scholars refer to as a timeline—without respect to the kind of underlying meter found in Western music.

The simplest example of polyrhythm is the "two against three" cross-rhythm. In this example one pattern follows a timeline pattern of two pulses while another pattern provides three pulses within the same time span. You can try this yourself or with a friend. Pat your left hand on your knee with an even duple pulse, "1-2-, 1-2-, 1-2-. …" Now, tap on the book with your right hand to an even triple pulse, "1-2-3-, 1-2-3-, 1-2-3-…," making sure to sound the "1" beats of both pulses simultaneously. As you will quickly discover, while each pattern is simple in and of itself, combining the two is a significant challenge.

When these two patterns are combined, they form a *rhythmic melody* that can be articulated as one idea, namely as a "1-2&3-, 1-2&3-, 1-2&3-…" pattern, in which the "&" falls between the last two pulses of the triplet. Try the cross-rhythm again by starting with the right hand triple meter, tap and just pat your left hand on the "&." This should be easier. Once you've gotten that down, add a pat on the "1" beat as well. The resulting rhythm is the same as the "two-against-three" pattern you initially tried, but the difference is that you are no longer thinking in terms of separate rhythms (duple vs. triple), but in terms of a unified whole (see Table 1). This latter conception is more in line with the way African musicians approach performance: for them, each individual musical element is part of the collective whole. Of course, however Africans themselves perceive of polyrhythmic music, understanding the intricacies of individual timeline patterns leads to a greater appreciation of the music's complexity.

Table 1. Two against Three Cross-Rhythm

Left Hand	1			&		
Right Hand	1		2		3	

DONDO
A double-headed hourglass-shaped drum found in Ghana and elsewhere in West Africa.

MARACA
(Also, SHEKERE)
A gourd rattle from Ghana with an external beaded netting.

Often times it is easier to recognize the individual timeline patterns when the musicians can be seen. In our cross-rhythm example, you can say the phrase "Look to the left" in rhythm as you play. The visual reference of seeing your left hand play the duple pattern will help you to hear it more clearly. Now say, "Look to the right" in rhythm and watch your right hand sound the triple pattern. Your ears will focus on that pattern more clearly. The absence of visual references requires that you listen for different timbres, i.e., drums versus bells, in a musical performance, to hear the individual patterns.

Our example of an Akan recreational band from Ghana features voices and several instruments: the *dondo*, a double-headed hourglass variable-pressure drum played with a

The *mpintin* drum group of the Asantehene in Kumase, Ghana. The *mpintin* consists of several *dondo* (hourglass pressure drum; left), *mpintintoa* (membranophone with gourd resonator; right), and other drums (not pictured) (Joseph S. Kaminski)

hooked stick and capable of producing more than one pitch; the *tom-tom*, a pair of tall, single-headed hand drums; the *afirikyiwa*, an iron clapper bell; and the *maraca*, a gourd rattle with external beaded netting. Together, the musicians create complex polyrhythms, far more difficult to perform than our cross-rhythm example. In order for the musicians to collectively play the correct rhythmic melody, each individual musician must interlock their particular pattern very precisely with the other musicians' patterns.

A helpful analogy is that of a bicycle wheel. One rhythm typically functions as a density referent, a pattern that is like the center of a bicycle wheel. Because drumming ensembles tend to be loud, this part is usually played by a loud instrument with a distinctive timbre, such as a bell or a rattle. When the central rhythm is established, the other musicians play their parts in relation to it; held together by this central reference point, these other parts are like the spokes of the wheel. (Complicating our analogy, however, is the fact that musicians often use more than one reference rhythm to play their part, and thus interlock their pattern with multiple instruments at once.)

Once all the patterns are added together, forming the collective analogous to the rim of the wheel, the music spins along without trouble. If, however, one of the patterns falls out of sync, then the wheel starts to wobble. The music starts to feel unbalanced, and if the troublesome part does not drop out and reenter correctly, the entire ensemble is in danger of "crashing." This frequently happens when amateur ensembles in the United States attempt to play African music. The music may spin easily for a while, but a slight distraction may cause one musician to lose concentration and fail to play his/her simple pattern in sync with the complex whole. As a result, the music falls apart like a house of cards, and the musicians must start over, typically by reestablishing the density referent and then gradually adding the other patterns until the music flows again.

The musicians in our recorded example are obviously quite skilled. The vocal parts follow a call-and-response pattern, while the instruments perform polyrhythm. It is not necessary to know what the specific rhythms are to appreciate the music as a whole. Notating all the parts of the music in a meter, as is frequently done by Western musicians, too often inhibits the listener from hearing this music as an African might. African musicians generally perceive a rhythm without breaking it into even-metered pulses. Nonetheless, focusing on specific instruments and parts can be a helpful way of explaining how polyrhythm works in a complex example such as this.

Turning to the bell (afirikyiwa) part first, we hear a rhythm that could be written as "1-2-3-(4), 1-2-3-(4), 1-2-3-(4) …" This three-pulse pattern with a silent fourth pulse can be heard as a reference point for the hand claps, which sound only once in the course of the bell pattern. When is the clap heard? The clap follows its own timeline, which is just one clap per cycle. If you think in terms of meter, then the clap in isolation can be considered to follow a duple meter, "1-(2)-, 1-(2)-, 1-(2)-…," in which the second pulse is silent.

Alternatively, you can consider the clapping as falling slightly ahead of the "&" after the third bell pulse. But the tempo of the music is moving very quickly. Trying to count "1&2&3&4&, 1&2&3&4&, 1&2&3&4&…" in order to clap in the correct place is difficult and quite unnecessary. If you forget counting and just listen to the bell, you can "fit" your part in much more easily. Sometimes it also helps if you think of a phrase that suggests the rhythm as a whole. For example, try thinking of the rhythm as the phrase, "What do you think?," with the bell part sounding on "What do you" and the clap falling on "think." Easier? It should be, because when you do this you are hearing the rhythmic melody created by the combination of bell and handclaps.

While this discussion places the bell pattern as the reference point in order to more easily hear how the handclaps work in relation to it, the central density referent in our audio example is *actually* the handclaps themselves. The bell pattern, as well as the triplet pattern of the rattle, anticipate the claps, leaving space for them to sound and thus be heard clearly. The call and response form of the voices also references the handclaps to fit their "timeline" in the peformance correctly, emphasizing the third syllable of the vocal phrase in conjunction with the handclaps. The drums (*dondo* and *tom tom*) alternate between high-pitched and low-pitched sounds in a duple pattern, the lower drum corresponding to the handclaps. The alternating drum sounds may either be created by a single drummer, or by two drummers in tandem. Without seeing the performers, it's hard to know which was the case in our example.

Throughout the performance, the drummers slightly alter their patterns to make the performance more dynamic, but then return to their initial pattern. The music spins like a bicycle wheel, or perhaps the aural equivalent of a kaleidoscope: it uses the same "pieces," but changes them just enough to make the music "different" each time the cycle repeats. Once you feel you can identify each of the parts individually, try listening to the whole ensemble again as a collective performance.

Cultural Considerations. Polyrhythm is the basis for musical creation throughout much of sub-Saharan Africa. For those who grow up in cultures where polyrhythmic music is common, understanding comes "naturally" because these insiders are surrounded by it in various contexts, i.e., festivals, funerals, in the market, and so on. For outsiders, however, polyrhythm is perhaps the most impenetrable form of musical organization found in any world music tradition.

Our example is typical of music performance among the Akan—a linguistically based category that includes many ethnic groups, such as the Asante (Ashanti), Fante, and Denkyira—as well as among non-Akan speaking peoples of Ghana, such as the Ewe and the Igbo. Even though they are an amateur group comprised of villagers from a small farming community, the musicians nonetheless display a high degree of music skill. These "recreational bands," as they are often called, play at wakes, funerals, and for annual festivals, as well as for social clubs, special community events such as weddings, and purely for entertainment.

Polyrhythmic ensembles often have a master drummer who oversees all aspects of a performance, including vocal performance and dance. The master drummer knows a multitude of rhythms that work within the performance and is responsible for helping each musician to "fit" within the group. He may briefly play specific timeline patterns that correspond to those of other instruments, establish a new pattern that someone will then follow, or play within the overall polyrhythmic activity, frequently "speaking" with his drum to communicate with the other musicians, dancers, or audience.

The majority of musicians who play in polyrhythmic ensembles learn their craft in an informal manner. Continual exposure to polyrhythmic music throughout childhood gives most an innate sense of rhythm and timing, though only a few become specialists capable of leading an ensemble.

Track 32

Site 2: "Talking Drums"

First Impressions. This example alternates short sections of a text spoken by a young girl with drum passages that seem to mimic the girl's words, both tonally and rhythmically. What we are hearing are the

Adzewa group performing at a funeral at the Asante court in Kumase, Ghana (Joseph S. Kaminski)

famous "talking drums" (which usually are not coupled with spoken word passages; we have chosen this example because it makes the drumming's relationship to speech particularly clear). This is not music for dancing but for listening. In fact, it is not considered music at all, but rather speech in the context of a music performance.

Aural Analysis. Language is an integral part of music performance in Africa. Many African languages are "tonal," meaning that the intonation of the voice is as important to the meaning as the phonemes used.

Although tonal languages are encountered in many cultures, such as China and Thailand, European languages are not tonal. One way to understand how intonation can change the meaning of a word is to listen to the different ways the word "yes" is pronounced, depending on whether it is used as a question or an answer. When it is used as a question, the speaker's inflection has a rising tone, whereas when it is used as an answer the tone is even or slightly falling.

In Ghana, a drum capable of tone-bending is used to imitate the rising and falling inflections of the voice, in order to communicate words through music. Double-headed hourglass pressure drums, such as the *dondo*, are especially equipped to accomplish tonal variation, as the pitch can be altered by squeezing the strings that secure the faces and thus changing the tension of the drum. If the drum can only produce one pitch, two drums of differing pitches can be used to imitate the direction in inflection, e.g., a low pitch followed by a high pitch would convey a rising tone. Additionally, drummers replicate the "speech rhythm" of the words they imitate. By coupling the tones and rhythms of specific phrases, drummers can create surrogate speech comprehensible to native speakers of the language.

A nonnative speaker will not always recognize when linguistic meaning is being conveyed through musical performance. Musicians may do this in a variety of contexts: while praise-singing, announcing the passing of a royal family member, recounting historical events, and so on. These performances may be solo or occur in the context of ensemble playing.

Atumpan drums from Ghana, often used as a speech surrogate (Amy Unruh)

The "talking drums" in this example are *atumpan*, a pair of goblet-shaped, hollow logs with tightly stretched animal skin, typically that of an antelope. The particular piece is in praise of a king and may be performed with or without the vocalist. In this case, the musician speaks in Twi, a common tonal language found throughout Ghana, before playing each phrase on the drums. The novice listener may perhaps be better able to appreciate the musical relationship between the language and music by first listening for the drummer's imitation of the speech's tonal aspect. Keep in mind that rising and falling pitches require two consecutive drum strokes, going from low to high or high to low, respectively.

Cultural Considerations. In Ghana, drums are used as a surrogate for speech to give the words more power and to enable the praise-singing to be heard by ancestral spirits as well as the living. "Talking drum" performances often occur to honor someone of royal lineage or to praise a powerful ancestral spirit. Because royalty are often considered descendents of powerful spirits, praise-singing or praise-drumming frequently accomplishes both objectives in a single performance. Prior to the colonial period, chiefs would include in their entourage musicians capable of rendering poetic performances in honor of themselves and their lineage. This practice has diminished considerably, but is still found among some groups, especially the Asante.

Here is a transcription and translation of the words in our example, which were recited in honor of the king of the Denkyira people, and echoed by the *atumpan:*

Greetings to Those Present

Me ma mo atena ase, Nana ne ne mpaninfoo
I welcome you, Nana and his elders
Owura dwamtenani,
Mr. Chairman,
Enanom ne agyanom
mothers, fathers
ne anuanom a yeahyia ha,
and brethren here gathered
yegye me asona
the response to my greeting is "asona"
Saa atweneka yi fa Odeefoo Boa Amponsem, Denkyira hene ho
This drum language is about Odeefuo Boa Amponsem,
    King of Denkyir
Odomankoma kyerema, ma no nko
Creator's drummer, let it go!

Actual Drum Language Glorifying the King of Denkyira

Adawu, Adawu, Denkyira mene sono.
Adawu, Adawu, Denkyira the devourer of the elephant
Adawu, Adawu, Denkyira pentenprem, Omene sono, ma wo ho mene so
Adawu, Adawu, Denkyira the quicksand, devourer of the
    elephant, come forth in thy light, exert yourself
Pentenprem, ma wo homene so,
Quicksand, come forth in thy light,
Ma wo ho me ne so
Exert yourself, in glory
Kronkron, kronkron, kronkron;
Your holiness, holiness, holiness;
Amponsem Koyirifa, ma wo ho me ne so
Amponsem Koyirifa, come forth in thy light in glory
Ako nana ma wo ho mene so
Grandsons of the Parrot, come forth in thy light
Ako nana a ho a ne mframa mene boo, ma wo ho me ne so
Grandsons of the Parrot whose winds sweep and devour
    even the stones, come forth in thy light
Wo a wofiri dodoo mu
you who came from many,
Wo a wutu a ewiemu den se asamando, ma wo ho me ne so
You who fly and the skies become still like the cemetery

come forth in thy light

Amponsem nana a "odi sika to," atomprada, ma wo ho me ne so

Amponsem's grandson who "eats mashed gold dust," and
uses only freshly mined gold in his daily transactions,
come forth in thy light

Agona adegyekan nana

First grandson of the Agona line,

Wo a wode osee ye oyo

You promise and you fulfill it

De nkoden akyekyere Denkyiraman, de ape no sibre, ma wo ho me ne so

Having fought hard to establish the Denkyira state, and having
found it a place among the nations, come forth in thy light

Ayekra Adebo nana

Grandson of Ayekra Adebo [first ruler, fetish priestess
of Denkyira]

Ahihi Ahaha nono

Grandson of Ahihi Ahaha

Wirempi Ampem nana a owo ntam na yenka, ma wo ho me ne so

Grandson of Wirempi Ampem whose oath is not to be sworn,
come forth in thy light

Otibu Kwadwo nana

Grandson of great King Kwadwo Otibu, [accompanying audio
ends here]

Wo a wode Denkyiraman firii Abankesieso baa Jukwaa,
ma wo ho me ne so

who led the Denkyira people in their great migration from
Abankesieso to settle in Jukwa, come forth in thy light

Odeefoo, ma wo ho me ne so

Benefactor, come forth in thy light

Ma wo ho me ne so Agona,

The Agona clan,

Denkyiraman da wo ase,

The Denkyira state

Yeda wo ase a ensa,

Expresses its endless

Esie ne kagya nni aseda

Gratitude to you

(Text and translation from *Rhythms of Life, Songs of Wisdom: Akan
Music from Ghana, West Africa.* Smithsonian-Folkways SF 40463,
1996, pp. 17–18.)

This translation provides the literal meaning of the message conveyed by the "talking drum"—but these words also have a deeper level
of symbolic meaning that is unintelligible to cultural outsiders. The
attempt to understand the extramusical aspects of musical performance
is one of the most fascinating challenges of ethnomusicology, and of
linguistics and anthropology as well.

Track 33

PALM WINE GUITAR
A popular guitar style known for its association with folk musicians who frequently played for drinks, i.e., palm wine.

HIGHLIFE
A broad label applied to a variety of urban popular music traditions throughout Western Africa, especially in Ghana.

Site 3: Palm Wine "Highlife Song"

First Impressions. Palm wine guitar music is easy-going. While other genres of "Highlife" may use larger ensembles and electrified instruments, the palm-wine style continues to be popular in many parts of sub-Saharan Africa as an amateur musician's pursuit, due to its minimal instrumentation—usually just guitar and a supporting percussion instrument—simple melodic content, and breezy, light-hearted feel. The music inspires you to "sway," rather than dance, as you lose yourself in its hypnotic melodic polyrhythms and lyrical vocal harmonies.

Aural Analysis. Palm wine music features varied instrumentation, but its traditional format uses the acoustic guitar in the central role with an accompanying percussion instrument, oftentimes just a bottle tapped with a small stick or coin. A bass instrument is commonly included to contrast with the guitar, along with a small drum or tambourine for additional rhythmic support. Our example uses the ubiquitous acoustic guitar, a pair of wooden sticks *(claves),* a small drum, and a low-pitched lamellophone called the *apremprensemma.*

Just as it is in Ghanaian drumming traditions, polyrhythm is the fundamental organizational principle grounding this melody-oriented music. Each instrument follows its own rhythmic pattern, which is played continuously with occasional variations. The woodblocks articulate this approach most clearly, by playing a syncopated rhythmic pattern throughout. The *apremprensemma* also plays a repeated patternwhich supports the harmonic movement of the guitar. The guitar focuses on the interlocking of parts played by the thumb and index finger, and essentially establishes two additional "timeline" patterns. The thumb plays a repeating bass pattern primarily using two tones, while the index finger interlocks an upper part that also uses two tones. The combination provides a steady undercurrent of melodic motives that support the vocals.

While its most distinctive feature is its guitar-based sound, palm-wine music is primarily vocal. The lead vocalist comments on a variety of subjects, in this case in the Twi language, and sings the primary melodic line during the sung refrains. These refrains are supported by responding vocalists who add harmony. Because of the polyrhythmic phonic structure, a variety of "meters" can be heard, such as duple, triple, and compound (six beats). The voices seem to follow a triple-pulse pattern, whereas the underlying melodic motives played by the guitar keep a steady duple pulse. The interweaving polyrhythmic melodic lines of the voices and instruments create a gently flowing sound that feels solid, yet never stagnant. It is the unique use of polyrhythm with melody instruments that makes palm wine music one of the world's most distinctive guitar-based traditions.

Cultural Considerations. Palm wine music is considered to be a type of Ghanaian highlife music. The term *highlife* is essentially a broad label applied to a variety of popular musical styles found not only throughout Ghana, but also in several other West African countries.

Early highlife music was strongly European-derived—the name itself refers to the social events of the European elite—and centered on dance bands that played ballroom music, such as foxtrots and waltzes. This music thrived during the 1920s and 1930s and continued its popularity as new Western styles, such as swing and jazz, fused with the African popular sound.

Palm wine represented the opposite end of the social spectrum, and was performed primarily for lower-class audiences who often "paid" the musician by buying him drinks, such as palm wine, an alcohol made from fermented palm tree sap. The palm wine style has long been overshadowed by the dance band sound, but during the 1950s, when Ghana achieved its independence, a few palm wine musicians became well known due to the social commentary included in the lyrics of their songs—most notably Kwaa Mensah, who released hundreds of records. As electrified instruments began to take center stage in the guitar-based highlife bands, palm wine all but vanished. By the mid-1970s, however, a roots music revival had reinvigorated the genre, and artists such as Koo Nimo, heard in our example, achieved a modicum of popularity.

Palm wine guitarist, Koo Nimo, of Ghana
(David Copland)

Palm wine music continues to have a loyal following throughout Ghana and elsewhere in sub-Saharan Africa. Because its primary performers are amateur musicians, it is often compared to acoustic blues in the United States, even though its sound is quite different.

Arrival: Central Africa

The spread of modernization to Central Africa that began during the twentieth century has caused the destruction of much wildlife, most notably the endangered silver-backed gorilla, probably the best-known animal to inhabit the Congo basin rainforests. Even so, this region still maintains some of the most pristine areas of tropical vegetation on the planet and is home to one of the most intriguing and talked-about peoples of Africa, the pygmies.

The total pygmy population is unknown. Whatever their true numbers—estimates range from as few as 40,000 to nearly 600,000—they are spread across several countries in Central Africa, including the Congo, the Democratic Republic of the Congo (DRC), Gabon, Cameroon, and the Central African Republic (CAR). *Pygmy* is a generic term that denotes a diverse population of forest-dwellers who are short by Western standards, being on average less than five feet tall. Contrary to popular belief, many pygmies

Pygmies of the Bangombe ethnic group in the forests of southwestern Central African Republic (Gerhard Kubik)

241

can be found in villages and living as farmers, interacting with surrounding ethnic groups on a daily basis. Many pygmy cultural groups, however, still live within the forest and maintain a nomadic lifestyle.

A number of Western anthropologists, such as Colin Turnbull, have been intensely interested in the typical social structure of nomadic pygmy groups, which provides one of the few examples of an egalitarian society. An egalitarian society is one in which every member of the community is considered equal. Certain individuals may take a leadership role depending on the context, for example, a strong young man may lead a hunting party, but no formal hierarchy exists. Cooperation, rather than competition, guides the social interaction of a pygmy community, because each person is dependent on the others for his or her survival.

Track 34

Site 4: Pygmy Music from the Democratic Republic of the Congo

First Impressions. The aspect of pygmy music that generally first strikes the listener is the intricacy of the vocal performance. The "hoots and hollers" swirl around the listener as the vocalists sing, yodel, and clap. Few instruments are heard in pygmy music, usually only flutes, an occasional rattle or pair of clapsticks, or small drums.

Aural Analysis. Pygmy music is dominated by vocal performance. Although pygmy singing frequently employs a call-and-response organization like many other African traditions, it also features a unique polyrhythmic vocal style that makes it quite distinctive. As with other African traditions, polyrhythm is central to the structure and creation of pygmy music. Since few instruments are used, the voice creates the basic timeline patterns that would be produced instrumentally among other ethnic groups in sub-Saharan Africa.

PYGMIES

A general term describing the many ethnic groups of forest-dwellers in the rain forests of Central Africa.

In our example, performed by a group of Mbuti pygmies from the Democratic Republic of the Congo (DRC), a set of clapsticks plays a repetitive rhythm with minor variation that acts as the aural center. If you consider it to be in a duple meter (though the musicians by no means think in terms of meter) with eight pulses, the basic clapsticks rhythm would be 1 2 - 4 - 6 7 -. A lead vocalist provides the essential lyrical content necessary for the ritual while the rest of the singers interweave a complex polyrhythmic structure. As with instrumental performance elsewhere in Africa, each person performs a short repeating melodic pattern. Some performers may sing a basic theme, while others sing variations. Each pattern interlocks with and overlaps those of the other performers, resulting in the unique rhythmically dense layering of melodic lines typical of pygmy vocal performance. Handclaps or instruments may function as a density referent, as in our example, but often the basic theme acts as the aural center for the performers. Though soloists are not always distinguished, call-and-response singing often occurs in addition to the polyrhythmic singing.

Cultural Considerations. The nomadic lifestyle and egalitarian social structure characteristic of pygmies are reflected in their musical performances, which are considered community activities. Each person plays an "equal" role, contributing his or her individual talents to the collective performance. The creation of complete melodic lines and thick rhythmic density requires the interlocking of parts, and thus a dependency on other performers. The pygmy's nomadic lifestyle is also reflected in pygmy music's emphasis on the voice; after all, large instruments are not easily transported, but the voice can travel anywhere.

Communal performances among the pygmies usually include dance as well as music, especially circle dances. These dances are often performed for ritual occasions, such as puberty ceremonies, or in anticipation of an important event, such as a hunt. As animism predominates in the pygmy spiritual belief system, music is often sung in conjunction with related ritual activity.

Victoria Falls on the border between Zambia and Zimbabwe (Max T. Miller)

Arrival: Zimbabwe

Much of Zimbabwe consists of vast grasslands inhabited by a variety of animals, such as impalas, hippopotamuses, crocodiles, hyenas, and baboons. The rainy season occurs from November to March, creating an average annual rainfall of between twenty-three and thirty-three inches. Mining is a major industry, though most people earn a living as farmers, growing tobacco and various foodstuffs. The great Victoria Falls is found in Zimbabwe's western region bordering Zambia, and is one of the most attractive tourist destinations anywhere in Africa.

Known as Rhodesia until achieving independence in 1980, Zimbabwe was a colony of the British. Consequently, the official language is English, though many native languages are spoken as well. The predominant indigenous languages include Ndebele and Shona. The Shona ethnic group has been of particular interest to ethnomusicologists due to a distinctive musical instrument that they play known as the *mbira dza vadzimu*.

Site 5: Mbira Dza Vadzimu

First Impressions. The gentle sound of the *mbira dza vadzimu* (often simply referred to as *mbira*) is much like that of a child's music box. The music seems to float in an endless cycle, punctuated by an occasional somber cry from the performer. The sound of a small rattle helps maintain a steady pulse, while a distinctive "buzzing" sounds

ZIMBABWE

MBIRA

A general reference to lamellophones found throughout Africa, in particular those common to the Shona and other ethnic groups from Zimbabwe.

Track 1

243

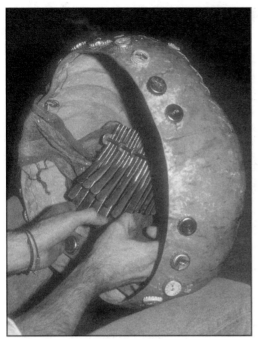

Mbira dza vadzimu (lamellophone) from Zimbabwe

BIRA

A spirit possession ceremony of the Shona ethnic group from Zimbabwe.

throughout the performance. This is hypnotically soothing music, that makes you feel as if you were rocking in a chair on the front porch watching and listening to heavy raindrops fall from the eves to puddles of water below.

Aural Analysis. It is accurate to describe the *mbira dza vadzimu* as a music box. As with a Western music box, tones are produced through the plucking of flat metal strips of various lengths. These instruments are known as lamellophones, a subclassification of the idiophone family. Similar instruments are found among many ethnic groups throughout sub-Saharan Africa and are called by various names, such as *likembe* or *kalimba*. The term *mbira* has become popular in the Western world to denote all of these lamellophones.

Performers pluck the tongs of the *mbira dza vadzimu* with their thumbs and forefingers. The vibrations then carry through the instrument to the large resonating gourd. Small seashells or pieces of metal, such as bottle caps, are affixed to the resonator to create the "buzzing" timbre, a characteristic sound of many instruments found throughout the continent. Oftentimes bottle caps are also found on a metal bridge attached to the keyboard. The percussion instrument that enters shortly after our example begins is the *hosho*, a gourd rattle with internal beads. Usually, two *hosho* are used to maintain a steady cross-rhythm (two against three) throughout a performance.

Mbira dza vadzimu music has a minimum of two parts. The lead part, known as the *kushaura*, is most often played in the higher range of the instrument and is most easily heard. The *kutsinhira*, or "following" part, is typically played on the lower-pitched keys of the instrument. These two parts interlock and overlap to create polyrhythm. In our example, the higher *kushaura* pattern plays with a triple pulse, while the lower *kutsinhira* pattern follows a duple pulse. The accents of the *hosho* fall on the duple pulse with a deemphasized interlocking pulse.

The *hosho* reinforces the "following" part, and thus helps clarify the underlying harmonic rhythm of the piece. Harmony is a term most commonly associated with European music traditions (see Chapter 10), but harmonic movement can be perceived in *mbira dza vadzimu* music as well. A *mbira dza vadzimu* piece often has four harmonic segments that repeat with endless variations. In our example, each segment has four beats articulated by the lower *kutsinhira* pattern and the *hosho* accents.

Try to hear the four four-beat segments of this *mbira dza vadzimu* song. Tap the duple pulse of the *hosho* with your right hand. Once you have established this reference point, listen closely to the upper *kushaura* melodic pattern. The melodic pattern starts in the high end of the instrument's range and then switches to slightly lower pitches. When you hear the melodic line of the lead part lower in pitch, start counting to four with your right-hand fingers. This change in the melody of the *kushaura* part marks the middle point of the four segments. The theme begins when the melodic line rises again. When you hear the melody return to higher pitches, use your left hand to count each segment as your right hand counts the "one" pulse again. The first two four-beat segments of the song use higher notes, while the second two segments use lower notes before the entire theme is repeated.

The *kushaura* and *kutsinhira* parts provide the basic structure of the music. Variations are often added, especially to the lead part. A single musician may even add a third "middle" part to increase the rhythmic density of the music. The ability to add variations and rhythms is the sign of a skilled performer. A second *mbira dza vadzimu* performer may also add variations and interlocking rhythmic patterns to the basic theme, as is heard in the background of this example.

The musician may also sing. In our example, the musicians' voice enters just after the second pulse of the first harmonic segment and drops out at the end of the four-segment theme. In most *mbira dza vadzimu* performance contexts, an accompanying singer is the primary focus. Call and response is common in group singing, but solo vocal performances are frequent as well.

Cultural Considerations. The Shona use the *mbira dza vadzimu* in a variety of contexts, such as storytelling, entertainment, and rituals. The most important ritual context is the Shona spirit possession ceremony known as *bira*. The example heard here is from a *bira* ceremony in which ancestral sprits are invited to appear to the community through the body of a spirit medium. These spirits are believed to guide and protect the community members in their day-to-day activity.

Perhaps because of this association with spirit possession, the Shona consider the *mbira dza vadzimu* a specialists' instrument, one that requires a high level of skill for performance in ritual contexts. Many *mbira dza vadzimu* musicians are "called" to learn the instrument by an ancestral spirit and thus feel obligated to become proficient at performance to help facilitate possession at these rituals. Certain pieces are only to be played for these ceremonies and are prohibited from performance in other contexts.

Arrival: *Uganda*

UGANDA

Uganda, along with Kenya and Tanzania, borders Lake Victoria, the second-largest freshwater lake in the world. Chimpanzees roam through its jungles, and leopards hunt in its grassland regions. Most inhabitants are agriculturists, though fishing provides a significant income for those along the lake. Thatched huts can still be found in rural areas, though as the country develops they are becoming increasingly rare.

Uganda's known history dates to the fourth century A.D., when it was a major crossroads connecting northern Nilotic cattle herders and southern Bantu agriculturists via the Nile river, which flows from Lake Victoria through the region. The kingdom of Bunyoro became a powerful unifying force in the late fifteenth century, but was eventually overshadowed by the kingdom of Buganda, which became the region's major power in the early nineteenth century. The kings of Buganda (known as *kabaka*) soon had to deal with British colonialists, who arrived on the heels of the Christian missionaries who had begun proselytizing throughout the region during the middle of the nineteenth century. By 1890 the kingdom and the areas around it had become a British protectorate, and Uganda's present boundaries were set.

After achieving independence in 1962, the country survived some rather notorious political and economic misdirection. Idi Amin, a brutal ruler, seized control of the government in 1971 and orchestrated a reign of terror that abolished the former kingdoms, ousted more than 70,000 "Asians," and massacred more than 300,000 Ugandan citizens. By the end of the decade, he was at war with neighboring Tanzania, whose forces, allied with Ugandan rebels, drove him from power. Since then, Uganda has struggled to regain its footing as a regional power and trade partner.

Track 2

AKADINDA
A large, heavy log xylophone from Uganda that uses interlocking patterns that can approach nearly 600 beats per minute.

Site 6: Akadinda Xylophone

First Impressions. This music is like a sped-up film of a busy New York City street corner during rush hour. Looking for "space" in this continuous welter of sounds is futile. It is crowded and unrelenting. This is the type of music that inspired minimalist composers such as Steve Reich, Philip Glass, and Terry Riley, who in the 1970s and 1980s created music that wove simple, repetitive phrases into intricate, interlocking, densely textured patterns of sound.

Aural Analysis. The *akadinda* is a large, heavy log xylophone with between seventeen and twenty-two bars. The heavy wooden bars are arranged on banana tree trunks that rest on the ground. Long sticks are driven into the ground to separate the bars and keep them from shifting sideways during performance. The largest bars can be more than two feet long, and the instrument itself is nearly seven feet long. *Akadinda* are also found in sets, in which each instrument produces pitches in different ranges, so that all together between four and five octaves are covered. The lowest ranged *akadinda* is often placed in a shallow pit, which serves as a resonator and gives the instrument a deeper sound.

While most xylophones in sub-Saharan Africa have bars with a flat surface, *akadinda* bars frequently have a carved "dip" in the center, and *akadinda* performers may strike the center of the bar at the "dip," which gives the instrument its unique "hollow" timbre. The mallets are either made of a straight piece of soft wood or have a "hook" shape to better strike the center of the bars.

Akadinda performance requires substantial interlocking of parts.

Two groups of three men stand opposite each other with the xylophone between them. The first group plays a repetitive rhythmic pattern, typically in octaves, while the second group fills in an interlocking pattern to create a thick polyrhythmic structure. *Akadinda* performance usually also involves a third group of performers playing yet another interlocking pattern, and as a result the tempos of such music can approach nearly six hundred beats per minute. This triple-interlocking technique is unique to *akadinda* performance, whereas other traditions have fewer performers and are only based on double-interlocking of rhythmic patterns.

Performers on the *amadinda* xylophone of Uganda
(Moya A. Malamusi)

It is nearly impossible to decipher this fast-moving music merely by listening to it. To unravel the intricacies of the interlocking parts really requires seeing the performers in action. Nevertheless, as with all polyrhythmic music, just by listening you can begin to hear some of the subtleties. The music may initially strike you as chaotic, but if you focus on just one or two distinct sounds, you can start to hear how they work within the whole.

In our example, the highest-pitch strand is played with a steady pulsation on just one pitch in what can be thought of as a duple meter. While this pulse is part of a larger pattern, following it is a first step toward hearing individual parts. In the low-pitched patterns, a longer cycle can be heard that can be articulated as a pattern of high (H), center (C), and low (L) pitches, and can be rendered as: HC-HC-HL-HC-HCCC-. To put it in "Western" terms, the high pitch anticipates the main beat, which corresponds to the earlier single-pitch pattern in duple meter. This "beat" falls on the center pitches of the first two pairs, the low pitch of the next, the center of the following pair, and the first and third center pitches of the four-beat finish. You might sound this out as "&1-&1-&Low-&1-&123," with the main beat on the ones and three.

Again, keep in mind that this way of singling out particular patterns is not how the African musician thinks about musical creation. A Ugandan musician is concerned with how the patterns "fit together," rather than with how they can be "pulled apart."

Cultural Considerations. Xylophones are among the most common instruments found throughout sub-Saharan Africa. Many, such as the *balafon* common to West Africa, are small enough to be carried and played as solo instruments. Others, such as the *timbila* of Mozambique, exist in a variety of sizes and are typically played in larger ensembles. The polyrhythmic nature of xylophone performance combines with the use of melodic pitches to create some of the most complex music on the planet.

Uganda is home to many xylophone traditions, but the *akadinda* is perhaps the most difficult and highly respected of them. Before the colonial period, *akadinda* musicians were part of the musical entourage that accompanied the *kabaka* (king) of Buganda. Their music was considered "royal" and was not played outside of courtly functions. The

JALI
(Also, JELI; pl. JALOLU)
A poet/praise singer
and oral historian from
the Mandinka of
Western Africa.

melodies played on the *akadinda* are believed to be derived from vocal music; thus, through their association with specific texts, *akadinda* performances could convey a story or offer praise of the *kabaka* without the need for a singer. Our example would be understood by Ugandans to have a specific meaning, despite being purely instrumental; according to the Africa volume of the *Garland Encyclopedia of World Music,* it "celebrates the rough justice meted out to Gganga, a young page of the palace who was caught sexually molesting the Princess Nassolo" (p. 824). The *akadinda* (consisting of seventeen or twenty-two individual keys, usually played with three interlocking parts) is closely related, both physically and in its performance practices, to the *amadinda* (only twelve individual keys, and played with two interlocking parts), a type of xylophone found in Uganda and other nearby regions, though usually in less formal contexts.

SENEGAL-GAMBIA

Arrival: *Senegal-Gambia*

The Gambia is a sliver of a country embedded in the southern portion of Senegal at the western edge of the African mainland. Approximately two hundred miles from east to west and only thirty miles wide from north to south, the country surrounds the mouth of the Gambia River, which flows into the Atlantic ocean. Most of the population are agriculturists, with the primary crop being peanuts. Because the country was formerly a British protectorate, English is common, as is French, the national language of Senegal, which surrounds the Gambia on three sides. Indigenous languages are commonly spoken as well, especially Wolof, Jola, and Mandinka, the predominant ethnic groups of the Senegal–Gambia.

Of particular musical interest in this region is the tradition of the *jali* (or *jeli*), a type of specialized musician associated with the Mandinka populations. In Mandinka society, the *jali* (*pl., jalolu*) serves as an oral historian, a role held by similar artisans throughout many parts of Western Africa. The history of most African populations is passed from generation to generation through oral tradition rather than through writing or other forms of empirical evidence. Though members of the community are usually familiar with the major events of their ethnic group's history, the responsibility of maintaining this history usually falls on one particular family lineage. In some societies, such as the Mandinkas, this activity is considered a family trade, involving skills and knowledge that are passed down just as a blacksmith might pass on his skills to the next generation.

KORA

A harp-lute or bridge-harp played by a jali during his poetic recitation.

Site 7: *Jali with Kora*

First Impressions. The music of the *jali* offers proof of the diversity of African music, which is frequently thought by outsiders to invariably revolve around drumming. No percussion is heard at all, merely a

Track 3

vocalist and his instrument, a plucked chordophone known as the *kora*. The opening flourishes on this instrument lead to a steadily repetitive melodic groove. This churning repeated pattern underlies the rapid-fire delivery of the vocalist. He has something impor-tant to tell you, and displays his virtuosity with words rather than melody. His shouting praises are meant for everyone to hear.

Aural Analysis. *Jalolu* play a variety of instru-ments, such as the *balafon*, a small xylophone, or the *koni*, a lute, depending on their geographic location and preference. The *kora*, however, is the most dis-tinctive of *jali* instruments and one of the few examples of a harp-lute in the world of musical instruments. The *kora* is constructed of a large res-onating calabash (a type of gourd), which is cut so that the face of the instrument can be covered with cowhide. A wooden pole is passed through the top of the calabash and fixed with leather straps that are used for tuning the strings. Most *kora* have twenty-one strings that are made of nylon fishing line, though they were once made from thin strips of twisted antelope hide. The strings are fixed to the bottom of the resonator, pass over the bridge, and

Kora (lute-harp) performed by *jali* (praise singer) Amadu Bansang
(Roderic Knight)

are attached to the individual tuning straps on the neck. While most lutes have the string plane running parallel to the face of the instrument, the strings of the *kora* are arranged in two planes, both running per-pendicular to the face. Thus, the *kora* is organologically classified as a harp-lute, or can be described as a bridge harp as most harps do not have a bridge.

The perpendicular planes of strings enable the performer to use the forefinger and thumb of the left-hand to play one set of strings while the right-hand forefinger and thumb play the other. The strings are tuned in a manner that requires the per-former to alternate from left to right planes to produce ascending and descend-ing scales. The left-hand strings, for exam-ple, might be thought of as odd numbers, while the right-hand strings are even. To ascend consecutively, the per-

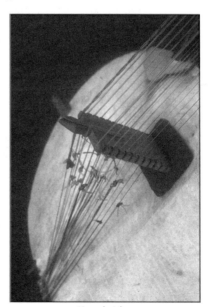

Kora bridge

former must interlock between left and right string planes. Two stick "handles" are placed on either side of the neck, which the performer grips to keep the instrument vertical. The musician may tap these pegs to add a percussive sound to his performance. Finally, sometimes a *kora* will have a metal plate punctured with metal ringlets attached to the bridge. As the *jali* plays, the string vibrations cause the ringlets to vibrate, producing a "buzzing" timbre that is common to many sub-Saharan African instruments.

The performer generally sits to play, resting the *kora* on the ground or on his lap. A performance has two distinct sections-- referred to as *birimintingo* and *kumbengo*--that allow the performer to show both his skills as a musician and as a praise singer. The *birimintingo* sections are marked by the flourishing solo runs of the *kora*. A performer may solo for an extended period of time in order to collect his thoughts, or survey the audience, or merely for his own enjoyment.

During the *kumbengo* sections, the performer plays a steady repeated pattern on the *kora* while singing praises that relate the history of the Mandinka or of individual family lineages. The steady rhythm of the *kumbengo* is maintained throughout the performance and underlies both the *birimintingo* solos and the vocalist's melodic passages. The *kumbengo* rhythm is yet another demonstration of the tendency of African musicians to use polyrhythm in performance.

In our example, the *kumbengo* is established after a short introductory *birimintingo* "flourish." A low and high part can be heard. The lower part provides a root rhythmic pattern, while the upper part interlocks with it to produce a cross-rhythm. The repetitive nature of the *kumbengo* allows the performer to focus on his singing without thinking much about his *kora* performance. During *birimintingo* sections, the *kumbengo* is usually maintained in the lower part with the thumbs while the fingers play the upper melodic runs.

The melodic contour of the vocal part can generally be described as descending. The *jali*'s praises start high and fall to a long sustained tone at the end of the phrase. The performer does not sing continuously; rather, the vocal phrases are separated by instrumental sections that allow the musician to collect his thoughts before the next bout of praise-singing. The text setting tends to be syllabic with little or no melisma. A performance will usually end with a final birimintingo section.

Cultural Considerations. Among the Mandinka, a person's surname will often indicate the nature of his family trade; Kouyate or Suso are well known names for *jali*. Even if a person chooses another occupation, his family name indicates a link to ancestors who at one time practiced that trade. Once a *jali* learns the name of an individual, he can extemporize a musical performance that praises the contributions to the community of that individual, and of his family and ancestors. For example, Smith is a common name in the United States. The name is derived from the word "Blacksmith," a common occupation of settlers to North America. As a result, many of these early settlers in this trade took the name Blacksmith, shortening it later to Smith. A present-day "Smith" is not likely to be a blacksmith, but in tracing his genealogy, he is likely to reveal that his ancestors pursued such an occupation.

The texts of praise songs are extemporaneously drawn from a pool of poetic verses learned over the course of a lifetime. Praise songs are most often reserved for members of royal lineages or, in modern times, for wealthy patrons, though almost anyone can be praised in this fashion. The person praised responds with gifts, usually money, which enables a *jali* to earn a living.

As already mentioned, the texts of *jali* praise songs may relate to a specific individual, but frequently they deal more generally with the great deeds of the Mandinka people and with Mandinka history. In our example, "Salieu Suso," the *jali* sings of a Mandinka warrior who battled against the Fulani, another ethnic group in West Africa. The warrior, Kallafa (or Kelefa), captures many prisoners who refuse to return to the Mandinka stronghold. Kallafa ties the prisoners together and has to "pull" them back home, and in so doing causes great dust clouds on his approach to the kingdom. The people mistake the dust clouds for smoke from fire until Kallafa is within sight. After recounting this episode, the *jali* then sings of the great deeds Kallafa performs as he enters the city. While the *jali's* praises are improvised, they are based on a set of phrases and images known as "Kuruntu Kallafa" ("Kallafa Pulling"), which has been passed down through generations.

Through such stories, the *jali* is able to pass on knowledge of historical events to future generations and enhance community pride in the accomplishments of the Mandinka peoples. More specifically, however, since it is the descendents of Kallafa who are especially honored in this song, the song's performance obligates those descendants to reward the musician for his gracious praises. This is done by "spraying" him, either by placing money on his forehead, usually after a performance, or by putting money in his instrument through the resonator hole.

"Spraying" is important not only for the economic subsistence of the musician, but also for the well-being of the community. A common belief throughout sub-Saharan Africa is that ancestral spirits can be brought into the presence of the community by invoking their names. These spirits have the power to help the community by keeping people healthy, maintaining good crops, warding off natural disasters, and so on. If, however, the spirits are not respected properly, they may become malevolent and cause disease, drought, or harmful accidents. The *jali's* ability to praise the names of so many hundreds of ancestors is viewed by the Mandinka populations as a kind of supernatural power. A great warrior spirit, such as Kallafa, can protect the community from outside evils, or, if not respected properly, reveal his anger by, for example, making community members sick or causing a fire to spread throughout the village. Thus, the *jali* must be appropriately compensated for his services as a praise-singer in order to help ensure the security of the community.

Arrival: The Republic of South Africa

THE REPUBLIC OF SOUTH AFRICA

The Republic of South Africa is the southernmost country on the African continent. Just smaller than twice the size of Texas, the country

AFRIKANERS
The descendents of
Dutch colonialists
in South Africa.

has a diverse landscape marked by tall mountain ranges that separate its high interior plateaus from its extensive shoreline. As with much of sub-Saharan Africa, wildlife, including unique small black rhinoceroses, ostriches, and baboons, are found in several game reserves, such as the more than 7,500-square-mile Kruger National Park along the Mozambique border. Parts of the Western Cape (north and northeast of Cape Town) resemble the wine country of Europe.

South Africa is home to diverse ethnic groups of a variety of races. The main ethnic groups comprise more than three-quarters of the population and include the Zulu, Xhosa, Sotho (North and South), Tswana, Tsonga, Venda, and Ndebele. White South Africans are primarily of British and Dutch descent. In addition, the country is home to more than a million people of Asian Indian ancestry as well.

Squatter's area in Soweto Township near Johannesburg, South Africa

Archaeological evidence dates South Africa's earliest inhabitants, *Australopithecus africanus*, one of mankind's earliest ancestors, to more than three million years ago. More recent historical evidence indicates that hunter-and-gatherer groups, such as the San and Khoikhoi, inhabited the region along with Bantu-speaking peoples from West Central Africa, who settled as agriculturists and are believed to be the ancestors of the modern Nguni peoples, who include the Zulu, Xhosa, and other ethnic groups. Though explorers passed through the region in the late fifteenth century, the first colonialists to settle there arrived only in 1652. These settlers were Dutch and are known as the Boers, meaning "farmers." They landed at the Cape of Good Hope, where they established a fort and a provision station for trading ships on their way to Asia. In 1814 the British bought the Dutch territories and within a decade thousands of British colonialists arrived, who soon demanded that English law govern the region's affairs. Many of the descendants of the Boers, known as Afrikaners, refused to accept the new government's authority and began migrating north during the 1830s, shortly after the British abolition of slavery in 1833, with plans to reestablish their own colony. By this time, indigenous peoples had asserted their dominion over the northern territories, and thus the migrating Afrikaners became embroiled in conflicts with various African groups.

The best known of the African kings who held sway in the northern regions was the Zulu warrior Shaka (1787–1828), who had uprooted many indigenous groups in the process of establishing one of the area's

SHAKA
Zulu warrior king of
the late eighteenth and
early nineteenth centuries
who reigned over much
of South Africa.

most powerful kingdoms. Shaka's repressive ruling tactics and impressive war machine have made him one of the most important historical figures in South Africa's history. Though viewed as a cultural hero by many, for others he is a tyrant, whose remembered brutality still influences spiritual and social matters. His successors were defeated by the Afrikaners, who soon established their own independent territory where they maintained strict segregation of blacks and whites.

After the discovery of diamonds in 1867 and of gold deposits by 1886, the Afrikaner and British communities were continually at odds. By 1902 the British had overwhelmed the Afrikaner armies with a "scorched-earth" policy that destroyed Afrikaner farms and forced many women and children into concentration camps where an estimated 20,000 Afrikaners and roughly 14,000 indigenous Africans died. To help end the war with the Afrikaners, the British agreed to allow the Afrikaners to continue their practice of strict segregation. By the middle of the twentieth century, this social separation was instituted as a set of laws, referred to as Apartheid (Afrikaans for "separation"), which resulted in the segregation not only of blacks and whites, but also of "Asians" (i.e., East Indians) and "Coloureds" (people of mixed racial descent). Many Afrikaners attained positions of political power and succeeded in promoting governmental support of apartheid legislation.

Apartheid policies were maintained for the next few decades in the face of increasing disapproval from the international community. During this time, several anti-Apartheid organizations struggled to find ways to end the oppression by South Africa's white minority of the rest of its population. The African National Congress (ANC), in particular, began seeking nonviolent means for ending racial and social discrimination in South Africa after its inception in 1912. Opposition to the Apartheid government finally reached its peak in the mid-1980s after half-hearted reforms resulted in numerous riots and hundreds of deaths. The government found itself in a perpetual state of emergency as it tried to maintain order and eventually lost the support of nearly all its foreign investors.

Nearly bankrupt, unable to maintain civil order, and finding itself increasingly isolated from the international community, the Apartheid government finally became untenable. In 1989 Frederick Willem De Klerk, soon after accepting the South African presidency, began serious reforms that eventually led to an end of Apartheid in 1992. He and newly freed ANC leader Nelson Mandela received a joint Nobel Peace Prize in 1993, for their cooperation in ending racial segregation and Apartheid rule. Mandela became the first truly democratically elected president of South Africa the following year.

APARTHEID
A policy of racial segregation and political/economic discrimination against non-European in South Africa.

Site 8: Mbube Vocal Choir

First Impressions. The lush harmonies of Zulu choral singing are immediately attractive to most Western audiences. No instruments are heard, just an all-male choir with a dominant lead vocalist and bass-

Track 4

MBUBE
A genre of choral
performance common
among migrant workers
of South Africa.

heavy backing vocals. The performance is obviously well-rehearsed, with precise attention paid to tone, timbre, and rhythm. Though these are amateur vocalists, they have a professional sound. This is music for the stage, not an informal communal event.

Aural Analysis. Though some female vocal groups exist, most *mbube* is performed by all-male vocal groups. A solo voice (referred to as the "controller") leads the group (called the "chord"), following the call–and–response organization typical of sub-Saharan African vocal performance. In this case, however, the responding group may also sing backing harmonies as the lead singer "tells his story." This is heard throughout this example, in which the lead vocalist laments the suffering of black people in apartheid South Africa.

By varying the interaction between the lead vocalist and the group, the performers are able to create definite changes in mood. In our example, the opening verse follows a call-and response-format, with the group responding to the leader's call in harmony. This section is then repeated. In the next section, the lead vocalist is featured, as supporting group harmonies establish a beat behind him. The third section models the first with the group responding to the lead vocalist then blending with this voice in the concluding harmonies. This section is also repeated. In the final section, the lead vocalist makes his final declaration before the "swooping" harmonies of the group carry the music to its conclusion.

While Zulu choral singing existed prior to the colonial period, its harmonies and strong cadences (closing phrases) reveal European musical influence. A distinctive feature of the *mbube* sound, however, is an emphasis on the lower vocal range. (The vocal ranges are described using European musical terminology: namely, *soprano, alto, tenor,* and *bass.*) The lead vocalist generally sings in a middle or upper register, though bass leads are found as well. One or two voices in the choir will represent the other upper parts, while the rest of the performers sing bass. For every one of the upper parts, there are often five or six bass voices that give the music its rich harmonic foundation. This distinctive emphasis on the lower range of voices is considered to be a characteristic of Zulu choral performance that predate the colonial period.

The *mbube* style is also distinctive for its frequent changes in tempo. The lead singer commonly begins his phrases in a "loose" manner approximating speech, that is, he does not emphasize a definite beat. The ends of vocal phrases often feature a slight slowing of the tempo, and a short pause afterward that does not follow the established beat. The closing repeated refrain follows a tempo different than the rest of the performance, especially in competition pieces when the performers walk off stage (the footsteps of the exiting vocalists can be heard toward the end of our example).

Cultural Considerations. As with much of Zulu traditional culture, the roots of *mbube* are considered to have originated during the lifetime of Shaka. Whether this belief is accurate, it is an indication of the degree to which Zulu people identify themselves with this great king. Shaka was regarded not only as a powerful warrior, but also as a great dancer and strong singer. Much of the Zulu traditional repertoire is often attributed to him, as he was said to have composed many songs to help keep morale high among his soldiers.

More recent influences on the sound of *mbube* are traceable to the 1920s, when migrant workers began holding evening singing competitions as a form of entertainment after long arduous days of hard labor in the gold and diamond mines found throughout South Africa. Many unique music traditions came from the labor camps, known as townships, that many blacks were forced to live in during the years of Apartheid. The segregation was so strict that armed guards were often found at the gates leading to the townships. The townships were also divided into black and "coloured" (Indian or mixed descent) encampments. Soweto, meaning "Southwestern Townships," is a vast area near Johannesburg where millions of people live in housing that varies from cardboard shacks to mansions. This area was home to Nelson Mandela before his imprisonment in 1962.

By the late 1930s, the nighttime *mbube* singing competitions were characteristic of the Zulu encampments and hostels. One of the earliest recordings of this style of singing, "Mbube," was made by Solomon Linda and his Evening Birds vocal group. The song became very popular and later inspired two American hits, "Wimoweh" by the Weavers (1951) and "The Lion Sleeps Tonight" by the Tokens (1961). The song's title came to categorize the "bombing" vocal style (so-called for its frequent descending melodic contour) exemplified by Solomon's group, with its deep four-part harmonies and soprano lead voice.

The best known derivative of the *mbube* style is *iscathamiya*, popularized by Ladysmith Black Mambazo, a vocal group from Ladysmith, South Africa, which first gained international prominence

The well-known South African vocal group, Ladysmith Black Mambazo, ⓒ performing onstage in New York City (© Jack Vartoogian/FrontRowPhotos)

for their collaboration on American artist Paul Simon's *Graceland* album (1986), and soon after won a Grammy for their own album, *Shaka Zulu* (1988). The name *iscathamiya* means "to walk like a cat" (i.e., stealthily), and is derived from a description of the dance that accompanies the singing. This style of dancing uses "tiptoeing" choreography and flowing gestures, in contrast to traditional Zulu dancing, which frequently features hard stamping and vigorous "warrior" movements. The *iscathamiya* sound reflects this subdued dance style and tends to be "softer" and "smoother" than *mbube*.

Questions to Consider

1. How do the principal musical manifestations found in sub-Saharan Africa reflect the collective community and encourage group participation?

2. How is polyrhythmic music created in sub-Saharan Africa?

3. What linguistic elements are required to make a drum "talk?"

4. In what ways do Highlife and other types of popular music in sub-Saharan Africa draw on traditional music for inspiration?

5. What role does music play in maintaining oral histories and legitimizing royalty?

6. In what ways has music in South Africa reflected the particular history of the country?

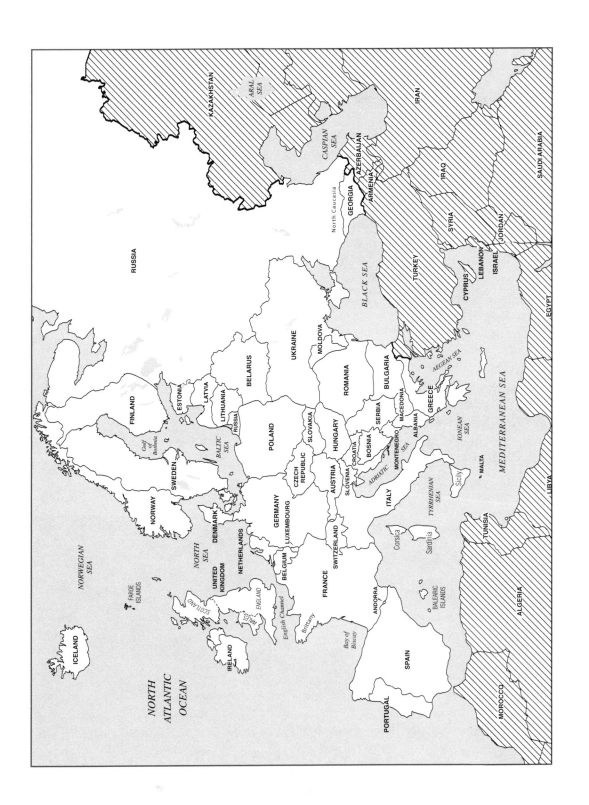

Lübeck, center of the 14th century Hanseatic League, is traditionally entered through the Holstentor, a mid-15th century double tower

CHAPTER 10

Europe:
Harmony and Hierarchy

Background Preparation

Exactly what do we mean when we say "Europe"? If a friend were to tell you, "I'm going to Europe this summer," he or she would probably mean "Western" Europe, especially the United Kingdom (casually called Britain), France, Germany, Italy, Spain, and perhaps Switzerland and Austria. When a news reporter uses the term *European Union*, he or she refers not to all European nations, but to a specific group of countries (which may even come to include Turkey, a country not considered geographically part of Europe). In music history courses, when we refer to "European music," we mostly mean the "classical" tradition of "Western Europe." What, then, is Europe: a political entity, a geographical unit, a cultural area, or all of these things?

There are today some forty-one nation-states that constitute Europe, ranging from Russia, the world's largest country, to miniature city-states like Monaco and Luxembourg. While forty-one may seem like a high number, before many modern nations such as Germany and Italy were created in the nineteenth century, Europe consisted of dozens, if not hundreds of tiny statelets headed by various kings, princes, dukes, and so forth. Many of the territories that are now part of nation states were also successively part of the Roman, Holy Roman, and Austro-Hungarian Empires—though the "unity" of these empires was tenuous at best. During the nineteenth and early twentieth century many nation states were cobbled together out of linguistically, culturally, and ethnically distinct regions. This process has recently begun to reverse itself: over the past ten years or so, many small nations, particularly in Central and Southeast Europe, have been formed after breaking away from larger ones. Even so, there are numerous other ethnic groups that would prefer to have their own nations as well, including the Basque, the Russyns, the Vlachs, and other minorities.

Europe is also home to several groups who are not associated with any one region, but are spread throughout the continent. One such group are the Rom—usually called "Gypsies"—a traditionally migrant people who originated in India. In those countries where the Rom have settled, whether they live in their own communities or are integrated into the mainstream, they have become an important part of the indigenous musical culture. Historically at least, the position of Jews in European society was similar; like the Rom, they were simultaneously insiders and outsiders and were important for their music making.

Sorting out Europe's peoples is challenging, but one possible way to subdivide Europeans is by language family. While most Europeans speak languages that belong to the great Indo-European family, some, such as the Finns, Hungarians, and Estonians (members of the Altaic family) and perhaps the Basque as well, speak non-Indo-European languages. Most Indo-European languages are members of one of four families: Germanic, Italic (or Romance), Balto-Slavic, and Celtic. In addition, there are at least three Indo-European languages that do not belong to any of these families: Greek, Albanian, and Rom. The below table classifies nations according to their primary language; some nations, such as Switzerland and Belgium, have more than one official language, however.

European Countries by Language Group

Germanic	Italic (Romance)	Slavic	Slavic	Celtic
Germany	France	Russia	Macedonia	Ireland (in part)
Austria	Italy	Latvia	Serbia	Wales (UK)
Switzerland	Belgium	Lithuania	Montenegro	Scotland (UK, in part)
Denmark	Spain	Belarus	Slovenia	Cornwall (UK)
Sweden	Portugal	Poland	Croatia	
Norway	Romania	Czech Republic	Bosnia-Herzegovina	**Independent**
United Kingdom	Andorra	Slovakia	Georgia	Greece
England (UK)	Monaco	Moldova		Albania
Scotland (UK)		Ukraine		
Netherlands		Bulgaria		
Iceland				
Luxembourg				

While Ireland is listed in the Celtic category, relatively few Irish people still speak Gaelic. Celtic languages are also spoken (or were until recently) in the highlands and islands of Scotland, in French Brittany, in Wales and Cornwall in England, and in small pockets elsewhere.

While categorizing European peoples into language groups does help us to understand certain broad strands in European music, it is also essential to understand that none of these strands is isolated. As Hungarian composer and ethnomusicologist Béla Bartók (1881–1945) discovered early in the twentieth century, national musics cannot realistically be

In Telgart, Slovakia, the musicians are of Gypsy (Rom) descent, but they continue to play music similar to that collected by Béla Bartók in the early twentieth century

considered self-contained and unique unto themselves. Bartók came to see that an understanding of Hungarian music was impossible without accepting its obvious relationships with the musics of rival neighbors such as the Serbs, Romanians, Bulgarians, and even the "hated" Turks. National boundaries within Europe have changed so many times over the years that it is all but impossible to think of any area as culturally "pure." On the other hand, it is also difficult to think of all these over-lapping regions as comprising one "culture." Bearing all this in mind, is it ever reasonable to use the term "European music"? The short answer is, probably not.

"Classical" versus "Folk"

As with music everywhere else in the world, music in Europe is closely connected with notions of nation, region, ethnicity, and social

An Inside Look
Morag MacLeod

I was on the staff of the School of Scottish Studies at the University of Edinburgh, Scotland, from 1964 to 2001. I was appointed as a transcriber of Scottish Gaelic texts and later of music attached to Gaelic song texts, and gradually moved up

Morag MacLeod, transcriber and editor of Gaelic song

to the status of Senior Lecturer in Gaelic Song, my position on retirement. During my time at the school, I became very much involved in its series of publications of cassettes and CDs, becoming responsible to a large extent for selection and annotation of items, but especially in the transcription and translation of song texts. The School's audio publications have been produced by Greentrax Limited, and the productions with which I was particularly involved were: *Gaelic Bards and Minstrels,* a double CD of William Matheson's vocal illustrations of two types of poetic metre in Gaelic, 17 of one, 18 of the other; *Seonag NicCoinnich* (Joan MacKenzie), a CD of 21 songs sung by one of Gaeldom's favourite singers; and *Clò Dubh Clò Donn,* a collection of popular songs by a variety of singers. I am, howev-er, particularly interested in the unique way of singing the metri-cal Psalms of David using precenting, or "putting out the line," which is practiced in Gaelic-speaking congregations of the Presbyterian church in Scotland. Another of my special interests is *waulking* songs, which were used to accompany the finishing process in the production of Harris Tweed, a cloth made from the wool of black-faced sheep in the Scottish Highlands. The cloth is rubbed and thumped onto a wooden board by the hands of a team of women who use the songs as a way of coordinating the rhythms. These items appear on *Gaelic Psalms from Lewis* and *Waulking Songs from Barra* respectively. A few years before retirement, I became editor of *Tocher,* a magazine for publishing items from the archives, with each issue usually focusing on a theme, in Scots, Gaelic, or English. The magazine started life as a quarterly, but teaching and other commitments have made it difficult to get one out in a year. At the same time it is a much more substantial production now.

I now live on Scalpay, a small island in the Hebrides where lovely, varied views of hills, rivers, and the sea compensate for difficulty of access to colleagues, libraries, and other facilities to be enjoyed in Edinburgh.

class. The all-too-freely used terms *classical, folk*, and *popular* derive from European conceptions of how music exists in society. It is important to realize that these categories exist only in peoples' minds, and are based on implicit value judgments and hierarchical ways of thinking. The term *classical* refers to what is considered the highest class of music. This music is judged by standards that privilege complexity and "sophistication," and that rate a long composition for a large ensemble a "greater" achievement than a short piece for a small ensemble. Because music scholarship has primarily focused on this sort of music and music scholars primarily work in universities, music students in universities, colleges, and conservatories worldwide study "classical" music almost exclusively. Consequently, for them "classical music" is European music—and, by the same token, European music *is* "classical music." Because classical music only flourished where there were wealthy courts and aristocracies, little of it is found in southeastern Europe or much of eastern Europe, or in other places where such contexts were mostly missing, such as Ireland, Finland, Portugal, and Greece. The areas formerly under Ottoman control, some until the early twentieth century, naturally could not develop a "classical" music in the European tradition.

What the field of ethnomusicology adds to the study of European music is a focus on what is usually designated "folk music," as well as an anthropological perspective on classical music. *Folk* is a demographic concept based on the assumption that there are "folk" and "nonfolk." What is implicit is an evaluative hierarchy that places "folk music" in a humble position relative to "classical music." The notion of a "folk"— and by extension of "folk music"—is an outgrowth of Romanticism, an aesthetic orientation that flourished in the latter part of the eighteenth century and throughout much of the nineteenth century. Romanticism originated in the northern sectors of Europe, especially German-speaking areas, and was viewed as an antidote to the domination of "classical" French and Italian culture. Most spoken drama at the time was in French and most opera was in Italian, even in places like England and "Germany" (in quotes because Germany as a unified nation did not yet exist). Germanic peoples were made to feel that their culture and languages were inferior to Mediterranean cultures and languages—but with the rise of Romanticism they began to assert their cultural independence.

The term *folksong* (*Volkslied* in the original German) was coined by the philosopher Johann Gottfried Herder (1744–1803), who believed that the essence of a culture was in its peasants—whose pure souls were uncorrupted by the Industrial Revolution that had created poverty, pollution, and the destruction of traditional patterns of life. The "folk" were the antidote to the ills of the modern world. This notion stimulated a great deal of field research into Northern roots, especially seen in the collecting of folk tales and folk songs. Many of these tales and songs were published in influential collections, such as *Grimm's Fairy Tales* and *Des Knaben Wunderhorn* (The Youth's Magic Horn), a compilation of songs collected from the "folk" by Arnim von Achim and Clemens Brentano early in the nineteenth century. *Folk*, then, is a category that existed only in the minds of "nonfolk" advocates such as Herder.

Our view, however, is that European music cannot really be divided into discrete "folk" and "nonfolk" categories—there is, rather, a continuum from the music of the "lowliest" villager in Slovakia to the most sophisticated music of the aristocracy in Paris. Indeed, some of the historical musics studied in music history classes as part of the "classical" evolution were actually the music of non-aristocrats. Likewise, in Europe "classical music" was everyone's music: reed bands organized by factory workers played excerpts from symphonies, amateur choruses sang excerpts from operas, and player pianos and other automatic musical instruments included classical excerpts on their rolls and barrels.

When its regions are considered together and all layers of its music are explored, Europe is revealed as an incredibly musically rich continent. Extensive as the classical orchestral instruments are, their number pales in comparison to the endless variety of instruments seen at the village level, from medieval survivals to the many exotic instruments that came to Europe from the Middle East via the Ottoman

France's Chartres Cathedral built between 1194 and 1260, has mismatched towers.

Empire and Moorish Spain. Collectively, the various vocal styles found throughout Europe feature most of the sounds humans are capable of creating. "European music," then, encompasses everything from lullabies sung by grandmothers to operas, and its sounds range from the plaintive melody of a shepherd's flute to the power of a massed orchestra or pipe organ.

Planning the Itinerary

Europe consists of so many individual nations—many of which are home to several distinct peoples—that it is impossible in this brief survey to explore more than a few examples of European music. Of necessity, our itinerary must be highly selective.

Though Judaism exists in parts of Europe and Islam is important in the southeast, particularly Bosnia and Albania, and increasingly significant in France and Germany, Europe is predominantly Christian—thus we must include some music that is related to Christianity. From Europe's vast array of attractive and sometimes unique instruments, we have chosen two that allow exploration of several broad issues: the Russian *balalaika* and a representative of the *hurdy-gurdy* family. Because bagpipes are pervasive throughout Europe—and not just a Scottish phenomenon—including bagpipes is a must. We have chosen two types in order to contrast two methods of operation. Bulgarian choirs, particularly women's choirs, have been widely noticed outside Bulgaria, and for this reason we have chosen to include a discussion of them. Because we felt that, as much as possible, each of Europe's different regions should be represented, our European sojourn ranges far afield: it includes musical examples from the British Isles, and throughout the European mainland.

GREECE

Arrival: Greece

Greece can be seen in two ways: (1) as one of the classical cultures that forms the foundation of Europe, and (2) as a modern nation that shows much influence from its centuries under Ottoman Turkish rule. Classical Greek civilization centered on Athens from about 800 B.C. to 300 B.C., then spread throughout the Macedonian Greek Empire of Philip of Macedonia and his son, Alexander the Great, the latter of whom was responsible for spreading "Hellenistic" culture over a vast area of Central Asia and North Africa. When the succeeding Roman Empire divided into West and East, Greece became part of the latter. After 1453, when it came under Ottoman Turkish rule, Greece was profoundly influenced by its conqueror, and modern Greece, especially in the north, reflects this in its cuisine, architecture, and musical instruments.

Modeled after early Christian churches in the Eastern Roman Empire, this modern Greek Orthodox church is in downtown Athens

Site 1: Byzantine Chant

First Impressions If you were expecting something like the music from *Zorba the Greek* or *My Big Fat Greek Wedding,* than Byzantine Chant, an austere form of eastern religious music, might seem surprising. It is typical of the religious singing of the Greek Orthodox Church, also called the Byzantine Rite, as practiced in Greece. The presence of a drone pitch gives this singing an "otherworldly" feeling and calls up visions of an ancient church bathed in the colored light of stained glass windows.

Aural Analysis. In churches where a formal order of service is observed—what is called *liturgy*—the spoken and sung texts are regulated year round according to church season and feast. Among the most important seasons is Christmas, celebrating the birth of Jesus of

Track 5

265

Nazareth. The present example is a Greek Orthodox Christmas hymn, the text of which is "Come, faithful, let us see where Christ was born."

The first sound heard—let's call it E for simplicity (actually Ab)—continues to be held as the second (and upper) part begins the melody. This held part is called a drone. While drones can sound above or below the melody, low drones such as this are a typical feature of Byzantine chant. The melodic part ascends using pitches E, F, G#, A, B, C, D, and the upper octave, E, thus restricting the melodic range of the chant to one octave. Rhythmically, the chant is simple, with only two durations, the longer one being twice the length of the shorter one, creating an overall feeling of duple time, though not rigidly so. About three quarters of the way through there is a brief passage in which the C becomes a C#, giving the chant a "major" feel—but almost immediately C# begins alternating with C natural, and in the last part of the chant the scale returns to its original form.

High above the sea on a sheer cliff, the 14th century Monastery of Simonopetra (Simon and Peter) is one of dozens scattered throughout mountainous Athos peninsula, technically the Monastic Republic of Athos, a roadless enclave belonging to the Greek Orthodox Church

The scale heard here does not conform to any standard scale form known elsewhere in Europe. It is neither major nor minor, nor any variant of either type. Byzantine chant theory centers around a complex system of modes that provides both scales and a broader basis for melodic composition, a system somewhat like that of the Indian *raga*. These modes are called *echoi* (singular, *echos*). The scale of the present example is described as *kathisma*, chromatic fourth mode.

Cultural Considerations. Note that only male voices are heard. Following a strict interpretation of Paul's admonition to the Corinthians, "Let your women keep silence in the churches; for it is not permitted unto them to speak" (I Corinthians, 14:34), the early churches forbade women from speaking, singing, or preaching; this is still true in some denominations today. In the Greek Orthodox Church, the leadership is exclusively male.

Today's Greek Orthodox Church represents the survival of the old Byzantine Church, originally centered in Byzantium (later called Constantinople). For centuries, the Byzantine, or Eastern, Church was more or less unified with the Western Church under the control of the Pope in Rome. In 1054, however, the Eastern Church split off, and from then on it was controlled by a Patriarch based in Constantinople. After the fall of Constantinople in 1453 to the Ottoman Turks, Eastern Christianity retreated back into Europe, and as the Turks expanded into southeastern Europe bringing Islam with them, the center of the Eastern Church retreated to a mountainous peninsula off northern Greece called Mount Athos. Isolated from the Turks and Islam, thousands of monks built marvelous monasteries, many high above the sea and accessible only by dangerous mountain trails. Today Athos peninsula remains a technically independent religious entity, the Monastic Republic of Athos, administered by the Greek Church, mostly lacking roads and other forms of development, and is strictly off limits to women. There, a diminished number of monks preserve the Church's oldest traditions, including its chant.

This chant is also heard throughout Greece in numerous "Greek Orthodox" Churches and in some overseas churches. Byzantine chant, therefore, is one of the oldest continuously living song traditions in the world, linking us directly to the splendor of the old Byzantine churches still seen in modern Istanbul and in other areas of Turkey. The church buildings in which it is heard are also of great interest. In the northern city of Thessaloniki (recall Paul's epistles to the Thessalonians in the Greek Bible's New Testament), chant is still heard in mosaic-filled churches that date back to the fifth and sixth centuries, as well as in exotic-looking churches from the thirteenth century built in Byzantine style. During services, the small male choir stands near the front around a large wooden lectern reading from a large chant book. The congregation takes no part in the chanting, because in this ancient tradition, mass is said *for* the congregants, not by them.

Arrival: *Spain*

SPAIN

The beaches and bullfights of sunny Spain attract more than forty million visitors per year. The many holy days of the Roman Catholic calendar present numerous opportunities for *fiestas* throughout the country. Perhaps the best known of these includes the "Running of the Bulls" during the Feast of San Fermín celebrations in July in the northern city of Pamplona, reflecting the zest for life that permeates Spanish culture. Olive groves and vineyards are plentiful, especially in Andalusia in the south, where *cantaoras* sing late into the night to the accompaniment of a flamenco guitarist, and *tapas* bars serve wine and piquant delicacies until dawn.

Separated from the rest of Western Europe by the Pyrenees Mountains that form the border between the Iberian Peninsula and France, Spain exhibits a unique blend of European and North African cultural characteristics. The Romans occupied the peninsula for roughly seven hundred years (second century B.C. until the sixth century A.D.)

An architectural gem in World Heritage city Toledo, Spain, the 13th century Church of Santiago del Arrabal is described as Mudejar, that is, a blend of Visigothic Christian (Mozarabic) architecture and Arabic decoration

before the Christian Visigoths (Germanic peoples) spread into the region, reducing it to a nominal vassal state of Rome. In addition, most cities had a Jewish quarter after the destruction of the great Temple in Jerusalem in 70 A.D. The Moors (Muslims) invaded from North Africa in the eighth century A.D. and occupied much of the peninsula for more than seven hundred years (711–1492), diminishing Roman Catholic influence in Spain and establishing the Western front of the Islamic realm.

Arabic dominance began to recede in the eleventh century as the few remaining Christian rulers, encouraged by the Crusades, began to reestablish control of the peninsula. While Muslims, Christians, and Jews had lived in relative peace under Moorish rule, religious fervor came with the reconquest of Spain, resulting in the infamous Inquisitions (1478), the expulsion of the Jews and Moors (1492), and the aggressive conversion practices of the Roman Catholic missionaries who followed Spanish Conquistadors to the Americas beginning in the sixteenth century. The Spanish kings soon established Spain as a colonial world power dominating much of the "newly discovered" Western hemisphere.

Until recently Spain, along with Portugal, was the most isolated region of Western Europe. Long years of internal conflict and dictatorial leadership slowed its modernization and political development. Only after the death of General Francisco Franco in 1975 did Spain begin to catch up with rest of Western Europe, a process hastened by the country's gradual integration into the European Union. As a result, Spain still retains a strong "Old World" sensibility that is felt less and less in other parts of the continent.

Track 6

Site 2: Flamenco

First Impressions. Flamenco is a vibrant music. The powerful voice of the singer, the percussive performance of the guitarist, and the rhythmic clapping and heel-stomping of the dancers as onlookers shout "¡olé!" create a synergetic experience that propels the participants to heights and depths of emotion that can bring tears of both sadness and joy within the span of a single song. To feel this passion is to understand flamenco, no matter if you hail from Spain or elsewhere.

Aural Analysis. Flamenco includes one of the most virtuosic of guitar styles. Guitarists must have incredible dexterity with both hands in order to convey the power and delicacy the style demands. Performers use the fleshy part of the fingers for some sounds, while the characteristic strummed "flourishes" of flamenco and much of the solo work are produced using the fingernails. Percussive accents are commonly added by slapping the face of the guitar to emphasize a melodic passage or articulate a specific rhythm.

Flamenco dancers and guitarists perform in a club in Cadiz, Spain (Robert Garfias)

The guitar accompanies the *cantaora* (vocalist). The singer can be either male or female, though male performers predominate. The singer frequently sings in the higher reaches of his vocal range. This creates a strained timbre that encourages the sense that he is "giving it his all" by singing to the point where his voice nearly breaks. The heavy use of melisma is also a key feature of the flamenco singing style. The heavily ornamented melismas are intended to have an emotional effect, by making the singer sound as if he is crying, almost wailing, as he empties his soul into song. The lyrical content of flamenco is deeply personal, with death and devotional love, either accepted or rejected, being common themes.

Handclapping (*palmas*) as well as finger-snapping (*palillos* or *pitos*) are common in traditional flamenco performance. These gestures articulate the basic beat, though frequently the onlookers interlock their claps to create a thick rhythmic density that heightens the tension of the music. The dancers also add a rhythmic vibrancy through their toe- and heel-stamping choreography.

Flamenco music generally emphasizes minor keys, and triple meters are most common. Our example follows a twelve-beat pattern divided into two six-beat phrases, which can be heard from the opening guitar chords. The home chord changes on the third beat and returns on the ninth beat. The handclaps add syncopation before slipping into an interlocking pattern. The vocalist enters on the ninth repetition of the twelve-beat pattern and sings through three measures. Soon the tempo picks up dramatically as the dancers infuse their own energy into the music. While this particular example does not do so, many flamenco performances shift the meter from triple to duple and back to triple frequently within a single song. Rhythmically free passages are also often interspersed within a performance.

Improvisation is a key element of flamenco, on the part of the guitarist, vocalist, and dancers. While the vocalist generally leads a performance, any of these three elements, voice, guitar, or dance, can change the mood of a performance through shifts in meter, tempo, dynamics, or rhythmic complexity. This stark change in mood is best

FLAMENCO
A Spanish musical tradition featuring vocals with guitar accompaniment, characterized by passionate singing and vibrant rhythm.

illustrated in our example by a passage that occurs shortly after the dancers increase their tempo and rhythmic density. In this section, the guitarist plays alone, the dancers adding occasional foot stomps and finger-snaps to accent the rhythm. This quieter passage uses a different harmonic progression with a slightly fluctuating tempo. After a solo dance interlude, the performance then slips back to its initial energy level as the tempo increases, the original guitar accompaniment returns, the *cantaora* sings, and the dancers increase their intensity.

Cultural Considerations. Most Spanish musicians would likely assert that flamenco is the most passionate music on the planet. While a high degree of musicianship is essential, successful performances are judged according to the level of emotional intensity, or *duende*. Vocalists are expected to pour every bit of their emotion into a performance, whether the intent is to express extreme sorrow or exultation, and the goal is to achieve a state of catharsis for themselves and their listeners.

While modern flamenco is frequently performed on a concert stage, traditional contexts for flamenco are much more intimate. The ideal setting is a *juerga*, an informal event in which the separation between musicians and audience is blurred. Everyone participates, if only with clapping and shouts of encouragement known as *jaleo*. These gatherings can happen almost anywhere, on a side street, in a *tapas* bar, at a musician's home, and so on. They usually last late into the night, often until dawn, and are characterized by much laughter and a family feeling.

Flamenco was born in Andalusia, the southern region of Spain. Originally, flamenco featured the voice alone, in a song form known as *cante*. This traditional Spanish style of singing incorporates the strained timbre and heavy use of melisma typical of Arabic vocal traditions, reflecting the more than seven hundred years of Arabic influence in the region. Arabic influence is also reflected in the style's generally vibrant rhythmic activity. *Cante* is typically divided into three forms—deep, intermediate, and light—determined by the subject matter and rhythmic structure. *Cante* performances frequently feature audience participation in the form of handclapping, dance, and vocal interjections.

The earliest evidence of flamenco in its modern form dates from the early nineteenth century, when Gypsy (*gitano*) musicians were observed singing the *cante* forms with instrumental accompaniment. The private "jam sessions" of the Gypsy musicians in the bars and brothels of some of the larger cities, such as Sevilla and Madrid, caught the attention of upper-class clientele. By the 1840s *Cafés cantantes*, clubs devoted specifically to flamenco performance, became popular throughout the country. The guitar became the standard accompanying instrument, a choice reflecting both the Arabic emphasis on intricate melodic passages and the European taste for harmony.

Since this time, flamenco has continued to develop in new ways. Theatrical productions of flamenco dance and song are common, and flamenco troupes are frequently found on international tours. Since the 1960s some artists have fused flamenco with other music forms, such as

DUENDE

A Spanish word meaning "passion," which refers to an emotional quality considered essential in performances by Spanish Flamenco singers.

jazz and rock, to create popular sounds with a global appeal. Artists such as Paco de Lucía and the Gypsy Kings have helped to widen the audience of flamenco through their innovative compositions, while remaining true to the roots of the music and the spirit of *duende*.

Arrival: Russia

RUSSIA

Russia is the largest country on the planet. While more than 80 percent of its territory is in Asia, it is European Russia, the part west of the Ural mountains, that represents Russia's political and cultural identity to the outside world. The two largest cities, Moscow and St. Petersburg, are the destinations for most tourists, who discover a unique juxtaposition of the architecture of Tsarist Russia, with its pastel-colored Baroque-like palaces and onion-domed Russian Orthodox churches, and Soviet Russia (1917–91), which exchanged color for monumental concrete buildings and statues of steel. Since the dissolution of the Soviet Union in 1991, Russia, still a world power, has striven to transform itself from a totalitarian Communist regime to a Democratic free market society. This transition has not been easy, but the Russian people are resilient, having dealt with many dramatic political changes in their history.

In Moscow, Russia, St. Basil's Cathedral, built by Tsar Ivan the Terrible between 1555 and 1561, sits at the edge of Red Square (Andrew Shahriari)

During the nineteenth and twentieth centuries, Russian nationalism inspired much artistic development, especially in music. Many Russian "art music" composers, such as Nikolai Rimsky-Korsakov (1844–1908), Pyotr Ilich Tchaikovsky (1840–93), and Igor Stravinsky (1882–1971), are counted among the greatest composers of the last two centuries. While many urbanites of modern Russia would rather consider these composers and their music as the essence of Russian musical identity, the work songs, *chastushki* (playful songs), and dance tunes of the Russian countryside inspired many of the most revered Russian composers and are in fact more indicative of Russia's distinctive musical culture.

BALALAIKA
A triangle-shaped, fretted plucked-lute from Russia.

Site 3: Balalaika

First Impressions. The "chattering," high-pitched sound of the *prima balalaika* is apparent even in a full *balalaika* orchestra, as is heard in

Track 7

our. This music may remind you of a German Oktoberfest as it has a "polka" feel. Though the instrumentation is certainly different, such dance genres are also a staple of Russian folk music.

Aural Analysis. As is typical of musical performance in Europe, harmony is the key musical element. In this case, the major instrument heard is the *balalaika*, the most popular folk instrument in Russia. The *balalaika's* most distinctive feature is its triangular-shaped resonating body. The instrument can be found in varying sizes, but the most common type is the *prima balalaika*, which has a wooden sound box a little more than a foot long on each side and a fretted neck that extends the instrument to nearly three feet. Most *balalaika* have just three strings. Two strings are tuned to the same pitch or an octave apart, while the third string is tuned to a fourth above the root. The strings are usually made of steel, nylon, or gut and are played with the fingers only, though sometimes a leather plectrum may be used.

Members of the St. Nicholas Russian Orthodox Church Balalaika Orchestra from Mogadore, Ohio, use instruments in several sizes. In the front row are seen the typical *prima balalaika* in triangular shape and the *domra* with a round body

Our example is performed by the St. Nicholas Church Balalaika Orchestra, which was founded in 1985. They perform a variety of folk music from Russia, though the ensemble hails from Mogadore, Ohio, in the United States. As is typical of European folk music, the melody is relatively short and repetitive. The double-bass *balalaika* plods along with the basic harmonic structure as smaller-sized *balalaika* and *domra* "chatter" out the melody. An accordion helps to fill in the harmony and adds another timbre to the overall sound. Of note is the near absence of "percussion" instruments other than the occasional rattling of a tambourine.

Cultural Considerations. Though polyphonic vocal ensembles are more characteristic of Russian folk music, the *balalaika* has become the distinctive visual symbol of Russian musical identity. The predecessor of the *balalaika* is a similar lute, known as a *domra*, which has a round resonator. The earliest records of the *domra* date to the seventeenth century. The primary performers on the instrument were wandering minstrels and jugglers who performed for weddings, festivals, and other celebratory activities. These entertainers, known as *skomorokhi* ("jesters"), commonly appeared in costume, dressed up as, for example, an animal or a witch, in order to attract an audience.

Unfortunately, the ruling powers of the time issued decrees that put strict restraints on various peasant activities, including the performance of music. In 1648 the Tsar ordered that all music instruments be burnt and decreed that anyone who dared to play music would be flogged and exiled to the outer reaches of the kingdom. The *balalaika* likely developed as a consequence because it was easier to make a triangular-shaped body than a round one, it could be more quickly made if a musician was forced to abandon his original instrument for fear of persecution. After the harassment of Russian musicians subsided in the eighteenth century, the instrument became quite popular for its distinctive look and characteristic "chatter-like" sound. The name *"balalaika"* is derived from the Russian word meaning "to chat," and is intended to contrast the instrument with the violin, which is considered to "sing."

The bass balalaika performed by a Russian street musician (Rex Shahriari)

The *balalaika* was most commonly used as a courting instrument but also was found among court musicians. Its popularity waned during the early nineteenth century with the introduction of the harmonica, until its cause was picked up by a Russian nobleman, Vasily Vasilyevich Andreyev (1861–1918), who is today nicknamed the "Father of the Balalaika." Andreyev first became intrigued by the instrument after hearing one of his workers play it. In the spirit of Russian nationalism, he promoted the *balalaika* as the distinctive musical instrument of Russia and succeeded in modernizing the instrument so that it could play a classical repertoire. Andreyev had five differently sized *balalaika* created, the largest being the size of a double bass. He debuted his ensemble in 1888 to great acclaim and by 1892 had won the support of the Russian royalty. His Russian Balalaika Orchestra toured Europe and even visited America.

Andreyev encouraged the dissemination of the *balalaika* among the populace by teaching soldiers and common folk to play the instrument, often giving them free instruments. Under Soviet rule, the *balalaika* continued to play a vital role in promoting Russian nationalism, and by the end of the twentieth century, it had regained its prominence as the most popular instrument in the country. Today it is frequently sought after by tourists and is used by *balalaika* "combos," which are popular in major cities throughout Europe. The film, *Dr. Zhivago,* featured the *balalaika* in its soundtrack helping to familiarize Western audiences with the instrument. Balalaika orchestras, such as the St. Nicholas Balalaika Orchestra in Ohio, have become an important means of expressing Russian identity for people throughout the United States and Europe.

SCOTLAND

Arrival: Scotland

Although Scotland is often thought of as a country, in reality it has not been one since 1707; rather, it is a constituent part of the United Kingdom (or Great Britain), along with England, Wales, and Ulster (Northern Ireland). During the Roman occupation of Britain—from the mid-first century until the fourth century—what is now Scotland was inhabited by the much-feared Picts and was considered a wild land. To keep the Picts at bay, the Romans built a stone wall from sea to sea across northern England during the 120s A.D.; remnants of this construction, known as Hadrian's Wall, can still be seen today.

Scotland was a hardscrabble land for most of its inhabitants, especially those trying to eke out a living in the rocky highlands or the bleak, peat-covered plains of the islands, the areas of "traditional" Scottish Gaelic-speaking highland culture. People working the land for a subsistence living were sheltered in "blackhouses"—sod or stone huts with thatched roofs and little light, but much smoke. At the end of the eighteenth century, the English gentry who owned most land in Scotland decided that raising sheep was more profitable than renting land to small farmers, and forced the Scots from their land, in what is called The Clearances (1790–1845). Some of the Scots pushed off their land died, while many others were forced to migrate. A segment of these Scottish immigrants settled permanently in northern Ireland, while others remained in Ireland for a time, then went on to North America to start a new life. Indeed, the "Scots-Irish" provided the backbone of Appalachian culture in the United States, while other waves of migration brought Scottish culture to Canada as well.

The medieval stronghold of the Macraes, Eilean Donan Castle in Dornie, Scotland, was reduced to rubble in 1719 by the English and only restored in the 20th century to become Scotland's most photographed castle

Modern Scotland, home of two great cities—industrial Glasgow and learned Edinburgh—is now as prosperous as England. Thanks to "devolution," the political process by which the United Kingdom's four regions have obtained more local governance, Scotland is able to define itself to a far greater degree than it could in the eighteenth century, when it was under the English yoke.

Site 4: Highland Bagpipes

First Impressions. Most North Americans have heard the Scottish bagpipes (called "pipes" for short), perhaps at a funeral, or at a festival, and certainly on television. Scotland's highland pipes have become almost inseparable from public funerals, especially those for police and other public officials. If you've ever been around someone playing these pipes, you know they are more appropriately played outdoors, because their strident tones are rather deafening. As with most bagpipe performances, our example features a highly ornamented melody together with constant drone pitches. Most of the time pipers play "Scotland the Brave" or "Amazing Grace." They stand or walk proudly, dressed in colorful kilts, with a *dirk* (dagger) in their sock and greater or lesser amounts of regalia, depending on whether or not they are connected with the military or police.

Aural Analysis. The Scottish highland pipes, called *an piob mhór* in Gaelic, are just one of dozens of types of bagpipes found throughout Europe, North Africa, and Turkey, though they are the best known. European bagpipes can be of two kinds: (1) lung-driven, and (2) bellows-driven. The highland pipes are the former and the Irish *uilleann* pipes (see Site 5)) are the latter.

Bagpipes illustrate well the concept of a "folk instrument," in that all their parts (melodic chanter, drone pipes, and bag windchest) can be obtained locally. The melody line is created on a *chanter,* a wooden pipe with finger holes powered by a double reed made of cane, which is set in vibration when air passes through it. The European double reeds, unlike many of those found in Asia, are not particularly loud, making them difficult to hear in outdoor situations. Further, they require a good bit of lung power. The bagpipe solves these problems with a reservoir of air that is driven through the double-reed pipe and additional drone pipes with single reeds by arm pressure. The air is stored in a bag traditionally made from the skin, stomach, or bladder of various common farm animals, especially goats and sheep. Cloth—usually a tartan—covers the animal-skin bag to hide its "unpleasant," if natural appearance. The

Track 8

BAGPIPES
A reed aerophone consisting of an airbag, *chanter* (melody pipe), and drone pipes.

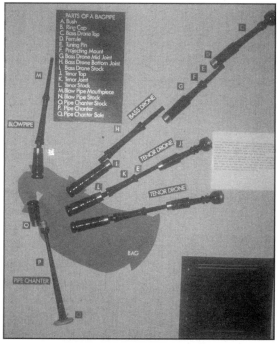

An "exploded" display of Scottish bagpipe parts in the Pipe Museum on the Isle of Skye off the northwest coast of Scotland

apertures—or leg holes—into which the chanter and the three drone pipes were placed were a natural part of the animal. To fill the bag with air, the player blows into a fifth pipe, which incorporates a nonreturn valve to prevent the air from escaping when the piper is drawing more breath. When the player inflates the bag through the blowing pipe and squeezes the bag with his left arm, air is driven through the drone pipes and *chanter,* producing the exciting din of highland bagpipe music.

To operate the bagpipes, the player must first fill the bag with air and begin pressing on it. The three drone pipes—one bass and two tenor—are the first part of the instrument to sound. These use single reeds comparable to those used with the clarinet or saxophone, and the pipes are built in sections, allowing the player to tune them differently by lengthening or shortening them (shorter being a higher pitch, longer being a lower pitch). The drone pipes often sound squawky at first, until full pressure gives them constant pitches. Once a full, steady drone is achieved, the performer begins playing melody on the *chanter.*

The most familiar bagpipe music consists of tunes, such as "Scotland the Brave," "Mull of Kintyre," and "Amazing Grace." There is also much dance music for bagpipes, including jigs, reels, marches, waltzes, and even polkas, as well as the famous "sword dance." Little known but highly developed is the *pibroch* (*piobairèachd* in Gaelic), an elaborate form of theme and variations, in which the "theme" is actually a "ground" (a sort of bass line) rather than a tune. In all cases, the piper embellishes the melody extensively with quick ornamental notes made possible by the motions of the fingers on the *chanter.* This suggests that ornamenting a melody is as much a physical act as it is a melodic one, since the typical ornaments are remembered more in the muscles than in the brain. In this example, piper Sean Folsom plays three tunes: "Busk Busk Bonnie Lass," a slow air; "Faill Illo Agus O'Ro Eille," a *waulking* song (traditionally sung while working on wool); and "The Kilt is My Delight," a reel. You can distinguish the pieces easily because the first is slow, the second is faster, and the last is still faster.

Virtually all Scottish bagpipe music is in meter. In some *pibroch* compositions, the tempo may be very slow but with extensive ornamentation, so that the basic pulse is difficult to ascertain. Individual pipers or, more likely, pipe bands are often accompanied by bass and snare drums, especially for marching. Virtually all highland piping is done outdoors because it is so loud. Some have called the highland pipes the "war pipes," and claim that pipers led clan troops into battle. Whether this is true or not, the term "war pipes" comes from a misunderstanding of *mhór,* a Gaelic word that sounds like war but means "great."

Cultural Considerations. The old Gaelic language and culture, part of the larger Celtic culture and family of languages, typically represents Scotland to the outside world, but Scotland also includes the lowlands where a form of English has always been spoken, the English of poet Robert Burns that is difficult for outsiders to understand. Gaelic culture, to the extent that it survives today, is found in the north and northwest and in the Hebrides Islands off the northwest coast, including Skye, Lewis, Harris, Uist, and Barra. The health of Gaelic culture depends on the survival of the language, and in recent years, despite efforts to reverse the trend, there has been a steady decline in the num-

PIBROCH

(pronounced pee-brohk): A form of Scottish bagpipe music with an elaborate theme-and-variations structure.

ber of native speakers. Much of the classic Gaelic culture is now seen only on special ceremonial occasions and in tourist shows.

Inextricably linked to Scotland, the highland pipes serve as a symbol of Scottish identity, both visually and aurally. While it is true that piping was associated with clans and with both martial and festive occasions, the original Scottish musical instrument was not the

Scottish highland pipers march for visitors in Portree, Skye, in the Hebrides Islands off the northwest coast of Scotland

pipes but the Celtic harp. In early times Scottish culture was an extension of Irish culture, and the harp was the basic instrument of both. Bagpipes are no more intrinsically Scottish than Scotland's other major instrument, the fiddle (or violin). Indeed, the highland pipes can be dated back only to the sixteenth century.

In North America the highland pipes have come to be linked with funerals, particularly those of public officials and policemen killed in the line of duty. Pipers and pipe bands routinely play "Amazing Grace," a melody that originated in North America and is not known to be Scottish. Highland pipes have also become associated in North America with St. Patrick's Day, a celebration of Ireland's patron saint. While it is true that Irish police bands have used the highland pipes since the nineteenth century, this association is a stretch. It is as if all Celtic areas have been melded together, so that pipes from Scotland can now symbolize Ireland as well. In fact, Ireland has its own pipes, but they are less commonly encountered.

Arrival: Ireland

IRELAND

Ireland, often called the "Emerald Isle," is a mostly rural island generously speckled with castles, monasteries, and great houses, some in ruins. It also boasts the rugged beauty of the western seacoast, including the unforgettable Cliffs of Moher. One of Ireland's most enduring cultural attractions is its music, including everything from that played in local pubs by amateurs to sophisticated versions of traditional tunes by groups such as The Chieftains. Indeed, there has been an explosion of new types of Irish-based music generally labeled "Celtic."

But Ireland was not always a placid locale for music. Over the centuries Ireland endured successive waves of invasions, as the many ruined "round towers" and other fortifications attest. In spite of this fate,

Celebrated in song as well as visited by thousands of tourists each year, the Cliffs of Moher in western Ireland is among Europe's most dramatic sites

Ireland was one of the most developed and cultured places in medieval Europe, with many great centers of learning, religion, and the arts.

While the Republic of Ireland has been independent from the United Kingdom since 1922 (technically, it formed in 1949), one of its original four counties, Ulster, remains a constituent part of the U.K., a testament to an incomplete revolution. It is nonetheless important to recall that until the twentieth century Ireland itself was not independent and that English speakers far outnumber the fabled Gaelic speakers, who were mostly found in the west of the country.

Track 9

Site 5: Union Bagpipes

First Impressions. Compared to the Scottish bagpipes, the Irish pipes sound mellower, much fuller in sound, and warmer in tone. Along with the expected melody and drone, one hears occasional "chords," groups of consonant notes sounded together. If this instrument sounds less martial, it is because the Irish pipes are played indoors for domestic occasions. In fact, you are just as likely to encounter these pipes playing with other instruments, such as the fiddle, banjo, wooden transverse flute, and perhaps even spoons, as to hear them solo.

Aural Analysis. Irish pipes, known in English as "union" and in Gaelic as *uilleann* (meaning "elbow"), are bellows-driven, meaning they have less power than mouth-driven pipes and as a result are played indoors. A players sits with the bellows on the right hip secured with a belt, the drones lying across his lap. While the instrument's history goes back to the

Irish "union" or *uilleann* pipes

eighteenth century, its present form stabilized during the nineteenth century. Without doubt, the union pipes in their fully developed form are the most complex bagpipes in the world.

Disassembled for storage, the pipes consist of the bag, the bellows and strap, a *chanter* pipe, three drone pipes, and—in full sets—an additional three pipes fitted with a series of large metal keys. These additional pipes, called *regulators,* allow the player to produce the chords that are the union pipes' most distinctive feature. Thus a player must be exceptionally coordinated, because they have to pump the bellows with their right arm, press the bag with their left arm, play the melody on the chanter with the fingers of both hands, and sometimes press the regulator keys with the side of their right hand.

Irish music is one of the world's most developed melodic traditions. The repertory is vast, though numerous individual tunes are actually variants of other tunes. Sometimes the same tune is known by different names depending on the region, and sometimes tunes with the same name are musically distinct. Those that are not lyric songs with texts are likely to be one of the several types of dances tunes found in Ireland: namely, the jig (quick 6/8 or 12/8 time), the reel (quick 2/4), the hornpipe (6/8 or 12/8 time), and the polka (quick 2/4 time). Some tunes fall into the major-minor tonality system, but there is a tendency for them to be structurally pentatonic (five-tone scale) with the possibility of additional notes.

In our example piper Sean Folsom uses a Taylor Brothers instrument made in Philadelphia in 1890 to play a medley of three pieces: "An Cailin Deas," a slow song air; "The Mountain Road," a reel; and "Anything for John Joe," also a reel. The first piece begins with the sound of the chanter alone, followed twelve seconds later by the entrance of the drone pipes. Thirty-five seconds into the piece the pipes take on a fuller sound resulting from the use of the "regulators" to provide harmony. The first piece is slow and is played freely in a song-like fashion. The two reels that follow are fast and steady and are both duple metered; the first of these commences at 1:29, the second at 2:00.

Cultural Considerations. If much Irish music seems sad or sentimental, Irish history has provided many reasons for it to be so. Although blessed with natural beauty and generous rainfall, Ireland has experienced more than its share of violence over the course of history, from the Anglo-Norman invasions of the twelfth century, to English Protestant Oliver Cromwell's scorched-earth policy of the seventeenth century. Between invasions there were numerous intertribal battles, as various peoples and clans tried to gain dominance over one another and fought over land and religion. All of this provided Irish songwriters with more than ample subject matter. The Great Famine that lasted through much of the 1840s not only starved many to death but also drove much of the population—reduced from 8.5 million to around 4 million in less than five years—from the island to the New World. The Irish population in North America, particularly in places like Boston, New York, and

"UNION" or UILLEANN BAGPIPES
The bellows-driven pipes of Ireland.

Chicago, then struggled as a Roman Catholic underclass in a predominantly Protestant nation before eventually rising to prominence and power. While the Irish are widely associated with police work, they also had to labor in the most menial of jobs before harvesting the fruits of upward mobility. Nonetheless, they were luckier then their compatriots overseas, because Ireland remained impoverished until the late twentieth century, when it became a fast-growing, technologically savvy leader in the European Union.

Local amateur musicians play a "session" in a Limerick pub (public house). From L to R: *uilleann* pipes, accordion or button box, fiddle, and small percussion. The guitarist has his back to the listeners

As already mentioned, the original Irish instrument was the courtly harp, but this fell into oblivion by around 1800. In the twentieth century, there was revival of the harp, which was reconstructed on the basis of pictures and written descriptions, and inaccurately portrayed as a folk instrument. Besides this and the union pipes, there are several other prominent Irish instruments: the fiddle (really just an inexpensive violin), the vertical tin whistle (a kind of metal recorder), the "timber" flute (a wooden transverse flute), and a variety of bellows-driven free reed instruments such as the melodeon, concertina, and accordion. Over time several foreign instruments have been adopted, including the Mediterranean mandolin, the American tenor banjo, the guitar, and a hybrid lute derived from the mandolin and called *bouzouki* after the Greco-Turkish lute. Percussion is limited to the well-known but recently introduced *bodhran*, a goatskin-covered frame drum played by the right hand with a wooden beater, and a pair of wooden "bones" (possibly borrowed from America along with the banjo), or spoons.

Traditionally, Irish music was played communally for family and friends in various settings, many private. Visitors are most likely to encounter Irish music in a public house (pub), where local musicians gather in their reserved corner in the evening to play for each other, the rest of the pub patrons being casual listeners rather than an audience. These gatherings are called "sessions" (*seisiún ceoil*). Because they are informal and ad hoc, the instrumental makeup varies greatly. The Irish pipes are one of the possible instruments found and blend well with the quieter sounds of other indoor type instruments. When an evening event features dancing and a named band, the group is called a *céilí* band; these events are the most likely context for Irish music in North America today.

Music has become an important element of Ireland's tourist industry, and in areas where tourists tend to congregate, especially in the west, there is a conscious effort to have music every evening during the summer. Nowhere is this more so than in the village of Doolin in County Clare, where enormous crowds gather nightly. Visiting musicians may join a session, though there are unwritten rules for participating. Outside the tourist pubs, visitors should also request permission before taping or photographing musicians.

With the rise in popularity of all things "Celtic," another kind of music has also arisen that is better described as "pan-Celtic," meaning it vaguely sounds Irish but in fact reflects a variety of influences. This phenomenon includes Michael Flately's popular "River Dance" shows.

Arrival: Hungary

HUNGARY

Like Hungary itself, the Hungarian people stand astride both West and East. Descended from the semi-nomadic Magyars who originated in the Ural Mountains of present-day central Russia, the Hungarians arrived in the Danube Valley and the Great Plain in the late ninth

century. Over time they mixed with Germanic and Slavic peoples and during the late tenth century they settled into a stable agricultural life under their first king, Stephen. But their location at the crossroads of Europe made them victim to competing armies and subject to invasion. These invaders included the Mongols in the thirteenth century, the Ottoman Turks in the fifteenth, and finally, through marriage and

A typical Hungarian village house in Oskü, north of Lake Balaton in central Hungary

other alliances, the Hapsburgs of Austria in the sixteenth. As a consequence Hungary remained more oriented toward Central and Western Europe than to the East. Independence was achieved in 1919, but for much of the twentieth century Hungary was dominated by first Nazi Germany and then the Soviet Union. Rural Hungary preserves a lively folk music culture. Budapest is also home to a mature, European classical music establishment, and throughout the country the Rom (Gypsies) practice their own forms of music.

Site 6: Hurdy Gurdy

First Impressions. With its nasal tone and constant drones, the *hurdy gurdy* (or *tekerö*) might strike some as sounding like bagpipes. If

Track 10

281

you saw a hurdy gurdy player, you would note that he was turning a crank with the right hand and pushing keys with the left, suggesting the well-known but little understood "organ grinder." The sheer volume of sound can be deceiving; only one player is required to play this seeming "symphony in a box." Indeed, a medieval name for the instrument was *symphonia*.

Aural Analysis. The *hurdy gurdy* is classified as a chordophone because its sound emanates from three or four strings. Specifically it is a lute, with an only slightly differentiated body and neck, the latter being very short and thick. The *hurdy gurdy*'s continuous tone indicates

that it is a bowed, rather than plucked, lute—but its creators have solved the two most contentious problems associated with playing these instruments: bowing smoothly and accurately stopping the strings. As such it is the ultimate "user-friendly" instrument, a foolproof fiddle with the added bonus of drones to eliminate the need for an ensemble. These instruments have a long history in Europe dating back to medieval times, when they were even used in church, but by the eighteenth century they had begun to die out, except for two prominent forms: the French and the Hungarian versions of the instrument. To some extent both forms have been in continuous use as traditional instruments right up to the present time, and both also played a prominent part in twentieth-century folk music revivals in their respective countries.

American musician Sean Folsom explains the part of the Hungarian *tekerö hurdy gurdy*

To allow for smooth and continuous bowing, the makers of the *hurdy gurdy* installed a resin-coated wheel turned by a crank held in the right hand. The strings are tensioned against the wheel and sound continuously, though some models allow for the disengagement of the drone strings. The melody string is stopped not by the player's fingers, but by a series of wooden *tangents* (or keys) placed along the bottom side of the instrument so that they fall back after being pressed against the string. Consequently the *hurdy gurdy* produces both melody and drone in a continuous sound. In addition the player can produce accents by moving into place a "buzzing bridge" that lifts one drone string enough for a buzzing sound to be created when the crank is "jogged" (jerked) as it is turned.

Much of the traditional instrumental music of the Hungarian Great Plain is intended to accompany dance, but players often begin by playing a section that lacks a regular beat before beginning the metrical dance section. Hungarian ethnomusicologist/composer Béla Bartók

HURDY GURDY

A chordophone common in France and Hungary that uses a wheel turned by a crank to vibrate the strings.

called the unmeasured section *parlando-rubato*, that is, "in speech rhythm," and the measured or metrical section *tempo giusto*, meaning "precise tempo," a phrase suggesting that a regular beat is present.

The track heard here consists of a series of tunes played on an instrument with one melody string and three drone strings, with the drones tuned A, e, a (the A being the tonic). Most of the melodies heard use the scale A, B, c#, d, e, f#, g, a, which is equivalent to the medieval mixolydian "church mode," but in some passages the c# changes to c natural, producing the scale A, B, c, d, e, f#, g, a, which has no church mode equivalent.

The track consists of five short melodies played without break, beginning with a *parlando-rubato* "song air." A second "song air" begins when the "buzzing bridge" is activated at 0:25. As the tempo picks up, you hear three "jumping dances" (at 0:58, 1:13, and 1:27), with the repeat of the last one slowing down slightly. Completing the set is a "fast czardas" beginning at 1:59. The *czardas*, with its simple side steps, is Hungary's best-known "popular" dance. The meter is duple, but the phrasing of the fast *czardas* breaks the monotony of 4/4 time. The initial descending phrase, played twice, has four beats. Then follow three phrases of two beats each, producing a phrase with six beats. Thus, the dance shifts phrase groupings from four to six and back.

Cultural Considerations. Although traditional Hungarian music possesses certain distinct instruments and styles, it is best understood as part of a larger Central and Southeast European cultural sphere. When Béla Bartók began his research into Hungarian folk music, his goal was to isolate those elements that were quintessentially Hungarian. His research was inspired by Hungarian nationalism and colored by the typical Hungarian antipathy toward non-Hungarian neighbors, especially the Romanians and Slovaks. To his surprise, however, Bartók discovered that Hungarian music had to be seen in a context that encompassed not only the music of Hungary's immediate neighbors but the music of Central and Southeastern Europe as a whole. Owing to the Ottoman Turk influence on Hungarian music, he also conducted further work in Turkey and North Africa.

ROM
(Also, ROMANI)
An ethnic group originating in India characterized by a semi-nomadic lifestyle; popularly known as Gypsies.

Collecting songs in the village of Darázs (now Drazovce), Slovakia, in 1907, Hungarian ethnomusicologist-composer Béla Bartók has the singers project directly into the horn of a cylinder recording device.
(© Archivo Iconografico, S.A./Corbis)

Local musicians playing the *citera* (left) and Köcsög (right) in Bugac, Hungary, a village near Kecskemet on the Great Plain (*Puszta*)

Bartók's research into "true" Hungarian village music did, however, reveal a side of Hungary that had been hitherto ignored: namely, traditional Hungarian folk music that was distinct from the music of the Rom (Gypsies). During the nineteenth century a number of composers, especially those working in Vienna, had a certain fascination with exotic sounds and styles they considered "Hungarian"—that in fact were Rom in origin. Franz Liszt, for example, wrote music in a "Hungarian" style, such as the *Mélodies hongroises* (1838–9) and *Ungarische Rhapsodien* (1846–7)—but most of the sounds he understood to be "Hungarian" were actually Rom. Likewise, the German composer Johannes Brahms' "Hungarian Dances" (1880) were really Rom in style. The same was true for most other "Hungarian" compositions of the time.

The old "folk" world that Bartók knew has largely disappeared after the tremendous disruption of World Wars I and II, changes in national borders, the rise and fall of Communism, and, more recently, the modernization that has come from Hungary's joining the European Union. While there are undoubtedly rural areas where ordinary local people continue to play folk music, much of Hungary's "traditional" music is revivalist in nature. Young musicians have sought to reenact the old culture of their grandparents by forming strictly old-fashioned ensembles specializing in music that might have been transcribed from Bartók's field recordings. These ensembles employ a number of fascinating instruments—some of which are otherwise obsolete—including bagpipes (*duda*), friction drums played by vibrating a wet stick that passes through the membrane (*köcsög*), a zither (*citera*), a large hammered dulcimer (*cimbalom*) played both by Hungarians and Rom, a struck lute (*gardon*), and long end-blown flutes (*hosszú furulya*).

CIMBALOM

A hammered zither from Eastern Europe, commonly associated with Rom (gypsy) music. Also, the national instrument of Hungary.

Arrival: Bulgaria

BULGARIA

Bordering Turkey and the Black Sea on the southeast and east, Bulgaria is about as far "southeast" as you can go in Southeast Europe. Modern day Bulgaria is the size of Ohio (USA), and has its capital in Sofia (also spelled Sofija). A part of the Roman Empire from around 50

A.D., the region came to be inhabited by Slavs during the 500s, then was conquered by the Bulgars from the north shore of the Black Sea in the 600s. The Bulgars converted to Christianity and established the Bulgarian Orthodox Church, an independent body within the greater family of Byzantine (Eastern) churches. After reaching its peak in the 800s, the Bulgarian Empire was conquered by the all-powerful Ottoman Turks in the 900s and was not free from them until 1878, some nine hundred years later. Bulgaria's history during the two world wars is too complicated to relate here, but after World War II the country came under communist rule, which lasted until the collapse of the Soviet Union in 1991. Originally an agricultural nation where colorful regional cultures created some of Europe's most attractive and vibrant music, Bulgaria industrialized during the twentieth century, and aspects of its musical culture were reformulated for the stage to serve state purposes during the Communist period.

Site 7: Women's Chorus

Track 11

First Impressions. The singing of a Bulgarian women's chorus is quite striking to first-time listeners because it sounds so forceful and has an unusual tonal quality: it is open-throated and yet pinched, almost reed-like. As different as these characteristics are from the usual warm tones and vibrato of Western European and American voices, this singing is strangely attractive to many people. Perhaps you are already familiar with these sounds from a television commercial or a recording of a performance of arranged folksongs by the group *Les mystère des voix bulgares.* Such Bulgarian singing was included in the recording sent into space with the Voyager space-probe in 1977.

Aural Analysis. Work songs are found throughout the world. In some places their rhythm helps coordinate a group activity, in order to make the work more efficient, to sustain it, or to discourage uncoordinated movements that might result in injury. In other places work songs are simply commentary on the task at hand, as is the case here. This harvest song is from the Shop (rhymes with "hope") region in western Bulgaria, which lies not far from Sofia. Its singers comment on how the sun is coming up earlier and earlier, scorching the fields and making them miserable in the heat. Other songs might focus on any part of the work-

Colorfully dressed members of a Bulgarian women's chorus perform onstage (© Jack Vartoogian/FrontRowPhotos)

day, from going to the fields in the morning, to the fatigue experienced at the end of the day.

The singers, all female, divide into two groups. One performs a low drone, which is established with a quick rising glide at the beginning; the singers call this "following" or "bellowing." The other singers perform the melody, rising as high as an octave, but often dwelling on the seventh scale degree, which the singers call "crying out." Throughout our example, there are sudden glides down from the seventh on the sound "eee," a typical trait in Bulgarian singing. Two other characteristics contribute to an intriguing, admittedly "mysterious" quality: the music's nonmetrical flow and its use of both the minor second and major second intervals, which create an exhilarating tension with the drone/tonic. When singers perform these close intervals, they seek to "ring like a bell." There is also a bit of *ululation*, that is, the performing of a single pitch repeatedly with glottal stops.

Cultural Considerations. Bulgaria, because of its specific history and geopolitical location, offers some of Europe's most attractive and colorful music. Long embedded in the Turkish Ottoman Empire, Bulgaria absorbed instruments and stylistic influences from Western Asia, both from the Turks and from the Rom, the latter of whom still provide many of the musicians heard in Bulgarian villages today. In addition to the close harmonies of its vocal music, Bulgaria is also known for its lively and driving instrumental music, often played on the bagpipes called *gaida*. Much of the dance music, especially that of the southwest, matches intricate step patterns to melodies based on "asymmetrical" time units. Instead of using phrases that are evenly divided or consistently in two or four beats, these melodies use a meter in which there is an uneven or asymmetrical grouping of beats, such as 3 + 3 + 2 or 4 + 2 + 3. Some refer to these meters as "additive," because the meter is created by adding together two, three, or four short groupings of beats. This instrumental music forms quite a contrast to vocal music of the type we have heard, which is usually slow and unmetered.

Bulgarian music made a strong impression on Hungary's Béla Bartók, who did extensive collecting in Bulgaria, especially the southwest region, the area that borders Macedonia, now an independent nation that was formerly part of Yugoslavia. The complex asymmetrical meters he encountered, recorded, analyzed, and transcribed were usually labeled "Bulgarian meter." They are especially prominent in such works as his String Quartet Number 5, movement 3; the "Six Dances in Bulgarian Rhythm" from his pedagogical work for piano, the *Mikrokosmos*; and in many works whose title includes the word "dance."

In Eastern Europe under Communism, music became a potent tool for state expression and control. Because the masses ("peasants") were privileged under Marxism, their music was sometimes used to symbolize the power and unity of the state. As a consequence most Communist regimes in Eastern Europe founded and supported "folkoric" ensembles that represented the nation's culture both to the internal population and to the world at large. Though staffed by people who in many cases had learned folk music in a "traditional" way, these state troupes were designed to perform arranged music on stage or for television or radio. The intent of their performances was to reinforce state philosophy in some manner, be it subtle or obvious. Many types of Bulgarian music were so treated, including the music of the women's choruses. Some performers, such as the group known as *Les mystère des voix bulgares*, achieved widespread recognition through tours and recordings. Because Bulgarian women's choral singing is so attractive to many non-Bulgarians, it has become one of most prevalent facets of "world music." Consequently, Bulgarian singing is now performed by many non-Bulgarian groups, used in advertisements to sell goods, and sometimes combined with other kinds of music to create multiethnic "world beat" recordings.

Questions to Consider

1. How is the history of European and Arabic cultural contact revealed through musical characteristics in places like Spain and Bulgaria?

2. What determines a music as "classical" versus "folk" in the European context? How has "classical" music influenced "folk" music style and performance and vice versa?

3. Drone is especially prominent in many European music traditions. What are some specific manifestations and how does drone relate to the overall sound?

4. Some "folk" instruments are designed to be easy to play but others require advanced techniques. Discuss examples of European instruments that typify both ends of the spectrum.

5. How are music and musical instruments used to express national identity in Europe?

6. Is language a reliable demarcation of musical style in Europe? If not, why?

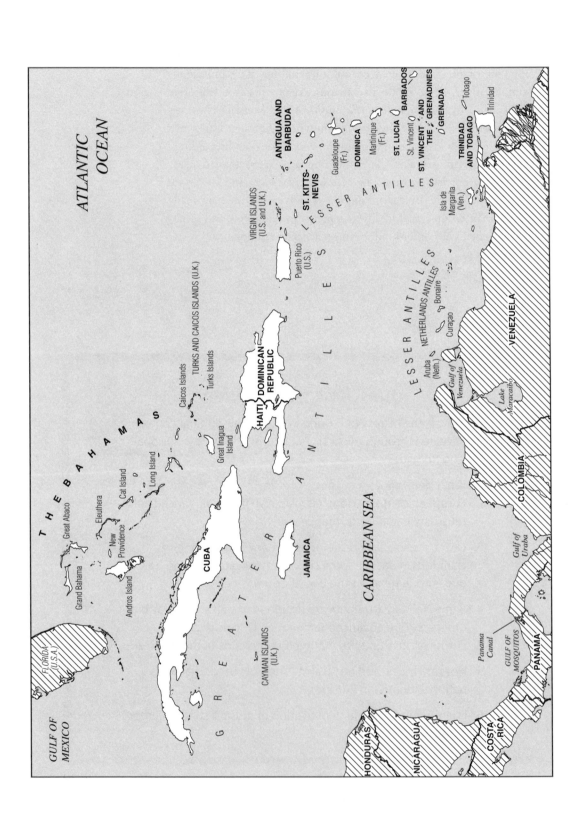

A typical fishing village on the tiny Caribbean island of St. Vincent, the main island of St. Vincent and the Grenadines

CHAPTER 11

The Caribbean: Musical Energy of Island Peoples

Background Preparation

*T*he Caribbean represents many things to different people: white sandy beaches with clear blue water, dreadlocks and reggae music, cruise ships, Cuban communism and Fidel Castro, sugar cane, steel bands, or perhaps even offshore financial havens. For Americans none of it is geographically very far away and yet most of it remains little known. There is much physical poverty but the region is a cornucopia of colorful and dynamic cultures. Despite a history of brutality against the native population and of slaves being forcibly brought from Africa, the mixing of different peoples occurs more easily there than practically anywhere else in the world, and this mixing has produced tremendous cultural and artistic energy. Tiny islands have developed stentorian cultural voices, producing music appreciated worldwide. Most readers will have likely heard steel band music, calypso, reggae, and salsa.

A map of the Caribbean shows a curving string of islands running from the Bahamas off the coast of Florida down to Venezuela. The largest islands—Cuba, Jamaica, Hispaniola (comprising Haiti and the Dominican Republic), and Puerto Rico—are in the center. The pre-contact population consisted of several indigenous groups, including the Arawak and Carib, but attempts to enslave them only led to their deaths or deportation. Today there are still black Caribs—a mixture resulting from contact with Africans—in a few places such as Honduras and St. Vincent. Contact with Europeans resulted first from the four voyages of Christopher Columbus, who between 1492 and 1503 "discovered" not "America" (meaning North America) but the Caribbean islands, Central America, and a bit of South America. After that, Spain claimed virtually all of the New World, though over time its rivals, the English, Dutch, and French, took possession of certain islands. Today, the Caribbean remains virtually the world's last bastion of colonialism; Martinique and Guadeloupe remain French possessions and the Dutch Antilles (Curacao, Aruba, and Bonaire) belong to The Netherlands.

The diversity of languages spoken in the Caribbean reflects the region's complex and colorful history. The main language currently spoken in any given place is the language of that country's most recent colonial master, but in many places a layering of languages can be heard; for example, in Trinidad and Tobago, one finds many Spanish place names, and some Spanish terms have infiltrated the English spoken there. Spanish predominates in Cuba, Puerto Rico, and the Dominican Republic, whereas French predominates in Haiti, Martinique, and Guadeloupe. English is the main language of most of the remaining islands, including the Bahamas, Jamaica, the Virgin Islands, Dominica, St. Lucia, Barbados, Grenada, St. Vincent and the Grenadines, and Trinidad and Tobago, to name only the better-known ones. Dutch and English predominate in the Dutch Antilles. In many islands one also finds linguistic blends, often called Creole, or forms of English or French impenetrable to outsiders. Anyone who has listened to reggae "dub" or "dancehall" will know how difficult it can be to understand some forms of island English.

Most Caribbean islands have predominately African-derived populations. After their failure to enslave the Arawak and Carib, Spanish colonialists, attempting to establish tobacco and sugar plantations, began importing African slaves in 1451, as part of a trading triangle. The Europeans exported manufactured goods to Africa in exchange for human cargo that was shipped primarily to South America and the Caribbean, after which sugar and rum produced by slave labor were exported back to Europe. Slave trading reached its peak during the eighteenth century. Periodically there were violent slave rebellions, and many slaves escaped into the hills, mountains, or other remote areas; escaped slaves were called by the Spanish term *cimarrons,* Anglicized as *maroon.*

The English abolished slave trading in 1807, the French in 1818,

ANTILLES
The islands of the Caribbean, excluding the Bahamas.

and the Spanish in 1820, but Brazil allowed it until 1852 and the United States until 1862. Slavery ceased in 1834 in all English colonies and in 1848 in the French possessions, but it lingered until 1865 in the United States, 1873 in Puerto Rico, 1886 in Cuba, and 1888 in Brazil. Amazingly, the number of slaves emancipated in the United States (some four million) is greater than the combined total for the rest of the Americas. Following the end of slavery, the English brought indentured laborers from other parts of the world, especially India and China, while the Dutch brought them from Java. Indentured workers were only a step above slaves but could work themselves to freedom. As a result there are significant populations of people from India in Trinidad and Guyana (in South America), from China in Trinidad and Jamaica, and Javanese in Suriname.

The Caribbean, with its incredible mix of peoples, also retains aspects of old culture from Europe, Africa, and India. In the Bahamas and other nearby English-speaking islands, people of African descent sing old English traditional ballads and perform *mummer* plays during Christmas. In Trinidad, also during Christmas, people still sing *parang* songs from Spain and Portugal. African traditional religions, surviving intact or in part, flourish in such places as Trinidad, Grenada, Jamaica, Haiti, the Dominican Republic, and Cuba. Aspects of eighteenth-century English hymn-singing and some early "Negro spirituals" survive in the Bahamas, because during the Revolutionary War British loyalists left the rebellious colonies and settled in the Bahamas, taking their slaves with them. Many kinds of Spanish music survive in Cuba, the Dominican Republic, and Puerto Rico.

MUMMER
A type of street theater actor, usually in performances staged during the Christmas season.

Planning the Itinerary

While the Caribbean is home to numerous little-known, though fascinating, kinds of music, it is also a wellspring of some of the world's best-known music genres. Steel band music, calypso, reggae, and merengue all originated there and exemplify the idea that small countries can have big voices. The worldwide fashion for Latin-based ballroom dance music—cha-cha, mambo, rumba (or rhumba), merengue, bolero—derives from Cuban, Puerto Rican, and Dominican styles. Granted, some of these musics are better described as "popular" rather than "traditional," but reggae and calypso, to name only two, are thoroughly embedded in the cultures of their homelands, Jamaica and Trinidad respectively. We therefore survey most of these well-known musics, along with the Bahamian rhyming spiritual, which is especially interesting because of its roots in the United States.

Arrival: Haiti

Haiti, a nation of around seven million people, occupies the western end of Hispaniola. Originally Spanish, it was ceded to France in

HAITI

1697. Following a slave-led revolution that lasted more than ten years, Haiti became the first independent nation in the Caribbean in 1804. While the official language is French, most Haitians speak Creole, a blend of French, Spanish, Portuguese, English, and various African languages that is incomprehensible to outsiders. Today Haiti remains one of the world's most impoverished nations, in part because of frequent natural disasters, such as earthquakes, floods, and hurricanes, and the low value of its main crop, sugar cane; its population has also suffered through a series of brutal political regimes. Virtually all Haitians are of

An Inside Look

P. Olivia Ahyoung

I was born on the South American mainland in Guyana, formerly British Guyana, but destiny took me to Trinidad and Tobago. My current day-to-day life as a Research Associate living in the United States is in the area of statistics. However, I also maintain a professional life as a musician. My love of music was fostered at a very early age, having grown up in a household where my father was an organist and choir master. My musical life began with private piano lessons in the English-speaking Caribbean, and later led to undergraduate studies in England in preparation for a teaching career. My principal instruments are organ and piano, but along the way, I flirted with violin, viola, flute, and more seriously steel pan. After a few years of teaching in high schools in the Caribbean, I pursued postgraduate studies in Music Education here in the United States. This led to a position as a lecturer at a teacher's training college in the Caribbean, and a professional musical life that has embraced the areas of teaching, performing, research. and composition.

P. Olivia Ahyoung,
clinician, pianist, organist
and choir master

The challenge of teaching teachers-in-training how to adapt English- and American-styled lessons and texts led to my first serious stint of research into native folk melodies and rhythms. I had always been fascinated by the stories behind the country's folk songs, and captivated by performances by local folk groups. My attendance at a workshop given by Olive Lewin of Jamaica cemented my interest and set me on the path of research. As a lecturer, I found one of the more satisfying uses of folk tunes was in arrangements for Orff instruments/recorders accompanied with singers.

I left the Caribbean many years ago, but have continued to keep abreast and remain informed about my culture. As a clinician, I relish every opportunity to talk to music teachers and Middle and High School-aged children about my rich heritage and to get them involved in performing. My church choir also affords me the opportunity to hone my skills in vocal composition on a regular basis. Whether teaching, performing, composing, or researching, music informs and consumes my life.

Ellie Mannette

In 1937, when I began participating in the steel drum art form, I had no idea how it would impact the world of music. I was little more than an adolescent who had, along with my brothers and other young men in our working class neighborhood of Trinidad, West Indies, wanted to simply express the music that was inside us. Between the years of 1941 and 1946 I created several key innovations in the realm of pan (also called steel drums), such as inverting the playing surface from convex to concave, wrapping sticks with rubber for the first time, and building the first instrument from a 55-gallon drum. Little did I know these advancements would usher in the era of the modern steel drum instrument. When I was offered a scholarship to study music at the Birmingham School of Music in England in 1946, I turned it down so that I could devote my life to furthering the steel drum art form. However, I did make it to London a few years later, in 1951, along with 11 other panmen as members of the Trinidadian All-Star Percussion Orchestra (TASPO), which represented Trinidad in the Festival of Britain. As my reputation spread across the island, I was asked to provide music for audiences at the Little Carib Theater and for the first radio program to include steel band music. I also crafted a band for the U.S. Navy upon their request.

Dr. Ellie Mannette, Artist-in-residence, West Virginia University; founder and CEO, Mannette Steel Drums

My career has lead me all around the world where I have received countless awards and recognitions including from the Queen of England (in the 1960s), the National Endowment for the Arts (in 1999), an Honorary Doctorate from the University of the West Indies (2000), and my induction into the Percussive Arts Society Hall of Fame (2003). That desire to express the music within me led to my creating 7 of the 10 voices in the modern steel band, and when I moved to the United States in 1967 that passion fueled my desire to spread the art form in the public education systems across the United States. In 1982, I formed a partnership known as the Mannette Touch with then-freelance journalist, Kaethe George, that enabled me to continue being at the forefront of the steel band movement in this country for 35 years.

In 1992 my appointment as an artist-in-residence at West Virginia University's Creative Arts Center allowed me to form an innovative apprentice program know as the University Tuning Project, and through it realize my dream of training future tuners and builders And now as I near retirement I can see the fruits of my teaching and training in the scores of steel band programs across the world and in the handful of gifted builders and tuners that have been fully trained at Mannette Steel Drums, a for-profit company that works in partnership with West Virginia University's Research Corporation.

I would feel proudest if my legacy indicates that I passed along my skills to young people so that our art form was able to progress and that I created instruments that made people happy by enabling them to express the music within them.

African descent, but class differences based on skin color remain, and as a result Haitians with lighter skin (from mixing with Europeans) retain more wealth and power than the rest of the population. Nonetheless, Haiti's capital, Port-au-Prince, is alive with music and dance.

Track 12

Site 1: *Vodou Ritual*

First Impressions. *Voodoo* (or *Vodou* as it is more correctly spelled) is associated in North American minds with satanic rituals in which pins are placed in dolls to hurt someone, or a mysterious powder is sprinkled on someone's doorstep to turn them into zombie slaves. In fact, this stereotyping of *Vodou* as black magic is unfair and inaccurate. As for our recorded example, if you listen to it objectively, you will no doubt be struck by its similarity to African music—which it essentially is. The performance features drumming and singing in a language that certainly does not sound French.

Aural Analysis. The track consists of two sections, the first vocal with drums, the second vocal with a bamboo wind instrument. Basically there are two musical elements in the first part of the example, the rhythmic accompaniment played on drums and other instruments, and the vocal parts, which in this case contrast a male soloist and a group made up mostly of women. The structure of the vocal parts is therefore responsorial—that is, it is based on a call-and-response pattern in which the soloist begins a sentence or thought that the group then completes. These songs are passed on through oral tradition, making them vary somewhat from one group to another, even as certain elements that maintain the song's identity are preserved. The language is a combination of Creole and *langaj*, the latter being a ceremonial language derived from several West African and Central African religions.

A display of various drums used in Haitian *Vodou* ritual

ANIMISM
Belief systems in which natural phenomena as well as both animate and inanimate objects are considered to possess a spirit.

The accompaniment in *Vodou* rituals typically consists of three *rada* drums, sometimes along with an African iron bell or similar object, and some kind of shaken rattle, usually with the shells or seeds fastened to an external net. The largest drum is the leader, the middle drum provides additional rhythms, and the smallest provides a steady beat off of which the others play. As with other types of West African music, these polyrhythmic patterns are organized into short units called "timeline patterns," rather than being in a continuous meter such as 2/4. Individual accompaniments and songs are specific to particular deities, and are played to invite those deities to a ritual. In a typical *Vodou* ritual, a succession of deities will be invited, each with their own music. Participants seek to be possessed by the deity they are invoking, and when this happens their dancing incorporates gestures and actions that express the character of that deity. Our recorded example features a song for Legba and part of a dance for Ogoun (see below).

The second part of the track again has responsorial voices, but there are no drums. Instead you hear a group of bamboo "trumpets" called *vaksin*, each capable of playing a single note. When a group of players, each with a different pitch, play them, a melody results from the interlocking patterns of these single pitches. The occasion is called *Rara*, processions of singers and players who go from one sacred spot (e.g., a cemetery) to another during the period between Carnival (just before Ash Wednesday, the beginning of Lent) until just before Easter.

Cultural Considerations. *Vodou* is an African-derived religious system incorporating influences from Roman Catholicism. Although at least 10 percent of the Africans brought to the New World were originally Muslims, the vast majority practiced traditional African religions. Some of these systems involved interaction with the spirits of ancestors, whereas others focused on a pantheon of personified natural forces, called *orisha* in the Yoruba language but called *loa* in Haiti. For example, in the Yoruba tradition found in present-day Nigeria, thunder and lightening is personified as the god Shango. In predominantly Roman Catholic colonies (which comprised most of South and Central America and much of the Caribbean), Africans vastly outnumbered their masters, because great numbers of slaves were required to work the sugar plantations. As a result, the Africans in these colonies were able to retain a fair amount of their African heritage, including their religions. More precisely, while many Africans professed Catholic Christianity, most saw Christ, the Virgin, and the Saints and Apostles as equivalents to African gods—an example of a process called *syncretism*. For example, in some traditions Shango is equivalent to John the Baptist. Thus the *Vodou* practioners considered there to be no contradiction between attending Mass in a church and participating in African rituals at an African temple.

Haitian *Vodou*, which blends the spiritual tradition focusing on ancestors with the one focusing on a pantheon of gods, derives mostly from Benin (formerly Dahomey) and nearby areas of West Africa. The two gods invoked in our example, both *loa* in the *Vodou* tradition, are Legba and Ogoun. Both are well-known Yoruba-derived deities classified into the "Rada" group in *Vodou*. Legba, the guardian of the crossroads and barriers, is depicted as a handsome old man with a flowing beard who likes meat and alcoholic drinks and limps while walking with a cane. Ogoun, the god of iron, is often depicted with a sword, and can be quite fierce and active. While it is true that most African religions include some aspect of destructive power, they are actually predominately positive in focus, as the principal goals are good health and

SHANGO
A Yoruba name for the god of thunder and lightning in the West African pantheon. Consequently, also the name for a West African-derived religion found primarily in Trinidad.

In Trinidad two musicians play drums and sing for a Shango ceremony, a syncretistic religious tradition distantly related to Haiti's *Vodou*

At the seacoast of Trinidad, six leaders of the African-derived Shango religion bow before ritual offerings about to be floated into the sea for Oshun, the goddess of the sea

healing, social cohesion, successful harvests, and the like. Participants reaffirm the power of the gods in rituals that involve dancing, singing, drumming, and possession. During possession a person's essence temporarily leaves the body, allowing the *loa* (deity) to "mount" the believer, who is considered to be the "horse." The possessed person acts out the personality of the god and demonstrates the god's traits in dance and gesture. At the conclusion of a possession, the "horse" may suddenly fall to the ground, after which it is given time to reunite with its human essence.

As already mentioned, each deity is associated with a particular drumming pattern and song. Performing their music invites a god to appear and hopefully to possess one or more lucky "horses." Despite myths to the contrary, *Vodou* music itself does not cause possession, because, if it did, anyone hearing it would be possessed. Indeed, the percussionists—almost always male—stay outside the ritual circle and are not subject to possession. What music in a *Vodou* ritual does do is *regulate* possession—that is, it makes the process of possession more even and efficient. Before a person can be possessed, he or she must learn how to become possessed; otherwise the experience of a *Vodou* ritual can be useless or even dangerous.

A full ritual must begin with a song to Legba, the guardian of the crossroads and gatekeeper to the spirit world. This is followed by a series of songs for other deities, presented in a prescribed order. These deities are both nature gods and ancestors; some are violent or energetic, while others are calm. During possession, the "horse" may receive healing energy. Others nearby may also benefit or may ask the deity questions about life and the future.

There are a great many African-derived religions in the New World, though admittedly *Vodou* is the best known and most notorious because of negative stereotyping. Other African-derived religions include *Santeria* and *Abakwa* in Cuba, *Batuque*, *Umbanda*, and *Candomblé* in Brazil, *Shango* in Trinidad, and *Cumina* in Jamaica. Some of them, including *Vodou*, have been transplanted to the United States, Canada, and England by Caribbean immigrants. Although not advertised, rituals associated with these religions may be found in cities such as New York, Miami, Toronto, and Los Angeles, as well as in many smaller cities.

Arrival: Jamaica

JAMAICA

For most North Americans, Jamaica means the white sand beaches along the north coast at Montego Bay, Ocho Rios, or Negril, classy resort hotels, and smiling local musicians playing gentle calypsos and limbo dance music. For most Jamaicans, life is a different reality, one of hardscrabble poverty and crime. The population of this Connecticut-sized island is 2.5 million, of which fully one third live in the greater Kingston area. In Jamaica, as in Haiti, there is a stark contrast between the very wealthy and the very poor. The country's colonial past, the low prices fetched by its principal exports (sugar cane and bauxite), and overpopulation in the Kingston area are all partly responsible for this situation and together comprise a recipe for tension and violence. Kingston can, unfortunately, be a dangerous city for foreign visitors. Nonetheless, it was in Kingston's slums that Jamaica's most vibrant music—reggae—originated.

The majority of Jamaica's population is of African descent, their forebears having come shackled in slavery. Spanish colonialists controlled Jamaica until the mid-seventeenth century, when English pirates drove them from the country. The country then became a British colony in 1670. Throughout Jamaica's history there were occasional slave rebellions, and many slaves escaped into the Blue Mountains in the east and into the still uncharted "Cockpit Country" in Trelawny Parish in the west. In these regions, they were able to reestablish an African way of life, including what remained of their ancestral religion called, *Cumina*. Since achieving independence in 1962, Jamaica has struggled politically, going through--among other things--a disastrous experiment with Socialism under Michael Manley. Not surprisingly, a great number of Jamaicans have left the island seeking a better life, principally in Miami, New York, Toronto, and London.

REGGAE
A popular music from Jamaica characterized by a rhythmic emphasis on the off-beat and by politically and socially conscious lyrics.

Site 2: Reggae

Track 13

First Impressions. Many North Americans enjoy the easy-going "laid-back" beat of reggae, with its emphasis on beats 2 and 4, and know the names of major reggae artists such as Bob Marley and Jimmy Cliff. Some of you may even know a little about of reggae's immediate predecessors, *ska* and *rock steady*. But while the sound of reggae may be familiar, the cultural context out of which it comes and the meaning its lyrics have for many Jamaicans are probably much less known to you.

Reggae artist Buju Banton with his trademark "dreadlocks" of Rastafarian origin
(© Jack Vartoogian/FrontRowPhotos)

Reggae artist Carlos Jones of Cleveland, Ohio (Larry Koval)

Reggae is much more than a form of pop music. The long, tangled hair (called *dreadlocks*) worn by most reggae musicians, the prevalence of the colors red, green, and gold, the frequent references to "Jah," even the celebration of *ganja* (marijuana), are not merely fashion statements or fads—they are part of a system of beliefs and a way of life called Rastafarianism.

Aural Analysis. Reggae is different from most other types of music featured in this book, first because it has been commercially successful, and second because songs usually come from known, individual creators who infuse their life experiences into their work. Our example, "Torchbearer," written by Carlos Jones, is such a song. Jones is a North American reggae musician from Cleveland, Ohio, who was attracted to reggae music as a teenager. After hearing a live performance of Bob Marley and the Wailers in 1978, he became a reggae musician, first joining a local band called I-tal, then joining a spin-off group called First Light, which performed for fifteen years. "Torchbearer" is a product of his recent work with a new band, The PLUS Band, and is a tribute to his role model, Bob Marley.

Bob Marley (a.k.a. Tuff Gong), born Robert Nesta Marley on February 6, 1945, is considered the most important of reggae's many stars, especially for the quality of his lyrics and his articulation of fundamental Rastafarian concepts (explained below). His career began in 1960 after he joined with a childhood friend, Bunny Wailer (born Neville O'Riley Livingston), to form The Wailers. Later joined by Peter Tosh (born Winston Hubert McIntosh), they recorded songs that encapsulated their life experiences in Kingston's most notorious slum, Trench Town. Through international tours, including one to North America called "Babylon By Bus," they spread their music to non-Jamaican audiences. Marley's 1981 death from cancer at the age of thirty-six was a devastating blow to both reggae and Jamaica, because, although establishment Jamaica shunned the Rastafarian "rude boys," the public had embraced Marley. Eventually a statue in honor of him was placed outside the National Stadium in Kingston.

In our example, Jones uses several examples of the language peculiar to Rastafarians, or *Rastas* as they are called for short. The phrase *I and I* serves as both a singular and plural pronoun, its use signifying that Jah (the Rastafarian term for God) is always present with the speaker. In plural form it refers to the mystical relationships within a group and between the group and

Jah. *A Nyabinghi* (referred to in the line "Nyabinghi shakes the ground") is a ritual convention at which chanting and drumming occur. The term, which is derived from the name of an anticolonial movement in Rwanda, also refers to dreadlocked Rastas and may be shortened to "Nya-man," as heard in "Torchbearer." References to "vibration" in the song highlight the metaphysical goals of peace, brotherhood, and love espoused by Rastas generally. Jones also mentions Marley's biracial background (Marley had a white father and a black mother), and refers to Peter Tosh using his original surname, McIntosh.

In a communication written in 2003, Jones explained how his songs come into being:

> Songs come to me in many different ways: Some seem to just spring up out of nowhere and plant themselves in my brain, while another may come completely intact in a dream and become imprinted on my waking consciousness. … Many times, I'll just go straight to the tape deck and record whatever idea I have as it's developing. … This is a part of my own small contribution to the cause of forwarding the positive vibration. It was through reggae music that I received the reawakening of spirit in my late teens. … Carry it and pass it on. One Love, One Peace, One Consciousness—*Carlos*

HAILE SELASSIE
An Ethiopian king considered by Rastafarians to be the second coming of Jesus Christ.

Cultural Considerations. Although some might view reggae as simply a Jamaican popular music, it is steeped in very particular aspects of Jamaican history and culture. Real reggae, not the sanitized form usually offered to audiences in North America, is challenging on several fronts, including the spiritual and the political. Many lyrics combine elements of Jamaican vernacular English with the peculiar vocabulary of the religion that informs reggae, Rastafarianism. Reggae's roots are complex and tangled, as it draws on many contradictory styles, including 1950s American rock and roll, evangelistic hymns and choruses, and African drumming and singing.

A full understanding of reggae is impossible without a discussion of Marcus Garvey and the roots of Rastafarianism. Garvey (1887–1940), a major force for West Indian nationalism and a promoter of black social pride, founded the Universal Negro Improvement Association (U.N.I.A.) in Kingston in 1914. In 1916 he traveled to New York City where he founded a branch of the U.N.I.A. and started a number of businesses (such as the Black Star Shipping Company), a newspaper *(Negro World)*, and a church (the African Orthodox Church). His arrest in 1925 on fraud charges led to his being deported back to Jamaica in 1927. It is reported that after returning home he proclaimed, "Look to Africa, where a black king shall be crowned." Indeed, Garvey's teachings led to the notion of Afrocentrism and the beginning of a "back to Africa" movement.

Many in Jamaica thought Garvey's words had been fulfilled when,

Half-Way Tree district of Kingston typifies the grinding poverty of Jamaica's capital, the breeding grounds for Reggae music

in 1930, they read that an Ethiopian tribal chieftain named Ras Tafari Mekonnen had been crowned Haile Selassie I, the King of Kings, the Lord of Lords, Conquering Lion of the Tribe of Judah. Many came to believe that Haile Selassie (meaning "Power of the Holy Trinity") was the black reincarnated Christ, and that the black peoples of the Diaspora were the lost children of Israel held captive in Babylon, awaiting deliverance by Jah (God) and their return back to Zion—in this case Ethiopia or Africa, the spiritual home of all black people. The colors red, green, and gold became associated with Zion, because they are Ethiopia's national colors.

Those who embraced this loosely organized faith were called Rastafarians. In addition to their core beliefs, they adopted a lifestyle that included the wearing of dreadlocks and the smoking of *ganja* (the Hindi term for marijuana). *Ganja*, or "herb," was already a traditional medicine in Jamaica, but was brewed as a tea or eaten with food. Rastafarians believed, however, that smoking "herb" would put adherents into a more prayerful state and bring them closer to Jah. Rastas justify their use of *ganja* with passages from the Bible, such as Revelation 22:2, which asserts that "The leaves of the tree were for the healing of the nation."

Ethiopian Emperor Haile Selassie I, "Lion of Judah," born Lij Tafari in 1892, crowned emperor in 1930 until his death in 1970 (Rastafari Archive and Ras Adam Simeon)

In Jamaica, the Rastas are considered a disreputable underclass by the establishment, and their close association with reggae has meant that much of the music expresses challenges to the social order. Because Rastas consider the white world to be Babylon (referring to the captivity of the chosen people) and Africa their true home, reggae lyrics also often challenges white hegemony. While not every reggae musician is necessarily a practicing Rastafarian, virtually all are sympathetic to this spiritual system.

Because live performances of reggae were long prohibited in Jamaica, the music was a phenomenon of Kingston's many small recording studios. There the musicians, using both acoustic and electric instruments, laid down tracks that were mixed to the liking of the audio engineer. Reggae music was then disseminated on vinyl recordings. Many party venues and dance halls hired soundmen to bring sound trucks to provide reggae music for dancing. By the 1980s these DJs had discovered that by turning down the melody track and boosting the bass and rhythm track, for them to talk over the music through a microphone. Eventually recordings without the vocals of so-called "dub" versions were made. This led to the creation of "dub" poetry, later called "dancehall." Some DJs became virtual reggae poets, creating long, complex poems that commented on life. Reggae "dub" also has a close relationship with the origin and rise of African-American rap and "toasting."

Reggae music derives in part from a number of earlier styles that were not associated with Rastafarians and rarely had political lyrics. The oldest style was *mento*, a Creolized form of ballroom dance music that was popular in the 1940s and continues to this day as "hotel music." With independence in 1962 and the increasing concentration of the population in Kingston's burgeoning slums came *ska*, a Jamaican response to American rhythm and blues and rock and roll. By the mid 1960s *ska* was slowing down and incorporating more politically charged lyrics; these changes led to a new style called *rock steady*. Reggae, the name of which is attributed to Toots Hibbert, emerged around 1968. It incorporated not only these older styles, but also new forms of blues, Latin American music, and Jamaican religious music. Reggae was also influenced by the music of Rastafarian religious gatherings, which blended the choral style of Christian revival meetings with *Cumina*, African-derived drumming and singing.

Arrival: Trinidad and Tobago

Trinidad, smaller than Delaware (USA) and with only 1.1 million inhabitants, has more than made up for its small size by contributing two of the world's favorite musics, steel band and calypso. The nation consists of two islands: Trinidad, the larger, is only about fifty miles by thirty miles, and Tobago is a mere twenty-five miles by eight miles. The name of the capital, Port of Spain, suggests something of the island's history. "Discovered" by Christopher Columbus during his third voyage in 1498, Trinidad was held by Spain until the English wrested it away in 1797, holding it as a colony until 1962. The native population, the Carib, disappeared after the first Spanish colonists brought their slaves to Trinidad to establish sugar plantations. Even after the end of slave trading, Britain brought more than 134,000 East Indians, 8,000 Africans, and 1,000 Chinese as indentured laborers to work the land. As a result, today's population is around 40 percent East Indian. The range of religions found is quite varied as well: the country boasts a colorful landscape of Christian churches, Muslim mosques, and Hindu temples along with many African ritual centers.

Most visitors to Trinidad come for Carnival, a festival preceding Lent, when Port of Spain comes alive with near nonstop music and

DUB
(Also, DANCEHALL)
Recorded music that emphasizes the bass and rhythm tracks so that a DJ can talk over the music through a microphone.

CALYPSO
A popular music from Trinidad characterized by improvised lyrics on topical and broadly humorous subject matter.

TRINIDAD and TOBAGO

dancing. Because the beautiful beaches on the north coast of Trinidad remain little known and undeveloped, Tobago has been the main destination for swimmers and surf lovers. Trinidad's Great Pitch Lake is perhaps the world's largest pitch (tar) deposit, and is the source of material that has paved roads in both Europe and the Americas.

Site 3: *Calypso*

Track 14

First Impressions. Our example of calypso opens with the sounds of a small dance band dominated by winds. Soon a male vocalist is introduced, who speaks as much as he sings; in a simple but direct manner, he gives his personal view of money and its corrosive influence on people. The repetitious music behind him sounds almost incidental, more a vehicle for conveying the words than an attempt to charm the listener with a sophisticated melody.

Aural Analysis. Studio-recorded in New York City in 1979, using an eclectic group of pan-Caribbean musicians, our example opens with a simple melodic line consisting of four short instrumental phrases; this melody returns periodically during brief interludes and also serves as a coda to the song. While the trumpet and clarinet dominate the purely instrumental sections, quieter instruments, including violin, piano, guitar, and electric bass, are heard accompanying the singing. Throughout, a conga drum reinforces the beat.

CONGA
A tall, barrel-shaped, single-headed drum used often in Latin American music.

The singer's stage name is The Growling Tiger, but he was born Neville Marcano in Siparia in southern Trinidad. A prizefighter and sugar cane worker in the early 1930s, he was inspired to become a calypso singer ("calypsonian") in 1934 during a trip to San Fernando, the largest city in the south. Within a short time, his talents as a lyricist and singer had become apparent, and in 1935 he and other singers were sent to New York City to record for Decca Records. Among these early recordings, now considered classics, is Tiger's calypso "Money is King." The present track is a rerecording of this song done some forty-four years later when Tiger was at least in his sixties.

"Money is King" is a Depression-era commentary on the lives of the haves and the have-nots, with the calypsonian, of course, speaking for the latter. Organized into five stanzas, the lines of the song are not consistent in length or in rhyme pattern, but nonetheless they are clearly lyrics. Even so, the words do not fit neatly with the music, and the singer forces some lines into the allotted time by rushing the words in speech rhythm. Each stanza has eight lines, and thus the melody consists of eight phrases. The first four melodic phrases, however, are the same, whereas each of the second four are different, leading to a melodic structure that can be expressed as A, A, A, A, B, C, D, E.

In the first stanza Tiger declares that if you have money, you can get away with murder, and people will not even care if you have the disease *kokobe* (yaws)—but if you are poor, you are little more than a dog. The latter theme reappears in the third, fourth, and fifth stanzas. In stanza

The hills above Port of Spain, Trinidad's capital, gave birth to Calypso and Steel Drums. Because the higher up one lives in the hills the lower one's social status, the poor naturally came from here

two Tiger asserts that if you have money, the storeowner will treat you like a king, and will even go as far as sending your goods to your house on a motorbike. The third stanza declares that even a college-educated man with no money will not be given credit at a Chinese restaurant (" 'Me no trust-am,' bawl out the Chinee [sic] man"). In the fourth stanza Tiger says that even a dog can find scraps of food around and if it's a good breed, people will take it in as a pet—but a "hungry man" will be treated worse than a dog. Finally, without money a man cannot attract a woman, buy her gifts, or show affection. His conclusion: "If you haven't money, dog is better than you." (These lyrics are quoted in Hill 1993, 259–60.)

Cultural Considerations. Trinidad's particular history of kinder and gentler colonialism helped create the more relaxed attitude reflected in its arts, quite unlike Jamaica where an oppressed underclass continues to seethe with anger against the wrongs of both today and the past. Although Spain originally claimed the islands of Trinidad and Tobago, few Spanish actually settled there. After the English drove the French out of certain islands of the Lesser Antilles group during the mid-eighteenth century, the French and their slaves resettled in Trinidad, bringing Roman Catholicism with them. The French had a relatively laissez faire attitude toward their slaves, but tolerance of slave customs declined after the Protestant English took control of the island in 1797. Slavery was abolished in Trinidad in 1843, after which great numbers of indentured laborers, especially from British India, were

During the annual Carnival parade in Ⓒ
Trinidad's capital, Port of Spain,
The Gladiators display the dramatic costumes
typical of this event (unknown)

His costume more than twelve feet high and Ⓒ
ten feet wide, Anthony Paul portrayed the
"Splendour of Moonlight" during Trinidad's
annual Carnival parade (unknown)

CARNIVAL

A pre-Lent festival
celebrated primarily
in Europe and the
Caribbean. Known as
Mardi Gras in the
United States.

brought to the country. Thus, the population of nineteenth-century Trinidad consisted of freed slaves, indentured workers (free or still under contract), and a small number of French and English colonials.

Carnival, the period of celebration before Lent begins—called Mardi Gras in New Orleans—is widely celebrated in Roman Catholic countries, and although Trinidad had become English, its French heritage remained strong. Early Carnivals were polite affairs celebrated publicly by the upper classes while the working classes were left to their own devices. By the mid-nineteenth century, however, the "rowdy" classes had taken over Carnival, now celebrated through street dancing, the singing of songs that often mocked the upper classes, stick fighting, and a great parade of costumed revelers. The British authorities attempted to bring this growing chaos under control by passing and enforcing laws against excessive noise. In 1883 the government passed a "music bill" that permitted "drums, tambours, and chac-chacs [rattles]" to be played only under license and forbade all such music at night. The prohibitions on drumming led to protests, riots, and the singing of increasingly critical songs. Not to be outwitted by the British, Trinidadians denied drums began beating or stamping on bamboo tubes, creating the "tamboo bamboo" band—the term *tamboo* being derived from the word *tambor,* meaning drum.

During the latter part of the nineteenth century government officials, especially Norman Le Blanc, began a process of both co-opting and civilizing Carnival activities. By creating competitions among singers and bands, held in tents during Carnival, he simultaneously harnessed calypso song and provided an acceptable place for its expression. At the same time, the language of the songs was changed from *patois* to English. Eventually, these now tamed topical songs became one of Trinidad's national musics.

Thus, a "calypso" is a topical song or musical commentary on current events, the foibles of the upper classes, recent scandals, or odd fashions. As such they have a short shelf life, but during their brief existence they often sting. Yet calypso is rarely an angry music like reggae; parody, satire, and ridicule are its methods, though, as is often pointed out in the lyrics, these are used *sans humanité* ("without mercy"). Because calypso songs were created in response to particular events close to home, they also did not export well, and calypso recordings have not had the wide distribution that recordings of, say, steel band have. However, when the Andrews Sisters rerecorded Lord Invader's "Rum and Coca Cola" in the United States and sold millions of copies, they showed that some songs could appeal to a broad market. (Lord Invader, who had not received any royalties, later sued and won a settlement.) Jamaican-born Harry Belafonte has also made a career of singing watered-down calypso music for a mass audience in North America.

Many calypsonians took on bombastic names, to match their sometimes bombastic lyrics. Major figures have included Attila the Hun (Raymond Quevedo, a labor leader and politician), The Mighty Sparrow (Slinger Francisco), Lord Protector (Patrick Jones), The Mighty Chalkdust (Hollis Liverpool, a school teacher), Lord Kitchener (famous for his "Pan in A"), and others with names like Roaring Lion, Lord Executor, Houdini, Calypso Rose (a rare female singer), and Immortal Spoiler. Because they were considered thoughtful commentators rather than popular stars, many have continued to perform into old age.

Trinidad, however, has not been immune to other musical currents, and calypso has faced stiff competition from North American rock, soul, and jazz, as well as reggae, Afro-Cuban music, and *zouk* (from the French Lesser Antilles). In the late 1970s some singers began blending calypso with aspects of rock and reggae, creating soca (soul-calypso), a more danceable style with less consequential words. New blends of calypso and other genres continue to be produced, but because the calypsonians retain a significant place in Trinidadian society as commentators, the pure calypso tradition continues. However, because calypso is mostly performed during Carnival, the singers can rarely make a living through their art. Many work in other sectors the rest of the year, and some live abroad, returning to Trinidad only for Carnival.

PAN
A musical instrument from Trinidad made from a steel oil drum.

Site 4: Steel Band

First Impressions. Uninitiated listeners may mistake the sounds of a steel band for a calliope, a theater organ, or some sort of automatic pipe organ contraption. In fact, the steel band is an unlikely orchestra,

Track 15

Three views of steel orchestras:

a. Full ensemble with bass pans in front (Right) Ⓒ

b. Lead pans in the front row (Below)

c. A lead or melody pan showing many "dents," each representing a pitch (Bottom)

MARACAS
A pair of small Caribbean gourd rattles with interior beads.

made up, in part or entirely, of fifty-five-gallon oil drums, whose heads have been beaten into a series of convex circles. Steel band music is usually energetic, highly rhythmic, and pop music–flavored—but it can also be serene, even "classical." In existence now for more than fifty years, steel band has soared in popularity in North America recently, resulting in an increasing number of schools, colleges, and universities that sponsor steel band ensembles. This music is tiny Trinidad's most famous gift to the rest of the world.

Aural Analysis. All but the rhythm instruments of the steel band began life as fifty-five-gallon oil drums. A steel band ensemble consists of multiple steel drums, also called *pan* (pronounced like "pawn"), plus a rhythm section known as the "engine room," which is comprised of a conventional drum set, conga drum, automobile brake drums, and possibly other kinds of percussion such as *maracas* (rattles), *claves* (sticks beaten together), the *guiro* (scraped gourd), and the cowbell (an echo of the African iron bell). There is no fixed number of *pan,* nor are their names used consistently. The higher-pitched *pan* are cut from the full drum, leaving a short "skirt" (side of the drum), whereas the lowest pans use the full skirt. Notes of definite pitch are produced by striking tuned dents that have been carefully hammered into the head of each pan; the higher-pitched instruments are capable of producing many more pitches than lower-pitched ones, because the area required for a high pitch is small and for a bass pitch large. Some pitch ranges require multiple *pan*, because bass pans often can produce only four pitches. The leading melodic *pan* are known variously as the *tenor, ping-pong, lead, soprano,* and *melody pan.* Those creating harmony or "strumming" effects in imitation of guitars are called variously *guitar, double second, double guitar, quadraphonic, triple guitar,* and *cello.* The bass line is provided by the bass *pan.* Because the tuning process is most critical, and the ensemble's overall sound depends on good tuning, skilled tuners are highly sought after.

The title of our example, "Jump Up," refers to the kind of dancing also known as "breakaway," which is performed in the streets during Trinidad's Carnival. This is the joyful, outdoor kind of music that really epitomizes Carnival: fast, rhythmic, full of syncopation. Because performances are typically extended and because players have to learn all compositions by memory, repetition is naturally a part of most pieces. "Jump Up" is no exception. Listen carefully and you'll be able to follow its progression.

The piece begins with an eight-measure introduction with much syncopation, played four times. Then follows the main tune, also eight measures in length, which is played twice. Following this a third section of eight measures, perhaps best called an interlude, is played four times, after which the melody is repeated twice and the interlude four more times. The main melody then returns before fading out in our excerpted example.

Cultural Considerations. The steel band, locally called *pan,* is doubtless the best-known and most widely distributed kind of ensemble invented in the New World. *Pan* were originally made from the thousands of oil drums left behind in Trinidad, first by the British, then during World War II by Americans, who had built a forward base west of Port of Spain for flights to Africa. Like the *tamboo bamboo* instruments, their invention was due to the British ban on drum playing during Carnival. In the 1930s revelers began picking up various discarded metal cans such as "biscuit tins" and beating rhythms on them; these groups became known as "dustbin bands." Creative Trinidadians soon discovered that by pounding (or "sinking") circles into the tops of oil drums abandoned as junk, it was possible to produce multiple pitches on a single surface. Obviously, these instruments were not as portable like the dustbin instruments. Over the next few years, however, the makers developed *pan* of various sizes to allow for a full range of pitches and to enable performers to produce full chords. Little did the British or Americans know that their refuse would be recycled into the voice of a nation: in 1992 *pan* became the official national instrument of Trinidad.

In its early years, however, *pan* was not so respectable, for, like the *tamboo bamboo* and dustbin bands, it was associated with the slums in the hills above Port of Spain and with gang violence. As with calypso, the authorities gradually tamed pan by integrating it into the country's social fabric, especially by arranging competitions. The earlier "Pan Is

A "panyard" where steel bands in Trinidad assemble to practice
(M. Tyler Rounds)

Beautiful" competition has given way to the current "Panorama" competitions. These are held near the end of Carnival, when dozens of bands, both amateur and near professional, compete by playing three currently required numbers: a Western classical composition of their choice, a mandatory test piece specific to that year, and a calypso of their choice.

Most players are amateurs who learn their parts by rote. Important to the process, then, is an arranger who creates the piece (more often than not in notation) and painstakingly teaches it one measure at a time to the ensemble. Many bands can play (from memory) extended and sophisticated European compositions as long as symphony and concerto movements, and some now play entirely original compositions in a relatively modern style.

Steel bands have spread throughout the Caribbean, and some islands, such as Antigua, have had them since the late 1940s. The use of a single tenor (melody) pan as part of an unrelated ensemble is now common too, sometimes just to invoke the idea of the "West Indies." Steel bands also flourish wherever West Indians have settled, especially in New York, Toronto, and London. Additionally, in recent years ensembles directed by non–West Indians and featuring non–West Indian players have sprung up in high schools, colleges, and universities throughout the United States. Steel bands are becoming prevalent in Europe as well, especially Sweden and Switzerland, although they have also been seen on the streets of Paris.

THE BAHAMAS

Arrival: The Bahamas

The Bahamas were the first islands of the "New World" visited by Christopher Columbus in 1492. At that time, the region was inhabited by the Arawak people, who after contact with Europeans were quickly wiped out by European diseases. The Spanish, despite having funded Columbus's voyage, did not lay claim to the islands, and it was the British who eventually settled Eleuthera and New Providence Islands during the mid-seventeenth century. The region became a stronghold for marauders, most notably the British-born pirate Edward Teach, better known as Blackbeard.

By the eighteenth century, the British government had asserted its control over the entire region and claimed the Bahamas as a colony. The

A *kecak* or "monkey chant" performance derived from the Indian epic, *Ramayana* (Jerrold Moore)

The statue of China's greatest philosopher and teacher, Kong Fuzi (Confucius), in the ancient Kong temple of Quanzhou, China

A *Jiangnan sizhu* (silk and bamboo) ensemble playing
informally in its meeting room, Shanghai, China (Phong Nguyen)

Jingju (Beijing Opera) performance: a red-faced general is flanked by a painted face *(jing)*
to his right and a young man *(xiao sheng)* to his left

A performance of a military style play in Taipei's Military Theater as seen from the lighting booth

Military *jing*
painted face character

Military scene with numerous generals

The hero character in the Revolutionary Beijing Opera *Taking Tiger Mountain by Strategy* challenges his oppressor (Peking: Foreign Languages Press)

A Japanese *gagaku* court ensemble
performs on stage, Taipei

Tseyen Tserendorj playing the
Mongolian *morinhuur* (two-stringed,
"horse-head" fiddle), New York City
(© Jack Vartoogian/FrontRowPhotos)

Japanese
kabuki actors
(Unknown)

Kabuki musicians: (back row) singers, *shamisen* players; (front row) *taiko* drum, *o-tsuzumi* side-held drum, *ko-tsuzumi* shoulder-held drum (© Jack Vartoogian/FrontRowPhotos)

Tibetan Buddhist monks of the Gyuto sect performing the *dung-chen* (long trumpets)
(© Jack Vartoogian/FrontRowPhotos)

Jerusalem's Dome of the Rock, a part of the Temple Mount called Qubbat As-Sakhrah in Arabic and built between 687 and 691, is a revered shrine *(mashhad)* for both Muslims and Jews.

Sufi Muslims of the Mevlevi ('Whirling') sect from Turkey perform the *Sema* ritual on stage in New York City
(© Jack Vartoogian/FrontRowPhotos)

The Nsuase *kete* drum group performing at an Asante funeral in
Kumase, Ghana (Joseph S. Kaminski)

The well-known South African vocal group, Ladysmith Black Mambazo, performing onstage
in New York City (© Jack Vartoogian/FrontRowPhotos)

Flamenco dancers and guitarists perform
in a club in Cadiz, Spain (Robert Garfias)

Bodhnath Stupa, a temple frequented by Tibetans living in exile near Kathmandu,
Nepal. A man chants on the left while a man turns a prayer wheel on the right

Members of the St. Nicholas Russian Orthodox Church Balalaika Orchestra from Mogadore, Ohio,
use instruments in several sizes. In the front row are seen the typical *prima balalaika* in triangular shape
and the *domra* with a round body

Scottish highland pipers march for visitors in Portree, Skye, in the Hebrides Islands off the northwest coast of Scotland

Colorfully dressed members of a Bulgarian women's chorus perform onstage (© Jack Vartoogian/FrontRowPhotos)

At the seacoast of Trinidad, six leaders of the African-derived Shango religion bow before ritual offerings about to be floated into the sea for Oshun, the goddess of the sea

During the annual Carnival parade in Trinidad's capital, Port of Spain, The Gladiators display the dramatic costumes typical of this event (unknown)

His costume more than twelve feet high and ten feet wide, Anthony Paul portrayed the "Splendour of Moonlight" during Trinidad's annual Carnival parade (unknown)

Steel orchestra: full ensemble with bass pans in front

Four musicians accompany Merengue dancing in the Dominican Republic's capital, Santo Domingo. L to R: the *tambora* drum, tenor saxophone, button box accordion, and *guiro* scraper (Martha Ellen Davis)

Amazonian Indians (Kayapo-Xikrin) native to the Brazilian rainforest (Courtesy of Alamy)

The Argentine tango dance, unlike the regularized ballroom form,
requires rapid changes of emotion, from control to inflamed passion
(© Jack Vartoogian/FrontRowPhotos)

Maypole dancers perform to the accompaniment of a *mariachi* ensemble on a city street in Merida, Mexico, on the Yucatan peninsula (Christina Shahriari)

Members of a *Gongada* from Minas Geraes perform during Carnival celebrations in Brazil (Welson Tremura)

Dancers re-enact a grand Samba dance during a performance
of the revue "Oba Oba '93" (© Jack Vartoogian/FrontRowPhotos)

A fiddler leads two friends playing guitar (center) and
mandolin (left) in playing an old string band tune

Old Regular Baptist elders at Pleasant View Church near Medina, Ohio,
prepare to baptize a new member after having broken six-inch thick ice

Typical of a powwow, dancers representing many tribes join together
to celebrate their Native American heritage (Andrew Shahriari)

islands became an important refuge for loyalists to the British crown after the American revolutionary war in 1776. Many Carolinians fled to the islands with their African-descended slaves. Baptist missionaries accompanied them as well, establishing churches throughout the islands. After slavery was abolished in 1833, many British-descended residents left as economic prosperity declined. As a result, more than 90 percent of today's population in the Bahamas is of African descent.

Today, the Bahamas, with its roughly seven hundred islands, is one of the most popular tourist destinations in the Western hemisphere. More than three million tourists visit the country each year to enjoy the white sand beaches and spectacular coral reefs and the splendors of Caribbean cuisine. Grand hotels and luxury cruise ships contrast with chalky stucco houses and solitary sailboats drifting offshore. Seafaring activity has long faded as the primary economic activity of the country as tourism brings in revenue of more than 1.3 billion dollars annually.

The huge emphasis on tourism has greatly affected cultural activities throughout the Bahamas. Most musicians seek employment at hotels or with tourist shows, resulting in a disinterest in music that does not "sell" to the predominantly American audience. Thus, reggae, calypso, and popular music from the United States and Europe dominate the musical landscape of the Bahamas, whereas the "quaint" rhyming spirituals, *goombay* ensembles, and "rake and scrape" bands of the locals usually remain unheard by the average tourist.

Site 5: *Rhyming Spiritual*

Track 16

First Impressions. Enthusiasm characterizes this performance. The reverent opening quickly moves into a rousing rendition of "The Lord's Prayer" from the Christian tradition. Sounding either slightly inebriated or "caught in the spirit," this male vocal trio performs a rhythmically vibrant rhyming spiritual that is raw rather than sanitized for tourist consumption.

Aural Analysis. The focus of a rhyming spiritual is on the lead tenor voice, known as the *rhymer.* While the music does not strictly follow a call-and-response form, the rhymer starts each phrase and guides the changing tempo. Though each rhyming spiritual has an established melody and basic narrative, the rhymer is free to extemporize the lyrical and melodic content of a performance. In this case, the rhymer begins with the expected lyrics of the spiritual and then uses "The Lord's Prayer" as the basis for his improvisations after the sixth refrain. He also extends his vocal phrases to make them overlap the refrain provided by the accompanying voices.

As the rhymer "bobs" along, the supporting cast adds unique vocal timbres: a deep growling lower voice and a near-falsetto upper voice repeating the refrain, "My Lord help me to pray." Rhyming spirituals are expected to have at least the rhymer and the lower voice, known as the *basser,* but are frequently enhanced by the addition of one or more upper voices. The inclusion of the upper voices helps clarify the vocal harmony rooted in the lower voice and allows the rhymer more freedom to elaborate his melodic content.

Cultural Considerations. Many hymns and spirituals common to the southern United States can be found in the Bahamas as well. The slaves of British Loyalists exiled after the American Revolutionary War brought these songs with them and maintained their performance in many contexts before and after slavery was abolished. The influence of the Baptist church, with its emphasis on energetic singing, emotionally extemporized sermons, and congregational participation, is especially pronounced. Anthems sung in church are the best-known reminder of the Bahamas' historical link with the United States.

The church's influence was felt in secular realms as well. Rhyming spirituals were most often sung by sponge fisherman who roamed the western coast of the island of Andros. Biblical themes were most common, though some songs focused on local events, such as a shipwreck. The spirituals are essentially narratives told through song rather than speech. The rhymer recounts the tale through his improvisations as the other voices provide harmonic and rhythmic support. The bass voice is likened to the earth while the upper voices are considered to be the sky. The rhymer weaves between the two with a rhythmic freedom akin to the ever-changing movement of wind or waves.

When the sponge-fishing industry declined, a major context for the performance of rhyming spirituals was diminished as well. Consequently, the art of rhyming now has a limited number of practitioners. Today, extemporized rhyming spirituals are most commonly heard at funeral wakes. Some professional groups, such as the Dicey Doh Singers, continue to perform rhyming spirituals, but their music has a slick polished sound intended to appeal to tourists. The raspy voices, improvised rhymes, and ambiguous harmonies heard in our example from the 1960s have been replaced with full voices, composed lyrics, and regular harmonic progressions. Nonetheless, though they have lost some of their raw energy, rhyming spirituals continue to be a distinctive aspect of Bahamian musical identity.

CUBA

Arrival: Cuba

Although only about ninety miles from Florida, at this writing Cuba remains largely off limits to American visitors, though tourism by non-Americans has actually once again become a major moneymaker for an otherwise destitute country. Before the revolution in 1959, when Fidel Castro swept away the American-supported government of Fulgencio Batista, Cuba was a playground for rich North Americans, and Havana was one of the most enticing cities in the Western Hemisphere, with its grand hotels, homes, and resorts.

An island slightly larger than Indiana with a population of around eleven million, Cuba was first "discovered" by Christopher Columbus in 1492. At that time its inhabitants were Arawak Indians, but with the influx of Spanish and Africans, the Arawak were wiped out over time. Following the Spanish-American War of 1898, Cuba was controlled by the United States until 1901, after which political instability and military dictatorships were the norm until 1959. Cuba has remained under Castro's rule for nearly fifty years. Whatever else we might say about its government, post-1959 Cuba has shown generous support for the traditional arts, particularly music, and in recent years the country's energetic musical styles have begun to attract the attention of connoisseurs the world over. Today, travelers to Cuba can enjoy performances by vintage musicians of the highest professional level.

What makes Cuba's music distinctive is its successful blending of European and African musical traditions. This mixing began with Santeria, a syncretistic religion combining traditional Yoruba practices with Roman Catholicism. Later, secular Afro-Cuban music developed, which gave rise to many of the so-called "Latin styles" that became popular in North America, particularly in the context of ballroom dance. American jazz also absorbed much from Cuba, leading to the Latin jazz movement of the 1940s brought to the north by players such as percussionists Chano Pozo and Machito (Frank Raul Grillo) and trombonist Juan Tizol. "Latin" music remains popular today, not just in North America but throughout the world, although sometimes in the popularized forms represented by Ricky Martin, Marc Anthony, and Gloria Estefan. The Latin music that accompanied ballroom dance was a major contributor from the 1940s on to the formation of popular song styles throughout the world, especially in Asia.

SANTERIA
An animistic belief system found primarily in Cuba and the United States.

Site 6: Afro-Cuban-Derived *Salsa*

Track 17

First Impressions. This recording is perhaps more rhythmically complex than any of our other examples of music from the Americas. As danceable as it is listenable, it offers both African-derived polyrhythmic patterns and European- and jazz-inspired harmonies, played in a crisp fashion with everything from brass "punches" to a florid flute solo.

Aural Analysis. Because the Caribbean is known for its cultural fusions, it comes as no surprise to hear European brass and the piano combined with a *slit-gong* wood block. Other instruments, such as the cowbell, are perhaps African in origin, but the clarinet, trumpet, trombone, string bass, and flute are European. This mixing of instruments representing different cultures (European, African, and Amerindian) is typical of the music we know as *salsa,* a term that otherwise denotes a colorful, pungent sauce much associated with salty chips. Our example also includes a solo male voice that works in a kind of call-and-response pattern with the melodic instruments and a small chorus.

While the melody and harmony are Euro-American, with a clear influence from jazz, the whole metrical-rhythmic structure is from another source: Africa. True, the music is ostensibly in duple meter—4/4

A local Salsa band plays on the stage of the Eastman School of Music in Rochester, New York, a bastion of Western classical music

time—but this is no march, with a heavy, obvious downbeat. Here and there beat one is easy to find, perhaps by focusing on the melody, but in other passages it becomes obscure. Accented sounds are heard on the off beats, giving the music a highly syncopated feel. This is because the underlying organization is closer to African timeline patterns than to European meter based on units of four beats each (i.e., measures). The basic organizational unit in this music is a two-measure pattern called the *clave*, which consists of either 3 + 2 or 2 + 3 beats played in a syncopated fashion. Other percussion instruments play their particular patterns in opposition to the *clave*, giving the rhythm section a changeable complexity that is as hard to sort out as it is to ignore. Indeed, in many compositions, beat one is de-emphasized or even omitted, requiring the listener to feel the missing pulse in order to know where the measures begin.

Our example begins with a melody played twice by piano and string bass, underpinned by the *clave* pattern (called *clave son,* 2 + 3) played on a wood block (called a *slit-gong* because the block has a deep slit cut in it near one edge). As the piano-bass pattern is repeated twice more, a tall barrel-shaped, single-headed drum called *tumbadora* or *conga* enters, playing its own *tumbao* pattern accompanied by the *maracas* (rattles). When the brass instruments begin playing melody, the *timbales* also enter, these latter being a pair of metal-framed drums of European military origin. The pattern that the *timbales* play, called *cascará,* is categorized as a *palito* because it is struck on the side of the drum. After this, the solo voice alternates with brass "punches" and flute. Finally, a section begins in which the voice alternates with a chorus comprised of several singers, while the *timbale* player adds a bell pattern.

Entitled "Quítate de la vía Perico," the song is a mock lament for someone nicknamed Perico (meaning "parakeet"). *Perico*, perhaps a local odd fellow, was sucking sugar cane while walking on the railroad tracks, didn't hear the train, and was killed. After an opening that sounds like a train whistle, someone calls out "And here comes Perico again; let's have fun once more! And what a machine [locomotive], man." The vocalists then warn Perico in a sung "call": "Move away from the train track, Perico; the train is coming … Later you may not say that you were not warned." In the response section the group sings, "If I had known that Perico was deaf, I would have stopped the train." The rest of the song more or less repeats these ideas, though we will spare you certain gris-

CLAVE

Rhythm pattern in Salsa music. Also, an instrument consisting of two sticks beaten together.

ly details. This song was originally recorded by Puerto Rican musicians, including singer Ismael Rivera and bandleader Rafael Cortijo Verdejo, but its text includes phrases associated with Cuba, not Puerto Rico. It is classified as a *guaracha*, a type of dance discussed in the next section.

Cultural Considerations. Most listeners would describe this music as *salsa,* but its roots are Cuban and its tendrils lead elsewhere, particularly to two forms of dance popular worldwide (*cha-cha* and *mambo*) and to Puerto Rican musicians living in New York. As we have already noted, in Cuba European melody and harmony, first introduced by Spanish colonialists, have long been combined with African rhythms brought to the country by African slaves. The mixing of these two influences produced new and exciting genres that are quintessentially Caribbean, but popularly called *Latin.* Cuba is also well known for *Santeria,* a syncretistic faith that combines traditional African pantheism with Roman Catholicism, somewhat like Haiti's *Vodou.* Unlike *Vodou,* however, *Santeria* is derived from the Nigerian Yoruba pantheon, which makes it a variation of similar religions found elsewhere in the Americas, particularly Trinidadian Shango and Brazilian Candomblé. As in all of these faiths, each god in Cuba (*orisha*) is associated with a particular *orus,* a rhythmic pattern played by a percussion group consisting of three *bata* drums, an iron bell (*ekón*), and rattles

The percussion instruments used in playing Salsa music. Top photo: (front) a pair of *tumbador* or *conga* drums, (right rear) a pair of *timbales* or *pailes* with metal cowbell attached, (left rear) a pair of *bongo* drums. Bottom photo: (from top clockwise), *concerro* (metal cowbell), maracas (shakers), *claves* (wood sticks), *cabasa* (gourd shaker), and *guiro* (scraper)
(Andrew Shahriari)

(*chéqueres*), and elaborated on through call-and-response singing.

The music of *Santeria* is generally called "Afro-Cuban" music and has given rise to numerous secular genres, including *rhumba, comparsa*, and *son*. These genres, too, came to be associated with various dance styles, both folk and ballroom. Following the Spanish-American War of 1898, Cuba became a playground for wealthy North Americans, and Havana developed into one of the hemisphere's most vibrant cities. During this period, various kinds of Cuban music, especially the softened and more popularized forms played by such band leaders as Xavier Cugat, became widely known outside Cuba and influenced classical, jazz, and popular music in North America and Europe. They also gave rise to several dance crazes—including the *rhumba, cha-cha,* and *mambo*—which were eventually absorbed into the ballroom dance canon. Though the music was Cuban, the ballroom dances themselves were actually created and codified by Anglos and only loosely based on the original dances of Cuba.

Afro-Cuban styles attained increasing popularity in New York in the 1970s among Puerto Rican musicians, who added Puerto Rican and jazz elements to the music to create what is known colloquially as *salsa*. Among the best-known proponents of this style are Willie Colón, Tito Puente, Johnny Pacheco, Ruben Blades, and Mongo Santamaria. Salsa is no longer emblematic of Puerto Rico alone, because it was adopted by musicians in many parts of the Caribbean and South America, and is today perhaps the most generally known form of Latin music worldwide.

Salsa music generally, including our example, is closely associated with dance. Today there are numerous Cuban-derived Latin dances, including the *rhumba, cha-cha, mambo, guaracha, merengue,* and *bolero,* but before these became popular during the twentieth century, Cubans danced the *contradanza, danza, danzón,* and *danzonete.* Modern Latin dances have little or nothing to do with any original "folk" dances found in Cuba or elsewhere, having been co-opted by North Americans and the British, stripped of undesirable elements, and redesigned and codified for the ballroom. For example, the *rhumba* craze began in Cuba in the 1920s as a watered-down form of *son,* while the *cha-cha* was developed in New York in the early 1950s. "Salsa dance," though closely related step-wise to ballroom dance, is quite separate from ballroom dance, because the ballroom is a highly regulated dance world that strictly differentiates its dances. Most salsa dance is a blend of what ballroom dancers differentiate as *mambo* and *cha-cha.* The present example is strictly speaking a *guaracha,* but because the ballroom world generally does not recognize this dance, our recording would be used for *mambo* dancing in a ballroom setting.

GUARACHA
(pronounced GWAH-RAH-CHA)
A Latin American ballroom dance, as well as a song type emphasizing call-and-response vocal organization.

ORUS
A rhythmic pattern associated with an *orisha* in the *Santeria* religious tradition.

Arrival: The Dominican Republic

THE DOMINICAN REPUBLIC

The island of Hispaniola is divided into two countries: Haiti and the Dominican Republic. Whereas Haiti is dominated by an African-descended populace, the Dominican Republic's population is largely a mix of Spanish and African heritage. While African cultural influence is strong throughout the country, Dominicans tend to emphasize their European roots and associate themselves with Hispanic culture, largely due to the cultural policies promoted by the former dictator Rafael Leonidas Trujillo Molina (r.1930–61). These policies instilled a fear of anything Haitian, especially anything associated with the widespread practice of *Vodou*. Trujillo's influence is still felt today, though many youth are embracing their African roots.

Site 7: Merengue

Track 18

First Impressions. *Merengue* is fast-paced. The "scraping" sound of the *guiro* is the primary timekeeper and perhaps the genre's most distinctive feature. The accompanying drum (called a *tambora*) plays in "bursts," with a thudding fundamental sound and interlacing slaps. The repetitive melodic line moves at a frenetic pace, pausing only when the voices enter. As with much Caribbean music, merengue is highly danceable.

Four musicians accompany Merengue dancing in the Dominican Republic's capital, Santo Domingo. L to R: the *tambora* drum, tenor saxophone, button box accordion, and *guiro* scraper (Martha Ellen Davis)

Aural Analysis. The identifying feature of *merengue* is the pairing of the *guiro* and *tambora*. The *guiro* is a rasp idiophone, typically with a cylindrical shape. The "scraping" sound is produced when a piece of wood or metal is rubbed along the coarse outside face of the instrument. The *guiro* provides the fundamental tempo and typically emphasizes the off-beats with a long "scrape." The *tambora* is a small barrel drum made with thick leather faces and is held in the lap. Deep tones are produced by playing one face with a stick, while slapping sounds are created by striking the other face with the hand. The "bursts" typical of the instrument are played with the stick, and are followed by hand-slap punctuation. In rural performances, the *guira* and *tambora* not only provide the fundamental rhythm but also are frequently featured in improvisatory passages. Ballroom dance *merengue* styles do not generally include such vibrant improvisation on these instruments.

The melodic content in our recorded example is provided by a button-box accordion, as well as by the voices. The melody is rhythmically dense and contributes to the fast-paced feel of the music. The voices follow a call-and-response format, which is imitated by the accordion at the conclusion of its solo sections. The quickly repeated tone imitates the call, while the subsequent harmonic chords corre-

GUIRO
(pronounced
GWEE-ROH)
A scraped
gourd idiophone.

MERENGUE

A Latin American
dance and music form,
originally from the
Dominican Republic.

315

spond to the group's response. Other styles of *merengue* use guitars or saxophones as the primary melodic instruments.

Merengue form is typically divided into three sections: *paseo*, *merengue*, and *jaleo*. These equate to an introduction, verse, and chorus. The *paseo,* or "walking" section, emphasizes the melodic instruments and often begins at a slower tempo, sometimes in free rhythm. This quickly leads to the *merengue* section, which is established by the *guira-tambora* rhythms. Vocalists sing different verses in this section followed by a refrain, the *jaleo*, which is repeated throughout the piece. The accordion (or saxophone) improvises its own *merengue* section and follows with a *jaleo* refrain before the voices return. This alternation between *merengue* and *jaleo*, which may be performed either by vocalists or instrumentalists, can continue indefinitely. The concluding *jaleo* often quickens in tempo as a sign that the performance is about to finish.

Cultural Considerations. While there are several styles of *merengue,* they are all generally categorized as either folk or ballroom. Ballroom *merengue* is characterized by a large orchestra, often backing a crooning vocalist, and a consistent *guira-tambora* rhythm. The ballroom form still follows the *paseo-merengue-jaleo* pattern, but has less improvisational freedom. Ballroom *merengue* was strongly promoted during the Trujillo years as a "national" dance in order to help establish a unique Dominican identity. Today, long after the end of Trujillo's rule, *merengue* remains the most popular music in the country.

As with many Caribbean music genres, *merengue*'s name also refers to a dance. The dance is a simple side-step in which the leg that follows drags on the ground. The modern form of the dance requires exaggerated hip movement from side to side. It is often danced in pairs, with the dancers' upper bodies poised in a standard ballroom dance position with one hand on the hip and the other held out at shoulder height. The dancers move to the left in a circle around the floor, but may rotate in a single spot, which allows for numerous couples in a small space.

The origin of *merengue* and its associated dance is not entirely agreed upon, but many believe that the dance is a combination of West African circle dances and European salon dances. The side-step shuffle seems to evoke a time when slaves' feet were chained together while working in the sugar-cane fields. The upper body movements mimic the dance positions of a French minuet. One of the step patterns in ballroom merengue is called the *ibo*, a term that, interestingly, refers to the Ibo ethnic group of West Africa. The music is also a blend of African and European elements. The *tambora* is believed to derive from similar West African instruments. The *guiro* is thought by some to be a Dominican creation, while others consider it an innovation based on scraped gourd idiophones found in West Africa. The call-and-response vocal organization is reminiscent of West African vocal performance. On the other hand, the inclusion of the button-box accordion and the use of the guitar and saxophones as primary melodic instruments reveal musical connections with Europe.

Questions to Consider

1. Where do "African Survivals" appear in music of the Caribbean? What makes them African?

2. How did differences in colonial rule affect the course of musical development in the Caribbean?

3. What role does music play in spirit possession in religions such as Vodou and Santeria?

4. Which Caribbean musics best exemplify the idea that music can express discontent and challenge authority? How are the examples chosen different in content and attitude?

5. How can you account for the fact that the most prominent music types in the Caribbean are popular in nature?

6. How has modern ballroom dance been influenced by music of the Caribbean? What ballroom dances derive from "Latin" music?

CARIBBEAN SEA
LESSER ANTILLES
TRINIDAD
CARACAS
ATLANTIC OCEAN
VENEZUELA
GEORGETOWN
FRENCH GUIANA
PARAMARIBO
GUYANA
CAYENNE
BOGOTA
SURINAME
COLOMBIA
MARAJO ISLAND
QUITO
ECUADOR
AMAZON RAINFOREST
Amazon River
Gulf of Guayaquil
ANDES MOUNTAINS
PERU
Recife
BRAZIL
LIMA
Salvador
BRAZILIAN HIGHLANDS
BRASILIA
Lake Titicaca
LA PAZ
BOLIVIA
SUCRE
Belo Horizonte
Rio De Janeiro
PACIFIC OCEAN
Sao Paulo
CHILE
PARAGUAY
ASUNCION
Curitiba
Porto Alegre
ARGENTINA
SANTIAGO
URUGUAY
BUENOS AIRES
MONTEVIDEO
Gulf of San Matias
ISLA GRANDE DE CHILOE
Gulf of San Jorge
TIERRA DEL FUEGO
calypso
Samba
Tango
MEXICO
MEXICO CITY
CARIBBEAN SEA
BELIZE
BELMOPAN
HONDURAS
GUATEMALA
TEGUCIGALPA
GUATEMALA
EL SALVADOR
SAN SALVADOR
NICARAGUA
MANAGUA
SAN JOSE
COSTA RICA
PANAMA
PANAMA

Established by the ancient Incas in Peru at least by the 13th century, Machu Piccu, a ruined city at 9,000 feet in the Andes Mountains, was forgotten following the Spanish conquest in the early 16th century and only rediscovered in 1911 (M. Tyler Rounds)

CHAPTER 12

Central and South America: New World Recipes

Background Preparation

I n the western hemisphere, Central and South America, as well as Mexico, are frequently overshadowed by the global attention given to the United States. While tourism is increasing steadily, most travelers choose the United States or islands of the Caribbean for their vacation destinations. Many areas south of the U.S. border are still regarded as "developing," yet the region boasts some of the world's most beautiful natural wonders, such as the Amazon, the largest river in the world, and its surrounding rainforests (mostly in Brazil); Angel Falls (Venezuela), the highest waterfall in the world; and the Andes Mountains, second only to the Himalayas in peak height and the longest system of high mountains in the world, running all along the western coast of South America.

Perhaps Mexico's most famous Mayan ruin, the pyramid at Chichen Itza was begun about 900 A.D. and testifies to the advanced technological development of this early civilization (Andrew Shahriari)

While the generally accepted theory is that the indigenous populations of the Americas crossed from Asia, recent archaeological evidence indicates that there were people living in modern Brazil some 30,000 to 50,000 years ago and in Chile and Venezuela roughly 13,000 years ago. Though little can be said for certain regarding the activities of these earliest inhabitants, the ancient empires of the Western hemisphere, namely the Maya, Aztec, and Inca empires, are better known and continue to influence the cultural identity of the present populations of Mexico, Central, and South America. Remnants of these ancient civilizations are visited by thousands of tourists every year, and archaeologists work tirelessly to uncover clues to the cultural activities of these early indigenous peoples. Evidence of advanced knowledge in astronomy, mathematics, and agriculture, as well as of highly structured political and religious systems dates to as early as

In Cusco, Peru, the Iglesia de la Compania de Jesus in the Plaza de Armas was built in the late 1570s and rebuilt later after an earthquake (Max T. Miller)

200 B.C. and suggests that at their peak each empire may have rivaled those of ancient China or Rome.

Spanish conquerors, however, put an end to the development of these civilizations soon after Christopher Columbus "discovered" the New World in 1492 A.D. Coupled with the military conquests of the Spanish conquistadors, Old World diseases—such as smallpox and measles—decimated many indigenous populations who had no biological resistance to the foreign diseases. Throughout the region, Roman Catholic missionaries found fertile ground in which to establish new churches. By the end of the eighteenth century, the Spaniards had settled in far-reaching areas of North, Central, and South America that have since grown into some of today's largest cities, such as San Francisco, Los Angeles, Mexico City, Lima, and Buenos Aires.

In addition to subjugating native peoples, Spanish and Portuguese colonialists also brought many African slaves to the Americas to work in gold and silver mines, to raise cattle, and to farm plantations growing crops such as tobacco and sugar cane. Other European colonialists followed suit, and brought with them laborers from other colonized countries such as India and Indonesia, while the French transferred many prisoners to the region. Because of this, many areas of South America today, Guyana, Suriname, and French Guiana in particular, reveal strong cultural connections with non-European peoples. Eastern coastal areas, especially in Brazil, are densely populated with peoples of mixed African and Iberian ancestry *(mulattos),* while Central America and much of the interior of South America is comprised mainly of indigenous populations, many of whom also have Spanish ancestry (those of mixed ancestry are known as *mestizos*). The rainforests of Brazil remained largely immune to the influx of foreigners until the late nineteenth and early twentieth centuries. Rapid deforestation in the 1980s led to increased interest in the protection of wildlife and the preservation of the traditional lifeways of the many indigenous Amazonian tribes.

The musical activities of the diverse peoples of Central and South America reflect these historical interactions. Indigenous populations in the rainforests and in rural areas of the Andes preserve musical traditions believed to predate the arrival of Columbus. Music found in urban areas reveals influences from Europe, specifically Spain and Portugal, as well as West Africa.

Planning the Itinerary

The music of Central and South America, and of Mexico (geographically part of North America), is comprised of three major ingredients: indigenous traditions; European-derived music; and African-inspired musical activity. The music of the Amazonian tribes and Andean rural communities dates to pre-Columbian times and has presumably remained little changed for centuries. Spanish influence is felt in numerous music traditions, especially those found in urban areas. African influence can be seen in the creation of new instruments modeled after African ones and in the use of musical traits, such as polyrhythm, commonly associated with various ethnic groups from Africa.

Our introduction to the music of this region begins with a discussion of the Kayapo-Xikrin, an Amazonian indigenous tribe found in the rainforests of Brazil. Next we travel to the upper reaches of the Andes Mountains, where descendants of the ancient Inca civilization continue to play the *siku* (panpipes), which are believed to date from at least the thirteenth century. Moving to urban areas, we discuss the Spanish-influenced music of *mestizo* populations throughout Mexico and South America by examining the Argentinean *tango* and the Mexican *mariachi*. Finally, we turn to the coastline of Brazil, which is home to two of the clearest examples of African influence in South America: the unique

THE AMAZON

martial arts dance-form known as *capoeira* and the celebratory music of Carnival known as *samba*.

Arrival: The Amazon

The Amazonian rainforest of Brazil is one of the largest remaining tropical forests on the planet. It is home to thousands of wildlife species, such as jaguars, toucans, and macaws, and numerous nomadic and semi-nomadic hunter-gatherer human communities. During the latter decades of the twentieth century, the Amazon became a flashpoint for environmental activists concerned about the deteriorating ecosystem of the earth. Logging companies destroyed millions of acres of rainforests and consequently displaced many Amazonian tribes. Some of these tribes were forced to integrate into modern society, while others retreated further into the rainforest. Still others, such as the Kayapo Indians, managed to resist the encroachment of the modern world by actively protesting against the intruders and organizing events that drew international attention to the plight of their peoples. Today, many Amazonians have managed to straddle both worlds by educating themselves about modern society while maintaining their traditional way of life. The romantic vision of the Amazonian Indian as a bare-footed, spear-toting, loin-clothed hunter-gatherer is no longer a realistic portrayal of the native population, who can often be found in T-shirts, hunting with rifles, and sitting in classrooms learning to read and write. Still, ceremonial activities based on traditional belief systems remain at the heart of the community life of each individual group of Amazonians.

There are many distinct tribes of Amazonian peoples, and cultural traits, such as language, dress, belief system, kinship practices, and so on, vary widely from group to group. Many commonalities do exist, however, and thus some general cultural tendencies can be represented by individual groups. In our case, we focus on the Kayapo-Xikrin, who live in the southwestern area of the state of Para in central Brazil, to gain a better understanding of the music of Amazonian peoples.

Site 1: Amazonian Indian Chant

Track 19

First Impressions. Our example begins with an "eagle cry," followed by group chanting. The singing seems to be part of a community ceremony or shaman ritual—which is usually the case. To a non-specialist, the vocal performances of Amazonian tribes may seem indistinguishable from those of North American native groups, and indeed there are some parallel musical traits.

Aural Analysis. A first listening to an Amazonian musical performance reveals several identifiable features typical of the majority of Amerindian tribes of the Brazilian rainforests. Unison group singing is most common and is often unaccompanied. The singing is in a style characterized as chant and uses only a few pitches. Unaccompanied unison (monophonic) group chanting is not unique to Amazonian Indians, but it is a recognizable trait of most tribes of the Brazilian rainforest. Men and women usually sing separately, and indeed our example includes only male voices.

Many songs have a descending melodic contour, while others consist of only one or two pitches. A melodic drop-off usually closes a vocal phrase. The text setting is

Amazonian Indians (Kayapo-Xikrin) native to the Brazilian rainforest (Courtesy of Alamy)

most often syllabic. The dynamic level is usually consistent, though shouting sometimes occurs but not usually as a central feature of the performance. Vocal pulsation (a slight volume amplification) is sometimes employed to add a rhythmic element to purely vocal performances. Rattles, flutes, or small drums sometimes accompany these performances, though none are heard in this example. Handclapping and foot-stomping are also frequently employed to maintain a steady pulse during performance. Additionally, large sticks or hollow tree branches are sometimes pounded on the ground to add a rhythmic element. Though the music follows a steady pulse, metrical units are frequently irregular as they follow the phrasing of the text rather than being organized into a set number of pulses.

Cultural Considerations. The music of Amazonian peoples is integral to their ritual activities. Some familiarity with these rituals is useful for a better understanding of the meaning of musical performance. The recording we have selected is the concluding section of a Kayapo-Xikrin naming ritual. Known as *takak-nhiok*, this ritual occurs in five stages over a period of five years. Each stage enables the initiates to participate in and gain new knowledge of a growing number of activities practiced by elder members of the community, such as feather handicrafts and hunting. The status of the initiates increases, and they are given secret knowledge regarding the community's history and belief system in the form of myths, dances, song, body-painting, and featherwork.

The concluding chant of the naming ritual begins at sunset and continues until dawn. It is identified by the opening call, which imitates the screech of a Harpy Eagle. The name-recipients, in this case female, form a semi-circle with their backs to the setting sun. The male vocalists complete the circle while a select group of "jaguar men," generally the elder community leaders, dance counter-clockwise around the interior of the circle, approaching each female in turn with a symbolic "clawing" gesture that completes their naming. The Harpy Eagle's chant translates as: "The claws of the Harpy Eagle will claw the Nhiok / Breathe and come through the path / Breathe and keep seeing hummingbird's feathers being born." The reference to the hummingbird is significant: the Kayapo-Xikrin believe that the hummingbird is "the jaguar remedy." (*Ritual Music of the Kayapo-Xikrin, Brazil. SF 40433.* Washington DC: Smithsonian-Folkways, 1995, p. 59). The hummingbird is considered unique; indeed, it is the only bird capable of flying backward. As such, it is quick and elusive. Hummingbird feathers are burnt and mixed with a plant to produce an ointment believed to protect an individual from jaguars. The Harpy Eagle call proclaims the final stage of the ceremony and sends the initiation of the newly named participants into a higher status among the community.

For most Amazonian tribes, music is an important means of communicating with natural and spiritual forces. Totems are acknowledged and respected through music. Shamans often use music to communicate with or appease spirits of the rainforest. Indeed, some tribes believe that songs are taught to them by these spirits through dreams. Music, then, is central to the lives of Amazonians and integral to their cultural identity. The chants of the Kayapo are stepping stones to a larger cultural canvas that deals with issues common to the realm of anthropology, such as kinship systems, social organization, and gender and age classifications. Many cultural aspects of the Kayapo are reflected in their music, as they are with any group, not just in the Amazon, but around the globe.

TOTEM
A plant, animal, or natural object used as an emblem for a person or group of people.

PERU

Arrival: Peru

Peru's landscape varies widely. Urban areas are found on the western coast, while much of the eastern interior is taken up by the tropical rainforests of the Amazon. Between these two zones are the highlands, where descendents of the ancient Inca Empire still live in adobe huts among llamas and alpacas, surrounded by the snow-capped mountains of the Andes. Peru's native and mestizo peoples form the majority of the population. Both Spanish and Quecha, an indigenous language formerly associated with the Inca Empire, are recognized as official languages of Peru.

The Inca Empire dates to roughly the thirteenth century and reached its peak in the last decades of the 1400s. Important centers of power and culture included the city of Cusco in southeastern Peru near Lake Titicaca, and the stronghold of Machu Piccu some fifty miles to the northwest and nearly 2,000 feet above sea level. Spanish conquistadors began arriving in the early 1500s and quickly toppled the ruling powers of the Inca, beheading the last Inca Emperor, Túpac Amaru, in 1572.

Though Inca heritage is still a vital aspect of the cultural identity of the native population, the Spanish influence is also felt in many ways. Roman Catholicism is especially prominent throughout the region, though in a form that reveals many influences from pre-contact religious systems. The numerous religious holidays associated with both Roman Catholicism and the earlier traditions provide ample opportunities for small- and large-scale festivals in both urban and rural areas. Among the most popular are Easter celebrations, which incorporate a variety of musical activities.

Site 2: Sikuri Ensemble

Track 20

First Impressions. Aside from the pounding drum beat, the breathy sound of the melodic panpipes, called *siku*, is the most distinctive feature of this example. The short repetitive melody with its "calliope-like" timbre sounds joyfully out of tune and is reminiscent of a carousel ride spinning non-stop.

Aural Analysis. The *sikuri* panpipe ensemble is common to many Andean communities throughout Peru and elsewhere in South America. *Sikuri* ensembles normally have around twenty *siku* players, though the group in our example is quite large, consisting of fifty-two musicians. The *siku* is made of several cylindrical reeds of varying lengths tied together to form one or two rows of pipes—in this case two. The performer holds these vertically and blows across the tops of the open pipes to produce breathy pitches, just as you would with a soda bottle: the shorter the pipe, the higher the pitch.

Descendants of the ancient Inca still live today in the Andes mountains of Peru (Max T. Miller)

One *siku* is not typically capable of playing all the notes of a scale. Rather, a second *siku* must complement it. The two performers use an interlocking technique to produce the entire melody. If, for example, the first player sounds the odd-numbered pitches, say 1-3-5, while the second player sounds the even ones, 2-4-6, then the two musicians must alternate in order to play pitches 1 through 6 consecutively. The musicians try to overlap their pitches slightly so that no gaps are heard between pitches. The breathy sound of the *siku* makes it easier for performers to smoothly connect successive pitches.

Another common feature of Andean music is the use of parallel polyphony. Parallel polyphony occurs when two melodic lines follow the same melodic contour but start on different pitches, thus moving in parallel but with a polyphonic structure as well. The interval between the two parallel lines that is most commonly used is either a fourth or fifth. The interval used here, however, is a third, which is typical of the

SIKU
Panpipes common among indigenous populations from Peru and throughout the Andes.

The panpipes *(siku)* are perhaps the most common indigenous instrument of the Andes

BOMBOS
(Also, SURDO)
A large drum used in *sikuri* performances from Peru as well as *samba* music from Brazil.

Conima style of which this music is an example. Intentional tuning variances often occur, sometimes as wide as a quartertone or more, giving the music a slightly dissonant quality. As is typical of native Andean music, the melodic line is short and repetitive and features only minor variations.

In our example, a large bass drum *(bombos)* and a snare drum *(cajas)* provide a driving beat. Drums in Peru are often made with a llama- or alpaca-skin face and are struck with a wooden mallet. Different genres of *sikuri* performance use different types of drums; in fact, the bass and snare drum accompaniment heard here rarely occurs outside of Easter celebrations. In most performances, occasional whistles are heard, most notably toward the end of the performance, to signal the musicians to increase their tempo.

Cultural Considerations. Evidence of *siku* and other types of flutes date to pre-Columbian times, while the many chordophones and brass instruments found today arrived only after the 1530s with Spanish conquistadors and Roman Catholic missionaries. The *sikuri* ensemble is most common among the Aymara-speaking peoples surrounding Lake Titicaca, the largest lake on the continent and the highest navigable lake in the world (at 12,500 feet above sea level). Living and farming in these highland rural areas requires collective effort and social cooperation, and scholars consider the *sikuri* ensemble a reflection of this social structure.

Sikuri is most often performed during monthly festivals associated with indigenous ceremonial rites that frequently are combined with Roman Catholic holidays. Instrumental performance is considered a male activity, while women generally dance or sing. During a *sikuri* performance, any man from the village can participate, regardless of his musical ability or familiarity with the tune. The emphasis of the performance is on social interaction rather than on a strict adherence to musical accuracy. The interlocking parts of the *siku* express the Aymara ideal of "playing as one."

Inter-community festivals may feature several *sikuri* ensembles, each representing a different village. The performers dance in one or more circles around the drummers, who stand in the center. Friendly competitions often occur between the different ensembles as non–performers dance and cheer. The choice of a "winner" is based primarily on who has given the most energetic performance and on the general reaction of the crowd, rather than on strictly musical qualities. In short, the response of the community is the essential factor in determining a successful *sikuri* performance.

Arrival: *Argentina*

The pre-contact history of Argentina is sketchy. None of the ancient empires of the Americas held dominion over the territory, which was sparsely populated by hunters and gatherers and a few agricultural settlements. Spanish colonization of the region began in the early sixteenth century with the first attempt at a permanent settlement, Buenos Aires, in 1536. Five years later the settlement was abandoned, due in part to conflicts with the indigenous populations. Eventually, the region was successfully colonized and Buenos Aires was resettled in 1580. In time, the growing city became an important port and gained a reputation as a haven for smugglers. By the middle of the eighteenth century its population had swelled to more than 20,000.

The British attacked the city in 1806, but were ousted only a few months later by a citizen army. Succeeding attempts by the British to overtake the city failed, and indeed encouraged a strong patriotic sentiment among the city's inhabitants. In 1810 the people of Buenos Aires rebelled against the Spanish crown and only a few years later they succeeded in gaining their independence. It is this spirit of rebellion that drives the *tango* in its purest form.

ARGENTINA

Site 3: *Tango*

First Impressions. Tango is a music of passion. The original form of the dance it accompanies symbolically represents a battle between two men for the affections of a fickle woman. At one point in the dance, one of the male dancers lustfully looms over the helpless woman before she is torn away by the other jealous suitor. Even in its simplest form, the music evokes the predatory stares of the men and the indecisiveness of the woman through variations of dynamics, tempo, and phonic structure.

Aural Analysis. Tango ensembles vary in size, and tango itself comes in a variety of styles. A distinctive feature of most tango orchestras is the inclusion of the *bandoneon,* a type of button-box accordion. The *bandoneon* was invented in Germany in the mid-nineteenth century by Heinrich Band and was brought to South America around 1890, initially in the hands of missionaries who found it a portable alternative to the organ. The instrument has two hexagonal wooden manuals (keyboards) separated by a bellows usually made of cardboard. Larger *bandoneon* have up to seventy-two buttons, with the right-hand buttons playing melody and the left-hand buttons playing chords. As the performer alternately compresses or draws out the bellows, air passes through a series of "free" metal reeds to produce the tones; thus, the *bandoneon* is a free-reed aerophone. Dynamic variations are produced by squeezing or drawing the air through the instrument more quickly for greater volume or more slowly for a quieter sound. In addition to the *bandoneon,* the violin, guitar, flute, and piano are frequently found in *tango* ensembles and a vocalist is often present as well.

Track 21

BANDONEON
A type of button-box accordion.

TANGO
A dance and associated music originating in Argentina, but now commonly associated with ballroom dance.

Tango rhythms are frequently syncopated, meaning some accents fall between the regular beat. Our example employs a common *tango* rhythm by emphasizing the off-beats of the first and second pulses. In order to hear this, you must first find the regular pulsation to establish a meter, in this case a duple meter with four beats. The melodic line anticipates the first beat of each four-beat grouping; therefore, it is probably easier to find the first pulse by listening to the underlying chords. The tempo is rather quick and fluctuates frequently, as is typical of tango.

The *bandoneon*, an accordion common in Argentina, is the most prominent instrument that accompanies the tango
(© Jack Vartoogian/FrontRowPhotos)

The syncopated tango rhythm falls within the four-beat grouping. Once you have established the meter by counting the four-beat grouping, divide this by saying "and" between each pulse, i.e., 1&2&3&4&. The "and" division indicates the "off-beat." The tango rhythm, articulated by the underlying chords, displays a fairly constant pattern of 1&-&3-(4)-. The "2" beat is absent, as is the "4&." Most of the melodic phrases also begin on the "off-beat," typically the "and" of the third beat. This emphasis on syncopation creates an off-balance feel throughout the performance: the musicians constantly flirt with the regular beat, but never commit to it. Indeed, this aspect of *tango* music parallels the fickle affections of the female character in *tango* dance's symbolic courtship battle.

The indecisive seductions of the female tango dancer are also manifested through fluctuations in dynamics, tempo, phonic structure, and even key. Bursts of volume with strong chord accompaniment at a quick tempo contrast with soft, sultry, slow passages with only a single melodic line. Though *tango* music is dominated by minor keys, the performers will often slip in brighter passages that utilize major keys, again keeping the music off-balance. As the dancers embrace in a loving gaze characterized by a major key, they suddenly turn from each other as the music abruptly shifts back to minor. Such variations of mood are essential to the unique character of the *tango*.

Cultural Considerations. Buenos Aires, Argentina, is the birthplace of *tango*. Since its resettlement in 1580 by Spanish sailors, this city has been a port of call for sea sojourners navigating around South America. As a hub of maritime trade for more than four hundred years, the city has attracted a variety of immigrants, primarily Spanish, but also Italian. Trade with European cities boomed after Argentina was officially proclaimed independent from Spain in 1816. By 1880, when it emerged as the capital city of Argentina, Buenos Aires was one of the most important economic and cultural centers of Latin America.

As often happened with port cities during the nineteenth century, the transient lifestyle of seamen encouraged a seedy subculture characterized by taverns and bordellos where sailors could unwind before heading to their next port of call. Knife fights and bar brawls over women were common occurrences among the *porteños* (people of the port area), typically initiated by inebriated sailors vying for the affections of a single seductive strumpet. Tango dance reflects these possessive relationships, originally casting two men and a woman in a sensual choreography with a distinctly predatory nature: the "vertical expression of horizontal desire" as it is often described. Tango music also suggests such seduction as the musicians thrust and parry through dynamic variations and tempo fluctuations, echoing the love triangle narrative of the dance.

Because of its lurid association with the vagabonds of the brothels, *tango* was disdained by aristocrats, who considered the music and its dance to be vulgar. Yet, the lure of bohemian nightlife attracted many, especially among the younger generation who flocked to *tango* just as teenagers in the United States later flocked to rock 'n' roll. By the end of the nineteenth century, *tango* had captured the youthful passions of popular culture in Buenos Aires and quickly spread throughout Argentina and the urban centers of many South American countries (including Uruguay, from which our example derives).

The attraction to *tango* was not limited to South America. By 1910 *tango* was tantalizing the playboys and dilettantes of salons in Paris, France, and it soon made its screen debut together

The Argentine tango dance, unlike the regularized ballroom form, requires rapid changes of emotion, from control to inflamed passion
(© Jack Vartoogian/FrontRowPhotos)

with Rudolph Valentino in *The Four Horsemen of the Apocalypse* (1926). Carlos Gardel (1887–1935) became an international superstar as *tango-canción* (tango song) was popularized on the radio and in the cinema. But in the United States, where puritan moralists have long considered dance to be sinful, Vernon and Irene Castle, who brought *tango* into the ballroom dance world, felt obligated to reassure readers of their *tango*-instructional booklets that this new and exceptionally sensual dance would not corrupt anyone's morals:

> The much-misunderstood Tango becomes an evolution of the eighteenth-century Minuet. There is in it no strenuous clasping of partners, no hideous gyrations of the limbs, no abnormal twistings, no vicious angles. Mr. Castle affirms that when the Tango degenerates into an acrobatic display or into

salacious suggestion it is the fault of the dancers and not of the dance. The Castle Tango is courtly and artistic, and this is the only Tango taught by the Castle House instructors. (Marbury 1914, p. 20)

By the 1940s tango had seduced every social class, but the Golden Age of tango was nearing its end. After World War II, rock 'n' roll pushed *tango* (as well as jazz) from the airwaves and dance clubs, although it still found an audience in Argentina and among many of the upper classes who had accepted it as the sultry side of ballroom dance. Tango never regained its former popularity, although composers such as Astor Piazzolla (1921-1992) helped to establish it as a music genre independent of the dance itself. Interest in tango briefly surged in the 1980s, and it has consequently maintained its visibility to the present day through movies with tantalizing *tango* scenes included in hit films like The *Scent of a Woman*, starring Al Pacino, and *Moulin Rouge*, starring Nicole Kidman and Ewan McGregor.

MEXICO

Arrival: Mexico

Mexico is the fourth largest country in the western hemisphere. Mexico City, the largest urban area in the world today with more than fifteen million people, is built on the ruins of Tenochtitlán, the center of trade and military activity of the Aztec empire, which dominated the region for nearly one hundred years. The Aztec era (ca.1427—1521) remains an important source of cultural pride for much of the population, many of whom are direct descendents of the Aztec.

While the native heritage of the Mexican population is important, the influence of Spanish culture is also quite prevalent. Many of the soldiers of the Spanish explorer Hernán Cortés, who conquered the Aztec, intermarried with the native populations, as did the Spanish colonialists who followed in their wake. As a result, more than 80 percent of Mexico's present population is *mestizo,* that is, a mix of Spanish and native ethnic heritage. The influence of the *mestizo*'s Spanish ancestry is visible in many aspects of Mexican culture. The architecture of Mexico's churches, the fact that Spanish is the national language (though many indigenous languages continue to flourish, including Nahuatl, the language of the Aztecs, spoken today by more than a million people), and, certainly, Mexico's music are all indicative of strong Spanish roots.

MARIACHI

An entertainment music associated with festivals and celebratory events in Mexico.

Site 4: Mariachi

First Impressions. *Mariachi* is a festive music. Whether in instrumental form or with a vocalist, *mariachi* is contagiously peppy. A single listen can conjure images of confetti and firecrackers, of revelers holding their margarita glasses high and singing along with sombrero-topped musicians. No frowns here: this music is all smiles.

Track 22

Aural Analysis. *Mariachi* is heavily imbued with European musical characteristics. This is shown most obviously by its instrumentation, which incorporates such familiar instruments as the violin, the trumpet, and the guitar. Guitars appear in a number of forms, including the *vihuela* (small guitar) and *guitarrón* (large guitar), both of which have convex resonators. Frequent changes in instrumentation are characteristic of *mariachi* music as different instrument sections are highlighted to produce contrasting textures. Melodic passages are exchanged between the violins and the trumpets with the guitars as a constant rhythmic and harmonic accompaniment. Few percussion instruments are heard in *mariachi,* because the percussive sound of the guitarists as well as the hand-clapping and foot-stomping of the dancers (absent from our recording) usually provide enough rhythm.

A Mexican mariachi group performs in a North American restaurant

Vocalists use a full, often operatic voice, complemented by the occasional catcalls and laughter of fellow band members, who chime in to help make the music more festive. During vocal sections, the violins and trumpets generally play a secondary role to avoid overshadowing the singer. Song texts are generally idealistic portrayals of romance, but they may also be about work, as with our example, *Los Arrieros* (The Muleteers), and sometimes contain political or religious references. Due to the Iberian descent of mestizo musicians, Spanish is the language of the *mariachi* singer.

Another key feature of *mariachi* is the use of clear, often memorable melodic lines, such as the melody of "La Cucaracha" (The Cockroach), a well-known *mariachi* tune. These melodies are generally carried by the violin, though modern *mariachi* bands frequently use the trumpets to play the main melody. Shifts in tempo corresponding to variations in instrumentation are also common. These changes in tempo typically correspond with changes in the movements of dancers and are reminiscent of the frequent tempo changes found in Spanish flamenco music. *Mariachi* music follows a variety of meters, which are usually clear-cut and in duple or triple meter and which occasionally shift along with changes in tempo. Our example belongs to a particular category of *mariachi* known as *son jalisciense,* which tends to be more rhythmically active than most *mariachi* music, with its frequent subtle shifts of meter and tempo.

Mariachi music is almost always in a major key, which is characteristic of "happy" music in European-related music traditions. Dynamic variation result from changes in instrumentation, as the trumpet-highlighted sections are louder than those sections emphasizing the violins or vocalist. The form of our example includes many distinctive sections,

VIHUELA

A small, fretted plucked lute from Mexico, similar to a guitar but with a convex resonator.

GUITARRÓN

A large fretted plucked lute from Mexico, similar to a guitar but with a convex resonator.

331

essentially strophic, meaning that the music repeats with each new verse sung by the vocalist. Purely instrumental *mariachi* also usually follows a repetitive form of this type.

Cultural Considerations. While Mexico is much more than merely *mariachi*, it is the decorative *charro* suits, wide-brimmed sombreros, and operatic serenades of the *son* singers that have come to characterize Mexican music to the outside world.

The origin of the term *mariachi* is unknown. A popular theory is that the term is a corruption of the French term *mariage*, because the music was frequently found at weddings and other festive events. Others believe the name comes from an indigenous word referring to a type of social event that features dancers stomping on a wooden platform. Whatever the etymology of its name, *mariachi* first appeared in the southwestern state of Jalisco.

Maypole dancers perform to the accompaniment of a *mariachi* ensemble on a city street in Merida, Mexico, on the Yucatan peninsula
(Christina Shahriari)

Various instruments found in *mariachi*, such as the violin, harp, and guitar, were originally brought by Spanish missionaries for use in church services but soon became common in secular musical activities as well. The early *mariachi* bands were primarily string bands, with the violin as the dominant melodic instrument. The harp was originally the principal instrument accompanying the violin, but with the addition of trumpets to the ensemble, the *vihuela, guitarrón,* and other guitars became the instruments of choice because they could be played with greater volume. The inclusion of the trumpet also encouraged the use of several violins in an ensemble, so that today it is common to see *mariachi* orchestras that include a dozen or more performers.

Early *mariachi* groups played primarily for festive events and in restaurants and taverns. These contexts are still the most common places in which to find *mariachi* music. Musicians serenade their patrons with the expectation that they will be paid for each song they perform. During the 1950s, *mariachi* reached its peak of popularity, as it was the featured music in a number of Hollywood films set in Mexico. As a result, the elaborately decorated *charro* suits and sombreros presented in these films have become the standard dress for *mariachi* musicians throughout the country.

STROPHIC
The use of distinct units (strophes) that have the same number of lines, rhyme scheme, and meter.

Audiences in the United States lost interest in the music of Latin America following the appearance of rock 'n' roll, and thus *mariachi,* like *tango,* mostly slipped off the radar screen as far as North Americans were concerned. The most prominent North American pop star to promote mariachi in recent years has been Linda Ronstadt, whose

L to R: The *vihuela, guitarron,* and guitar common to *mariachi* ensembles."

album *Canciones* included many *ranchera* songs, *ranchera* being a style of "country" mariachi that emphasizes vocal performance.

Arrival: Brazil

BRAZIL

Brazil is the largest country in South America and home to roughly 200 million inhabitants. Our earlier visit to the Amazonian rainforests presented a stark contrast to the bustling activity of the urban centers that dot the eastern half of the country. Brazil's largest cities are mostly found along the coastline, and include Rio de Janeiro, São Paulo, and Salvador. The country was colonized by the Portuguese, who began arriving in the region around 1500. They discovered a land rich in natural resources and with fertile soil. Within fifty years Portuguese colonialists began to import slaves from Africa to work on sugar, tobacco, and coffee plantations. Gold was discovered in the late 1600s, encouraging the enslavement of more Africans to work as miners. African populations were imported to Brazil for more than three hundred years, resulting today in the largest African Diaspora in the world.

Brazil became an independent nation in 1822. The government was then ruled by a succession of emperors descended from members of the Portuguese royal family. The abolition of slavery in 1888 was followed the next year by a revolution initiated by the military, which ousted the monarchy and created a federal republic in Brazil. The new government struggled to fairly represent its diverse population. Most of the political power resided with the wealthy landowners, invariably of European descent, while the vast majority of the population, either *mulatto* or of purely African descent, occupied the slum areas of the urban centers and had little or no political voice. By 1930 discontent among the masses had come to a head, while a collapse in the economy, brought on by the global depression that began in 1929, caused the landowning elite to lose confidence in their elected officials. A disgruntled military once again encouraged revolution, which was personified by the rise to power of a single man, Getúlio Vargas (1883–1954).

Vargas was a central figure in the revolution of 1930 and became president and ruled as an elected official until 1937. Rather than risk losing power, Vargas initiated a revolution of his own with the help of the military and with the support of the urban working and middle classes. He eliminated the congress and ruled by decree as a dictator for the next eight years. Vargas began many social and economic reforms that were, ironically, modeled after the policies of the Italian dictator Benito Mussolini, against whom the Brazilian military fought (in aid of the United States) during World War II. His *Estado Novo* (New State) encouraged a strong sense of a unified national identity among the masses and a feeling of pride in being Brazilian, no matter a person's ethnic background or social class. His propaganda machine was instrumental in the promotion of *samba* as a music for all Brazilians.

Site 5: *Samba*

Track 23

First Impressions. *Samba* is dance music. Its boisterous beat, wailing whistles, and shouting *sambistas* encourage the party atmosphere associated with its most notable context, Carnival (see below). The driving *samba* beat conjures up images of revelers parading through the streets of Rio de Janeiro in frenetic celebration. Samba music makes you move from the bottom of your feet to the top of your head.

Aural Analysis. *Samba* is strongly Afro-Brazilian, meaning that its musical characteristics are primarily drawn from African ingredients but have a unique Brazilian flavor. Polyrhythm underlies the instrumental organization; thus, the majority of instruments in *samba* are percussion. African-derived double bells (*agogo*), tambourines, scraping instruments (*rêco-rêco),* and drums large (*surdo* or *bombo*) and small (*caixa*) are all instruments commonly found in a wide variety of *samba* styles. The most distinct *samba* instrument is the friction drum (*cuíca*), which is a membranophone that has its face pierced in the center with a long, thin stick. When the stick is pushed, pulled, or twisted, it rubs against the membrane to produce a unique squeaking sound. Call-and-response vocals, generally in Portuguese, are standard, and are generally accompanied by a guitar.

SAMBA
A popular music from Brazil.

AGOGO
A double-bell found in Western Africa and used in African-derived musics in the Western hemisphere.

RÊCO-RÊCO
A notched scraper idiophone found in Latin American music traditions.

A prominent "*samba* rhythm," usually played by the largest drum or an electrified bass guitar, is what most differentiates the music from other Latin American dance musics. The *samba* rhythm is based on a standard duple meter but emphasizes the third beat by inserting a short pause just before it. In a four-beat pattern (though Samba moves so quickly, it is typically thought of as having only two beats), the samba rhythm would sound on the first beat, the "and" of the second, and the top of the third beat, i.e., 1—&3—. The rhythm is infectious and seems to call out: "Mooove your feet! Mooove your feet!" Other instruments add several other more rhythmically dense patterns to this fundamental samba groove.

Cultural Considerations. *Samba* traces its roots to Angola and the Congo in Africa. Its name is believed to be derived from the term *semba*, a Bantu word describing the distinctive "belly bump" found in some circle dances of the region. The navel is considered a spiritually significant body part, and contact between two navels symbolically links two dancers together. In Brazil, the *samba* folk dance begins with this gesture of bumping bellies as a dancer invites another dancer to enter the circle and dance together as one.

Members of a *Gongada* from Minas Geraes perform during Carnival celebrations in Brazil (Welson Tremura)

Initially, the ruling powers of Brazil viewed *samba* as a vulgar dance performed by slum-dwellers who lived in the *favelas* on the hills surrounding the city of Rio de Janeiro and in the *bairro*, a section of the city known as "Little Africa" due to the large number of African-descended inhabitants. The popularity of *samba* was especially visible during the Carnival season (see below), when music and celebration in the streets was more tolerated by government authorities. The driving rhythms of the music and the erotic appeal of the dance gradually attracted members of the rising middle class, many of whom were *mulatto* (of mixed African-Iberian ancestry), so that by the mid-1920s, composing *samba* had become a full-time occupation for many talented artists. Each year, neighborhood associations would parade through the streets during Carnival playing music and dancing to popular *samba* melodies, usually composed by one of their own members. By the end of the decade, these associations were referring to themselves as *escolas de samba* (*samba* schools).

After taking power in 1930, Getúlio Vargas actively encouraged samba as part of his *Estado Novo* campaign to promote a unified Brazilian national identity. In 1934 he made Carnival an official national event and decreed that only *samba* schools legally registered with the government could perform in parades. He further encouraged *samba* and its association with Carnival by offering public funds to support the registered *samba* schools, which were strongly encouraged to create costumes and compose music that stimulated national pride by glorifying national heroes and promoting patriotic symbols. Though such overt nationalism has fallen out of fashion, public support of the *samba* schools and a focus on Carnival as the hallmark event of the Brazilian calendar year have remained.

Dancers re-enact a grand Samba dance during a performance of the revue "Oba Oba '93" (© Jack Vartoogian/FrontRowPhotos)

Today, *samba* is nearly synonymous with Brazilian popular music. The term covers a variety of styles in much the same way the term *jazz* is used to describe a broad range of styles in the United States. The best-known styles, namely *samba-carnavalesco* (carnival samba), *samba-baiana* (Bahian samba), and *samba-enredo* (theme samba), are still associated with Carnival. Also popular is *samba-canção* (song samba), which is a staple of Brazilian nightclubs and the origin of *bossa nova,* a particularly popular style for ballroom dance. Since the 1990s *samba-reggae,* the Brazilian version of Jamaican reggae, has become widely known as well.

Carnival

Carnival is a pre-Lenten festival associated in the Americas with countries where Roman Catholicism was the primary religious tradition of the colonizers. The tradition originates in Europe but has come to be most associated with the grand parades and intense revelry of places like Rio de Janeiro, Port of Spain (in Trinidad), and New Orleans (where it is known as *Mardi Gras*).

Traditionally, Carnival celebrations were considered the last "party" before the forty days of Lent, during which Roman Catholics are supposed to renew themselves spiritually by abstaining from activities such as drinking alcohol, eating meat, dancing, and playing music. Weddings and other celebratory events were also forbidden during the Lenten season. The elite social classes held masked balls to indulge themselves before the commencement of Lent. Among the "common folk," outdoor festivals were held, which typically included a variety of "Carnival" games, jugglers, comedians, storytellers, and so on, much like the Renaissance Fairs of today. Among those to encourage the Carnival celebration were Gypsies (see Chapter 10), many of whom made their living by performing as entertainers and musicians. The Carnival season, which typically lasted four or five days, was considered a time to "forgive and forget" any animosity between individuals, and the authorities also tended to be more lenient during the celebrations.

This carefree attitude was transferred to the New World. The European colonialists maintained their tradition of masked balls and indoor revelry in many cities throughout the Caribbean, while the lower classes, most of whom were of African descent, were usually allowed to celebrate with out-door activities. A common feature of these outdoor activities was the street parade, which has since become the highlight of nearly every Carnival celebration in the Americas.

The Brazilian Carnival celebrations are considered by many to be the pinnacle of the festivals the world over. Thousands of people travel to Rio de Janeiro to participate in the nonstop partying that characterizes the Carnival Season (between February and March, depending on the date of Ash Wednesday). Body paint, confetti and streamers, lots of alcohol, and continuous dancing to the *samba* beat mark the annual activities, which are capped with a parade through the city center featuring the most extravagant costumes found in any festival the world over. *Sambistas* dance through the city streets followed by batteries of deafening percussion. *Samba* schools compete for prizes based on their music performance, dance choreography, and costumes. Each school's performance is organized around a specific theme, typically one that promotes Brazilian identity and revolves around national, historical, or political figures and events.

Site 6: *Capoeira*

Track 24

First Impressions. *Capoeira* is music with a groove. Whereas the *samba* music of Carnival pushes the body to a frenetic extreme, *capoeira* music embodies the laid-back attitude Brazilians often take during the rest of the year. The music constantly bobs and weaves as if the listener is relaxing on a small fishing boat along the Brazilian coastline. The waves bring him closer and closer to shore, gradually picking up momentum as he casually steers himself onto the beach. Fluid motion is the general feel, but there is also a constant awareness that the waves can tip the boat at any moment.

Aural Analysis. Among the key features of *capoeira* music are the call-and-response organization of the vocal performers and the subtle polyrhythmic organization of the African-derived instruments. These instruments include the *pandeiros* (tambourines), *agogo* (double bell), *rêco-rêco* (notched scraper), and *atabaque* (drum), as well as the most distinc-

CAPOEIRA
A dance that developed from a style of martial arts created by runaway slaves in Brazil.

Members of Brazil's Balet folclorico da Bahia
re-enact a *Samba* dance during Carnival
(© Jack Vartoogian/FrontRowPhotos)

PANDEIROS

A hand-held frame drum
with attached cymbals
(i.e., tambourine), used
in *capoeira* music.

ATABAQUES

A drum of West African
origin used in *capoeira*
music as well as
candomblé rituals

BERIMBAU

A musical bow used
in *capoeira* music.

tive instrument of the *capoeira* ensemble, the *berimbau* (musical bow). All of these instruments were recreated in Brazil by African slaves taken from Central Africa, Angola, and the Democratic Republic of the Congo (formerly Zaire) in particular.

In our example, which is in the *Capoeira Angola* style, three *berimbau* are played, to provide low, middle, and high parts. The *berimbau* is made from a wooden bow with a steel string. A piece of twine is looped around the base of the bow to attach a gourd resonator, which is pressed against the body to change the timbre and pitch of the instrument's sound. The smallest finger of one hand, usually the left for a right-handed player, balances the instrument on this loop during performance. A large coin or stone is held between the thumb and forefinger and is pressed against the string in order to change the acoustic length of the string and consequently alter the pitch. This coin is sometimes only lightly pressed against the string, so as to produce a buzzing timbre.

The other hand strikes the string with a small stick several inches long. This hand also holds a small wicker basket that encloses a handful of either pebbles or small seashells. The performer simultaneously shakes this rattle as he strikes the string of the bow with the stick. The timbre of the *berimbau* is much like the "boing" sound of a large spring. The use of the coin, rattle, and open string, along with the varied resonances produced by the gourd, allows the *berimbau* to provide a great variety of simultaneous timbres.

Though the vocalists carry the primary melody, the unique "springy" timbre of the *berimbau* is the focus of the dancers that this music typically accompanies. In the *Capoeira Angola* style, the lowest-pitched *berimbau* plays the basic pattern, while the middle *berimbau* plays a complementary rhythm. The highest *berimbau* ornaments these basic patterns with improvisation, paying close attention to the movements of the dancers the music accompanies.

The steady groove of the music is provided by the other instruments. The fundamental rhythm, 1—&3-4-, is set by the drum with three low tones and a "slap" on the fourth beat. This rhythm is common to most *capoeira* music as it corresponds to the basic *ginga* movement of the dancers (see below). The other instruments follow their own rhythms, being careful not to overshadow the fundamental beat or the sound of the *berimbau* trio.

As the music progresses, the tempo often gradually increases. The *berimbau* pattern will subtly shift throughout, urging the dancers to heighten their performance. The basic *ginga* pattern of the drum does not change, but the other instruments may shift their patterns, typically creating denser rhythms to correspond with the increased intensity of the music. The dynamic level typically remains constant, though the *berimbau* may increase its volume as the dancers "play" harder.

The vocal organization remains in call-and-response form through-

out a performance. The text setting is primarily syllabic and has a descending melodic contour. The melody will change as the music progresses, but generally keeps the same phrase length. The lyrics are generally sung in Portuguese, the national language of Brazil, and tend to focus on the dancers, the musicians, or other aspects of *capoeira* performance. Often times the singers use symbolic language, such as describing a large dancer as a tall immobile tree, to prod the dancers to better or faster movements.

Cultural Considerations. *Capoeira* is a unique form of dance that developed from a distinctive style of martial arts created by runaway slaves in Brazil. Before abolition, many slaves who escaped the oppression of the sugar and coffee plantations would take refuge in the mountains near the country's coastline. Not having guns or swords, they developed a martial arts system that drew upon various fighting styles from Africa. The system that was created, which is known as *compé*, emphasizes the use of the feet during combat. The movements are characterized by cartwheels, handstands, flips, and spinning motions.

The Brazilian *berimbau* (musical bow) played during a *capoeira* performance (© Jack Vartoogian/FrontRowPhotos)

After slavery was abolished in Brazil, many of the *capoeira* artists continued to utilize their skills as bodyguards for Brazil's social elite. Many others formed gangs, which led to *capoeira* being associated with street fighting and vandalism. The authorities, of course, frowned on such disturbances, so the gangs attempted to disguise their practice sessions and street fights by simultaneously performing music. Because the music and fighting styles were African-based, the European-descended officials were fooled into accepting the *capoeira* movements as an unusual dance style rather than a combat technique. Eventually, the inclusion of music in the performance of *capoeira* became standard practice, so that today the genre is often times regarded as more of a dance style than a martial arts system.

GINGA
(Also, JENGA)
A back-and-forth motion used as the basis for *capoeira* dancing.

A *capoeira* performance takes place in a *roda*, a large circle approximately eighteen feet in diameter that is outlined by the *capoeira* musicians and other participants standing in observation of the dancers. The two dancers typically begin the performance by "bowing" to the *berimbau*, typically the lowest sounding one, which is usually played by the senior *mestre* (master) of the group. The dancers then perform opening movements intended to assess the abilities of their opponent. This initial section is described as "cooperative," because the opponents do not attempt to strike their partner but rather work together to execute interesting moves, such as back flips and back-to-back body rolls. Throughout the performance, only the hands, feet, and head of the *capoeira* artist are allowed to touch the ground.

Capoeira artists in the midst of "combat." Berimbau performers and other musicians are pictured in the background
(© Jack Vartoogian/FrontRowPhotos)

As the performance progresses, the dancers slow their movements in conjunction with a shift in the music. This "control" section is intended to develop the strength and balance of the performers as they slowly move through cartwheels and handstands, still making little attempt to strike their opponent. Finally, the music urges the performers to move to the "confrontational" section of the dance, in which the *capoeira* artists execute their movements with full force. The objective during this section is to knock the opponent off-balance and send him to the mat or into the ring of observers.

The basic beat of the music, which is articulated as 1—&3-4-, corresponds to the dance movement known as *ginga*. This movement requires the performer to cross one leg behind the other and lean back before springing forward to repeat the same movement with legs crossed in the opposite direction. The *ginga* is the starting position for all strikes, because it allows the performer to keep in constant motion and attain more momentum from the back position as he strikes forward.

The music is intended to encourage the performers, and the vocalists prod the dancers to higher feats of skill and comment on the action. If, for example, a smaller opponent topples a larger one, the lead vocalist may sing about the "falling of a tree" to tease the defeated foe. The *mestre* may shift the music to bring a performance "down" if he feels the dancers' performance is becoming too competitive, and is threatening to turn into genuine fighting. While novice dancers focus on the *ginga* rhythm, advanced performers focus on the sound of the *berimbau* to spur themselves to perform more intense choreography. The sound of the *berimbau*, bobs in and out of the basic rhythm in much the same way the performers weave in and out of each other's strikes.

Capoeira has achieved an international reputation in the past decade as a unique martial art worthy of inclusion in competitions around the world. *Capoeira* clubs are increasingly popular in the United States and throughout the Western hemisphere. Though there is no direct relation, the similarities between some of the *capoeira* moves and break-dancing, popular in the United States in the 1980s and experiencing a resurgence of interest in the early twenty-first century, has helped bring the *capoeira* tradition to the attention of many young Americans, especially because *capoeira* artists sometimes integrate their moves into dance club performances.

Questions to Consider

1. To what extent do each of the musics in this chapter reflect pre-Columbian, European, or African musical traits?

2. How does *siku* performance reflect community cohesion among Andean populations?

3. How does *tango* music reflect the essence of *tango* dance?

4. Is *capoeira* a dance or a martial art? Why might it be considered both?

5. How does *mariachi* affirm or challenge American stereotypes of Mexican culture?

6. How is the survival of indigenous music and culture related to the challenges of modernization and environmental degradation?

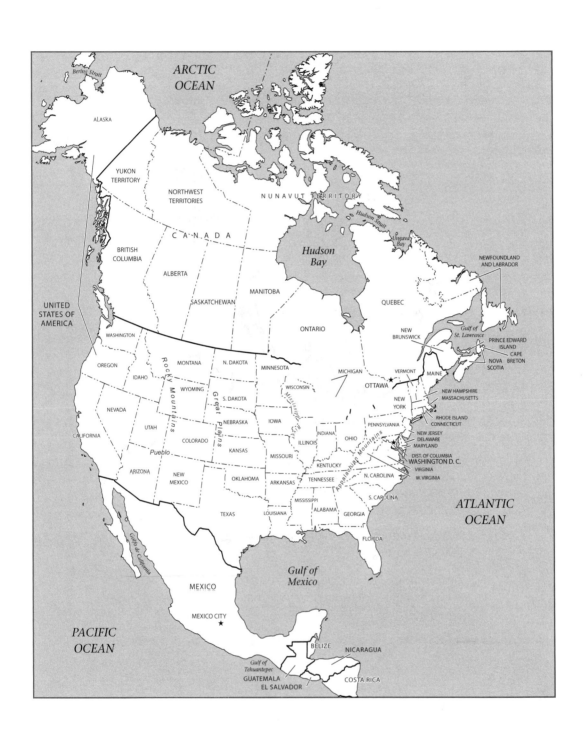

Built in 1866, the 460-foot Cornish (NH)-Windsor (VT) covered bridge spans the Connecticut River between the two states and typifies the spirit and creativity of America's pioneer generations

North America:
Diverse Peoples, Diverse Musics

Background Preparation

For most readers this chapter covers what is essentially "home," the United States of America and Canada. Though Mexico is geologically part of North America, it is culturally part of South and Central America and thus was covered in the previous chapter. It used to be said that the earliest people to inhabit North America, those who are called Native Americans, crossed the Bering Strait about 11,500 years ago, but recent excavations throughout the Americas have called this belief into question. Indeed, excavations at Meadowcroft, Pennsylvania, thirty miles south of Pittsburgh, have uncovered evidence of human civilization dating back to between 12,000 and 15,000 years. It is now thought that migrations from Northeast Asia could have begun 30,000 to 50,000 years ago.

By the end of the fifteenth century, Europeans—starting with Italian-born, but Spanish-backed Christopher Columbus—found their way to what was called the New World, though there is evidence of earlier arrivals by Scandinavians in the late tenth century. From the early sixteenth century onward Spanish, Portuguese, French, Dutch, and English colonists came in increasing numbers. By the 1600s, England, France, and Spain had become the dominant powers in North America. With the development of sugarcane and tobacco plantations, a need developed for large numbers of laborers. Because the number of colonists was still small, Europeans attempted to force Native Americans into slave labor. When this attempt failed, because Native American slaves resisted, died, Europeans started importing slaves from Africa. The slave trade was at its peak from 1701 to 1810, though during that time the vast majority of Africans were sent to South America and the Caribbean.

A fiddler leads two friends playing guitar (center) and mandolin (left) in playing an old string band tune

Eventually people from all over the world began immigrating into North America, making the United States and Canada two of the world's most diversely populated countries. Indeed, it can be said that in North America everyone's roots are somewhere else (except perhaps for Native Americans). The experience of starting a better life in a "new world" imbued many immigrants to North America with a spirit of energetic optimism. Many brought and preserved musical traditions from their homelands, some of which can be observed to this day. But it is also true that what is truly "American" (in the broadest sense) is the result of the mixing of peoples and traditions to create new forms of musical expression. Indeed, America's musical culture has long been one of its most influential and lucrative exports.

North America's musical prominence is not borne of an immense population or size; the continent accounts for only about 13 percent of the earth's land surface and is home to only around 310 million people, a mere quarter of China's population. While Canada is the second-largest country in the world, its population of around 34 million is very modest. Even the population of the United States, barely 300 million, is small in comparison not only to China's, but to India's as well.

Both Canada and the United States began as colonies of Great

Britain, though parts of each were earlier under French control, and the southwestern United States was under Spanish control. Unlike much of the Caribbean and most of Central and South America, where the colonial powers were mostly Roman Catholic, North America was largely Protestant. The dominance of Protestantism had at least two results: first, a tendency to suppress the religious traditions of both Native peoples and African slaves, and second, the flowering of an incredible number of highly diverse religious groups, many of which developed highly innovative musical traditions

Planning the Itinerary

What *is* traditional North American music? Until recently, it would have been exclusively thought of as music from the British Isles, such as ballads and folk songs, fiddling and dance music, and some kinds of religious music. A broader view, however, must include Native American music, various African-American forms, and any number of other hybrid genres incorporating influences from Europe, Latin America, the Middle East, and Asia.

Despite this need for a broader perspective, it is of course still true that no tour of American "traditional" music would be complete without including the Anglo genres, even though many represent survivals more than they do American innovations. We will look at four examples from the United States: a ballad, an archaic lined-out hymn, a singing school shape-note song, and a bluegrass number. While all of these represent the heart of Anglo-American culture, the traditions they come from remain little known to the general population. Sadly, it is

Picturesque Peggy's Cove near Halifax, Nova Scotia, Canada, attracts numerous visitors to its peaceful fishing village atmosphere during the summer

possible to earn one or more degrees in music in most American institutions without being exposed to any (or more than a little) "traditional" music. A foreigner arriving in the United States would be hard-pressed to find evidence of any traditional styles except perhaps bluegrass. Even that is mostly known only to aficionados.

Canada's traditional music remains little known in the lower "48." What makes Canadian music distinctive is its abundance of Native American traditions. In addition, one finds various traditions associated with the *métis* (that is, people of mixed Native American and European ancestry). There is also, of course, much music that derives from the British Isles. The primary influence is Scottish, as seen in the relatively familiar fiddling and piping traditions, but there are also pockets of Gaelic culture. French traditions remain strong as well, more obviously in Quebec, but also in Nova Scotia. Here we present Scottish fiddling from the Cape Breton area of Nova Scotia.

Among America's greatest musical treasures are the contributions of people of African descent. Indeed, most musics that have come to represent America's energy and innovation have come from African-Americans. Because so many of these musics have been absorbed into "white" culture, it would not be too outlandish to describe the United States as an "Africanized" culture, in which people of all races participate in and appreciate African-American forms such as jazz, blues, and gospel, and in which commercial music has "black" roots. To represent African-American music we have chosen an old-time spiritual, a modern gospel choral song, and an old Delta blues.

An Inside Look

Hugh McGraw

I was born and raised in one of America's oldest and most enduring singing traditions, that of the *Sacred Harp,* a songbook first compiled by two fellow Georgians, Benjamin Franklin White and Elisha J. King, in 1844. Like a lot of other

books, most of them now forgotten, the *Sacred Harp* was printed using a system of shape notes, by which the different pitches of the scale—fa, sol, la, fa sol, la, mi—are indicated in four different shapes, one for each syllable. *Sacred Harp* singers are the last holdouts in America of this old "fasola" system that goes back to early England. Because this book has always been popular around the South, it has been republished as the *"Original" Sacred Harp,* and I served on the revision committees in 1960, 1971, and 1977. In 1991 I served as General Chairman, and in fact I've contributed eight compositions to these editions.

Hugh McGraw, Sacred Harp shape-note song teacher and singer, Bremen, Georgia

For over fifty years I've traveled throughout the United States teaching this treasury of early American sacred music to all kinds of people. In 1982 I was honored to receive a National Heritage Fellowship Award from the National Endowment for the Arts for my work. Since then I've also appeared in two films, *Lone Riders* and Bill Moyers' documentary *Amazing Grace.* Since 1958 I've served as Executive Secretary of the *Sacred Harp* Publishing Company, Inc. in Bremen, which continues to publish this wonderful old book that has been central to my life. *Sacred Harp* singings are open to all, and I invite any of you to come join in the singing, the fellowship, and the great food served in our "dinner on the ground." You can find out where and when singings are held at www.fasola.org.

People of Hispanic descent now constitute America's largest minority, as their population has recently exceeded the African-American population. Hispanics number at least thirty-two million and constitute some 12 percent of the population of the United States. They come from many places, though those from Mexico, Puerto Rico, and Cuba constitute the vast majority. Hispanics are dispersed throughout the

Buddy MacMaster

I was raised in a Gaelic-speaking home and was introduced to the old music of Cape Breton through the lilting "mouth music" of my mother. By the age of four I would "jig" tunes using sticks to pretend to play the fiddle. At eleven I found an old fiddle in my father's trunk and learned a tune that very day. By fourteen I was playing for local dances, often with another fiddler to reinforce the volume.

Buddy MacMaster, Cape Breton (Canada) fiddler

In Cape Breton you could recognize a player from Mabou if you heard him. Also somebody from the Iona area, Victoria County, you could know by their playing. That was in the horse and buggy days. I am from Judique, and I know that my style is somewhat different from that of Mabou. I formed my own style from listening to different players and trying to pick what I liked, trying to do what the better players were doing. Through the years I tried to be a dance player, as well as playing for concerts or house parties. So, I kind of combined all that. I tried to play lively and sweet, to put some expression in the music. I suppose I figured out for myself that music played sweet sounds nicer. I like to try to give the music a pretty good lift and try to make it sound sweet and good to listen to, as well as to dance to.

In Cape Breton, step dancing and square dancing have a lot to do with the way we play—we make it lively for the dancers. You have to give it a lift or a lively feel to make the dancers feel like dancing or performing better. When you see a dancer responding to your music, that puts you in a better mood to play. It's the same at the square dances; if you see the people enjoying themselves, it sure puts you in the mood to play.

I don't speak [Scottish] Gaelic myself, but I think the Gaelic had an effect on my music because my parents were Gaelic speakers. Gaelic is a musical language, and I think it comes out in the Cape Breton music.

I enjoy the Cape Breton music if it's played well. What's special about it? Well, it's cheerful, lively, and bright; and there's quite a variety of tunes—different kinds, like, airs and marches, strathspeys, reels, jigs, clogs, and hornpipes. If you are in the Cape Breton area of Nova Scotia, please watch for opportunities to hear some genuine fiddling by me or one of my many fiddling friends.

United States, though there are major concentrations in California, Florida, New York, and of course in all states bordering Mexico. Their influence on American music is pronounced. For example, a great deal of our ballroom dance music is of Cuban, Puerto Rican, Brazilian, Dominican, and Argentine origin. *Salsa* music, a North American Puerto Rican–inspired response to Afro-Cuban music, has become quite popular in some quarters. To represent Hispanic culture in the United States we have chosen Tex-Mex *conjunto.*

Franco-American culture has also produced some unique styles of music. We will focus on the French "Acadian" tradition of Louisiana and discuss an example of what is commonly called "Cajun" music.

Because the ancestors of today's Native Americans were forcibly moved from their land, and because their religious rituals and cultural activities were suppressed by zealous Christian missionaries and government bureaucrats, much of traditional Native musical culture has been lost. Nonetheless, numerous kinds of Native American music can be found throughout the United States. In recent decades interest in Native music has increased, as the Native American flute and drum circles based on Native traditions have come to be associated with "New Age" spirituality. We have chosen two examples to represent traditional Native American music: a powwow performance in the Plains style and a recording of Zuni flute music from the Pueblo region of the southwestern United States. We will also highlight the highly unusual "throat-singing" of the Inuit peoples from Canada and Alaska.

Arrival: *Canada*

CANADA

Although larger than its neighbor to the south, Canada is in many ways not well known by Americans. As similar as Canada's heritage and lifestyle are to those of the United States, Canadians proudly maintain a distinct identity. Like the United States, Canada is a nation that has attracted immigrants from around the world, and is home to many Native American peoples (called First Nations by Canadians). Because Canada's population is small, the relative importance of non-European immigrants and First Nations is much greater than in the United States. Also important is French Canadian culture, which is centered in Quebec but found elsewhere as well, such as in Nova Scotia. Canada's culturally modern and ethnically diverse urban areas contrast with rural areas, where more culturally uniform populations continue to maintain long-practiced traditions. Our example of Canadian music originates in one such rural area, Cape Breton Island in Nova Scotia.

Site 1: Cape Breton Fiddling

Track 25

First Impressions. This familiar-sounding dance-like music, which hardly seems exotic at all, features a violinist (known colloquially as a fiddler) performing with piano and guitar accompaniment. This music may sound vaguely "Celtic," though this term usually points towards Irish music.

Aural Analysis. Buddy MacMaster, one of Canada's best-known and most-loved fiddlers, plays a jig in our excerpted example: "The Golden Keyboard." Jigs are associated with a dance form (also called the jig) known for its vigorous rising and falling movements. Along with other types of Scottish music—such as hornpipes, strathspeys, and reels—they were brought to North America by immigrants who settled in Nova Scotia ("New-Scotland"), one of Canada's eastern maritime provinces. Jigs are written as 6/8 time, with each of the two main beats having three subbeats (1 2 3 / 2 2 3). A given jig tune might be known by several different names depending on locale, while two jigs of the same name can be musically distinct.

This jig is in the key of E minor. Its range is limited to less than two octaves because most folk fiddlers only play in "first position," meaning that they do not slide their left hand toward the instrument's body to play a higher range of pitches. In spite of their length in performance, most jigs consist of just two or three short sections, each of which is eight measures long. To keep the piece going, fiddlers repeat or alternate these sections. This jig can be charted as A A B B A A B B A A, though some of the repetitions incorporate variations.

Violins, in spite of their association with European classical music, were domestic instruments for centuries. While it is true that today famous solo violinists use instruments valued in the millions of dollars, in the past musicians usually played locally made instruments or bought them by mail order at a modest price. Because the violin (called the *fiddle* in folk music contexts) was so often used for indoor dancing, and because families with "properly furnished parlors" usually had a piano, it became customary for fiddlers to be accompanied by a pianist, who improvised a simple chordal or figured part.

Cultural Considerations. Atlantic Canada includes four eastern provinces: New Brunswick, Nova Scotia, Prince Edward Island, and Newfoundland. The population is relatively diverse, as it includes First Nations, particularly the Mi'kmaq and Maliseet, as well as French Acadians and a small community of African-descended people. The majority, however, are of British (especially Scottish) extraction. Many among this latter group are (or were) Gaelic speakers, and have maintained Gaelic song to the best of their ability. The traditional context for their music-making was the *cèilidh* (pronounced "kay-lee"), a kind of house party. Along with singing, fiddle music was especially popular. Several kinds of dance, including solo Scottish step dance, were enjoyed at these parties, accompanied by fiddle if possible. If no instrumentalists were available, someone could sing these dance tunes using nonsense syllables, called *peurt a beul* (pronounced approximately "porsht a boy") in Gaelic; some call this "mouth music."

Cape Breton, from which our example originates, is an island separated from the mainland by the narrow Strait of Canso. Although

JIG
A dance tune
in 6/8 time.

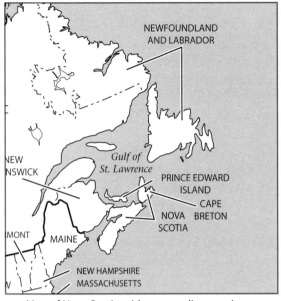

Map of Nova Scotia, with surrounding provinces

Gaelic Scottish culture once flourished throughout Atlantic Canada, Cape Breton has come to be most closely identified with it. A revival in the Gaelic arts—part of an international Celtic revival—has made music and dance the primary markers of Scottish identity there. Today there is an active Gaelic College—actually a summer school for the arts—at St. Anne just north of Baddeck in central Cape Breton.

The fiddling tradition in Cape Breton consists primarily of Scottish dance music, particularly waltzes, reels, jigs, polkas, square dances, and schottisches. Fiddle music found in Cape Breton is not purely Scottish in origin, however. There has been crosspollination between the French Acadian and Scottish styles, and in recent years there have also been a number of innovative younger players who draw on a variety of traditions. Fiddling was in rapid decline by the 1960s, but the Glendale Festival of 1973 stimulated a broad revival. In addition, Rounder Records of Boston has released a great number of albums of Cape Breton fiddling, which helped bring the music to the attention of the wider public.

THE UNITED STATES OF AMERICA

Arrival: The United States of America

Two areas of the United States have preserved traditional music more than others: New England and the Southern Applachians. Much of the

Buddy MacMaster, Canada's best-known fiddler, lives on Cape Breton, Nova Scotia, in maritime Canada and plays primarily music of Scottish origin (Buddy MacMaster)

traditional culture of both areas is disappearing as these once-isolated, relatively economically disadvantaged communities have increasingly been incorporated into "modern" American life. Nonetheless, a good deal of collecting of ballads, songs, and dance music over the last 100-150 years has preserved important examples of the music that once was common throughout these regions.

Site 2: Ballad-Singing

Track 26

First Impressions. This track may strike you as rather plain and unexciting. It features an unaccompanied vocalist, who sings with little ornamentation or rhythm, and whose words are hard to understand. Nonetheless, it is an example of a tradition, ballad-singing, whose influence is still felt in popular music today.

Aural Analysis. A ballad is a song that tells a story. Though sung by one person, it may incorporate both dialogue among two or more individuals and a narrator who comments on the story. The ballad we have chosen was recorded in Rhode Island sometime around 1950 by a Miss E. Price, who claimed to have learned the song from a friend living in Massachusetts. Since her generation of singers is now gone, most ballad singers today learned their songs from recordings and are better called "revivalists."

Listen carefully to our example and you will notice that the unaccompanied singer makes use of only five pitches, i.e., a pentatonic scale. Some might hear this scale as sounding "minor" because the three notes A, C, E outline a minor triad (three-note chord), but in fact pentatonic scales are neither major or minor.

The text is a poem organized in stanzas of four lines, but because the fourth line is repeated, the song actually has five lines. Though the basic meter is duple (divisible by two or four), sometimes there are extra words that seem to disrupt this flow. Ballad texts and tunes were all orally transmitted. Over time the words were sometimes changed, either when a singer sought to localize a song by changing place names or by bringing the story up to date, or when a singer made inadvertent changes based on misunderstandings. One such misunderstanding occurred with a ballad called "The Burley Banks of Barbry-O": the song was originally about a low class "rank robber," but in America the "rank robber" became a "bank robber."

Most ballads concern stories that are depressing, even violent, and the ballad we have chosen is no exception. The recording's original liner notes summarize the story:

> A mother sees blood on her son's clothing and asks him "How it came?" At first the son avoids giving a truthful answer but finally [he] confesses the murder of his father, brother, or, in this New England version, brother-in-law. Then follow a number of questions, each one bringing out a new fact.
>
> *Eight Traditional British-American Ballads, 1951*

Cultural Considerations. The ballad is one of Europe's most important song types, and its roots go back to medieval times. Ballads from continental Europe and the British Isles were primarily an orally transmitted folk form. With the rise of the Romantic Movement in the late eighteenth century, however, poets both major and minor began

PEURT A BEUL
(pronounced PORSHT A BOY)
An unaccompanied dance song with nonsense syllables used to substitute for fiddling.

BALLAD
A song that tells a story, usually performed by a solo voice.

writing ballads. Among them were two of the greatest poets of the time: Johann Wolfgang von Goethe (1749–1832) and Johann Christoph Friedrich von Schiller (1759–1805). Some of these literary ballads were set to music, most famously by Franz Schubert (1797–1828). Anyone who has taken a Western classical music appreciation class has no doubt encountered Schubert's ballad "Die Erlkönig" (1815). As with the traditional ballad, a single singer performs all the voices: a narrator, the father, the son, and the spirit of the Elf King.

British ballads were brought to the attention of American scholars by Francis James Child (1825–96), Harvard University's first Professor of English. Between 1882 and 1898 Child published a five-volume collection, *The English and Scottish Popular Ballads.* Child compiled more than 1,000 ballads, mostly collected from printed and manuscript sources and not from living singers. "Edward," the example used here, is number 13 in the collection, and thus it is labeled "Child 13."

Though American students poured over the Child collection, none seemed to recognize that these very same ballads were part of the American oral tradition and that singers throughout the United States (and Canada) were still singing them at home for friends and relatives. It took an English folksong collector, Cecil J. Sharp (1859–1924), to reveal to Americans this living tradition in their midst. Sharp's first visit to the United States took place during World War I and was followed by three more visits, during which he collected folksongs and ballads from singers in the Appalachian region. His publications, especially *English Folk-Songs from the Southern Appalachians* (1917), precipitated a gold rush in ballad and folksong collection throughout the United States. Most of the collectors, however, were professors of English, not ethnomusicologists, and because their goal was to collect texts, they usually paid little attention to the tunes. One important collector in New England was Helen Hartness Flanders, whose collection is housed at Middlebury College in Vermont and from which comes the present example, "Edward," collected in Rhode Island. It can be said that Sharp was especially responsible for this surge in collecting, which brought the new and little known field of Folklore to prominence.

Though there are still singers who know Child ballads, the golden age of collecting was more than seventy-five years ago, from around

APPALACHIA

A geographic region marked by the Appalachian Mountains, which extend throughout the eastern part of the United States.

Cecil Sharp and assistant Maud Karpeles noting downsongs from Mrs. Lucindy Pratt of Hindman, Knott County, Kentucky, 1917
(Courtesy of the English Folk Dance and Song Society, London)

1920 to 1950. It is the progenitors of these ballads that became important in the development of American music, both in a generalized sense and especially in the popular realm. More recent performers, such as Jean Ritchie, a Kentucky-born singer who has been important in the "folk revival" movement, have continued to sing Child ballads, but usually accompanied by instruments, especially the Appalachian lap "dulcimer," a three-stringed fretted zither played flat on the lap or a table.

Site 3: Old Regular Baptist Lined Hymn

First Impressions. Most first-time hearers of Old Regular Baptist lined hymns are puzzled or even put off by these seemingly tuneless and meterless sounds. As with the previous track, you hear only unaccompanied singing, but now by a group that seems unable to come together either melodically or beat-wise. This smudge of moving sound is occasionally interrupted by a male soloist who seems to be chanting rather than singing. However off-putting it may be on first hearing, this track, which was recorded by Kentuckians living in Ohio, represents one of the most archaic kinds of music still heard in the United States: a form of religious song with roots going back at least as far as the seventeenth century.

Aural Analysis. "And Must This Body Die?" is an eighteenth-century hymn by the eminent English poet Sir Isaac Watts (1674–1748). It is sung here by members of Pleasant View Old Regular Baptist Church near Medina, Ohio, led by their Moderator, Mr. Larry Newsome. The

Track 27

Elders of Valley Home Memorial Old Regular Baptist Church in Kurtz, Indiana, sing a hymn during a service. The second man from the left "lines out" the hymn from a words-only songbook

moderator simply begins singing, without announcing the hymn, since only he has a copy of the hymnal, a small paperback book without musical notation. Members join in as they recognize the hymn. At the end of the first line, the moderator "gives out" or "lines out" the next line of text—but uses a melodic formula to do this, *not* the tune. Because of differences in timing and degree of ornamentation, the singers produce simultaneous variants of the same tune (i.e., heterophony). The singing is quite slow, and therefore the music has little sense of beat or meter. Performers simply sing from memory, without even knowing the name or origin of the tune, which has been passed down through generations.

The words of this hymn are as elegant as they are depressing, and express the conviction that while the body is temporary, the spirit is timeless:

(Verse 1) And must this body die?
This mortal frame decay?
And must these active limbs of mine
Lie moldering in the clay?

(Verse 2) Corruption, earth, and worms, [accompanying audio
ends here]
Shall but refine this flesh,
Till my triumphant spirit comes
To put it on afresh.

PSALMS

A book of the Bible comprised of text praising God used as the source for songs in Calvinist churches.

Cultural Considerations. Martin Luther's attempt to reform the Roman Catholic Church was not the only cause of the Reformation. French theologian John Calvin (1509–64) had ideas far more radical than Luther's. He objected to most everything that was distinctively Roman Catholic, including vestments, stained glass, most Catholic rites, and everything sensual, such as incense and bells. He asserted that only the Psalms of the Old Testament, being the "inspired word of God," could be sung in church. These, being prose, had to be put into regular poetic verse ("versified") to allow for singing. Calvin's influence on the continent was great, but his influence in the British Isles was greater.

In England momentous changes had already taken place. King Henry VIII, desiring a divorce from one of his many consecutive wives and being denied one by the Roman Catholic Church, had broken away from Rome and created the Church of England. As Calvin's influence spread, England underwent a Reformation as well, which resulted in the founding of the "presbyterian-structured" Church of Scotland and a reform of the Church of England. (The "Presbyterian" form, which came out of an attempt to make the church less hierarchical, is a bottom-up system in which representatives are selected at four levels: session, presbytery, synod, and general assembly.) While these changes occurred, the radical Protestant and anti-monarchist Oliver Cromwell took power in England. Cromwell executed King Charles I in 1649 and began attacking Catholicism throughout the British Isles, including Ireland. Eventually, Cromwell's reforms were overturned in England and in 1660 the crown was restored, but Calvinism continued to develop deep roots in Scotland's rocky soil.

Interior of a Free Church of Scotland near Uig on the Isle of Skye has enclosed family pews. The three-tiered front area reserves the highest position for the minister, then for the elders, then the precentor, the latter "giving out the line" of the sung Psalms

It was in Scotland that a tradition of psalm-singing that is one of the roots of Old Regular Baptist singing first flourished. Cromwell had called for a conference to reform the Church of England, the Westminster Assembly of Divines, which ran from 1643 to 1648. In 1645 this conference published the *Directory for Publick Worship,* which prescribed how religious services were to be conducted. This book is not the first to document the performance practice of "lining out" a Psalm, but it was the first to sanction it. Because many church members lacked books or were unable to read, the writers of the *Directory* recommended that the "clerk" (pronounced like "clark") or minister "read" the Psalm passage before it was sung.

This led to a performance practice in which a leader (called "precentor" in Scotland) gave out the line of text in a chant-like manner just before the congregation sang the line to the tune. (In the United States this is called "lining out," because a leader "lines out" the words, one line at a time.) Furthermore, when the Scottish congregation sang, they sang without accompaniment. Reformed churches on the continent allowed for musical instruments, but most of those in Scotland forbade them. Because their singing was unaccompanied and without harmony, it was quite slow and had no recognizable beat. Further, some singers fell behind, some added ornamentation,

Old Regular Baptist elders at Pleasant View Church near Medina, Ohio, prepare to baptize a new member after having broken six-inch thick ice

some thought the melody went up when others thought it went down. The result was a "sonic smudge" of simultaneous variants of the tune.

These practices came to the American colonies almost immediately. Over time, and with the founding of various Baptist churches—a history far too long and complex to describe here—there was also a change from singing psalms to singing hymns, the difference being that psalms come from the "divinely inspired" Book of Psalms in the Bible's Old Testament, whereas hymns are poems of human creation. Over a long period and as people migrated to the South and West after the Revolutionary War (1770–82), isolated groups of Baptists found themselves in remote parts of Appalachia. The Old Regular Baptists were officially founded in 1870 in eastern Kentucky. There they continue to worship in a manner they believe was true of the first-century Christians, without instruments and observing most of Calvin's ideas of austerity and theology.

If this denomination is particular to eastern Kentucky, why in Ohio? After World War II as the troops returned from Europe and the Pacific, jobs were hard to come by in Appalachia. There was little more than coal mining, but the burgeoning auto plants in Indiana, Ohio, and Michigan offered jobs and could be reached by car. Many people from the "hollows" of eastern Kentucky found themselves working in places like the Detroit area, northern and central Indiana, and the Cleveland area. When enough Old Regulars settled in a new area, they founded a congregation, preferring to meet in a small building in the countryside. That is true of Pleasant View Church near Medina, Ohio.

Track 28

Site 4: *Singing School Shape-Note Music*

First Impressions. This track once again features unaccompanied vocalists, though this time their singing has an easily detectable beat. The first time through the song, they seem to be singing syllables, not words. Their tone of voice is quite nasal and strident, and the pronunciation has a Southern twang. All sing a line together, then each part comes in one after another and all four sing together to the end.

Aural Analysis. Arriving at a small wooden country church in rural Alabama near Cullman on a hot June morning in 1971, I (TM) could hear the singing some distance away, because all the windows were wide open. Hopewell Primitive Baptist Church was surrounded on two sides by a cemetery, the likes of which I had never seen before. All the grass had been scraped away, leaving the ground bare. This practice, typical of the rural South, is apparently an African-derived custom adopted by the white population as well. The singing I heard is also typical of the South, particularly northern Florida, Georgia, Alabama, Mississippi, and east Texas. People refer to it as "Sacred Harp singing" or "fasola singing," terms which will be explained presently.

SINGING SCHOOL

A tradition of teaching four-part harmony techniques, found in rural areas throughout the United States.

Among the many songs recorded that day was "Exhortation," a "fuging tune" composed by Eliakim Doolittle in 1800 using a hymn text written in 1709 by English poet Sir Isaac Watts. The title, "Exhortation," is actually the name of the tune or musical composition, because texts may be interchanged with other tunes. The singers are arranged in a square, and each holds a thick, oblong book entitled The *"Original" Sacred Harp, Denson Revision.* A male singer first intones the three pitches of the triad that defines the key, what is written as A minor, but the pitch level sung is set for the comfort of the voices, because there is no instrument in the building to sound a pitch anyhow.

"Exhortation," is an example of one of the most interesting song types in this tradition, called a "fuging tune." Although fuging tunes have a slight resemblance to a "round" (e.g., "Row, row, row your boat"), they are closer to the fugue, an instrumental genre of the Baroque period (ca. 1600–1750). Fugues begin with a single part called the "subject" that is then imitated by the second part, then the third, then the fourth, and so on (depending on how many voices the fugue

has). Fuging tunes are not fugues, but after a
first section in which all parts sing together
in harmony, a single voice part begins what
sounds like a simple fugue. Usually this is
the bass, who is followed by the tenors, then
either of the upper two parts (called counter [alto] and treble [often pronounced "trib-
ble"]). Fuging tunes, first developed in
England, but became a favorite of the early
New England singing schools.

In this example, all four parts begin
singing simultaneously, but they use syllables, not words. The first time through the
tune it is customary to sing the syllables
based on a scale of "fa, sol, la, fa, sol, la, mi,"
not the "do, re, mi" that is familiar today.
The singers then begin the first line of text,
"Now, in the heat of youthful blood,
Remember your Creator God." At this
point, the basses enter alone with the next
phrase, "Behold the months come hast'ning
on"; they are quickly followed by the

Hopewell Primitive Baptist Church near Cullman,
Alabama, and its "scraped" (grassless) cemetery,
site of annual *"Original" Sacred Harp* singings

tenors, then the altos, and finally the sopranos, each "imitating" the original bass phrase. After all four parts have gotten back together, they continue to the end with the words "When you shall say, My joys are gone."
The section with staggered entries, which resembles the beginning of a
fugue, is customarily repeated.

While the music seems to be in a minor key, in fact it is in the
Aeolian mode, one of the so-called "church modes" that preceded the
development of the major-minor tonal system. The seven degrees of the
scale are A, B, C, D, E, F, G, A. In A minor, the G would be sharp, but
here it is natural, giving the scale
an archaic sound. If you listen to
the first and last chords, you will
note that only two different
pitches are sounded, A and E; the
C that normally would be added
to make the chord sound full is
missing. Sometimes you also hear
nothing but the interval of a
fifth, which gives the music a
hollow sound. The way the
vocal lines move sometimes produces dissonance, caused by the
clashing of neighboring pitches.

A male singer (standing) leads a song from the *"Original"
Sacred Harp* at an all-day singing at Hopewell Primitive
Baptist Church near Cullman, Alabama

Cultural Considerations. Many of the early colonists in New
England were members of "dissenting" churches, that is, denominations

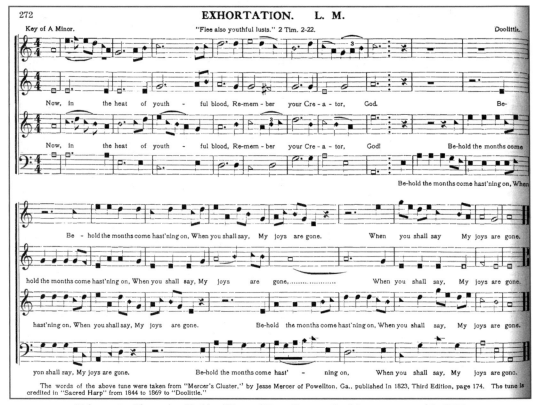

"Exhortation" from the *"Original" Sacred Harp*, Denson Revision, composed in 1800 by Eliakim Doolittle and notated in fa-sol-la shape notes

SHAPE NOTES

A music notation system that uses differently shaped "note" heads to indicate pitch.

other than the Church of England. Most of these denominations were Calvinist, and some were far more radical than John Calvin himself had been. The "Pilgrims" who came to Plymouth in 1620—in whose memory Thanksgiving is celebrated—were dissenters, believing in congregational independence and sharing Calvin's austere views. Consequently they and their brethren sang only the versified psalms, normally lined-out and sung heterophonically similar to the hymn in Site 3.

By the end of the seventeenth century, voices in metropolitan areas like Boston were raised against this practice, known then as the "Old Way of Singing." Ministers urged a turn away from what they felt was a moribund practice toward "Regular Singing," by which they meant singing by note, in parts, and in meter. In order for this change to be accomplished, however, a number of elements had to fall into place first. There needed to be a system of musical notation, a set of compositions, hymn books, and people to teach the congregations Regular Singing. These elements, which came into being during the first half of the eighteenth century, are still in existence today.

The old singing schools were taught by "singing masters"—though admittedly some had mastered very little. During the last third of the eighteenth century, however, a number of singing masters appeared who were also composers, and some published their four-voice compositions in oblong-shaped tunebooks.

Each book began with a substantial singing tutorial that offered instruction on notation and singing. From the earliest times singers in New England used the syllables—what is called solfège—customarily used in England. Instead of the series we know today (do, re, mi, fa, sol, la, ti, do), they used only four (fa, sol, la, fa, sol, la, mi, fa). In the singing schools it was customary to sing the syllables the first time the song was sung, before singing the verses.

After the Revolutionary War, many people migrated out of New England, and singing masters followed them. During the nineteenth century, singing schools were popular social events on the frontiers in the Midwest and the South. Around 1802 two clever singing masters, William Smith and William Little, authors of *The Easy Instructor*, created "shape notes," in which each of the four syllables of the "fasola"-system had its own shape.

After that most singing schoolbooks were published in shape notes, a notation style that continues to this day. Of the many collections published, the most prominent and successful was *The Sacred Harp*, compiled in Georgia by Benjamin Franklin White and Elisha J. King and published in Philadelphia in 1844. During the rest of the nineteenth century and through the twentieth, new editions were published. It became the custom to have annual "conventions" when singers assembled to sing from The *Sacred Harp* at an "all day singing with dinner on the ground" (that is, a potluck meal). This lively tradition continues into the twenty-first century throughout Georgia, Alabama, Mississippi, and parts of Florida, Tennessee, and Texas.

Sacred Harp singings are often held in rural Baptist churches, and because these only meet one weekend a month, the church is open for one-, two-, and three-day singings on the other weekends. The arrangement of the church pews, with the pulpit in the center, creates a square. With

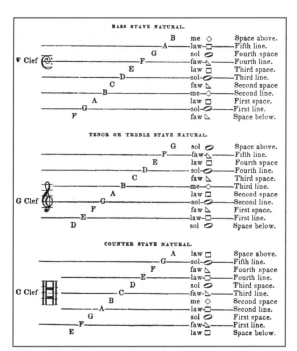

Chart from the singing tutor of the *"Original" Sacred Harp* showing the succession of pitches and shapes in three clefs, from bottom to top: C clef, G clef, and F clef

Singers still gather once a year at Cabe's Cove Missionary Baptist Church in Tennessee's Great Smokey Mountain National Park to sing from M. L. Swan's *The New Harp of Columbia*, a seven-shape book from 1867

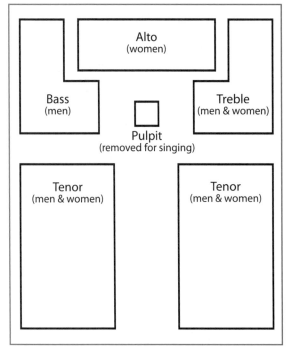

Bass (men)	Alto (women)		Treble (men & women)

Pulpit
(removed for singing)

Tenor (men & women)	Tenor (men & women)

Typical seating plan for a *Sacred Harp*
singing in a country church

Track 29

A bluegrass band plays for the National Folk Festival

the pulpit moved away, there is seating for each of the four parts. Anyone who wishes to do so is offered a chance to come up front and lead two songs. When lunchtime comes, everyone spreads his or her food on long tables outside. Afterward, they continue singing until late afternoon.

Site 5: Bluegrass

First Impressions. Bluegrass music is characterized by what is called the "high-lonesome sound": a high tenor harmony part over a baritone vocal melody, accompanied by a variety of stringed instruments. A bluegrass concert, typically a mix of "old-timey" tunes, "driving" instrumental solos, and the occasional gospel tune, is "down-home," a refuge from the hectic modern way of life. Perhaps you can picture the band in our recording set up under a gazebo in a town square on a sunny Sunday afternoon, surrounded by families on picnic mats.

Aural Analysis. Bluegrass music has clear melodic lines, simple harmonies, and a steady beat. Acoustic (non-electric) chordophones, namely the fiddle (violin), mandolin, banjo, guitar, and string bass, form the standard ensemble. Percussion instruments are rarely heard; the underlying rhythm is provided instead by the plodding bass line of a stringed bass or by the low strings of the guitar.

Each instrument has a unique timbre and different range. The bowed fiddle provides smooth melodies and countermelodies with frequent double-stops (the playing of two strings simultaneously) and sliding ornamentations. The other instruments are plucked, either with the fingers or with a plectrum. The five-stringed banjo has a "twangy" tone quality that contrasts with the mellow timbre of the six-string guitar. The banjo's unique timbre is due to the cowhide membrane used for the face of the resonator; this material brings out more high overtones than would be true of wood.

The bright timbre of the mandolin, the smallest instrument in the group, is primarily due to the high tension on the strings and the short neck, both of which contribute to the production of high, piercing pitches. The instrument has eight strings in four courses; this doubling of strings amplifies the mandolin's sound, allowing it to compete with the other instruments.

In vocal bluegrass music, the instruments play a secondary role, by supporting the voices with strummed harmony, "fills" (short melodic phrases played during pauses in the singing), and countermelodies (contrasting melodies played simultaneously with the vocalist at a lower volume). The string bass keeps the rhythm steady by playing on every first and third beat. The other plucked instruments often contribute to the rhythmic element by strumming on the upbeats (the second and fourth pulses), playing ornamented versions of the melody, or providing countermelodies.

A banjo player picks a tune during an outdoor wedding celebration in Nelson County, Virginia

Bluegrass musicians are expected to be highly skilled performers, and often play extremely virtuosic melodic passages. Each instrumentalist (except the bassist) is given the opportunity to perform a solo during sections without vocals, in which they play their own version of the melody at a greater volume than the other instruments. This alternation of the voice with instrumental solo breaks provides a clear example of a strophic form.

In our example, each verse has eight pulses. The fiddle opens the performance, anticipating very closely the main melody sung by the vocalists in the next verse. The banjo takes the next solo break and is followed by a second vocal verse. The mandolin is next, and is followed by the third vocal verse; the fiddle then returns, this time with a bit more improvisation. A fourth verse concludes the performance.

The vocal timbre of bluegrass music tends to be nasal, even pinched. This is characteristic of Appalachian vocal music in general, but the "high lonesome" tenor voice enhances this strained quality, as the vocalist intentionally sings in the upper reaches of his voice. The main melody is carried by the lower voice, while the harmony is usually a third or fifth interval above, moving in parallel

Brought from Italy, the mandolin became popular in the United States early in the 20th century, later becoming a mainstay of bluegrass music

motion. The texts usually focus on male-female relationships, or on the difficulties of having to "leave home" or family. Our example, "True Life Blues" performed by Bill Monroe and the Bluegrass Boys, focuses on the hardships of married life—interestingly, from the woman's perspective, even though the vocalist is male.

Bill Monroe (Courtesy of BenCar Archives)

BLUEGRASS
A style of American folk music characterized by virtuosic instrumental performance and the so-called "high lonesome" vocal style, in which a harmony pitch is sung above the main melody.

MANDOLIN
A high-ranged fretted lute commonly used in bluegrass music.

Cultural Considerations. Bluegrass music is truly an American music. Its elements are drawn from a wide variety of American music traditions, including the "old timey" tunes of Southern Appalachia, gospel, blues, jazz, and even mainstream pop. Bluegrass was inspired by nineteenth-century American roots music but was created during the booming economic era of the post–World War II years. Radio and television were integral to bluegrass's early success, but they have since mostly shunned its presentation. Bluegrass musicians generally prefer being ignored by the mass media and pop culture, which represent the hectic lifestyle of the urbanite. For them, the perfect environment is an outdoor performance in which technology is kept to a minimum and the music, rather than the presentation, is the focus.

The main figure of the bluegrass tradition is Bill Monroe (1911–96). Indeed, even the term *bluegrass* itself is derived from the name of Monroe's group, Bill Monroe and the Bluegrass Boys. Many of the most famous bluegrass musicians, such as Earl Scruggs and Lester Flatt, were members of the Bluegrass Boys at one time and all bluegrass musicians, from Doc Watson to Alison Krauss, acknowledge Bill Monroe as the standard for the style.

Bill Monroe was born and raised in Kentucky (the Bluegrass State). His older brothers, Charlie and Birch, already played fiddle and guitar, so Bill learned the mandolin as his major instrument. As is typical of most bluegrass musicians, Monroe acquired his musical skills informally. His mother and uncle were his primary influences—indeed, Monroe always credited his unique "shuffle" sound to his Uncle Pen (Pendleton Vandiver), who played fiddle for local dances. Having grown up in Appalachia, Monroe was inspired by a variety of musical traditions associated with the region.

Shape-note singing strongly influenced Monroe's "high lonesome sound," with its upper-voiced harmony and nasal timbre. Gospel tunes became a standard part of his repertory. The instruments common to Appalachian string bands formed the basis for his own band. Monroe even claimed to have been inspired by the Scottish bagpipes, which, while not normally associated with Appalachia, are indeed prevalent in the region due to the large number of inhabitants with Scottish ancestry.

The music traditions that Monroe drew from were associated with the white working-class rural populations of southern Appalachia. Beginning in the 1920s, large numbers of these Appalachians began migrating from rural areas to urban areas in search of work in factories. "Hillbilly" music, as the rural Appalachian music was then called, represented the life they had left behind. By mid-century, nostalgia for "country living" led to the popularity of radio and television broadcasts of this rural music, such as the Carter family, later dubbed "country." The most important radio station in the South for country music was WSM in Nashville, which produced a program called "The Grand Ole Opry."

Bill Monroe and his Bluegrass Boys became a prominent feature of this program, as well as of the subsequent television-version. Monroe also released recordings of numerous songs, many of which, such as "Blue Moon of Kentucky," have become standards of the bluegrass repertory.

The Phipps Family singers of Kentucky, successors to the Carter Family in performing country songs, the mainstay of the "Grand Ole Opry."

Discarding the "hillbilly" uniform of rustic overalls and worn-out shoes, Monroe dressed himself and his band in smart-looking suits and ties and donned clean, wide-brimmed cowboy hats. This polished stage presentation reflected the professional performances of the musicians in his band. Bluegrass, as the style was dubbed in 1956, was not "sing-along" music, it was concert music. The quick tempos and driving instrumental solos demanded exceptional virtuosity on the part of performers and serious attention from the listener. The solo breaks were infused with a competitive spirit, as performers vied to take the music to uncharted territory during each performance, an approach Monroe borrowed from jazz. Bluegrass had come to represent rural America, but with a sense of urban urgency.

Though overshadowed by the popularity of rock and roll, bluegrass acquired a large following during the 1950s and early 1960s. Interest in folk music surged in the mid-1950s with bands such as the Kingston Trio. The banjo became especially popular due to the success of folk singer Pete Seeger. Bluegrass became well known during this period, and musicians in particular gravitated toward its sound. Whereas the audiences for folk music performances were mostly made up of non-musicians, bluegrass concerts attracted musician-heavy audiences, who appreciated the high technical skills of the performers.

In 1965 the First Annual Bluegrass Festival was held in Fincastle, Virginia. At this event, Bill Monroe was deservedly dubbed the "father of bluegrass." Since then, bluegrass festivals and folk festivals in general have been the primary venues for the performance of bluegrass music. Though a few somewhat bluegrass-based musicians have achieved success in the mainstream music industry, such as the Dixie Chicks and

Alison Krauss, the majority of bluegrass musicians remain unknown to the general public. While even today "traditional" bluegrass continues to dominate the scene, since the 1950s there have been counter currents, collectively known as newgrass, associated with such groups as the Seldom Scene and the New Grass Revival.

Track 30

Site 6: African-American Spiritual

First Impressions. This track, which sounds something like the Old Regular Baptist track (site 2), once again features unaccompanied vocalists. Their singing is rhythmically rather free and without any clearly articulated meter, and the pitches they employ do not always sound "in tune." There is an almost improvisatory character to this performance. While it is religious in nature, it does not really sound like regular congregational church song.

Aural Analysis. This widely sung spiritual makes use of only five pitches within the narrow range of an interval of a sixth, rising a third from the central pitch and falling a fourth below it. The upper third, however, wavers between being major or minor and is closer to what it called a "neutral" third. These pitches, which are characteristic of African-American singing in general, are commonly known as "blue notes." It is this ambiguity between major and minor that gives spirituals and many other forms of African-American singing their distinct flavor.

BLUE NOTE

A pitch not standard to the Euro-American tradition, believed to derive from West African tuning systems.

As is typical of spirituals, the words are simple, because they must be memorized. They also follow a structure in which stanzas are repeated with only a few words changed. Spirituals can have an unfixed number of stanzas, and these stanzas can appear in many different orders. This performance has three stanzas. The first line, "Come and go to that land," is sung three times, then completed with the phrase "where I'm bound." The second stanza substitutes "I have a savior in that land" for the first part of the first line, but finishes again with "where I'm bound." The final stanza begins with the phrase "Peace and happiness in that land."

Spirituals incorporate freely interpolated comments here and there, such as "woe." Inserting these extra sounds allows individuals to express themselves while remaining part of a group. These spontaneous interpolations also reflect the African-American attitude toward performance, which is not thought of as an exercise in lock-step precision, but as a community event in which a certain amount of freedom is encouraged.

Cultural Considerations. While the term *spiritual* is usually associated with African Americans, it has also been used to denote a variety of Anglo pentatonic "folk hymns." But it was the African-American spiritual that caught the ears of travelers through America's south in the early nineteenth century, because its sound was so un-European. Although several scholars claimed these songs could not really be notated because of their free rhythms and non-European pitch intonations, several collections of transcribed spirituals were nonetheless printed during the nineteenth century.

The spirituals constitute what is perhaps the oldest extant form of black singing in America. Because Protestant Christians almost always suppressed any Africanisms, particularly religious ones, slaves had to express themselves in a form acceptable to their masters. This meant singing something that resembled European melody, with a text in English, usually taken from the Bible. Most spiritual texts were sorrowful, and looked forward to a release from earthly cares in Heaven. Some, however, were joyful, such as "Blow your trumpet, Gabriel"; this latter type of spiritual was often referred to as a *jubilee*. Many scholars have suggested that the texts of spirituals contained double meanings For example, the words "Didn't my Lord deliver Daniel?" or "Steal Away" were perhaps a coded expression of the desire to escape from slavery.

Ironically, as spirituals declined in popularity in African-American culture toward the end of the nineteenth century, more and more outsiders came to appreciate them. During the twentieth century "Negro spirituals" in many guises became a mainstay of American music, and were sung by high school choirs and great black soloists like Mahalia Jackson and Paul Robeson, and played in arrangements by bands and orchestras everywhere.

The old-time spiritual, however, has not disappeared, as is attested to by our recording. In African-American churches, particularly Baptist ones, many different kinds of music representing different historical and style periods coexist. One can encounter the old "Dr. Watts" or "long meter" lined-out hymns that go back to the eighteenth century, the timeless spiritual, standard hymns from the nineteenth and twentieth centuries, and gospel songs of all sorts in numerous guises within a single service. The old-style spiritual is most likely heard during "Devotions," a brief period of preparation led by the deacons before or just after the main service begins. In some churches these songs may also be accompanied by organ and piano.

Site 7: African-American Gospel Choir

Track 31

First Impressions. On this track a full and enthusiastic-sounding choir accompanied by an electric organ sings a rhythmically active religious song, apparently during a church service. Because it is so upbeat and joyful, this performance may not sound like typical American religious music to you. In fact, it may even remind you of a "popular" style of music, because of its strong rhythms and the style of the accompaniment.

Aural Analysis. As a visit to any record store will affirm, the bins marked "gospel" include two kinds of music, "white gospel" and "black gospel." The latter has had the wider appeal to audiences both inside and outside African-American churches. Indeed, there are now gospel choirs, especially on college campuses, whose members come from many backgrounds. African-American gospel has become, like jazz, everyone's music. The present example was recorded at New Hope Baptist Church in Akron, Ohio, a typical urban, northern, African-American church. "God is Good All the Time," composed by Paul Smith, a local musician, has been the church's theme song for some years and is sung every Sunday.

The choir, made up of approximately thirty adult members, is accompanied by a Hammond C-3 electric organ. The Hammond organ sound is still the preferred sound in African-American churches even though their electromagnetic tone-wheel technology dates to 1935 and was superceded by electronics in the 1970s. Combined with rotating drum speakers made by Leslie, an acoustic piano, and oftentimes a drum set, the Hammond organ provides accompaniments that range from straight "pipe organ" to nightclub stylings, and that are frequently played with much vibrato. Adding to the sound is the choir's clapping on beats two and four.

"God is Good All the Time" is a purely choral composition, consisting of a main section, which lasts half the song, a middle section based around the word "Hallelujah," and a closing section that partly restates the main theme. Many other gospel compositions, however, feature a solo vocalist who alternates with the choir. Both kinds are heard during a typical service at New Hope Baptist. "God is Good all the Time" also exemplifies the predominantly joyful side of gospel. Other compositions may be much more subdued, at least at the beginning, but usually become more animated and emotional by the end.

The Gospel Choir of Ocala, Florida's Covenant Missionary Baptist Church rehearses for the Sunday service. The director teaches the choir by rote while the organist improvises the accompaniment on an electric organ

For choir members, gospel is an aural tradition, transmitted by the director to the singers through demonstration. While some directors write fairly complete scores mostly for their own use, others write only skeletal "charts" and some use no notes whatsoever. Singers rarely use any kind of score. Directors typically use their own arrangements, which for the most part are based on recordings. Accompaniments are provided either by the director or by a separate person, and are mostly improvised from memory or based on an incomplete chart. Many directors also compose their own songs or create gospel-style arrangements of well-known hymns and old "Negro spirituals." Stylistically, there is no attempt to distinguish gospel from the contemporary popular genres heard outside the church, for the secular and sacred sides of African-American music have long influenced each other.

Cultural Considerations. The term "gospel," besides meaning the first four books of the New Testament of the Christian Bible, refers to a complex of musical types running the gamut from simple, unadorned hymns sung dispassionately to elaborate, passionately sung compositions/arrangements involving a soloist and choir and multiple instrumentalists. "Gospel" music has a single root that, over time, divided into separate histories for Anglo Americans and African Americans. Although "white gospel" remains a major musical force in the United States, "black gospel" has not only attracted greater attention, it has also

With its pastor, the Rev. Benny Williams, singing solo, the Gospel Choir of New Hope Missionary Baptist Church, Akron, Ohio, is directed by Mr. Robert Nation during the Sunday service

become one of the prominent forms of American "popular" music. It has been exported as well, as thriving gospel traditions can now be found in the Caribbean, the United Kingdom, and Africa.

As a musical term, *gospel* originally referred to the hymns and songs associated with American evangelism from the mid-nineteenth century onward. Gospel songs developed out of three sources during the first half of the nineteenth century: the simple but "correct" or "scientific" harmonies found in the hymns of white New Englanders like Lowell Mason ("My Faith Looks Up to Thee") and Thomas Hastings ("Rock of Ages"), Civil War–era Sunday School songs (such as William Bradbury's "Jesus Loves Me"), and the songs used in evangelistic services from the Civil War onward, such as "What a Friend We Have in Jesus," "Softly and Tenderly Jesus is Calling," and "Jesus, Keep Me Near the Cross." The term *gospel hymn* (or *gospel song*) was coined in the early 1870s by Ira D. Sankey, the musical associate of evangelist Dwight L. Moody. Gospel hymns are always in a major key and are characterized by the presence of a verse-chorus structure, the use of mostly simple chords (though some have extensive chromaticism), and by the use of *afterbeats*, that is, echo-like repetitions of short text phrases while one part holds a long note. One of the best known hymns is "The Old Rugged Cross."

Gospel hymns have been spread worldwide by evangelists, and in the South they were taken into the shape-note singing school tradition by the end of the nineteenth century. But it was their absorption into the Pentecostal movement, which was founded in Los Angeles in 1906, that caused them to flourish among African Americans. Some of the composers of standard gospel hymns were African Americans, but most of their songs were indistinguishable from white songs. One man, though, Charles A. Tindley, composer of "We'll Understand It Better By and By" (1905), brought black gospel hymns into the limelight. During this same period black street preachers began singing gospel hymns as part of their sermonizing, accompanying themselves on guitar. Among the best known of these preachers were Blind Willie Johnson and the Rev. Gary Davis first active in the 1930s.

Gospel hymns, now only the starting point for increasingly free performances, developed into other new forms from the 1920s on, especially the vocal "quartet" (called "quartets" even though some groups had more than four singers). The most prominent black composer of the time was Thomas A. Dorsey, formerly a barrelhouse pianist known as "Georgia Tom." His gospel hymn "Precious Lord, Take My Hand" remains the virtual anthem of black religious music today. Solo gospel singers, the most famous of them including Mahalia Jackson, Clara Ward, and Marion Williams, brought gospel to the concert stage. Gospel performances involving choirs, often combined with one or more soloists, became increasingly prominent in the 1950s. During the 1960s vocalist James Cleveland brought choral gospel to prominence not just within the African-American community, but within the outside world as well. Gospel music was increasingly influenced by and influential *on* popular genres. Indeed, much of black popular music, especially *soul,* derives ultimately from the old lined hymns and gospel performances of the churches.

Today "black gospel" mainly means choral music, with or without soloists. While it was originally associated with rough and ready street evangelists and "storefront" churches (small churches started in rented storefronts in the inner cities), over time it has been accepted by the mainstream denominations, including Baptists, Methodists, Roman Catholics, and even black Lutherans, Presbyterians, and Episcopalians. Gospel music remains one of the most exciting and creative of America's many musical expressions, and it is less and less restricted to the domain of black churches. Each year more and more colleges and universities add "gospel choir" to their list of official ensembles, and these attract students of every ethnic background. Gospel, like jazz earlier, has become an American music rather than an African-American music.

HYMN
A "humanly composed" religious work.

Site 8: Country Blues

Track 32

First Impressions. Blues music is raw. Though vocal prowess and musicianship are valued, the essence of blues music is emotion. Through his music and words, the blues musician reveals his innermost feelings, whether of sorrow, anger, joy, or lust. Blues is a music of hardship and heartache, and is born of the black experience in the United States.

Aural Analysis. Country or folk blues features a solo voice, typically male, and an accompanying instrument, virtually always a guitar or harmonica. The vocal timbre is often gritty, and the singing is declamatory and interspersed with melismatic moans. The lyrics are primarily sung in the first person. The vocalist expresses his emotions frankly and deals with serious subject matter. Our example, Lightnin' Hopkins's "Penitentiary Blues," is about false imprisonment.

The guitar acts as a second voice, responding to the vocal phrases with "riffs" that affirm the proclamations of the singer. Though based on European equal-tempered tuning, blues is characterized by the use of one or more "blue" notes, which fall between those pitches normally used in the Western tradition. These "blue" notes make the music neither major nor minor—yet suggestive of both—and create tension and an "edgy" sound that reflects the unsettled mood of the music. Though much of the blues music of today is quite polished, folk blues is raw-sounding.

Most blues music uses a minor-sounding key, because minor keys are perceived to indicate sadness. The typical blues song usually uses only five or six tones, with the second and/or sixth pitches of the scale being omitted. The "blues" notes are generally found between the fourth and fifth scale degrees or the sixth and seventh scale degrees. Pianists will use the "augmented" (raised) fourth and a flatted seventh to play these "blue" notes, because the pitches of the piano are fixed. The harmonic progression of most (but not all) blues follows a standard 12-bar blues stanza form. Each "bar" is comprised of four beats. The first four bars correspond to the first vocal phrase. The phrase is typically repeated in the second four bars, while the poetic response is sung in the last four bars. The harmonic structure of the blues utilizes the I-IV-V chords in the following form:

```
Line 1   I - - -| I - - - | I - - - | I - - - |
Line 2   IV- - -| IV- - - | I - - - | I - - - |
Line 3   V - - -| IV- - - | I - - - | I - - - |
(repeated for each succeeding stanza)
```

This structure is often modified, especially in the last four bars, frequently as V-V-I-I or by having the last bar be V, which acts as a "turn around" that leads into the next 12-bar stanza. The nonmusician can think of these chord symbols as representing tension and release. I is home, the most relaxed and comfortable chord. IV increases that tension, but then returns home. V increases the tension even more before returning to the I chord. Listen for this release of tension in the closing phrase [V-IV-I-I] of the first verse, in which Lightnin' Hopkins proclaims, "You know I'm gonna do time for another man [V], when there haven't been a thing poor Lightnin' done [IV]." The guitar riff response completes the verse on the home chord.

BLUES
A secular folk music tradition originating within the Africa-American community in the southern United States.

While the 12-bar blues is the standard model for performance, blues musicians frequently take liberties with various aspects of the form. Rhythmic flexibility is an essential feature—bars can be added or excluded and the tempo can be changed—and even the chord structure can be modified. In our selection, the tempo is roughly sixty beats per minute as the performance starts, but by the end it has increased to more than ninety beats per minute. This improvisatory element adds tension and enhances the unsettled mood of blues music.

Cultural Considerations. An appreciation of the blues requires only that the listener have empathy for the hurts, joys, desires, and frustrations the singer expresses through his music. Though the country blues originate from the experiences of being an African American in a racist and unjust world, the music's heartfelt and realistic perspective on the fundamental emotions of all human beings have given it broad appeal around the world.

The roots of much African-American music can be traced to the field hollers and work songs of slaves who labored under the broiling sun in the South, especially Mississippi, Alabama, Georgia, Tennessee, the Carolinas, and Virginia, as well as Louisiana and Texas. Singing was commonplace among slaves, who were forced to work long, hot days on plantations and elsewhere. The singing, especially the work songs, provided distraction from the tediousness of the work, while the music's regular beat oftentimes helped organize whatever physical activity the slaves were engaged in, be it pounding rocks or tamping railroad ties. The vocal style and melodic and rhythmic freedom of these work songs and field hollers, as well as many of the songs themselves, became the basis for early blues, spirituals, and gospel songs among African Americans after Emancipation in 1865.

By the 1890s, the blues form appeared in many places throughout the Deep South. While the instrumentation and harmonic progression of the music were inspired by the folk ballad traditions of Europe, the three-line form and use of an instrumental accompaniment as a "second voice" were African-American innovations. The characteristic "blue" notes are believed to derive from African conceptions of tuning. Even the itinerant lifestyle of the "bluesman" is thought to have its roots in the West African *griot* tradition (see Chapter 9, Site 7).

The "troubled" life of the bluesman provided a major resource for the lyrical content of blues music. Lost loves, promiscuity, alcohol and drugs, the bluesman's nomadic existence, racism, and death are all common themes in the country blues. Many of the early blues artists were blind, such as Blind Willie McTell, Blind Lemon Jefferson, and Blind Blake. Being blind undoubtedly made life difficult for a black man in the Deep South, as finding work was nearly impossible. Many other early blues artists chose the lifestyle as preferable to hard labor that paid little. A weekend's music performance at a picnic or other event could earn them as much or more than a week's worth of wages farming on plantations or building levees. The burdens of a nomadic life were preferable to the struggle to maintain a sedentary existence for the country bluesman. Sleeping in railroad cars, shacking up with a female admirer for a weekend or two, and avoiding the law or racist thugs all became fodder for the bluesman's songs.

Many venues for blues performances existed in the early years of the twentieth century. Traveling tent and medicine shows often hired blues musicians to accompany them to attract audiences, particularly black populations, as the vendors themselves were generally white.

A promotional photo of Lightnin' Hopkins (unknown)

Bluesmen frequently found work at house parties or in *juke joints*, the latter being the term for social clubs with a primarily black clientele. Brothels also commonly hired blues musicians to entertain, and became one of the earliest contexts for blues pianists.

An important activity for the blues artist was playing in what are called *cuttin' heads* contests. These contests pitted musicians against each other in a kind of duel judged by the audience, which determined who was the better player. Competitions were a necessary way for a musician to demonstrate his skills and gain a reputation in order to find work. However, if a musician was "cut" (i.e., if he lost), he generally had to hand over his guitar to the winner. Losing meant a musician would have to earn, borrow, or steal enough money to buy back his guitar from the local pawnshop. For obvious reasons, these contests were a great incentive for musicians to develop their skills and expand their repertory.

The popularity of the blues was recognized by the budding music industry of the 1920s and 1930s, which released a slew of recordings by country blues artists. These recordings were a staple of the "race record" industry, which featured primarily black artists, whose recordings were sold to black customers. As the industry grew, blues musicians saw

African-Americans dance at a "Juke Joint" or social venue. Notice the police observer. (Courtesy of Library of Congress)

an opportunity to make some quick cash (musicians were paid a one-time fee for their services) and maybe gain some notoriety through a successful record.

When the Great Depression of the 1930s hit the Deep South, many rural workers moved to distant cities to find employment. Northern cities, such as Detroit, Cleveland, New York, and especially Chicago, offered the greatest opportunities for work in factories and mills. As the black population left the South, the bluesman found that his audience was disappearing. Consequently, he followed his patrons to the city where he adapted his music to his new situation. Artists such as Muddy Waters, Howlin' Wolf, and Elmore James gave the blues a jolt of energy, literally, by adding electric guitars and forming combo groups that included less portable instruments, such as drums and piano. Creative use of the microphone gave great harmonica players, such as Little Walter and James Cotton, a new sound and a prominent role as soloists in many blues bands. Later this updated form of the blues came to be known as *rhythm and blues.*

These innovations led to the development of a new genre in the 1950s, namely rock and roll. Early American popular artists, such as Elvis Presley, Jerry Lee Lewis, Chuck Berry, and Little Richard, based much of their repertoire on the blues forms, as did later successful rock bands from overseas, such as the Rolling Stones, Cream, and Led Zeppelin. Not only rock was influenced by the blues, however: much early jazz was played in 12-bar blues form, and the distinctive piano style called *boogie-woogie* was essentially piano blues.

Blues was perhaps one of the most influential musics of the twentieth century and today is still a prominent feature of America's musical landscape. Many contemporary blues artists, despite usually traveling with a band, maintain the rural roots of the music by performing solo pieces drawn from recordings made in the early years of the twentieth century. Older artists such as Robert Johnson, Charlie Patton, and Blind Willie Johnson are still revered as the models for performance and are legends of the genre.

Track 33

Site 9: Conjunto from Texas

First Impressions. This recording may seem puzzling at first, because while the musicians are Spanish-speakers, the featured instrument is an accordion, and the tune sounds like a polka. How did this odd blend come about?

Aural Analysis. *Conjunto*, with or without words, is music for dancing. Because the *conjunto* ensemble is small, it is ideal for modest places, like the Texas *cantina*, basically what Anglos call a bar or small club. The most prominent instrument in *conjunto* is the accordion, a bellows-driven free-reed instrument invented in 1829 by Cyrillys Damian of Vienna, Austria. Czech and German immigrants, many of who became cowboys, brought the accordion to Texas during the nineteenth century. The preferred accordion models have three rows of buttons on the right (melodic) side and far fewer on the left (chord) side. Extending the bellows drives the air through one set of reeds and compressing them drives the air through another.

CONJUNTO

A popular dance music found along the Texas-Mexico border in North America.

While the sound of the accordion dominates *conjunto*, other instruments are typical of it as well. The resonant Mexican 12-string guitar, called *bajo sexto*, differs from standard guitars in tuning. Whereas the American 12-string guitar is tuned e'e'-BB-GG-DD-A1A1-E1E1, the Mexican guitar is tuned f'f'-CC-GG-Dd'-A1a'-E1e'. Basically it plays the bass note of the first beat of the measure and strums chords on the others. The drum (or "trap") set, already popular in local swing bands, came to conjunto in the 1940s; players use the bass drum to emphasize the downbeat and the snare drum to accent the offbeat. Finally, the electric bass guitar, which was invented in the 1950s, is used to emphasize the bass notes.

Playing for a New York audience, Mingo Saldivar (accordion) with Los Cuatro Espadas play *conjunto* music (© Jack Vartoogian/FrontRowPhotos)

Created and performed by Tony de la Rosa, one of the most prominent *conjunto* artists today, the song "Besos, besitos" is about two lovers who are apparently breaking up. The text is in five sections that are not exactly stanzas, as they vary in length. The first section translates as, "After me, you'll have lots of lovers, / With them will come a thousand new illusions. / But they will never erase from your mouth all those kisses / that made you tremble."

While the words might express sadness, the music certainly has a happy go-lucky feel to it. The dominant sound is the accordion, which plays continuous, even staccato-like melody notes while each of the other instruments performs its more routine function—playing bass notes, filling in chords, and emphasizing beats. As with basic polka, the dance movements are simple and repetitive, mostly skipping steps, making it easy for everyone to join in.

Cultural Considerations Because *conjunto* music originates in Texas, that is where we shall concentrate this study. The old Indian name for what is now Texas was *Tejas*, and Latin people from the region are described as *Tejano*, though many prefer to be called *Mexicano*. Although the area was first visited by Europeans in the early sixteenth century, *Tejas* was not settled by the Spanish until the early eighteenth century, when a Spanish Roman Catholic mission was established in San Antonio. Texas remained a part of the Vice Royalty of New Spain until Mexico's independence from Spain in 1821, after which it continued as a part of the Republic of Mexico. During the 1820s many people of non-Spanish European descent migrated there, and as a result the Texans sought and achieved independence from Mexico in 1836, becoming the independent Republic of Texas. Annexation by the United States in 1845 led to a two-year war (1846–48) with Mexico after which Texas was securely in American hands. Thus *Tejano* as a cultural term includes peoples of both Spanish-Mexican and general Anglo descent, though the dominant culture was virtually the same as that of northern Mexico.

Two Ohio conjunto musicians in a workshop. The button box accordion (right) is the leader, and the *bajo sexto* Mexican twelve-string guitar (left) provides accompaniment

Later there was considerable strife between the dominant, largely Anglo Texas Rangers and Spanish speakers. With such violent history now left to historians, it is *Tejano* food and *conjunto* music, often characterized as "Tex-Mex," that is this area's most prominent contribution to American cultural life as a whole.

Early dance bands, called *banda tìpica,* consisted of whatever instruments were available. They accompanied dancers doing the *schottische, waltz, polka,* and *mazurka,* these being the then-current ballroom dances of Europe. As time went on, the accordion and 12-string Mexican guitar became standard. Although the *polka* remains popular, the most fashionable dance now is the duple-metered *ranchera* (which, to the uninitiated, sounds like a polka). While *conjunto* continues to be popular among certain parts of the population, other genres have come to overshadow it. The Tejano swing band, called *banda* or *orquesta,* reached its peak by the 1990s and has been succeeded by a newer, mostly synthesized type called *el grupo,* of which the late Selena Quintanilla, murdered in 1993, was the best-known performer.

Track 34

Site 10: *Cajun Music*

First Impressions. This is relatively simple music with an infectious beat and a lot of forward drive, which, like *conjunto,* places the accordion at the center. The singing is in French, though it sounds like French with a southern twang. Cajun music, like Cajun food, has attracted a growing number of followers and, like the spiciness of the alleged "Cajun sauces" served in most American restaurants, has a certain spiciness of its own. This is music that practically pushes you out of your seat onto the dance floor.

Aural Analysis. Besides the voices, only two melodic instruments are heard, the accordion and fiddle, but if you listen carefully you will also hear the high, clear tones of a metal triangle. The accordion is even simpler than the one used in *conjunto,* having just one row of melody buttons. Like the basic and inexpensive accordions usually mail-ordered from "up north," the harmonies of Cajun music are simple, basically I and V, tonic and dominant. The melodic range is just one octave, rising a fifth above the tonic and descending a fourth below. Because such an accordion can be played in only one key, an instrument must match the singer's range. Much Cajun singing, as this example shows, is sung in the singer's upper range. The accordionist gives the vocal melody greater energy by repeating most notes.

Lousiana Cajun music played at the National Folk Festival near Cleveland, Ohio

A favorite Cajun expression is *laissez les bons temps rouler*, meaning, loosely, "let the good times roll"—but this sentiment masks the hard realities of life in southwestern Louisiana and seems contradicted by the sometimes distressing words to Cajun songs. Cajun musicians frequently quickly invent new songs to comment on local events and community scandals. Our example, entitled "The Blackberry Bush," deals with more general human foibles, as it concerns the misbehavior of a young woman who goes into the blackberry bushes with her boyfriend. They become lost in the briars—perhaps a metaphor for being lost in a broader sense.

Cultural Considerations. The term *Cajun* is a shortened colloquial form of *Acadian*, a word referring to the French settlers who first migrated to Atlantic Canada in 1605. Caught in the wrangling between the French and English during the seventeenth and eighteenth centuries, they were forcibly deported starting in 1755, and scattered south to various places including Louisiana, which was then a French colony. Although many of the French returned to Canada during the later eighteenth century, several thousand who had gone to Louisiana remained there. Louisiana was also home to French-speaking peoples of African or mixed ancestry who came from the French islands of the Caribbean. Today the latter are called Creoles, though the term once referred to all French speakers. The Cajun community is concentrated in southwestern Louisiana from Lafayette westward to the Texas border.

The older and more traditional context for Cajun music and dancing was the home, where parties called *bals de maison* were held. Visitors to Cajun country are now more likely to encounter the music on Saturday nights in public dance halls. These dance halls are called *do-do*, which means "go to sleep"—something parents probably told their children before going to the dance. There, ordinary folks danced a great variety of styles, at least in the past; today, waltzes and two-steps predominate.

BANDA TÌPICA

An early type of dance band that plays popular music from the Texas-Mexico borderland region of North America.

CREOLE

A term referring to populations of French descent that are found in the southern United States, primarily Louisiana.

Cajun button box accordion and
player from Louisiana

In the early days, long before accordions were available and before people could afford fiddles, Cajuns sometimes danced to wordless vocal melodies called *reels á bouche*, similar to the *peurt a beul* of the Gaelic Scottish of Cape Breton, Nova Scotia. Eventually the presence of one or two fiddles became usual. After contact with German settlers Cajuns absorbed the diatonic, single-row button box accordion, now the signature Cajun instrument. Contemporary Cajun music has also added electrical amplification, guitar, bass, and drums. At the same time, old-fashioned acoustic Cajun music has enjoyed a revival, because of tourism and the rise of folk festivals in the 1960s.

The Creoles had much in common with the white Cajuns, and their music was sometimes indistinguishable from that of the Acadian French. But over time they blended elements from the Caribbean, of both African and Spanish origin, into their music. Since their parties were called *la la* or *zydeco*, the latter term came to denote the music of Creole Cajuns. Today's *zydeco* also shows influence from blues and even rock. While they use the same instruments as their white brethren, Creoles are more likely to use the metal washboard, called *frottoir*, which is played with thimbles, bottle openers, or other kitchen utensils.

**NATIVE AMERICAN
RESERVATIONS**

ZYDECO
Creole dance music from
the southern United
States, primarily Louisiana

Arrival: Native American Reservations

Many Americans would be surprised to know that Native American (also, American Indian) reservations are found in more than half of the states of the U.S.A. Though the best-known reservations are found in Southwestern states, primarily Arizona and New Mexico, there are significant reservations throughout the country. Though many Native Americans choose to live on these reservations, more than two-thirds of the roughly nine million Native Americans in North America live elsewhere.

The American Indian population is the most diverse ethnic "group" in North America. Though unified by their Native American ethnicity, their cultural practices vary greatly. Distinctions in Native American dress, subsistence patterns, spiritual beliefs, marriage customs, language, kinship systems, and so on, have intrigued anthropologists and linguists since the start of their respective disciplines. The earliest ethnomusicologists (1890s–1930s) in the United States focused much of their attention on Native American musical traditions. With more than three hundred different tribes throughout North America, the research produced in the last one hundred years, while extensive, is still far from complete.

Scholars generally identify nine primary culture areas among the Native Americans of the United States, Canada, and northern Mexico: the Southeast, the Southwest, the Plains, the Plateau and Basin, California, the Northwest Coast, the Subarctic, the Arctic, and the Northeast.

Though a great variety of musical activity occurs throughout these regions, there are several generalizations that can be made about most Native American music traditions. The foremost characteristic of Native American music is the use of the voice as the primary focus of performance. While instrumental traditions exist, vocal solos and group singing are most frequent in both spiritual and secular contexts. The use of *vocables* or nonlexical (untranslatable; i.e., meaningless) syllables, such as *yaa, heh, daa, weh*, and so on, is common in many traditions. Vocables are often believed to hold a secret meaning that enables the performer to communicate with the spirit world. Drums and rattles are the most common instruments used to accompany the voice.

Musical performance, even in secular contexts, usually has a spiritual or symbolic significance for the musicians. Many songs are believed to have been taught by spirits and animals through dreams and by other means. Nature is often an inspiration for songs, and many songs are intended to honor and respect the environment. Other songs relate the history of a community or great deeds of warriors from the past. The myths and legends of a tribe are passed on through song, and frequently music plays an important role in male-female relationships and courting rituals. Practically all traditional music is passed on orally from generation to generation.

Though Native American musical practices are quite diverse, we will focus on two styles of performance. These are both styles that have become quite visible to the general public in the past few decades. The Plains Indian style is typical of singing practices originating among American Indian populations of the Midwest. It is the source for many of the musical traditions presented at the Native American powwow, which has become a pan-tribal event common throughout the United States. The second style we consider is represented by a courting song performed on the Native American flute by a Zuni musician from the Taos Pueblo region of the Southwestern United States. This music has become most associated with the "New Age" movement that flourished in the 1980s and continues today.

Site 11: Plains Chippewa: Rock Dance Song

Track 35

First Impressions. The striking features of this Plains Indian musical performance are the tense warble of the vocalists and the steady pounding drum sound, which almost seems to telegraph a message.

Aural Analysis. As with most Native American music, the voice is the focus of Plains Indian music performance. The singing style is chant-like with a distinctive "cascading" or "terraced" melodic contour,

A Volkswagen bus is dwarfed by the rock formations made famous in numerous films at Monument Valley on the border of Arizona and Utah near the "Four Corners" (Max T. Miller)

VOCABLES

Words considered only with regards to sound, not in terms of meaning.

POW WOW

A pan-tribal American Indian event celebrating Native American identity and culture, generally also open to non-Native Americans.

which starts high and remains primarily on one pitch before "falling" to successively lower pitch levels. The range between the starting pitch of a phrase and the closing pitch is wide in the Plains style. Vocal pulsation, in which a periodic slight increase in volume is used to create rhythmic accents, is common, especially when vocables are sung. This pulsation creates a warbling sound on a single pitch, but is not considered melisma, because melisma requires more than one pitch per syllable.

Vocal timbre varies between performers, but a strained sound is often desirable in the Plains singing style. Some practitioners will gently press on their throat to tighten the vocal cords in order to produce the preferred sound. This tense timbre is most strongly associated with the vocable sections, when the clear articulation is less important. During the translatable sections of performance, a tense voice and vocal pulsation is less noticeable as the extended vowels are fewer, and the emphasis is on the text itself rather than the singing style. Group performances in the Plains style usually feature a leader who begins a vocal phrase and is followed shortly thereafter by the other voices, who either enter at the end of the leader's initial call or overlap the lead voice to complete the phrase. Group singing is most prominent during vocable sections, while the leader may sing the translatable sections as a solo or with the group.

A large double-sided frame drum is the most common instrument found in Plains group performances. The instrument can be round or edged, even sometimes square or octagonal. The drum is placed on a stand with the face upward. The drummers sit around the drum and strike the face with a padded mallet. The beat is steady, often times with a dotted (short-long) rhythm that imitates the sound of a heartbeat, symbolic of Mother Earth. The accents of the vocal pulsation and of the drum do not necessarily correspond, creating a polyrhythmic interaction.

Cultural Considerations. The Native American group activity most open to the general public is the powwow. The modern powwow is a pan-tribal event central to the cultural identity of American Indians throughout North America. Public powwows are much like outdoor fairs. While music and dance performances are the central activity, there are also usually many vendors selling jewelry, crafts, clothes, books, food, and so on. For non–Native Americans, it is the most available opportunity to experience Native American culture.

The powwow was created by several Plains Indian tribes in the mid-1800s. During this period, the influx of white settlers into the Midwest was contributing to the decline of traditional Native spiritual, social, political, and economic practices. At the same time, intertribal

A typical inter-tribal powwow. The drum circle in the foreground provides the accompaniment for the dancers behind them

warfare had become greatly curtailed, because all tribes were threatened equally by the American military. As Native American populations dwindled, many groups were forced to resettle among other culturally distinct tribes.

The powwow events were created in response to these developments. They became a means of reinforcing the unity and strength of

Typical of a powwow, dancers representing many tribes join together to celebrate their Native American heritage (Andrew Shahriari)

Native American culture in order to ensure its survival. The many social differences among tribes were acknowledged, but were made secondary to the Native American identity shared by all. The events have changed over the years, but since the 1950s they have functioned primarily as a means of honoring and expressing Native American identity within and outside of the American Indian community.

Powwows usually last between one and four days. The public events can be held outdoors or indoors, in parks, on college campuses, in gymnasiums, or in conference centers. They are usually only minimally advertised, and public events are often free. Though variations in the proceedings occur, a powwow typically begins with a "Grand Entry" parade led by flag-bearers representing the participating tribes. These marchers are then followed by dancers, respected elders and tribal chiefs, and children.

Music and dance are the main focus of powwow events. Each tribe displays its unique traditions through regalia and performance. Intertribal dances are most common, usually using a basic toe to heel dance step that corresponds to the beat of the drum. The Plains style of singing is the most common musical accompaniment for these dances. Nonnatives are sometimes encouraged to participate in these dances as well.

Other group dances also encourage intertribal participation. Social dances are common, such as the Round Dance, which is performed in a circle and based on a basic side-step motion. In Rabbit Dances, a male and female dancer hold hands or interlock their arms as they dance to a love song and the beat of the drum. Contest dancing is a more specialized but important activity, in which dancers competing for prizes and prestige dress in elaborate regalia with sophisticated symbolic meanings. The most successful of these dancers often perform outside of the powwow context to earn a living, doing concerts and workshops around the United States and internationally.

Site 12: Native American Flute

First Impressions. If the sound of the Plains Indian drum is symbolic of Mother Earth, then the sound of the Native American flute

Track 36

represents the wind. This is the sound of sublime solitude, an escape from the hectic life of the city into a peaceful unity with nature.

Aural Analysis. Native American flute performance is one of the few solo instrumental traditions found among American Indians. End-

Inuit Throat-Singing

One of the more interesting vocal traditions to surface in the past decade is Inuit throat-singing. The Inuit, often referred to as Eskimos, live in several arctic areas of North America. Though modernization has considerably changed the Inuit lifestyle, hunting and fishing are still a primary means of subsistence as they have been for centuries. In the past, hunting expeditions would often last for more than a month. Throat-singing developed among the women of the Inuit communities as a means of entertainment during the long absences of the men.

Throat-singing among the Inuit (in contrast to the "two-tone" throat-singing found in Mongolia and elsewhere) is characterized by its deep, breathy sounds and rhythmically dense performance technique. Two women (sometimes four) face each other at a close distance, typically holding each other's arms. One woman leads while the other follows. The lead voice establishes a short, fast-paced rhythmic phrase and the second voice is expected to interlock with this phrase in the gaps between the sounds. The performance is considered a kind of game. The first person who runs out of breath or who cannot keep pace with the other loses. Good performers will subtly change the rhythm of their phrases.

Many variations of the throat-singing style are found throughout Canada, the most commonly known type being *katajjaq* from northern Quebec. In this style, the performers frequently imitate the sounds of nature and everyday life, such as the barking of dogs, the whistling of wind, or the buzzing of insects. For many years this tradition was strongly discouraged by Christian missionaries, but it is again finding popularity among the Inuit youth, who consider throat-singing an important means by which to express their cultural identity.

Recommended Listening

Canada: *Jeux vocaux des Inuit,* Ocora, 1989, C559071.
Canada: *Chants et jeux des Inuit,* Auvidis/Unesco, 1976/1991, D8032.
Musique des Inuit, La tradition des Eskimos du Cuivre, Auvidis/Unesco, 1983/1994, D 8053.

blown flutes are more common than side-blown flutes and are made from soft woods such as cedar. While each flute is considered unique, the type that has become most popular is modeled after flutes used by Plains tribes, which have five or six melody holes. This flute is distinctive for its "bird" ornament, which is tied firmly below the blow-hole. This ornament is vital to the sound production as it channels the air flow across an edge to create the sound vibrations. Since its newly established association with the "New Age" movement, Native American flute recordings frequently make use of electronic sound effects to add heavy reverb to the original sound. The effect creates a "distant" sound as if the music were echoing through a great canyon or from a remote past.

While the music does not always follow a steady beat, clear melodic phrases are the norm. Ornamentation is usually limited to an occasional trill or slight bending of a tone. Vibrato, a rapid wavering of the pitch, is often heard on extended tones. Most compositions use a scale of between five and seven pitches with a range of little more than an octave. Overtones are not commonly used, though special effects are sometimes employed to imitate the sounds of birds or natural elements, such as the wind. The music is mostly quiet with little dynamic variation.

Cultural Considerations. The flute is the most widespread melodic instrument found in Native American culture. The Plains Indian version has become most popular in the modern era, but is only one of many types. Some are made of bone, others are globular and made of clay. The end-blown flute made of wood, however, has been the most common since the resurgence of interest in American Indian flute traditions in the 1970s and early 1980s. The "New Age" movement of this period, which drew heavily on Native American culture for inspiration, encouraged the revitalization of Native American flute performance, which had practically disappeared.

This revival of interest has spurred much debate within Native American communities, as many who now play the flute are not of American Indian ancestry. Flute circles and social clubs of Native American flute enthusiasts are increasingly popular and open to anyone. Many American Indians, such as R. Carlos Nakai, the most famous Native American flute performer, support these organizations, taking the attitude that the instrument and its music are not the exclusive property of Native Americans, but are meant to be shared with everyone. Others take an opposing stance, asserting that the music has a sacred dimension and cultural value, and thus is only appropriately performed by Native Americans.

Traditionally, the flute was primarily used in courting rituals. Love songs were performed on the flute, which substituted for the voice. This usage dwindled to near nonexistence by the end of the nineteenth century and is little practiced today. Another important context was storytelling. Oftentimes an elder would tell a story that ended with a moral, much like Aesop's fables in the Western tradition. When the story

Michael Searching Bear (Smallridge), part Cherokee and Powhatan, plays a Native American Flute
(courtesy M. S. B. Smallridge)

was finished, the storyteller would play the flute while the listeners reflected on the meaning of the story.

The main characters of these stories are often animals or natural elements, revealing the affinity American Indians tend to have with their environment. Native Americans believe that humans can learn much from their surroundings if they only pay attention. Indeed, the "bird" decoration on the flute is a symbolic reminder of this symbiotic relationship between humans and nature. Today the Native American flute is frequently sold at powwow events and has become broadly representative of Native American musical identity.

Questions to Consider

1. What is "American" music and what differentiates it from European or African music?

2. How does music from the British Isles underlie music surviving today in the United States and Canada?

3. Compare and contrast the performance of "lined" hymns and "shape-note" singing. What makes these types of music especially archaic?

4. How have Protestant Christian values influenced music in the United States?

5. Compare and contrast African-American spirituals and gospel music. What elements of each might reflect the African heritage of their creators?

6. How does blues music express the social conditions of African-Americans in the United States?

7. Compare and contrast *conjunto* and *cajun* music in terms of origin, instrumentation, and function.

8. How have the *powwow* and the Native American flute shaped the outsider's view of Native American culture?

CHAPTER 14

Discovering Yourself
Through Music

U p to this point, you have been listening to the music of *other* people in places
mostly outside your own life and experience. Now has come the moment to
realize that *your* life is also bound up with music, that you are as "traditional"
a person as any found in this book, and that your music, be it rap, ragtime, or Rachmaninoff,
resonates within the larger culture in which you live. This chapter is offered as a guide to
self exploration through music. It introduces the techniques and tools used by ethnomusicologists to study music cultures. These same tools can easily by adopted by you to
study your own musical traditions.

The chapter is divided into three segments: 1) music and self-identity, 2) researching
your musical roots, and 3) disseminating your findings. Essentially, these three steps are those
followed by ethnomusicologists in researching any of the world's musics. The first step is
conceptual, the second is the active fieldwork phase of collecting material, and the third
involves sharing insights with a larger community. We suggest that you try out these three
steps in your classroom or on your own, treating the first step as an extended research paper,
the second as a project in field documentation, and the third as a live presentation for class
(or another public forum) and/or as a possible publication.

Music and Self-Identity

At its core, identity is self-awareness. Self-awareness develops over time—indeed, infants
do not initially have a sense of themselves which is separate from their mothers or their
general surroundings. In addition to a personal identity, a child develops a social identity
that is shaped by his or her sociocultural environment. Interactions with others helps the
child understand the social categories or "groups" to which he or she belongs. This belonging is determined partly by biological factors, such as race and sex, but is largely determined
by sociocultural factors like religion, language, gender, economics, and politics.

Most people are unaware how these social and personal identities are manifested

387

through their behaviors in daily activities. When you wake up in the morning and put on a pair of jeans and a t-shirt, you may think nothing of it, but this simple act says a lot about the kind of person you are as well as your cultural upbringing. The same can be said for music. The kind of music that you listen to says much about the type of person you are and your cultural background. Music, as much as anything else, is a manifestation of the personal and social identities of an individual or group. The function of the music, its structure, and the context in which it is performed all reveal significant information about social values. Music reflects a community's identity and expresses "who they are." Essentially, what we have striven to do throughout this text, is to "get to know" other people through their music.

But who are we? Turning the tables and trying to figure out how music reflects who we are is also important. Though our global journey has taken us to many places, we cannot realistically say that our chosen "sites" represent the music of all peoples of the planet. Our few selections represent only the kinds of music that stand out, to us, as most significant to the personal and social identities of the people who live in those regions. In addition to being choices made from our own subjective perspectives, the selections are of course limited in many other ways, too. The handful of examples that we have from India, for example, are not necessarily the types of music listened to by the majority of the Indian population. However, when you meet someone from India and ask "what is Indian music," our examples would easily qualify as appropriate for representing Indian culture to the outside world. Indian self-identity, both personal and social, is in part expressed through this music.

Let's look at American music as an expression of self-identity. As an American, what one example would you choose to reflect your "American" identity? Does rap define who we are as Americans? Britney Spears? Garth Brooks? Does the music of Mozart and Beethoven represent us, even though its origin is European? How about Jazz? What kind of Jazz? Which performer and from what style period? Defining "American" identity through one example of music is impossible, yet in this textbook (as in others) we have only enough pages to focus on a few examples from countries often much larger than the United States, places with histories much longer than our meager 230 or so years of existence as a nation. Yet, through just a few music examples, the spiritual beliefs, political philosophies, moral values, attitudes and activities of many aspects of life are revealed. No doubt, we are able to learn something about the people of other cultures and gain a greater understanding of "who they are," by studying their musical traditions. We can do the same by examining our own musical expressions.

So, how does music express your self-identity? Ask yourself some questions: What music do I like to listen to? What music do I like to perform (whether you are a musician playing for an audience or just singing to yourself in the shower)? Why does that music appeal to me?

How does this music reflect me personally, my philosophy of life, my goals and desires, my spiritual beliefs, my personal history and life experiences? How does the music I enjoy reflect my social identity, i.e., the friends I have, the organizations I belong to, the activities I participate in? What does this music say about my cultural upbringing as an American? What stereotypes does it suggest about my personality and behaviors? Start with some of these questions, and then try to pick one example that most accurately expresses all the facets of your self-identity. You will likely find this to be quite difficult. Trying to pick just one example to say to the outside world, "this is me," is a challenge for most. If it is for you, a little research may be in order.

Researching Your Musical Roots

Having situated yourself in a social context that ranges from being a Westerner, to being an American, to being something much closer to home, it is time to ask, what kinds of music express your own life and the lives of those around you, be they family members or friends. Sorting this out requires what we call *fieldwork*. Fieldwork is essentially the process of going into the environment in which a specific music normally occurs in order to observe musical activities and question individuals with knowledge of the tradition under study. Fieldwork is a method of studying music which is employed by ethnomusicologists wherever they work. It may include any or all of the following: (1) being an observer or participant-observer, (2) audio recording, (3) video recording, (4) still photography, (5) interviewing, (6) collecting and archiving of materials, be they instruments, books, recordings, or any other kind of memorabilia.

Observation and Participant-Observation. Typically a researcher observes musical activity from the sidelines, sometimes documenting it, sometimes merely absorbing impressions. It may sometimes, however, be appropriate for the researcher to join in an activity themselves, by learning to play an instrument or by singing. When they join in, they become what is called a *participant-observer*. In those circumstances, it is important for the researcher to maintain as much objective distance as possible. The researcher and the researched cannot become one.

Audio Recording. The equipment for making field recordings has changed dramatically over the last thirty years, having gone from analog recording—first on reel to reel tape, then on cassette—to digital recording on a variety of media. When one of the present authors (Terry Miller) began making field recordings in 1970, for example, stereo reel-to-reel tape recorders with twin microphones for stereo sound were considered state-of-the-art technology. After about 1980 audiocassettes became the norm, and reel-to-reel recording retreated to the recording studio. Because they were much smaller and lighter, and the media (cassettes) were also small, cassette recorders were a great improvement on reel-to-reel. The costs came down, too. A top-of-the-line Swiss reel-to-reel recorder cost $10,000 in 1970 dollars, while a comparable cassette machine cost less than $500 in the early 1980s. In the field the lighter and simpler is preferable to the complex and heavy. Field recording is not to be confused with studio recording.

Since the 1980s digital recording has gradually superseded all forms of analog recording, and costs have once again fallen. The first practical digital technology was DAT (digital audio tape), but DAT recorders were expensive, and for a long time their sale in the United States was held up while copyright questions were resolved. DAT tapes are small, but they, like audiocassettes, damage easily and wear over time as the

An Inside Look
Nguyen Thuyet Phong

Although I was born in a rice growing village deep in the Mekong River delta of southern Vietnam, I came from a family of skilled traditional musicians who performed the local ritual music in our province. My father began teaching me music at age 5, and at age 7 I began study with Tram Van Kien, a local master,

Dr. Nguyen Thuyet Phong, director, Institute for Vietnamese Music and independent scholar

concentrating on both instrumental and vocal music. When I was 7 my family sent me to a nearby market town where I continued my music studies while living in a Buddhist temple. By the age of 12 I had become proficient in many kinds of music including instrumental music, ritual music, theater music, folksongs, and Buddhist chant. After that I studied at the University of Saigon, earning a Bachelor of Arts in philosophy and literature in 1974. Most of these early years, however, were very stressful because of the war's increasing ferocity, and many times my family's village was bombed by American forces and our house destroyed.

I was working, in Japan when my country, the Republic of Vietnam, fell to the north in April, 1975. Fortunately, Vietnam's former colonial ruler, France, accepted me, and in 1983 in Paris I was able to complete a Ph.D. in Musicology from the Sorbonne University, writing my dissertation on Vietnamese Buddhist chant. Eventually, in 1984, I made my way to the United States and have lived here ever since. Although it is difficult to make a living performing traditional Vietnamese music, I have been fortunate to have been invited to play throughout the United States and in many other countries, including Canada, Norway, Korea, Hong Kong, Japan, Singapore, and Taiwan. In 1997 the National Endowment for the Arts awarded me a National Heritage Fellowship presented by Hilary Clinton. I and my ensemble continue to perform live and make recordings. I also remain a scholar, writing books, articles, compiling compact discs, and lecturing. Recently I had the honor of advising the National Conservatory of Music in Hanoi on creating the first program in ethnomusicology in Vietnam supported by an American-government Fulbright grant.

tape is wiped over a head. The rise of compact discs has made DAT technology mostly obsolete. Mini-disc recorders, which are inexpensive and tiny, work well in the field, but professional audio engineers tend to discount them because of how they compress the data. Recently, full-sized compact disc recorders designed for field use have become available, but at this writing their drawback is their size and the fact that they require a lead-acid battery weighing some seven pounds. An even newer machine records data to Flash Memory cards, but the most "hi-tech" approach is to use external hard drives, and the recorded files require manipulation on a laptop for playback and storage.

While the recording machine is obviously important, the choice of microphone is essential. The sound cannot be better than what the microphone can hear. One can use a pair of single-track microphones or a single-point stereo microphone, which allows some track separation microphone placement is extremely important for critical recordings, and researchers may need to experiment before choosing their setup.

Video Recording. Until about 1970 the only way to produce "moving pictures" short of a professional film crew was with a silent Super 8 film camera powered by a spring. The earliest video recorders consisted of a heavy camera connected to a heavy recorder connected to a car battery. The tapes were open-reel black and white and the sound was in mono. In addition, the recorders cost about $8,000 in 1970 dollars. Later, color videocassettes became available in two rival formats, VHS and Beta (Beta was soon beaten out by VHS). During the 1990s stereo 8-mm video, both in its regular form and in the enhanced Hi 8 form, largely supplanted VHS. Recently, in turn, Mini DV (digital video) and digital Hi 8 have supplanted analog Hi 8, which remains available only in mono. Whereas analog Hi 8 cameras allowed two hours of uninterrupted recording, Mini DV and digital Hi8 cameras unfortunately allow only one hour to a cassette—and with bottom loading cameras being standard now, changing cassettes is also a more time-consuming procedure than with the analog Hi 8. In 2003 DVD disc recording became available, but because of its expense it has not yet caught on.

The most important aspect of videography is the stability of the camera. Except when one needs to move around a subject a great deal, it is best to use a sturdy tripod to capture good images. Watching a jerky video will not appeal to you, your audience, or your students. A common mistake amateur videographers make is to pan too fast and too often. Similarly, avoid overusing the zoom feature. On the other hand, simply placing the camera on a tripod and letting it run for two hours on a scene will be excruciatingly boring to watch. Strive for smoothness and slowness of movement; do not emulate music videos or commercial advertisements with their obsessively fast scene changes. Try to capture some important details in close-ups as well as having other footage that gives a sense of the bigger picture--the space and feel of a performance.

Still Photography. There are currently two forms of photography, analog and digital. Analog photos may be black and white or color; in either case, film is required. Print film produces negatives that are printed onto photo paper while slide film results in transparencies (slides) that can be projected onto a screen. Both forms can be scanned into digital format as well, though slides are better scanned with dedicated slide scanners. Digital cameras have come a long way since they were first offered. They are small and light and will allow a great number of images to be captured on a single memory stick, card, disc, or other medium.

For fieldwork, digital photography is preferable to analog, because it provides the ability to make good photos in dim light and at night using available light. (While one may use flashes with analog cameras, on small cameras these are not strong enough to reach beyond about ten feet.) Whereas analog cameras require a supply of film, digital cameras require either a supply of memory devices—which tend to be expensive—or a laptop computer into which photos are downloaded daily. Digital photos can be stored and saved in multiple formats and in large or small sizes, and can be uploaded and mailed electronically.

Interviewing. Interviewing is essentially a conversation between the researcher and someone who can provide insight about the music under study. That person, sometimes referred to as an *informant,* can be either a musician or simply someone familiar with the tradition. The information gleaned in an interview is subject to all the limitations of human conversation and thinking. Information provided spontaneously from memory may or may not be reliable. Other factors may also distort the information: for example, someone may tell the researcher what they think the researcher wants to hear, or they may attempt to manage a music or culture's image by carefully selecting what facts they present. Regardless of these drawbacks, however, interviews can elicit valuable information.

Especially in an initial interview, questions should be kept short and open-ended, so as to encourage an informant to speak freely. Although it is wise to plan a series of questions in advance, researchers must also be prepared to alter the order of questions or take the conversation in unexpected directions if the informant seems interested in pursuing a particular topic. In short, they should not try to control the informant.

There are two ways to preserve an interview: taking notes and recording. The latter is far better in that it produces an exact record of what was said, and allows the researcher not to be distracted by the process of writing things down. However, it is always necessary to get an informant's permission before recording commences. A recording is especially valuable if the informant sings or plays an instrument during the interview. In fact, if there is to be much performance, the researcher is better off videotaping the interview. Whatever technology is used, the researcher must strive to keep it out of sight and out of mind as much as possible, so as to minimize the informant's self-consciousness.

Archives and Collections. The conditions under which you keep recordings, photos, and other documents affects how long they last. When such materials are subjected to extremes of heat and cold, humidity and dryness, and other changes, they deteriorate faster. Instruments are particularly challenging because they take up much space and when neglected fall into disrepair because of broken strings, warped or cracked wood, splits in bamboo, cracked reeds, etc. The most valued of resources are generally deposited at an archive, such as the American Folklife Center at the Library of Congress or Indiana University's Archives of Traditional Music, which is the nation's premier collection of ethnographic field recordings. Professional archivists maintain such collections to ensure their availability for future generations.

Disseminating your Findings

Discovering yourself through music is a challenging but ultimately rewarding experience. In the process of learning about your own musical roots, you undoubtedly learn much about other people who have contributed to the development of your self-identity. While this new knowledge is of great benefit for you, it may also be helpful for other people in knowing their own musical heritage. Disseminating your findings is an important way to help future sojourners learn from your experiences so that they can add new knowledge through their own inquiries rather than just repeating research you have already completed. There are many avenues in which to share your research, but the most pertinent ones in the field of ethnomusicology are through teaching, performance, and publishing.

Teaching. Many ethnomusicologists teach at institutions of higher learning around the world, but others teach in less formal environments. Teaching is merely a matter of sharing knowledge with others. It can take place in a classroom, at a local worship center, as part of a community program, or just among family and friends.

A common way of teaching or of communicating information to peers is to give presentations. Researchers often present their findings by reading "papers" at professional conferences. Most scholarly societies hold such meetings. The larger professional organizations may have both an annual national or international meeting and regional or chapter meetings. The latter are often more receptive to student papers than national ones. Upon receiving a "call for papers," the researcher submits an *abstract*, that is, a paragraph or so that explains their topic. If this is accepted, they are invited to present their paper at a conference; usually, their presentation is expected to last no longer than twenty minutes. Whenever possible, it is best for presentations to include audio and video examples of the music under discussion. This is particularly true when the audience is comprised of nonspecialists.

Performance. However useful audio and video examples may be, live performance is an even more effective means of teaching. For this reason, ethnomusicologists often invite "guest artists" to help them demonstrate a music tradition. Ethnomusicologists frequently find themselves in the role of manager or concert promoter as well. Through their research, they sometimes discover unknown artists of great quality and they may wish to organize opportunities for these musicians to perform publicly. Arranging performances at local schools or community centers is usually easy to do. By getting a musician to perform in public, they are helping to preserve the music that artist represents and are providing the musician with an opportunity to share his or her musical talents with others.

Publishing. The most permanent way to disseminate knowledge about a music tradition is through print publication. With the advent of desktop and electronic publishing, this is far easier than before, but it should be understood that not all publications are equal. In academia a clear distinction is made between publications that are "peer-reviewed" or "refereed," and those that are not. Peer-reviewed publications—be they article, book, or recording—are those that are reviewed by one or more people with expertise in the field before being accepted. Most peer reviews are done "blind," that is, the reviewers do not know the name of the author under review. With regard to book publishing, there is also a distinction between legitimate scholarly presses that subject manuscripts to close scrutiny and review and so-called "vanity presses" that publish whatever an author submits. Virtually anything written can find its way into some kind of print, physical or electronic, but being in print alone is not a measure of reliability.

A further distinction is made between scholarly and commercial publication. Professors are expected to publish the results of their research in scholarly journals. Even though these journals pay nothing for articles, publication in them is often the basis for promotion, tenure, and pay increases. On the other hand, when ethnomusicologists write for magazines and other commercial publications they can expect to be paid. Authors of academic press books can expect—or at least hope for—royalty payments based on copies sold. However, because academic publications are expensive to print and have limited sales potential, their authors rarely realize more than a token profit.

Today many individuals have created their own personal web sites where they maintain a collection of personal materials (e.g., their resume), family pictures, etc. It is possible to upload the results of your own research into your website. With today's powerful search engines (e.g., Google), interested readers are increasingly likely to stumble upon your work. This likelihood increases when your titles include key words that will snag the search engine.

Where to Go From Here

Most readers of this book are likely to be students having their first experiences with the musics of the world. In writing the previous pages, we understand that most of you are unlikely to become practicing ethnomusicologists working in academia. And, considering the relative dearth of jobs in higher education for ethnomusicologists, we are not suggesting you change your major and join us. Still, we hope you will become aware of music around you that is little known or that is important to your family, community, or ethnic group and decide to document it. Professional ethnomusicologists cannot be everywhere. The music you document may someday find its way into the local historical society, your family's treasure trove, your church's library, or your club's memento collection.

Documenting music may preserve the sound (and sight, if done with a video camera), but music that only exists in archives and is no longer heard live is not the same as a living tradition. Do what you can to encourage the continuation of the music that you like or discover. You might even consider learning it yourself. Most state arts councils offer small grants for "apprenticeships in the folk arts." These offer modest funds to a practitioner (called "the master artist") for passing on the tradition to a novice (called the "apprentice"). Because most "master artists" do not think of themselves as such, it will probably be up to you to obtain the application forms, fill them out, and encourage the master to make the application.

If you are (or become) a teacher, you can explore your community for individuals who carry interesting music traditions and bring them to the attention of others. Many states and localities offer modest funds to support artists in the schools. These "tradition bearers" can be brought to the school to give programs in classrooms or to present a concert for the whole student body. This recognition not only allows the students to learn about individual musicians but often encourages these practitioners to continue performing, because their skills are sometimes little known or appreciated.

On a more modest scale, you can do your part to preserve diversity in the musics of the world by purchasing (not "file sharing") audio and video recordings of traditional music. You can attend concerts, workshops, festivals, houses of worship, and other venues where you can hear the music live. Or perhaps you could purchase an instrument and buy an instruction book (or find a live teacher) and learn to play it. There's no telling where you could go by following an interest in world music. The path you follow is entirely up to you.

Glossary

Author's Note: As some transliterated words are difficult to pronounce or have no English equivalent, we have included some pronunciation approximations in parentheses for several of the glossary terms.

A

A-AK: A Confucian ritual ensemble from Korea. (Chapter 7)

ABAKWA: An animistic belief system found primarily in Cuba. (Chapter 11)

ABORIGINES: A generic term for an indigenous population, often used to describe native peoples of Australia. (Chapter 4)

ACCENT: An emphasized beat. (Chapter 2)

ACCORDION: A bellows-driven free-reed *aerophone* with buttons or keys that enable a performer to play melody and harmony simultaneously. (Chapter 10)

ACOUSTIC: Term used for non-electric instruments. (Chapter 13)

ADHAN (Also, AZAN): The Islamic call to prayer. (Chapter 8)

AEROPHONE: Ethnomusicological classification referring to instruments that require air to produce sound: namely, flutes, reeds, trumpets, and bellows-driven instruments. (Chapter 2)

AFIRIKYIWA: An iron clapper-bell from Ghana. (Chapter 9)

AFRIKANER: A South African of Dutch descent. (Chapter 9)

AGOGO: A double-bell found in Western Africa and used in African-derived musics in the Western hemisphere. (Chapter 12)

AKADINDA: A large, heavy log *xylophone* from sub-Saharan Africa, associated with the former kingdom of Buganda. (Chapter 9)

ALAP (Also, ALAPANA): The opening, freely rhythmic period of improvisation of *raga* performance in Indian classical music. (Chapter 5)

AL-'UD: See UD.

AMADINDA: A log *xylophone* similar to the *akadinda*, but with fewer pitches, from sub-Saharan Africa. (Chapter 9)

ANTHEM: A category of shape-note song that is *through composed*, meaning it has different music from beginning to end. (Chapter 13)

ANTHROPOLOGY: The study of all aspects of human culture, including music. (Chapter 1)

ANUDRUTAM: The first element of the *tala* in Indian classical music. (Chapter 5)

ANUPALLAVI: The second section of a *kriti* vocal performance from South India. (Chapter 5)

APARTHEID: The official South African policy of racial segregation, abolished in 1992. (Chapter 9)

APPALACHIA: A geographic region marked by the Appalachian Mountains, which extend throughout the eastern part of the United States. (Chapter 13)

APREMPRENSEMMA: A low-ranged *lamellophone* from Ghana. (Chapter 9)

ARABIAN PENINSULA: A geographic region in the Middle East that includes Saudi Arabia, Yemen, Oman, and the various smaller nations on the Persian Gulf. (Chapter 8)

ARADHANA: A South Indian festival. (Chapter 5)

ARAWAK: A pre-Columbian indigenous population of the Caribbean. (Chapter 11)

ATABAQUES: A drum of West African origin used in *capoeira* music as well as *candomblé* rituals from Brazil. (Chapter 12)

ATUMPAN: A pair of goblet-shaped drums often used as a speech surrogate by several ethnic groups from Ghana. (Chapter 9)

AULOS: A double-reed *aerophone* from Ancient Greece. (Chapter 3)

AVAZ: The improvised, non-metrical section of a performance in the Persian classical tradition. (Chapter 8)

AYATOLLAH: A high-rank clergyman in Islam. (Chapter 8)

AZAN: See ADHAN.

AZTEC: A pre-Columbian indigenous population found in central and southern Mexico. (Chapter 12)

B

BAGLAMA: A round-bodied lute from Turkey. (Chapter 3)

BAGPIPES: A reed *aerophone* consisting of an airbag, *chanter* (melody pipe), and drone pipes. (Chapter 10)

BAIRRO: A poor housing area found in the city of Rio de Janeiro, Brazil. (Chapter 12)

BALAFON: A *xylophone* from West Africa often played by oral historians. (Chapter 9)

BALALAIKA: A triangle-shaped, fretted plucked-lute from Russia. (Chapter 10)

BALLAD: A song that tells a story, usually performed by a solo voice and commonly associated with music from the Appalachian region of the United Sates. (Chapter 13)

BALS DE MAISON: A house party that typically has *Cajun* music as entertainment, found in the southern United States, primarily Louisiana. (Chapter 13)

BANDA TÌPICA: An early type of dance band that plays popular music from the Texas-Mexico borderland region of North America. (Chapter 13)

BANDIR: A frame drum common to Turkish and Arabic music. (Chapter 8)

BANDONEON: A type of button-box accordion. (Chapter 12)

BANJO: A fretted, plucked lute from the United States that uses a membrane face on the resonator. (Chapter 13)

BANSRI (Also, BANSURI): A transverse flute from North India. (Chapter 5)

BANTU: An African linguistic category. (Chapter 9)

BAR MITZVAH: A Jewish "coming-of-age" ceremony. (Chapter 8)

BASHRAF: An Arabic musical form. (Chapter 8)

BASSER: The lowest vocal part in a *rhyming spiritual* performance from the Bahamas. (Chapter 11)

BATA: Ritual drums used in *Santeria* ceremonies. (Chapter 11)

BATUQUE: An animistic belief system found primarily in Brazil. (Chapter 11)

BAULS: A group of itinerant musicians from India, especially noted for their poetry. (Chapter 5)

BAYA: A small bowl-shaped drum of the *tabla* pair of drums from North India. (Chapter 5)

BAYIN: The Chinese organological system. (Chapter 7)

BEAT: A regular pulsation. (Chapter 2)

BELLOWS: An apparatus for producing a strong current of air; used with the Irish bagpipes, as well as the pump organ and other *aerophones.* (Chapter 10)

BERIMBAU: A musical bow used in *capoeira* music from Brazil. (Chapter 12)

BHAJAN: Devotional songs from India. (Chapter 5)

BIBLE: The sacred text of Christianity. (Chapter 13)

BIN: A fretted plucked lute considered the origin of other popular lutes in India, such as the *sitar.* (Chapter 5)

BIRA: A spirit possession ceremony of the Shona ethnic group from Zimbabwe. (Chapter 9)

BIRIMINTINGO: The instrumental solo sections of a *jali* performance from West Africa. (Chapter 9)

BIWA: A fretted, pear-shaped, plucked lute from Japan. (Chapter 7)

BLUEGRASS: A style of American folk music characterized by virtuosic instrumental performance and the so-called "high lonesome" vocal style, in which a harmony pitch is sung above the main melody. (Chapter 13)

BLUES: A secular folk music tradition originating within the African-American community in the southern United States. (Chapter 13)

BODHRAN: A frame drum from Ireland, played with a beater. (Chapter 10)

BOLERO: A Latin American dance and music. (Chapter 11)

BOLLYWOOD: An informal name for India's film industry combining "Bombay" and "Hollywood." (Chapter 5)

BOLS: Mnemonic syllables corresponding to drums strokes in Indian drumming traditions. (Chapter 5)

BOMBARDE: A double-reed *aerophone* from France. (Chapter 3)

BOMBOS (Also, SURDO): A large drum used in *sikuri* performances from Peru as well as samba music from Brazil. (Chapter 12)

BON: Festive dancing from Japan. (Chapter 7)

BONANG: A rack gong found in *gamelan* ensembles from Indonesia. (Chapter 6)

BONES: A small pair of wooden slats struck together to create rhythm. Common to folk music in the United States as well as Great Britain. (Chapter 10)

BOSSED GONG: A gong with a bump-like protuberance. (Chapter 6)

BOUZOUKI: A round-bodied lute from Greece. (Chapter 3)

BUGAKU: A Confucian ritual ensemble from Japan that includes dance. (Chapter 7)

BUNRAKU: A popular form of puppet theatre from Japan. (Chapter 7)

BUZUK (Also, BUZUQ): A round-bodied lute from Turkey. (Chapter 3)

BYZANTINE CHANT: A chant style associated with the Greek Orthodox Church, centered on a complex system of *modes.* (Chapter 10)

C

CAIXA ("x" pronounced *sh*): A small drum from Brazil found in *samba* performances. (Chapter 12)

CAJAS: A small drum from Peru used in *sikuri* performances. (Chapter 12)

CAJUN: A term describing the cultural traditions, including music, of French-speaking Louisiana, USA. (Chapter 13)

CALL AND RESPONSE: A style of vocal organization characterized by a leader who "calls" and a group who "responds." (Chapters 9 and 13)

CALYPSO: A popular music from Trinidad characterized by improvised lyrics on topical and broadly humorous subject matter. (Chapter 11)

CANCIÓN: A general term for "song" in Mexico. (Chapter 12)

CANDOMBLÉ: An animistic and Roman Catholic syncretised belief system found primarily in Brazil. (Chapter 9)

CANTAORA: A vocalist in Spanish Flamenco music. (Chapter 10)

CANTE: A traditional Spanish style of singing incorporating a strained timbre and heavy use of *melisma*. (Chapter 10)

CANTINA: A social venue for drinking and dancing found in the Texas-Mexico borderland region of the United States. (Chapter 13)

CANTON: The term used for the states of the Swiss Federation. (Chapter 13)

CAPOEIRA: A form of dance that developed from a distinctive style of martial arts created by runaway slaves in Brazil. (Chapter 12)

CARANAM: The final section of a *kriti* vocal performance from India. (Chapter 5)

CARIB: A pre-Columbian indigenous population of the Caribbean. (Chapter 11)

CARNATIC (Also, KARNATAK): A term referring to the cultural traditions of South India. (Chapter 5)

CARNIVAL: A pre-Lent festival celebrated primarily in Europe and the Caribbean. Known as Mardi Gras in the United States. (Chapter 12)

CASCARÁ: A rhythmic pattern played on the *timbales* in *salsa* music. (Chapter 11)

CASTE SYSTEM: A system of social organization based on hereditary status found in India. (Chapter 5)

CÉILI: An Irish band that performs in a public house (pub) for entertainment and dance. (Chapter 10)

CÉILIDH (pronounced *kee-lee*): A kind of "house party" associated with fiddling traditions in Canada and Scotland. (Chapter 13)

CELTIC: A subfamily of the Indo-European language family that is associated with the Scottish and Irish peoples of Great Britain. (Chapter 10)

CHA-CHA: A Latin American ballroom dance. (Chapter 11)

CHAHAR-MEZRAB: A metered piece in the Persian classical music tradition. (Chapter 8)

CHANTER: The melody pipe found on various bagpipes. (Chapter 10)

CHARRO: A style of suit worn by *mariachi* performers from Mexico. (Chapter 12)

CHASTUSHKI: A category of songs from Russia considered "playful." (Chapter 10)

CHÉQUERES (Also, SHEKERE): A gourd rattle with externally beaded netting. (Chapter 11)

CHING: A pair of cup-shaped cymbals from Thailand. (Chapter 6)

CHIZ: The composed section of vocal performance in Indian classical music. (Chapter 5)

CHOBO: The narrator and accompanying shamisen performers of the Kabuki theatre in Japan. (Chapter 7)

CHORD: Simultaneous soundings of three or more pitches. (Chapter 2)

CHORDOPHONE: Ethnomusicological classification referring collectively to the four types of stringed instruments: lutes, zithers, harps, lyres. (Chapter 2)

CHOU: The comic role-type in Beijing Opera from China. (Chapter 7)

CH'UN HYANG KA: The five stories performed in Korean *p'ansori*. (Chapter 7)

CIMARRONS: A term for escaped slaves from the Spanish-colonized regions in the Caribbean and Americas. (Chapter 11)

CIMBALOM: A hammered zither from Eastern Europe, commonly associated with Rom (gypsy) music. Also, the national instrument of Hungary. (Chapter 10)

CIRCULAR BREATHING: A technique used to maintain a continuous airflow in *aerophone* performance. (Chapter 4)

CITERA: A small zither from Hungary. (Chapter 10)

CLAVES: A pair of hand-held wooden bars used as percussion instruments in many African and Latin American music traditions. (Chapters 9 and 11)

CLERK (pronounced *clark*): A religious leader in Calvinist churches in the United States and Scotland. (Chapter 13)

COBZA: A pear-shaped lute from Romania. (Chapter 3)

COLOTOMIC STRUCTURE: The organizational system of *gamelan* music from Indonesia. (Chapter 6)

COMPARSA: A Latin American dance music. (Chapter 11)

COMPÉ: A martial arts style from Brazil that emphasizes striking "with the foot." (Chapter 12)

CONCERTINA: A small hexagonal accordion with bellows and buttons for keys. (Chapter 10)

CONGA (Also, TUMBADORA): A tall, barrel-shaped, single-headed drum used often in Latin American music. (Chapter 11)

CONJUNTO: A popular dance music found along the Texas-Mexico border in North America. (Chapter 13)

CONTRADANZA: A Cuban dance form. (Chapter 11)

CORROBOREE: A nighttime ritual performed by Australian aborigines. (Chapter 4)

CREOLE: A term referring to populations of French or mixed African and French descent that are found in the southern United States, primarily Louisiana. (Chapter 13)

CRESCENDO: A gradual increase in volume. (Chapter 2)

CROSS-RHYTHM: A "two-against-three" rhythmic pattern often found in polyrhythmic performance in sub-Saharan Africa and Latin America. (Chapters 9 and 11)

CUÍCA (pronounced kwi-kha): A small friction drum used in *samba* music. (Chapter 12)

CULTURAL REVOLUTION: A ten-year period (1966–76) in China's history marked by severe social and political upheaval. (Chapter 7)

CUMINA: An animistic belief system found primarily in Jamaica. (Chapter 11)

CUTTIN' HEADS: A music contest found in African-American communities, typically involving blues musicians. (Chapter 13)

CZARDAS: A popular dance from Hungary. (Chapter 10)

D

DAN (pronounced *dahn)*: The female hero role-type in Beijing opera from China. (Chapter 7)

DAN CO: A fiddle from Vietnam. (Chapter 6)

DAN KIM: A fretted plucked lute from Vietnam. (Chapter 6)

DAN TRANH: A plucked zither from Vietnam. (Chapter 6)

DAN TYBA (pronounced *dahn tee-bah*): A pear-shaped lute from Vietnam. (Chapter 6)

DANCEHALL: See DUB.

DANZA (Also, DANZON and DANZONETE): A Cuban dance form. (Chapter 11)

DARABUKA: A goblet-shaped hand drum common to various Turkish music traditions. (Chapter 8)

DARAMAD: The freely rhythmic opening and conclusion of a *dastgah* performance in the Persian classical music tradition. (Chapter 8)

DASTGAH: A *mode* or system of rules and expectations for composition and improvisation in Persian classical music. (Chapter 8)

DECRESCENDO: A gradual decrease in volume. (Chapter 2)

DEFINITE PITCH: A sound with a dominating frequency level. (Chapter 2)

DENSITY REFERENT: A reference pattern heard in polyrhythmic music, usually articulated by a bell, rattle, or woodblock. (Chapter 9)

DERVISH: Turkish word literally meaning "beggar," but often used to refer to Sufi Muslims. (Chapter 8)

DHIKR (Also, ZIKR): A ritual commonly performed by Sufi Muslims in which believers chant the names of Allah with the goal of entering a spiritually ecstatic state. (Chapter 8)

DHRUPAD: A category of vocal music from India. (Chapter 5)

DIAO: The *key* used in a music performance from China. (Chapter 7)

DIDJERIDU: A long trumpet made from a hollowed tree branch and performed by aborigines from Australia. (Chapter 4)

DILRUBA: A bowed lute from India. (Chapter 5)

DIZI: A transverse flute from China.
(Chapter 7)

DOMBAK: A goblet-shaped hand drum used in Arabic music traditions. (Chapter 8)

DOMRA: A round-shaped fretted plucked lute from Russia. (Chapter 10)

DONDO: An hourglass-shaped pressure drum from Ghana. (Chapter 9)

DOUBLE-STOPS: The practice of playing two strings simultaneously on bowed lutes such as the violin. (Chapter 13)

DOULCEMELLE: A hammered dulcimer from France. (Chapter 3)

DR. WATTS: An informal term for a *lined hymn* employed in some African-American communities. (Chapter 13)

DREAMTIME: A term describing the Australian aboriginal spiritual belief system and concept of creation. (Chapter 4)

DRONE: A continuous sound. (Chapter 2)

DRUTAM: The second element of the *tala* in Indian classical music. (Chapter 5)

DUB (Also, DANCEHALL): Recorded music that emphasizes the bass and rhythm tracks so that a DJ can talk over the music through a microphone. (Chapter 11)

DUDA: Bagpipes from Hungary. (Chapter 10)

DUENDE: A Spanish word meaning "passion," which refers to an emotional quality considered essential in performances by Spanish Flamenco singers. (Chapter 10)

DUFF: A small, single-headed drum, sometimes having snares, common to Turkish and Arabic music traditions. (Chapter 8)

DULAB: A compositional form found in Turkish and Arabic music. (Chapter 8)

DUNG-CHEN: A long metal trumpet from Tibet. (Chapter 7)

DUNG-KAR: A conch-shell trumpet from Tibet. (Chapter 7)

DYNAMICS: The volume of a musical sound. (Chapter 2)

E

ECHOS (pl. ECHOI): *Mode* used for Byzantine Chant. (Chapter 10)

EKÓN: An iron bell used in *Santeria* rituals. (Chapter 11)

EKTARA: See GOPIYANTRA. (Chapter 5)

ELECTROPHONE: Ethnomusicological classification that refers to instruments that require electricity to produce sound, such as the synthesizer. (Chapter 2)

EMIC: A term borrowed from linguistics, used by anthropologists and ethnomusicologists to describe the perspective of a cultural insider. (Chapter 3)

ERHU: A fiddle from China. (Chapter 7)

ESCOLAS DE SAMBA: Samba schools of Brazil. (Chapter 12)

ETHNOCENTRISM: The unconscious assumption that one's own cultural background is "normal," while others are "strange" or "exotic." (Chapter 1)

ETHNOMUSICOLOGY: The scholarly study of any music within its contemporary context. (Chapter 1)

ETIC: A term borrowed from linguistics, used by anthropologists and ethnomusicologists to describe the perspective of a cultural outsider. (Chapter 3)

F

FAIS-DO-DO (pronounced *fai-doh-doh*): Literally meaning "go to sleep," a reference to a public dance hall that hosts performances of Cajun dance music. (Chapter 13)

FASOLA SINGING: A singing style that uses shape-note notation. (Chapter 13)

FAVELA: Poor housing areas in the hills around Rio de Janeiro, Brazil. (Chapter 12)

FIDDLE: A generic term used to describe a bowed lute. (Chapter 2) Also, a slang term for a violin. (Chapter 10)

FIESTA: A festival or celebration in Spain or Latin America. (Chapter 10)

FILMI (Also, FILMI GIT): Popular music taken from films in India. (Chapter 5)

FIRQA (pronounced *feer-kah*): Large orchestral ensembles consisting of traditional Arabic instruments from the Middle East. (Chapter 8)

FLAMENCO: A Spanish musical tradition featuring vocals with guitar accompaniment, characterized by passionate singing and vibrant rhythm. (Chapter 10)

FLUTE: A type of *aerophone* that splits a column of air on an edge to produce sound. (Chapter 2)

FOLKLORE: The study of orally transmitted folk knowledge and culture. (Chapter 1)

FORM: Underlying structure of a musical performance. (Chapter 2)

FREE RHYTHM: Music with no regular pulsation. (Chapter 2)

FRET: A bar or ridge found on the fingerboard of chordophones that enables performers to produce different melodic pitches with consistent frequency levels. (Chapter 2)

FRICTION DRUM: A type of drum with a membrane that is "rubbed" rather than struck. (Chapter 10)

FROTTOIR (pronounced *fwaht-twah)*: A metal washboard used in Cajun-Zydeco music. (Chapter 13)

FUGING TUNE (pronounced *fyu-ging*): A category of shape-note song in which individual voices enter one after the other. (Chapter 13)

G

GADULKA: A spiked fiddle from Bulgaria. (Chapter 3)

GAELIC (pronounced *gaa-lik*): The indigenous language of Scotland. (Chapter 10)

GAGAKU: A Confucian derived ritual ensemble from Japan. (Chapter 7)

GAIDA: Bagpipes from Bulgaria. (Chapter 10)

GAMELAN: An ensemble from Indonesia comprised primarily of *metallophones.* (Chapter 6)

GAMELAN GONG KEBYAR: An ensemble type from Bali, Indonesia, comprised primarily of *metallophones* and characterized by rhythmically dense performance technique. (Chapter 6)

GANJA: A Rastafarian word for marijuana, borrowed from the Hindu Indian term for "herb." (Chapter 11)

GARAMUT: A slit drum from Papua New Guinea. (Chapter 4)

GARDON: A struck lute from Hungary. (Chapter 10)

GAT (pronounced *gaht*): The composed section of instrumental performance in Indian classical music. (Chapter 5)

GEISHA: A Japanese girl or woman trained to provide entertainment, including musical entertainment. (Chapter 7)

GHAWAZI: Term in Arabic cultures for female dancers who specialize in very rapid hip-shaking movements. (Chapter 8)

GHUNUR: A string of bells worn around the ankle, commonly associated with the Bauls of South Asia. (Chapter 5)

GIG: A slang term referring to a job or performance-for-hire. (Chapter 10)

GINGA (Also, JENGA): A back-and-forth motion used as the basis for *capoeira* dancing. (Chapter 12)

GONG AGENG: The largest gong of an Indonesian *gamelan* ensemble. (Chapter 6)

GOOMBAY: A type of folk music ensemble from the Bahamas. (Chapter 11)

GOPIYANTRA (Also, EKTARA): A single-stringed *chordophone* with a membrane base found in India and often associated with the Bauls. (Chapter 5)

GOSPEL: An American religious music tradition associated with Christian evangelism. (Chapter 13)

GRIOT (pronounced *gree-oh*): The French term for a wandering minstrel, often used to describe the West African *jali*. (Chapter 9)

GUARACHA (pronounced *gwah-rah-cha*): A Latin American ballroom dance, as well as a song type emphasizing call-and-response vocal organization. (Chapter 11)

GUIRO (pronounced *gwee-roh*): A scraped gourd *idiophone*. (Chapter 11)

GUITAR: A fretted plucked lute common to American folk and popular music, as well as Spanish flamenco and various other traditions. (Chapter 13)

GUITARRÓN: A large fretted plucked lute from Mexico, similar to a guitar but with a convex resonator. (Chapter 12)

GUQIN (pronounced *goo-chin*): See QIN.

GURU: A teacher or spiritual guide, primarily associated with Hindu traditions from India. (Chapter 5)

GUSHEH: Short composed melodic phrases found in Persian classical music. (Chapter 8)

GYPSY: See ROM.

H

HACKBRETT: A hammered zither from Germany. (Chapter 3)

HAJJ: The Islamic pilgrimage to Mecca, Saudi Arabia. (Chapter 8)

HALILE: A pair of cymbals found in Sufi Muslim music performance. (Chapter 8)

HANUMAN: The "monkey-hero" in the Indian epic, *Ramayana*. (Chapter 5)

HARHIRAA: A type of throat-singing from Mongolia. (Chapter 7)

HARMONICA: A free-reed *aerophone* common to folk music from the United States. (Chapter 13)

HARMONIC: An *overtone* produced by lightly touching a string at a vibrating node. (Chapter 7)

HARMONIUM: A free-reed pump organ. (Chapter 5)

HARMONY: The simultaneous combination of three or more pitches in the Euro-American music tradition. (Chapter 2)

HETEROPHONY: Multiple performers playing simultaneous variations of the same line of music. (Chapter 2)

HICHIRIKI: A double-reed *aerophone* used in *gagaku* music from Japan. (Chapter 7)

HIGHLAND PIPES: Bagpipes from Scotland. (Chapter 10)

HIGHLIFE: A generic term describing urban popular music traditions throughout sub-Saharan Africa. (Chapter 9)

HINDUSTANI: A term referring to the cultural traditions of northern India. (Chapter 5)

HOCKET: A performance technique in which performers trade pitches back and forth to create a complete melody. (Chapter 12)

HOMOPHONY: Multiple lines of music expressing the same musical idea. (Chapter 2)

HOSHO: A gourd rattle from Zimbabwe. (Chapter 9)

HOSSZÚ FURULYA: A long end-blown flute from Hungary. (Chapter 10)

HULA PAHU: Hawaiian dance songs using drum accompaniment. (Chapter 4)

HURDY GURDY: A *chordophone* common in France and Hungary that uses a wheel turned by a crank to vibrate the strings. (Chapter 10)

HYMN: A "humanly composed" religious work. (Chapter 13)

I

IDIOPHONE: Ethnomusicological classification encompassing instruments that themselves vibrate to produce sound, such as rattles, bells, and various other kinds of percussion. (Chapter 2)

ILAHI: A Sufi Muslim hymn. (Chapter 8)

IMPROVISATION: An instrumental or vocal performance or composition created spontaneously without preparation.

INCA: A pre-Columbian indigenous peoples from the Andes region of South America. (Chapter 12)

INDEFINITE PITCH: A sound with no single dominating frequency level. (Chapter 2)

INDEPENDENT POLYPHONY: Multiple lines of music expressing independent musical ideas as a cohesive whole. (Chapter 2)

INTERVAL: The difference between two pitches. (Chapter 2)

INUIT: The term for specific Native American populations that live primarily in Canada and Alaska; often referred to as "Eskimos." (Chapter 13)

IQ'A (pronounced *eek-ah*): Rhythmic *modes* used in Arabic music. (Chapter 8)

ISAN (pronounced *ee-sahn*): A term referring to Northeast Thailand and its regional culture, including music. (Chapter 6)

ISCATHAMIYA (pronounced *is-kah-tah-mee-yah*): A term meaning, "to walk like a cat," i.e., stealthily, which describes a soft style of *mbube* all-male vocal performance from South Africa. (Chapter 9)

IST: The central or "home" pitch of a Persian classical music performance. (Chapter 8)

J

JALEO: Clapping and shouts of encouragement associated with a *juerga* ("happening") in Spanish Flamenco music. (Chapter 10) Also, refers to the closing section of a *merengue* performance from the Dominican Republic. (Chapter 11)

JALI (Also, JELI; pl. JALOLU): Term for a Mandinka poet/praise singer and oral historian from Senegal-Gambia. (Chapter 9)

JALTARANG: An instrument from India, consisting of a series of small china bowls each filled/tuned with a different level of water and struck with a small beater. (Chapter 5)

JAMACA (pronounced *yah-mah-kah*): In Islam, word used for an important *mosque*. (Chapter 8)

JANIZARY (pronounced *ye-nis-air-ee*); **(Also, JANISSARY or YENICERI):** A corps of elite troops commanded by the Ottoman caliphs from the late fourteenth century until their destruction in 1826. (Chapter 8)

JATI: The final section of the *tala* in Indian classical music where the number of beats in the cycle varies. (Chapter 5)

JHALA: Refers to a set of drone strings on Indian *chordophones*. Also, a reference to the climactic end of the *alap* section of raga performance in India. (Chapter 5)

JIG: A musical form in 6/8 time popular both in British and in North American fiddle traditions.

JING: The warrior role-type in the Beijing Opera from China. (Chapter 7)

JINGHU: The lead fiddle of the Beijing Opera's instrumental ensemble. (Chapter 7)

JINGJU (Also, JINGXI): Beijing Opera from China. (Chapter 7)

JOR: A regularizing of the beat in the opening section of *raga* performance in Indian classical music. (Chapter 5)

JUERGA (pronounced *hwair-ga*): An informal event associated with Spanish Flamenco music in which the separation between musicians and audience is blurred. (Chapter 10)

JUKE JOINT: An African-American social venue serving alcohol and hosting dance music, typically *blues*. (Chapter 13)

K

KABUKI: Popular music theatre form from Japan. (Chapter 7)

KAHUNA: A Hawaiian term for a ritual specialist. (Chapter 4)

KALIMBA: A *lamellophone* from sub-Saharan Africa. (Chapter 9)

KANG DUNG: A trumpet from Tibet made from human thighbones. (Chapter 7)

KANUN: See QANUN.

KAPU: Strict taboo system from precolonial Hawaii. (Chapter 4)

KARNATAK: See CARNATIC.

KARTAL: Indian percussion instrument consisting of a steel rod struck by a horseshoe-shaped beater. (Chapter 5)

KASIDE: Freely rhythmic melismatic passages performed by a vocal soloist in a Sufi Muslim ritual. (Chapter 8)

KATAJJAQ (pronounced *kah-tah-jahk*): An Inuit throat-singing style from northern Quebec, Canada. (Chapter 13)

KAYAGUM: A plucked zither from Korea. (Chapter 7)

KECAK: A Balinese theatrical performance of the *Ramayana*. (Chapter 6)

KEMENCE (Also, KEMANCHEH or KEMANJA): A spiked fiddle common to Turkish and Arabic music traditions. (Chapter 8)

KERESHMEH: A type of metered piece in the Persian classical music tradition. (Chapter 8)

KEY: A tonal system consisting of several pitches in fixed relationship to a fundamental pitch. (Chapter 7)

KHAEN: A bamboo mouth organ from Northeast Thailand. (Chapter 6)

KHANEGAH: A type of Sufi Muslim monastery. (Chapter 8)

KHAWNG WONG LEK/KHAWNG WONG YAI: Respectively, the higher- and lower-ranged gong circles found in classical ensembles from Thailand. (Chapter 6)

KHON: A classical masked drama based on the Thai version of the *Ramayana*. (Chapter 6)

KHOOMEI: Throat-singing tradition from Mongolia. (Chapter 7)

KHRU: A Thai teacher; the term is linguistically associated with the word *guru* found in Hinduism. (Chapter 6)

KHRUANG SAI: A classical Thai ensemble characterized by stringed instruments and rhythmic percussion. (Chapter 6)

KHYAL: A category of vocal music from India. (Chapter 5)

KILT: A knee-length skirt made of wool associated with Scottish Highlanders. (Chapter 10)

KILU: A small drum from Hawaii, usually made from a coconut shell with a fish skin face. (Chapter 4)

KISAENG: A professional entertainer from Korea. (Chapter 7)

KLEZMER: A European-derived dance music commonly associated with Jewish celebrations, influenced by jazz and other non-Jewish styles. (Chapter 8)

KONI: A plucked lute from West Africa. (Chapter 9)

KORA: A harp-lute or bridge-harp performed on by *jalolu* from Senegal-Gambia. (Chapter 9)

KORAN (Also, QU'RAN): The sacred text of Islam. (Chapter 8)

KOTO: A plucked zither from Japan. (Chapter 7)

KO-TUZUMI: A small, hourglass-shaped drum from Japan that is held on the shoulder. (Chapter 7)

KRITI: A genre of devotional Hindu poetry from South India. (Chapter 5)

KUDUM: A type of kettle drum common to Turkish and Arabic music. (Chapter 8)

KUMBENGO: The sung sections of a *jali* performance from West Africa. (Chapter 9)

KUNDU: An hourglass-shaped drum from Papua New Guinea. (Chapter 4)

KUSHAURA: The "leading" rhythmic pattern of *mbira dza vadzimu* performance from Zimbabwe. (Chapter 9)

KUTSINHIRA: The "following" rhythmic pattern of *mbira dza vadzimu* performance from Zimbabwe. (Chapter 9)

L

LA LA: A Creole dance party. (Chapter 13)

LAGHU: The final element of the *tala* in Indian classical music. (Chapter 5)

LAM KLAWN (pronounced *lum glawn*): Vocal repartee with *khaen* accompaniment from Northeast Thailand. (Chapter 6)

LAM SING (pronounced *lum sing)*: A popular music form from Northeast Thailand. (Chapter 6)

LAMELLOPHONE: A type of *idiophone* that uses vibrating "lamellae" or strips of material, usually metal, to produce sound. (Chapter 2)

LANGAJ: A ceremonial language found in the *vodou* (voodoo) tradition from Haiti. (Chapter 11)

LATA MANGESHKAR: Famous *filmi* singer from India. (Chapter 5)

LAUTO: A pear-shaped lute from Greece. (Chapter 3)

LAYALI: A vocal improvisational form in Arabic music traditions. (Chapter 8)

LIKEMBE: A *lamellophone* from sub-Saharan Africa. (Chapter 9)

LINED HYMN: An archaic form of singing found in Scotland and the United States, in which a leader "lines" out a verse and the congregation repeats it heterophonically. (Chapter 13)

LONG-METER SONG: An informal term for a *lined hymn*. (Chapter 13)

LUTE: A type of chordophone with a resonating body and a neck with a fingerboard that enables individual strings to sound different pitches. (Chapter 2)

LWA (Also, LOA): A category of deities in Haitian vodou (voodoo).. (Chapter 11)

LYRA: A spiked fiddle from Greece. (Chapter 3)

M

MAGHRIB: A geographic region in North Africa that includes Morocco, Algeria, Tunisia, and Libya. (Chapter 8)

MAHORI: A classical ensemble from Thailand characterized by melodic and rhythmic percussion, stringed instruments, and a fipple flute. (Chapter 6)

MAKAM (Also, MAQAM): A *mode* or system of rules and expectations for composition and improvisation in Arabic classical music. (Chapter 8)

MAMBO: A Latin American dance and music form. (Chapter 11)

MANA: Term for spiritual power in the Hawaiian belief system. (Chapter 4)

MANDOLIN: A high-ranged fretted lute commonly used in bluegrass music from the United States. (Chapter 13) Also the term for a medieval round-bodied lute. (Chapter 3)

MANEABA: Term for a communal meeting house in Kiribati. (Chapter 4)

MARACA: A gourd rattle from Ghana with an external beaded netting. (Chapter 9).

MARACAS: A pair of small Caribbean gourd rattles with interior beads. (Chapter 11).

MARIACHI: An entertainment music associated with festivals and celebratory events in Mexico. (Chapter 12)

MAROONS: Anglicized term for *cimarrons*. (Chapter 11)

MASHRIQ (pronounced *mah-shrik*): A geographic region in the Middle East that includes Egypt, Israel, Jordan, Lebanon, Syria, and Iraq.

MASJID: Term for a local *mosque* in Islam. (Chapter 8)

MAWLAM (pronounced *maw-lum*): A professional *lam klawn* singer from Northeast Thailand. (Chapter 6)

MAWWAL: A vocal improvisational form in Arabic music traditions. (Chapter 8)

MAYA: A pre-Columbian indigenous group from Central America, primarily Mexico and Guatemala. (Chapter 12)

MBIRA: A general reference to lamellophones found throughout Africa. (Chapter 9)

MBIRA DZA VADZIMU: A *lamellophone* from Zimbabwe. (Chapter 9)

MBUBE: All-male vocal groups from South Africa. (Chapter 9)

MEDIUM: The source of a sound, be it instrumental or voice. (Chapter 2) Also, the term for a person in a possessed or trance state.

MEHTER: Ceremonial music of the Turkish *Janizary.* (Chapter 8)

MELANESIA: A collection of islands in the Pacific Ocean. The term is derived from Greek, meaning "black islands," a reference to the darker skin pigmentation of the majority population. (Chapter 4)

MELE (pronounced *meh-leh)*: Poetic texts used in Hawaiian drum dance chant. (Chapter 4)

MELE HULA (pronounced *meh-leh hoo-lah*): Unaccompanied Hawaiian songs specifically associated with dance. (Chapter 4)

MELISMA: Term for a text-setting style in which more than one pitch is sung per syllable. (Chapter 2)

MELODEON: A small reed organ. (Chapter 10)

MELODIC CONTOUR: The general direction and shape of a melody. (Chapter 2)

MELODY: An organized succession of pitches forming a musical idea. (Chapter 2)

MEMBRANOPHONE: Ethnomusicological classification referring to instruments such as drums that use a vibrating stretched membrane as the principle means of sound production. (Chapter 2)

MENTO: A Creolized form of ballroom dance music considered a predecessor to *reggae.* (Chapter 11)

MERENGUE: A Latin American dance and music form, originally from the Dominican Republic. Also, the term for the middle section of a *merengue* performance. (Chapter 11)

MESTIZO: A person of mixed Native American and Spanish descent. (Chapter 12)

MESTRE: A Brazilian term for a senior *capoeira* artist considered a master of the tradition. (Chapter 12)

METALLOPHONE: An *idiophone* consisting of several metal bars graduated in length to produce different pitches. (Chapter 6)

METER: A division of music beats into regular groupings. (Chapter 2)

MICRONESIA: A collection of islands in the Pacific Ocean. The term is derived from Greek, meaning "tiny islands." (Chapter 4)

MIHRAB: A small "niche" or focal point found in a *mosque,* used to orient Islamic worshippers in the direction of Mecca, Saudi Arabia. (Chapter 8)

MINARET: The tall tower of a *mosque,* used for the Islamic call to prayer. (Chapter 8)

MIXOLYDIAN: A medieval church *mode* that predates the "equal tempered" tuning system used today as the basis of Euro-American music. (Chapter 10)

MODE: A set of rules or guidelines used to compose or improvise music in a particular tradition. (Chapter 5)

MODERNISM: In an academic context, a term for scholarship that emphasizes objective "truth" and objective description in favor of subjective interpretation. (Chapter 1)

MONOPHONY: Music with a single melodic line. (Chapter 2)

MORIN HUUR: A fiddle from Mongolia with a distinctive horse head ornament. (Chapter 7)

MOSQUE (pronounced *mosk*): A house of worship for Islamic believers. (Chapter 8)

MRIDANGAM: A barrel-shaped drum from India. (Chapter 5)

MUEZZIN: A person who calls Islamic believers to worship five times a day. (Chapter 8)

MULATTO: A person of mixed African and Iberian ancestry. (Chapter 12)

MULLAH: A low-rank clergyman in Islam. (Chapter 8)

MUMMER: A type of street theater actor, usually in performances staged during the Christmas season. (Chapter 11)

N

NAGASVARAM: A double-reed *aerophone* from India. (Chapter 5)

NEY (Also, NAY): A vertical flute found in Turkish and Arabic music traditions. (Chapter 8)

NGA BOM: A double-faced drum from Tibet. (Chapter 7)

NODE: A point of minimum amplitude on a vibrating string. (Chapter 7)

NOH: Classical drama form from Japan. (Chapter 7)

NOKAN: A transverse flute from Japan. (Chapter 7)

NONGAK: Style of folk music from Korea associated with farmers. (Chapter 7)

O

ORGANOLOGY: The study of musical instruments. (Chapter 3)

ORISHA: A category of deity in the animistic spiritual belief system of *Santeria* and in other African-derived religious traditions. (Chapter 11)

ORNAMENTATION: An embellishment or decoration of a melody. (Chapter 2)

ORQUESTA (Also, BANDA): A reference to "swing" bands from the Texas-Mexico borderland region of North America. (Chapter 13)

OSSIAN: Legendary Gaelic hero and bard of the third century A.D. (Chapter 10)

ORUS: A rhythmic pattern associated with an *orisha* in the *Santeria* religious tradition. (Chapter 11)

OTTOMAN EMPIRE: An empire centered in what is now Turkey that spread throughout West Asia, Eastern Europe, and Northern Africa from the fourteenth to nineteenth centuries. (Chapter 8)

O-TUZUMI: A small, hourglass-shaped drum from Japan that is held at the hip. (Chapter 7)

OVERTONE: A tone that is heard above a fundamental pitch, and that is one of the ascending group of tones that form the harmonic series derived from the fundamental pitch. (Chapter 7)

P

PAHU: A single-headed cylindrical *membranophone* from Hawaii that stands vertically on a carved footed base. (Chapter 4)

PALILLOS (pronounced *pah-lee-yohs*) **(Also, PITOS):** A type of finger-snapping commonly found in Spanish Flamenco music. (Chapter 10)

PALITO: The term for a rhythmic pattern played on the side of a drum in *salsa* music. (Chapter 11)

PALLAVI: The first section of a *kriti* vocal performance from India. (Chapter 5)

PALM WINE GUITAR: A popular music style from sub-Saharan Africa. (Chapter 9)

PALMAS: The term for the hand-clapping commonly found in Spanish flamenco music. (Chapter 10)

PAN: A musical instrument from Trinidad made out of a steel oil drum. (Chapter 11)

PANDEIROS: A hand-held frame drum with attached cymbals (i.e., a tambourine), used in *capoeira* music from Brazil. (Chapter 12)

PANORAMA: A steel drum orchestra competition held at the end of the Carnival festivals in Trinidad. (Chapter 11)

P'ANSORI: Narrative vocal performance style from Korea. (Chapter 7)

PARANG: A Portuguese-derived music sung during Christmas season. (Chapter 11)

PARLANDO RUBATO: A term meaning "speech-rhythm," indicating a fluctuating tempo. (Chapter 10)

PASEO: The opening section of a *merengue* performance. (Chapter 11)

PENTATEUCH: See TORAH.

PENTATONIC SCALE: A scale consisting of only five pitches. (Chapter 2)

PEURT A BEUL (pronounced *porsht a boy*): Unaccompanied dance song with nonsense syllables used to substitute for fiddling. (Chapter 13)

PHIN (pronounced *pin)*: A fretted plucked lute from Northeast Thailand. (Chapter 6)

PHLENG LUK THUNG (pronounced *pleng look toong*): A popular music form from Thailand. (Chapter 6)

PHONIC STRUCTURE: The relationship between different sounds in a given piece; can be either m*onophony* or some form of *polyphony*. (Chapter 2)

PI (pronounced *bee*): A double-reed *aerophone* found in the piphat classical ensemble of Thailand. (Chapter 6)

PIBROCH (pronounced *pee-brahk*): A form of Scottish bagpipe music with an elaborate theme-and-variations structure. (Chapter 10)

PIPA: A pear-shaped lute from China. (Chapter 7)

PIPHAT (pronounced *bee-paht*): A type of classical ensemble from Thailand characterized by the use of melodic and rhythmic percussion and a double-reed *aerophone*. (Chapter 6)

PITCH: A tone's specific frequency level, measured in Hertz (Hz). (Chapter 2)

PITOS: See PALILLOS.

POIETIC: The process of creating the meaning of a symbol. (Chapter 1)

POLYNESIA: A collection of islands in the Pacific Ocean. The term is derived from Greek, and means "many islands." (Chapter 4)

POLYPHONY: The juxtaposition or overlapping of multiple lines of music; the three types of *polyphony* are *homophony*, *independent polyphony*, and *heterophony*. (Chapter 2)

POLYRHYTHM: A term meaning "multiple rhythms"; the organizational basis for most sub-Saharan African music traditions. (Chapter 9)

PORTAMENTO: A smooth, uninterrupted glide from one pitch to another. (Chapter 4)

PORTEÑOS: A term for residents of the port area of Buenos Aires, Argentina. (Chapter 12)

POSTMODERNISM: A general term applied to numerous scholarly approaches that reject "modernism," with its emphases on objective "truth" and objective description, in favor of subjective interpretations. (Chapter 1)

POW WOW: A pan-tribal American Indian event celebrating Native American identity and culture, generally also open to non-Native Americans. (Chapter 13)

PRECENTOR: A song leader who recites the "line" of a *lined hymn* in Calvinist churches in the United States. (Chapter 13)

PROGRAMMATIC MUSIC: Music that has a "program," i.e., tells a story, depicts a scene, or creates an image.

PSALMS: A book of the Christian Bible used as the source for many songs in Calvinist churches in the United States. (Chapter 13)

PUK: Drum used to accompany Korean *p'ansori* performance. (Chapter 7)

PYGMIES: A generic term applied to a diverse population of forest-dwellers in Central Africa. (Chapter 9)

Q

QANUN (Also, KANUN): A plucked zither used in Turkish and Arabic music traditions. (Chapter 8)

QAWWALI (Also, KAWWALI): Sufi Muslim devotional songs. (Chapter 5)

QIN (pronounced *chin* also, **GUQIN**): A bridgeless plucked zither from China, the playing of which is characterized by the frequent use of overtones. (Chapter 7)

QU'RAN: See KORAN.

R

RADA: Ritual drums used in *Vodou (Voodoo)* ceremonies from Haiti. (Chapter 11)

RADIF: A collection of *gusheh* for each *dastgah* in Persian classical music. (Chapter 8)

RAGA: A mode or system of rules and expectations for composition and improvisation in Indian classical music. (Chapter 5)

RAKE AND SCRAPE: A folk music from the Bahamas. (Chapter 11)

RAMA: The central figure of the Hindu Indian epic *Ramayana*. (Chapter 5)

RAMAYANA: An Indian mythological epic about the Hindu god Rama found throughout South and Southeast Asia. (Chapter 6)

RANAT EK (pronounced *rah-nahd ek*): The lead *xylophone* of classical ensembles from Thailand. (Chapter 6)

RANAT THUM (pronounced *rah-nahd toom*): The supporting *xylophone* of classical ensembles from Thailand. (Chapter 6)

RANCHERA: A style of "country" *mariachi* from Mexico that emphasizes vocal performance. (Chapter 12)

RANGE: All the pitches that a voice or instrument can potentially produce. (Chapter 2)

RAQS SHARQI (pronounced *rocks shar-kee*): Middle Eastern dance form characterized as "belly dance" by outsiders to the region. (Chapter 8)

RASA: The mood or sentiment of an artistic expression in India. (Chapter 5)

RASTA: A believer in *Rastafarianism*. (Chapter 11)

RASTAFARIANISM: A religious cult centered in Jamaica, which purports that the second coming of Jesus Christ has already occurred in the form of Haile Selassie, an Ethiopian king. (Chapter 11)

RAVANA: The villain in the Indian epic *Ramayana*. (Chapter 5)

RAVI SHANKAR: A famous musician and composer from India. (Chapter 5)

REBAB: A fiddle commonly found in gamelan ensembles from Indonesia. (Chapter 6)

REBEC: A spiked fiddle from France. (Chapter 3)

RÊCO-RÊCO: A notched scraper *idiophone* found in Latin American music traditions. (Chapter 12)

REEDS: A type of *aerophone* that uses a vibrating reed to produce sound. (Chapter 2)

REELS: A type of dance music found in Scottish and Appalachian music. (Chapter 13)

REELS À BOUCHE: An unaccompanied song used for dance music in the Cajun region of Louisiana in the United States. (Chapter 13)

REGGAE: A popular music from Jamaica characterized by a rhythmic emphasis on the off-beat and by politically and socially conscious lyrics. (Chapter 11)

REGULATORS: The metal keys that "regulate" the drone pipes on the Irish bagpipes to produce different pitches. (Chapter 10)

RENAISSANCE LUTE: A pear-shaped plucked lute from Europe. (Chapter 3)

RHYMER: The lead vocalist in a *rhyming spiritual* performance from the Bahamas. (Chapter 11)

RHYMING SPIRITUAL: A vocal genre from the Bahamas. (Chapter 11)

RHYTHM: The lengths, or durations, of sounds as patterns in time. (Chapter 2)

RHYTHMIC DENSITY: The quantity of notes between periodic accents or over a specific unit of time. (Chapter 2)

RHYTHMIC MELODY: The complete musical idea of polyrhythmic music. (Chapter 9)

RIQQ (pronounced *rik*): A small, single-headed drum with pairs of small cymbals inserted into its frame (i.e., a tambourine), common to Turkish and Arabic music traditions. (Chapter 8)

RITARD: A musical term for slowing the tempo, normally at the end of a piece. (Chapter 2)

ROCK STEADY: A popular music from Jamaica considered a precursor to *reggae*. (Chapter 11)

RODA: A circular area used for the dancers in *capoeira* performance. (Chapter 12)

ROM (Also, ROMANI or GYPSIES): An ethnic group originating in India characterized by a semi-nomadic lifestyle; popularly known as *gypsies*. (Chapter 10) *Rom* is also the term used for large paired cymbals from Tibet. (Chapter 7)

RUMBA (Also, RHUMBA): A Latin American dance and music form. (Chapter 11)

RYUTEKI: A transverse flute from Japan. (Chapter 7)

S

SACRED HARP: The most popular collection of *shape-note* songs. (Chapter 13)

SACHS-HORNBOSTEL SYSTEM: Standard classification system for musical instruments created by Curt Sachs and Erik M. von Hornbostel, which divides musical instruments into four categories: *aerophones, chordophones, idiophones,* and *membranophones.* (Chapter 2)

SALSA: A Latin American dance music form. (Chapter 11)

SAMBA: A popular music from Brazil. (Chapter 12)

SAMBA CANÇÃO (pronounced *samba kahn-syao*): "Song samba" from Brazil. (Chapter 12)

SAMBA-BAIANA: "Bahian samba" from Brazil. (Chapter 12)

SAMBA-CARNAVALESCO: "Carnival samba" from Brazil. (Chapter 12)

SAMBA-ENREDO: "Theme samba" from Brazil. (Chapter 12)

SAMBA-REGGAE: "Reggae samba" from Brazil. (Chapter 12)

SAMBISTAS: Dancers in the *samba schools* that parade during Carnival in Brazil. (Chapter 12)

SAMUL-NORI: A type of folk music from Korea. (Chapter 7)

SANDOURI: A hammered zither from Greece. (Chapter 3)

SANJO: An instrumental form from Korea. (Chapter 7)

SANKYOKU: A classical ensemble type from Japan, consisting of *koto, shakuhachi,* and *shamisen.* (Chapter 7)

SANTERIA: An animistic and Roman Catholic syncretised belief system found primarily in Cuba and the United States. (Chapter 9)

SANTUR: A hammered zither from the Persian classical tradition. Often cited as the origin of hammered zithers found throughout Asia, Northern Africa, Europe, and the Western hemisphere. (Chapter 3)

SARANGI: A bowed lute from India. (Chapter 5)

SAROD: A fretless plucked lute from India. (Chapter 5)

SAW U (pronounced *saw oo*): A Thai fiddle with a coconut resonator. (Chapter 6)

SAZ: A fretted plucked lute from Turkey. (Chapter 8)

SCALE: The pitches used in a particular performance arranged in ascending order. (Chapter 2)

SCHALMEI: A medieval double-reed *aerophone* from Europe. (Chapter 3)

SCHEITHOLT: A spiked fiddle from Germany. (Chapter 3)

SEMIOTICS: The study of "signs" and systems of signs, including music. (Chapter 1)

SHAH: The title formerly given to hereditary monarchs in Iran. (Chapter 8)

SHAKA ZULU (1787–1828): Leader of the Zulu ethnic group from South Africa. (Chapter 9)

SHAKUHACHI: A vertical flute from Japan. (Chapter 7)

SHAM'IDAN: A Middle Eastern dance in which the dancer performs with a large, heavy candelabrum with lighted candles balanced on the head. (Chapter 8)

SHAMISEN: A fretless plucked lute from Japan with a membrane resonator face. (Chapter 7)

SHANGO: An animistic belief system found primarily in Trinidad. (Chapter 11)

SHAPE NOTES: A music notation system from the United States that uses differently shaped "note" heads to indicate pitch. (Chapter 13)

SHAWM: A medieval double-reed *aerophone* from Europe. (Chapter 3)

SHENG: A mouth organ from China. Also the term for the male hero role-type in Beijing Opera from China. (Chapter 7)

SHIAH: The fundamentalist branch of Islam. (Chapter 8)

SHO: A mouth organ from Japan. (Chapter 7)

SHOFAR: A Jewish ritual trumpet made of a ram's horn. (Chapter 8)

SIKU: Panpipes common among indigenous populations from Peru and throughout the Andes. (Chapter 12)

SIKURI: A type of ensemble from Peru, consisting of *siku* performers with accompanying drummers. (Chapter 12)

SINGING SCHOOL: A tradition of teaching four-part harmony techniques, found in rural areas throughout the United States. (Chapter 13)

SITA (pronounced *see-tah*): The wife of the Hindu God *Rama* in the Indian epic *Ramayana*. (Chapter 5)

SITAR: A fretted plucked lute from India. (Chapter 5)

SIZHU (pronounced *sih-joo*): An ensemble comprised of "silk and bamboo" instruments from China. (Chapter 7)

SKA: A popular music from Jamaica considered a precursor to *reggae*. (Chapter 11)

SOCIOLOGY: The study of human social behavior, emphasizing its origins, organization, institutions, and development. (Chapter 1)

SOLFEGE: Mnemonic syllables corresponding to individual pitches in a scale. (Chapter 5)

SON: An Afro-Cuban music genre from Latin America. (Chapter 11)

SONG LANG: A clapper *idiophone* from Vietnam. (Chapter 6)

SON JALISCIENSE: A category of *mariachi* that features frequent subtle shifts of meter and tempo, making it more rhythmically active than most *mariachi* music. (Chapter 12)

SPIRITUAL: A term for religious folk music. (Chapter 13)

SPOONS: A pair of spoons struck together to play rhythm. (Chapter 10)

STEEL DRUM: A musical instrument from Trinidad made from steel oil drums. (Chapter 11)

STRING BASS: A large fretless plucked lute heard in many music traditions from the United States. (Chapter 13)

STROPHIC: A song form in which the music repeats with each new poetic verse. (Chapter 13)

SUFI (pronounced *soo-fee*): The mystical branch of Islam. (Chapter 8)

SUNNI (pronounced *soo-nee*): The mainstream branch of Islam. (Chapter 8)

SUONA (pronounced *swoh-nah)*: A double-reed *aerophone* from China. (Chapter 7)

SURDO: See BOMBAS.

SUSAP: A mouth harp from Papua New Guinea. (Chapter 4)

SYLLABIC: A text setting in which only one pitch is sung per syllable. (Chapter 2)

SYMPATHETIC STRINGS: A set of strings most commonly found on Hindustani Indian chordophones that vibrate "in sympathy" with the vibrations of other strings on the instrument. (Chapter 5)

SYMPHONIA: A medieval European instrument similar to the *hurdy gurdy*. (Chapter 10)

SYNAGOGUE: A Jewish house of worship. (Chapter 8)

SYNCOPATION: The accenting of a normally weak beat. (Chapter 2)

T

TABLA: A pair of drums found in Hindustani music from India. (Chapter 5) Also, a goblet-shaped hand drum found in Arabic music. (Chapter 8)

TAHMALA: A compositional form found in Turkish and Arabic music. (Chapter 8)

TAHRIR: A freely rhythmic section emphasizing melismatic performance found in Persian classical music. (Chapter 8)

TAI THU (pronounced *tai tuh)*: A type of chamber music ensemble from Vietnam. (Chapter 6)

TAIKO: Generic term for *drum* in Japan. (Chapter 7)

TAKHT: A type of instrumental ensemble found in Arabic music traditions. (Chapter 8)

TALA: Rhythmic framework found in *raga* performance in India. (Chapter 5)

TAMBOO-BAMBOO: A type of ensemble developed after drums were banned in Trinidad, which used cane and bamboo tubes that were beaten with sticks and stamped on the ground. (Chapter 11)

TAMBORA: A small barrel-drum made with thick leather faces, commonly used in *merengue* from the Dominican Republic. (Chapter 11)

TAMBURA: A round-bodied lute used to provide the "drone" element in Indian classical music. (Chapter 5) Also, a term used to describe round-bodied lutes from Bulgaria, Croatia, and Serbia in Southeastern Europe. (Chapter 3)

TANBUR: A fretted plucked lute common to Turkish and Arabic music. (Chapter 8)

TANGO: A dance and associated music originating in Argentina, but now commonly associated with ballroom dance. (Chapter 12

TAQSIM (pronounced *tahk-seem*): An instrumental improvisational form in Turkish and Arabic music traditions. (Chapter 8

TARAB: Arabic word for a state of emotional transformation or ecstasy achieved through music. (Chapter 8)

TASLAM: A compositional form found in Turkish and Arabic music. (Chapter 8)

TAVIL: A pair of drums from India, often used to accompany the *nagasvaram*. (Chapter 5)

TEJANO (pronounced *teh-hah-noh)*: Term referring to populations and cultural activities from the Texas-Mexico borderlands in North America. (Chapter 13)

TEJAS (pronounced *teh-hahs)*: Native American name for what is now Texas in the United States. (Chapter 13)

TEKKE: A type of Sufi Muslim monastery. (Chapter 8)

TEMPO: The relative rate of speed of a beat. (Chapter 2)

TEMPO GIUSTO: A regular or "precise" metered rhythm following an unmetered section. (Chapter 10)

TEXT SETTING: The rhythmic relationship of words to melody; can be *syllabic* (one pitch per syllable) or *melismatic* (more than one pitch per syllable). (Chapter 2)

THEKA (pronounced *teh-kah*): The entire pattern or set of words *(bols)* for a given *tala* in classical Indian music. (Chapter 5)

TIMBALES: A pair of metal-framed drums of European military origin used often in *salsa* music. (Chapter 11)

TIMBER FLUTE: A wooden transverse flute from Ireland.

TIMBILA: A log *xylophone* from Mozambique. (Chapter 9)

TIMBRE: The tone quality or "color" of a musical sound. (Chapter 2)

TIN WHISTLE: A metal vertical flute from Ireland. (Chapter 10)

TOMTOM: A pair of tall, single-headed hand drums from Ghana. (Chapter 9)

TORAH (Also, PENTATEUCH, pronounced *peut-a-toik*): In Judaism, the first five books of the Bible, or more generally, all sacred literature. (Chapter 8)

TOTEM: An animal, plant, or other natural object used as the emblem of a group or individual, strongly associated with an ancestral relationship. (Chapter 13)

TRUMPET: A type of *aerophone* that requires the performer to vibrate his or her lips to produce sound. (Chapter 2)

TUMBADORA (Also, CONGA): A tall barrel-shaped single-headed drum used in *salsa* music. (Chapter 11)

TUMBAO: A rhythmic pattern played on the *conga* in *salsa* music. (Chapter 11)

TUNING SYSTEM: The pitches common to a musical tradition. (Chapter 2)

U

UD (Also, AL'UD): A fretless plucked pear-shaped lute found in Arabic music traditions. (Chapter 8)

UILLEANN PIPES (pronounced *il-en;* **Also, UNION PIPES):** Bagpipes from Ireland, called *uilleann* (meaning "elbow") because the performer uses an elbow to pump the bellows. (Chapter 10)

UKELELE: A high-ranged plucked lute from Hawaii. (Chapter 4)

UMBANDA: An animistic and Roman Catholic syncretised belief system found primarily in Brazil. (Chapter 11)

URTYN DUU: A Mongolian vocal form described as "long song"; performers are accompanied by the *morin huur.* (Chapter 7)

V

VENU: A transverse flute from South India. (Chapter 5)

VIHUELA: A small, fretted plucked lute from Mexico, similar to a guitar but with a convex resonator. (Chapter 12)

VINA: A plucked lute from South India, often associated with the Hindu goddess Saraswati. (Chapter 5)

VODOU (Also, VOODOO): An animistic belief system found primarily in Haiti. (Chapter 9)

W

WAI KHRU: A teacher-honoring ceremony from Thailand. (Chapter 6)

WAULKING SONG: Work songs from Scotland performed while working with wool. (Chapter 10)

X

XYLOPHONE: An idiophone consisting of several wooden bars graduated in length to produce different pitches. (Chapter 9)

Y

YANG BAN XI (pronounced *yahng bahn shi*): Chinese term for post-1949 Beijing Operas infused with Communist and nationalist political messages; translated as "Revolutionary Peking (Beijing) Opera." (Chapter 7)

YANG QIN (pronounced *yang chin*): A hammered zither from China. (Chapter 7)

YENICERI: See JANIZARY.

YUE QIN (pronounced *yweh chin*): A plucked lute from China. (Chapter 7)

Z

ZAKIRLER: A specialist group of male vocalists who perform metered hymns in unison during a Sufi ritual. (Chapter 8)

ZARB: A goblet-shaped hand drum used in Persian classical music traditions from Iran. (Chapter 8)

ZHENG (pronounced *jeng*): A plucked zither from China. (Chapter 7)

ZIKR: See DHIKR.

ZITHER: A type of chordophone in which the strings stretch across the length of the resonating body. (Chapter 2)

ZOUK: Popular music from the French Lesser Antilles in the Caribbean. (Chapter 11)

ZURNA (Also, ZOURNA): A double-reed aerophone from Turkey and Greece. (Chapter 3)

ZYDECO: Creole dance music from the southern United States, primarily Louisiana. (Chapter 13)

Resources for Further Study

*A*s comprehensive as this book seeks to be, there is no way to include enough material to cover all possible questions. Further, we have suggested that both teachers and students can supplement our Sites by constructing their own. Thirty years ago, when ethnomusicology was still young in American institutions and resources were severely limited, it was difficult to find additional information. Today, with the explosion of information and new technologies for delivering it, anyone can obtain further information on virtually any topic. Not all libraries will have all the print, audio, or video publications available, but anyone with access to the Internet can at least visit any of the better, more professional websites devoted to virtually any musical type or style in the world. The following, also found in part at the end of chapter 1, is a guide to some of the available resources that will lead you to further exploration of the world's musics.

We have arranged these resources into four categories: 1) print materials, 2) visual materials, 3) audio materials, and 4) additional resources. Our inclusion of an item does not necessarily include our complete approval of its contents, but we feel it offers something of value. Our exclusion of an item does not signal our disapproval; we are attempting to deal with limitations of space and our own knowledge. We have also limited ourselves to materials in English. Lastly, using the Internet as a research tool is quite valuable. Words of caution, however, articles on the Internet are generally not "refereed" for accurate content, so do not rely on the Internet as your only resource. Nevertheless, using a search engine, such as Google or Yahoo, to get started on a topic of interest can save you a lot of time digging through hard copy bibliographies for more information.

Print Materials
Encyclopedias and Dictionaries

Randall, Don Michael, ed. *The Harvard Dictionary of Music*. 4th ed. Cambridge: Belknap Press of Harvard University Press, 2003.

> Originally a slender book written entirely by one man, musicologist Willi Apel, it first appeared in 1944 and has undergone many revisions. The present volume supercedes

the previous edition, called *The New Harvard Dictionary of Music*. This resource provides lengthy but broad articles, such as "East Asia" "Folk Music," and "American Indian Music," but there are also short entries for particular instruments (e.g., "sitar"), ensembles (e.g., "gamelan"), and genres (e.g., "reggae"), but none on individuals.

Sadie, Stanley and John Tyrrell, eds. *The New Grove Dictionary of Music and Musicians*, 2nd ed. 29 vols. London: Macmillan, 2001.

Originally a small encyclopedia published by Englishman Sir George Grove in the 1870s, the "Grove" (as it is known familiarly) was long biased towards England in particular and Europe in general. The advent of the twenty-volume *New Grove* first edition in 1980 was a milestone in the study of world musics, for this edition included substantial entries by recognized scholars on most countries of the world. The second edition of 2001 incorporate those articles plus everything that had appeared in the earlier *New Grove American* and the *New Grove Dictionary of Musical Instruments*. Thus the Grove now includes articles at the level of continent (or sub-continent), nation, genre, ensemble, instrument, and individual performer/composer/innovator.

The Garland Encyclopedia of World Music. 10 vols. New York and London: Routledge, 1998-2002.

This monumental encyclopedia, each volume having from 900 to 1200 pages, is the first such work devoted entirely to the world's musics. Each volume has three sections, the first an introduction that includes overview articles, the second called "Issues and Processes" that includes articles on specific questions or approaches, and the third devoted to individual nations, cultures, or genres. Vol. 10, entitled *The World's Music: General Perspectives and Reference Tools,* includes articles by individual scholars under the heading "Ethnomusicologists at Work," and a section of "Resources and Research Tools" that combines the bibliographies, discographies, and videographies of vols. 1-9, those being devoted to a single continent or sub-continent (e.g., South Asia). Each volume, save for vol. 10, is liberally illustrated with photos, charts, and notations and includes a compact disc. The appropriate volumes will be cited under each of our chapters.

Books and Journals

World Music: The Rough Guide. 2 vols. [vol 1: Africa, Europe and the Middle East; vol. 2: Latin and North America, Caribbean, Indian, Asia and Pacific]. London: Rough Guides, Inc., 1999-2000.

While a few of the articles were written by known scholars and discuss traditional kinds of music, the bulk are devoted to contemporary forms, especially popular, revivalist, and innovative, with special attention to groups and individuals who make recordings. With its extensive illustrations, the two-volume set is nonetheless valuable for understanding at least certain aspects of each country's music scene. The Rough Guide has also produced a growing series of compact discs, mostly presenting popular and "worldbeat" forms.

Oxford University Press, Global Music Series. 17 vols. Oxford: Oxford University Press, 2004-2005.

This series of short books is intended to reach a non-specialist audience, providing in depth discussion of specific cultural areas as well as an accompanying CD of common musical types. The volumes have a strong "music education" approach as one of the series editors, Patricia Shehan Campbell, is well-known as a music educator specializing in world musics. Some of the volumes are mentioned below, but the areas covered include: East Africa, Central Java, Trinidad, Bali, Ireland, the Middle East, Brazil, America (United States), Bulgaria, North

India, West Africa, South India, Japan, China, and more specifically *mariachi* music in the United States.

We would be remiss if we did not include a few texts specific to various world music traditions discussed herein. We have intentionally limited the list to just a handful of resources as some areas have a wealth of material that the serious student will no doubt discover on his own. These, however, are a useful starting point. We have organized them according to chapters in the current book.

Chapter 1 Before the Trip Begins: Fundamental Issues

Blacking, John. *How Musical is Man?* Seattle: University of Washington press, 1973.

Hood, Mantle. *The Ethnomusicologist.* Kent, OH: Kent State University Press, 1982 [New York: McGraw-Hill, 1971].

Nettl, Bruno. *The Study of Ethnomusicology.* Urbana: University of Illinois Press, 1983.

Myers, Helen, ed. *Ethnomusicology: An Introduction.* New York: Norton, 1992.

Chapter 2 Aural Analysis: Listening to the World's Music

Kamien, Roger. *Music: An Appreciation*, 4th brief ed. New York: McGraw-Hill, 2002 [1990]. The opening sections of any number of "introductory" Euro-American art music texts, such as Kamien, are useful for understanding basic music terminology. The above-mentioned dictionaries also provide detailed discussion.

Kartomi, Margaret J. *On Concepts and Classifications of Musical Instruments.* Chicago: The University of Chicago Press, 1990.

Sachs, Curt. *The History of Musical Instruments.* New York: Norton, 1940.

Chapter 3 Cultural Considerations: Beyond the Sounds Themselves

Barz, Gregory F., and Timothy J. Cooley. *Shadows in the Field: New Perspectives for Fieldwork in Ethnomusicology.* New York: Oxford University Press, 1997.

Clayton, Martin, Trevor Herbert and Richard Middleton, ed. *The Cultural Study of Music: A Critical Introduction.* New York: Routledge, 2003.

Merriam, Alan P. *The Anthropology of Music.* Evanston, IL: Northwestern University Press, 1964. This text is particularly important to the "anthropology" branch of ethnomusicology and is considered fundamental to the field.

Chapter 4 Oceania: Voices of Land and Sea

Feld, Steven. *Sound and Sentiment: Birds, Weeping, Poetics, and Song in Kaluli Expression,* 2nd ed. Philadelphia: University of Pennsylvania Press, 1990.

Malm, William P. *Music Cultures of the Pacific, the Near East, and Asia,* 3rd ed. Englewood Cliffs, NJ: Prentice Hall, 1996 [1967].

Moyle, Alice M. *Songs from the Northern Territory.* Canberra: Australian Institute of Aboriginal Studies, 1974 [1967].

Chenoweth, Vida. *A Music Primer for the North Solomons Province.* Ukarumpa: Summer Institute of Linguistics, 1984.

RESOURCES

Moyle, Richard M. *Traditional Samoan Music.* Auckland: Auckland University Press, 1988.

Chapter 5 South Asia: Music with a Spiritual Dimension
Wade, Bonnie C. *Music in India: The Classical Traditions.* Englewood Cliffs, NJ: Prentice Hall, 1979.

Capwell, Charles. *The Music of the Bauls of Bengal.* Kent, OH: Kent State University Press, 1986.

Clayton, Martin. *Time in Indian Muisc: Rhythm, Metre, and Form in North Indian Rag Performance.* Oxford: Oxford University Press, 2000.

Kaufmann, Walter. *The Ragas of North India.* Bloomington: Indiana University Press, 1968.

_____. *The Ragas of South India.* Bloomington: Indiana University Press, 1976.

Sai Devotional Songs. Tustin, CA: Sathya Sai Book Center of America, n.d.

Chapter 6 Southeast Asia: A Land of Bamboo and Bronze
Becker, Judith. *Traditional Music in Modern Java: Gamelan in a Changing Society.* Honolulu: University of Hawaii Press, 1980.

Miller, Terry E. *Traditional Music of the Lao.* Westport, CT: Greenwood Press, 1985.

Morton, David. *The Traditional Music of Thailand.* Berkeley: University of California Press, 1976.

Nguyen, Thuyet Phong, ed. *New Perspectives in Vietnamese Music.* New Haven, CT: Department of International and Area Studies, Yale University, 1990.

Shahriari, Andrew. *Khon Muang Music and Dance Traditions of North Thailand.* Bangkok: White Lotus Press, Co., 2005.

Spiller, Henry. Gamelan: *The Traditional Sounds of Indonesia.* Santa Barbara, CA: ABC-CLIO World Music Series, 2004.

Tenzer, Michael. *Gamelan Gong Kebyar: The Art of Twentieth-Century Balinese Music.* Chicago: University of Chicago Press, 2000.

Chapter 7 East Asia: Ancient Echoes in the Modern World
Garfias, Robert. *Music of a Thousand Autumns: Togaku Style of Japanese Court Music.* Berkeley: University of California Press, 1975.

Heyman, Alan C. *Korean Musical Instruments.* New York: Oxford University Press, 1995.

Jones, Stephen. *Folk Music of China: Living Instrumental Tradition.* Oxford: Clarendon Press, 1992.

Liang, Mingyue. *Music of the Billion: An Introduction to Chinese Musical Culture.* New York: Heinrichshofen, 1985.

Mackerras, Colin. *The Rise of the Peking Opera, 1770-1870.* Oxford: Clarendon, 1972.

Malm, William P. *Japanese Music and Musical Instruments.* Tokyo: Tuttle, 1968 [1959].

Park, Chan E. *Voices from the Straw Mat: Toward an Ethnography of Korean Story Singing.* Honolulu: University of Hawaii Press, 2003.

428

Wichmann, Elizabeth. *Listening to Theatre: The Aural Dimension of Beijing Opera*. Honolulu: Hawaii University Press, 1998.

Chapter 8 The Middle East: Cradle of Great Religions

During, Jean. *The Art of Persian Music*. Washington DC: Mage Publishers, 1991.

Nettl, Bruno. *The Radif of Persian Music: Studies in Structure and Cultural Context*. Champaign, IL: Elephant & Cat, 1987.

Picken, Laurence. *Folk Music Instruments of Turkey*. London: Oxford University Press, 1975.

Shiloah, Amnon. *Jewish Musical Traditions*. Detroit: Wayne State University Press, 1992.

_____. *Music in the World of Islam: A Socio-Cultural Study*. Detroit: Wayne State University Press, 2003 [1995].

Touma, Habib Hassan. *The Music of the Arabs*. Portland, OR: Amadeus Press, 1996.

Chapter 9 Sub-Saharan Africa: The Rhythms of Community

Berliner, Paul F. *The Soul of Mbira*. Chicago: University of Chicago Press, 1993 [1981].

Charry, Eric. *Mande Music: Traditional and Modern Music of the Maninka and Mandinka of Western Africa*. Chicago: The University of Chicago Press, 2000.

Chernoff, John Miller. *African Rhythm and Sensibility*. Chicago: University of Chicago Press, 1979.

Erlmann, Veit. *Nightsong: Performance, Power, and Practice in South Africa*. Chicago: The University of Chicago Press, 1996.

Kisliuk, Michelle. S*eize the Dance! BaAka Musical Life and the Ethnography of Performance*. New York: Oxford University Press, 1998.

Locke, David. *Drum Gahu: An Introduction to African Rhythm*. Tempe, AZ: White Cliffs Media, 1998.

Nketia, J.H. Kwabena. *The Music of Africa*. New York: Norton, 1974.

Chapter 10 Europe: Harmony and Hierarchy

Bohlman, Philip V. *The Study of Folk Music in the Modern World*. Bloomington: Indiana University Press, 1988.

_____. *The Music of European Nationalism: Cultural Identity and Modern History*. Santa Barbara, CA: ABC-CLIO World Music Series, 2004.

Chuse, Loren. *The Cantaoras: Music, Gender, and Identity in Flamenco Song*. New York: Routledge, 2003.

Nettl, Bruno. *Folk and Traditional Music of the Western Continents,* 3rd ed. Englewood Cliffs, NJ: Prentice Hall, 1990 [1965].

Rice, Timothy. *May It Fill Your Soul: Experiencing Bulgarian Music*. Chicago: University of Chicago Press, 1994.

Slobin, Mark, ed. *Retuning Culture: Musical Changes in Central and Eastern Europe*. Durham, NC: Duke University Press, 1996.

Totton, Robin. *Song of the Outcasts: An Introduction to Flamenco.* Portland, OR: Amadeus Press, 2003.

Chapter 11 Caribbean: Musical Energy of Island Peoples

Béhague, Gerard H., ed. *Music and Black Ethnicity: The Caribbean and South America.* London: Transaction Publishers, 1994.

Hill, Donald R. *Calypso Calaloo: Early Carnival Music in Trinidad.* Gainesville: University Press of Florida, 1993

Johnson, Howard, and Jim Pines. *Reggae: Deep Roots Music.* London: Proteus Books, 1982.

Manuel, Peter. *Popular Musics of the Non-Western World.* New York: Oxford University Press, 1988.

Stuempfle, Stephen. *The Steelband Movement: The Forging of a National Art in Trinidad and Tobago.* Philadelphia: University of Pennsylvania Press, 1995.

Waxer, Lise. *Situating Salsa: Global Markets and Local Meaning in Latin Popular Music.* New York: Routledge, 2002.

Wilcken, Lois. *The Drums of Vodou.* Tempe, AZ: White Cliffs Media, 1992.

Chapter 12 Central and South America: New World Recipes.

Almeida, Bira. *Capoeira: A Brazilian Art Form.* Berkeley, CA: North Atlantic Books, 1986.

Clark, Walter Aaron, ed. *From Tejano to Tango.* New York: Routledge, 2002.

Perrone, Charles A., and Christopher Dunn. *Brazilian Popular Music and Globalization.* New York: Routledge, 2002 [2001].

Seeger, Anthony. *Why Suyá Sing: A Muiscal Anthropology of an Amazonian People.* Cambridge: Cambridge University Press, 1987.

Sheehy, Daniel. *Mariachi Music In America: Experiencing Music, Expressing Culture.* Oxford: Oxford University Press, 2005.

Stevenson, Robert. *Music in Mexico: A Historical Survey.* New York: Thomas Y. Crowell, 1952.

Turino, Thomas. *Moving Away from Silence: Music of the Peruvian Altiplano and the Experience of Urban Migration.* Chicago: University of Chicago Press, 1993.

Marbury, Elisabeth. "Introduction," in *Castle, Vernon and Irene. Modern Dancing.* NY: World Syndicate, 1914.

Chapter 13 North America: Diverse Peoples, Diverse Musics

Cantwell, Robert. *Bluegrass Breakdown: The Making of the Old Southern Sound.* Urbana, IL: University of Illinois Press, 1984.

Cobb, Jr., Buell E. *The Sacred Harp: A Tradition and Its Music.* Athens, GA: The University of Georgia Press, 1989 [1978].

Crawford, Richard. *The American Musical Landscape.* Berkeley: University of California Press, 1993.

Herndon, Marcia. *Native American Music.* Hatboro, PA: Norwood, 1980.

Koskoff, Ellen, ed. *Music Cultures in the United States: An Introduction*. New York: Routledge, 2005.

Nettl, Bruno. *Blackfoot Musical Thought: Comparative Perspectives*. Kent, OH: Kent State University Press, 1989.

Oliver, Paul. *Songsters and Saints: Vocal Traditions on Race Records*. Cambridge: Cambridge University Press, 1984.

Peña, Manuel. *The Texas-Mexican Conjunto: History of a Working-Class Music*. Austin: University of Texas Press, 1985.

Eight Traditional British-American Ballads. Middlebury, VT: Middlebury College, 1951.

Periodicals

There are several periodicals devoted to the study of world music. Among the most prominent are:

Ethnomusicology: Journal of the Society for Ethnomusicology
(www.ethnomusicology.org/),

Ethnomusicology Forum
(www.bfe.shef.ac.uk/),

Asian Music
(asianmusic.skidmore.edu/academics/asianmusic

The World of Music
(www.uni-bamberg.de/~ba2fm3/wom.htm).

The Scholarly Journal Archive
www.jstor.org

Project MUSE
muse.jhu.edu

The contents are varied and often include reviews of books, recordings, and video documentaries. Membership to the organizations that publish these journals is usually less than $100US and cheaper for students. As a member, you will also have access to electronic forums and contact lists that will allow you to network with ethnomusicologists around the globe.

Visual Materials
Video Collections

The JVC Video Anthology of World Music and Dance. 30 vols. (1990)

The original series of 30 video tapes and 9 books was produced in Japan by JVC, offering clips of 500 performances from 100 countries. While this collection is quite valuable, it is also heavily oriented towards dance and does not include some fairly basic kinds of music, e.g., Javanese gamelan. With 15 volumes on Asia and 2 on the Americas, it is obviously weighted away from the Western hemisphere. Certain features, such as "Soviet Union," date the collection a bit. The volumes are arranged as follows: East Asia, 1-5; Southeast Asia, 6-10; South Asia, 11-15; the Middle East and Africa, 16-19; Europe, 20-22; Soviet Union, 23-26; the Americas, 27-28; Oceania, 29-30.

The JVC Smithsonian Folkways Video Anthology of World Music and Dance of the Americas. (1995) 6 vols.

> Produced in the mid 1990s, this set of 6 videos and booklets offers 158 performances, making up for the paucity of clips for the Americas in the earlier set.

The JVC Smithsonian Folkways Video Anthology of World Music and Dance of Africa. (1995) 3 vols.

> This set of 3 videos and booklets was produced in the mid 1990s and offers 72 performances from 11 countries in Africa.

The JVC Smithsonian Folkways Video Anthology of World Music and Dance of Europe. (1996) 2 vols.

> Also produced in the mid 1990s, the set includes 59 performances to supplement those of the original set.

Multicultural Media has produced a series of 10 video documentaries on various topics. MCM, in conjunction with Lyrichord, has also re-released a series of documentary films by Deben Battacharya.
(www.multiculturalmedia.com)

Shanachie Entertainment Corporation. Numerous videos and DVDs including Jeremy Marre's documentary series *Beats of the Heart*.
(www.shanachie.com)

Audio Materials

(N.B. It is not possible to list all possible companies that produce world music audio materials. The following is a sampler of the best known companies.)

ARC Music
(www.arcmusic.co.uk)

Arhoolie
(www.arhoolie.com)

Auvidis
(www.auvidis.com)

Hugo Records (Hong Kong)
(www.hugocd.com)

King Records (World Music Library series)
(www.kingrecords.co.jp)

Lyrichord Discs
(www.lyrichord.com)

Multicultural Media
(www.multiculturalmedia.com)

Naxos Records (including the Marco Polo series)
(www.naxos.com)

PAN Records, Leiden, The Netherlands

Playa Sound Records (including the Air Mail Music series)
www.playasound.com)

Rounder Records
(www.rounder.com)

Shanachie Entertainment Corp (including Yazoo Records)
(www.shanachie.com)

Smithsonian-Folkways

(www.folkways.si.edu)

Additional Resources

We have prepared a website to accompany this book: www.routledge-ny.com/textbooks/world-music. It includes additional listening examples and articles, plus photos and weblinks, among other features.

There are several institutions around the country with ethnomusicology programs for those that are interested in turning their interest in world music into a career. Most prominent among these is the program at UCLA in Los Angeles, California
(www.ethnomusic.ucla.edu).

A complete list of programs is found on the SEM
(www.ethnomusicology.org) website under Resources
(webdb.iu.edu/sem/scripts/guidetoprograms/guidelist.cfm).

Archives are also a source of much useful information. Notable among these is the UCLA Ethnomusicology Archive
www.ethnomusic.ucla.edu/Archive/)

and the Ethnomusicology Institute at Indiana University
(www.indiana.edu/~folklore/ethnomusicologyinstitute.htm). Again, check the SEM website for a more complete list.

Index

A

D

S

T

X

Y

Z

Recorded Examples

CD 1

Chapter 4 Oceania: Voices of Land and Sea

1   (Site 1) **Australian Aborigine song with didjeridu**
"Bushfire" by Alan Maralung, from the recording entitled *Bunggridj-bunggridj Wangga Songs, Northern Australia* recorded by Allan Marett and Linda Barwick, SF 40430, provided courtesy of Smithsonian Folkways Recordings. © 1993. Used by permission.

2   (Site 2) *Susap* **from Papua New Guinea**
"Sounds of a *Susap*," performed by Amadu, recorded by Wolfgang Laade, Buji, Western Province, Papua New Guinea, 1964, from the recording *Music from South New Guinea,* Folkways 04216, provided courtesy of Smithsonian Folkways Recordings. © 1971. Used by permission.

3   (Site 3) **Hawaiian drum-dance chant**
"Kau ka hali'a I ka manawa" performed by Noenoe Lewis, drum, vocal, and Hau'oli Lewis, calls, dance, from the recording entitled *Hawaiian Drum Dance Chants: Sounds of Power in Time.* SF 40015 provided courtesy of Smithsonian Folkways Recordings. © 1989. Used by permission.

4   (Site 4) **Kiribati group song**
"E tataekinaki aron abara ae Onotoa" sung with clapping by men and women of Tanimaiaki Village, Abaiang Island, Kiribati, recorded by Mary E. Lawson Burke, 1985. Used by permission.

Chapter 5 South Asia: Music with a Spiritual Dimension

5   (Site 1) **Hindustani raga**
"Raga Ahir bhairav" played by Buddhadev DasGupta, *sarod*. From *The Raga Guide: A Survey of 74 Hindustani Ragas,* Nimbus NI 5536/9 (4 CDs and 196 pp. book), 1999. Used by permission.

6 (Site 2) Bhajan devotional song

"Jagatpatī Hari Sāi Gopālā," recorded by Terry E. Miller at the Sai Baba Temple, Longdenville, Trinidad, 1985. Used by permission.

7 (Site 3) Carnatic (South Indian) classical singing *(Kriti)*

"Dhikkutheriyatha," *Raga Behag, Adi Tala,* composed by Subramaniya Bharathi, performed by Sri V. Ramachandran, vocal; Sri S. Varadharajan, violin; Ramnad Sri Raghavan, *mrdangam;* Sri R. Balasubramaniam, *kanjira,* recorded at the 2003 St. Thyagaraja Festival by the Aradhana Committee, Cleveland, Ohio, 2003. Used by permission.

8 (Site 4) *Baul* Song from Bangladesh

"Bhana ghare," sung by Gangadhar Das, recorded by Charles Capwell, c. 1974. Used by permission

Chapter 6 Southeast Asia: A Land of Bamboo and Bronze

9 (Site 1) Upland bronze gong ensemble

Gong ensemble of the Jarai, Pleiku City, Pleiku province, recorded by Terry E. Miller and Phong Nguyen, from *Vietnam: Mother Mountain and Father Sea,* White Cliffs Media WCM 9991 (6 CDs and 47 pp. book), 2003. Used by permission.

10 (Site 2) *Tai tu* amateur chamber music

"Xuan tinh (Spring Love)" performed by Nam Vinh, *dan kim,* Sau Xiu, *dan tranh,* and Muoi Phu, *dan co,* recorded by Terry E. Miller and Phong Nguyen, from *Vietnam: Mother Mountain and Father Sea,* White Cliffs Media WCM 1991 (6 CDs and 47 pp. book), 2003. Used by permission.

11 (Site 3) Classical *piphat* music

"Sathukan" recorded by Panya Roongruang at Department of Music, Mahidol University, Bangkok, Thailand, 2003. Used by permission.

12 (Site 4) Northeast Thai *lam klawn*

"Lam thang san" (excerpts) sung by Saman Hongsa (male), Ubon Hongsa (female), and Thawi Sidamni, *khaen,* recorded by Terry E. Miller in Mahasarakham, Thailand, 1988.

13 (Site 5) *Phleng Luk thung* from northeast Thailand

"Love Dream, Bad Dream" sung by Honey Isan, from the recording entitled *Tears Drop on the Bed,* Yanavy sound cassette, n.d.

14 (Site 6) Javanese court gamelan

"Udan Mas" ("Golden Rain"), from the recording entitled *Music of the Venerable Dark Cloud: The Javanese Gamelan Khjai Mendung,* Institute of Ethnomusicology, UCLA, IER 7501, 1973. Used by permission.

15 (Site 7) Balinese gamelan gong kebyar

"Hudjan Mas." recorded in south Bali by a *gamelan gong kebjar* ensemble, from the recording entitled *Gamelan Music of Bali,* Lyrichord CD 7179, n.d. Used by permission.

Chapter 7 East Asia: Ancient Echoes in the Modern World

16 **(Site 1) The *qin* seven-string zither**
"Yangguang sandie" performed and recorded by Bell Yung, Pittsburgh, PA, 2002. Used by permission.

17 **(Site 2) The "Silk and bamboo" *sizhu* ensemble**
"Zhonghua liuban" recorded in Shanghai, People's Republic of China, by Alan Thrasher, from the recording entitled *Sizhu—Chamber music of South China—Silk Bamboo,* Pan 2030CD, 1994. Used by permission.

18 **(Site 3) Beijing opera *(jingju)***
"Tao Ma Tan (role), aria from *Mu Ko Chai* (opera)," from the recording entitled *The Chinese Opera: Arias from Eight Peking Opera,* Lyrichord LLST 7212, n.d. Used by permission.

19 **(Site 4) Revolutionary Beijing opera**
Scene 1, "A Rush Shipment," from the recording entitled *On the Docks: Modern Revolutionary Peking Opera,* performed by the "On the Docks" Group of the Peking Opera Troupe of Shanghai. China Record Company, M-958, n.d. Used by permission.

20 **(Site 5) Mongolian throat singing**
"Six types of hoomii demonstrated. . . . " From the accompanying CD with Carole Pegg. *Mongolian Music, Dance, & Oral Narrative,* Seattle: University of Washington Press, 2001. Used by permission.

21 **(Site 6) P'ansori**
"P'ansori, Ch'un-Hyang-Ka, Song of Spring Fragrance" sung by Mme. Pak Chowol with drum accompaniment by Han Ilsup, recorded by John Levy, from the recording entitled *Korean Social and Folk Music,* Lyrichord LLST 7211, n.d. Used by permission.

22 **(Site 7) *Gagaku***
"Entenraku," from the recording entitled *Gagaku: The Imperial Court Music of Japan.* Performed by the Kyoto Imperial Court Music Orchestra, Lyrichord LYRCD 7126, n.d. Used by permission.

23 **(Site 8) *Kabuki* theater**
"Excerpt from *Dozyozi [Dojoji]*" performed by the Kyoto Kabuki Orchestra, recorded by Jacob Feuerring, from the recording entitled *Japanese Kabuki Nagauta Music,* Lyrichord LLST 7134, n.d. Used by permission.

24 **(Site 9) Buddhist ritual**
"Genyen gi topa" "(In praise of Ge-nyen)" performed by the monks of Thimphu and nuns of Punakha, recorded by John Levy, from the recording entitled *Tibetan Buddhist Rites from the Monasteries of Bhutan, Volume 1: Rituals of the Drukpa Order,* Lyrichord LYRCD 7255, n.d. Used by permission.

Chapter 8 The Middle East: Cradle of Great Religions

25 (Site 1) Islamic "Call to Prayer"
5 Ezan/5 Kamet, recorded by Mehmet Emin Güler, published on cassette tape under Remak name, Istanbul, Turkey, n.d.

26 (Site 2) Arab modal improvisation
"*Maqam* Kurd" performed by Ali Jihad Racy, *buzuq,* and Simon Shaheen, *ud,* from *Taqasim: Improvisation in Arab Music,* Lyrichord LYRCD 7374., n.d. Used by permission.

27 (Site 3) *Dastgah Shur* for *santur* and voice
"Dastgah of Shour" by Mohamed Heydari, *santour,* and Khatereh Parvaneh, voice, from the recording entitled *Classical Music of Iran: Dastgah Systems,* SF 40039, provided courtesy of Smithsonian Folkways Recordings. © 1991. Used by permission.

28 (Site 4) Islamic song with *Takht* instrumental accompaniment
"Bashraf" (instrumental composition), performed by the Arabic Music Ensemble of Cairo, from the recording entitled *Egypt: Echoes of the Nile* Multicultural Media, MCM 3005, 1997. Used by permission.

29 (Site 5) *Dhikr* ceremony
"Sufi Hymn (Turkish)" performed by the Jarrahi Dervishes. Recorded by J. During, Konya, Turkey, 1982, from the recording entitled *The Silk Road: A Musical Caravan,* SF 40438, provided courtesy of Smithsonian Folkways Recordings. © 2002. Used by permission.

30 (Site 6) Jewish liturgical cantillation
"L'dor vodor" sung by Dr. Peter Laki, recorded by Terry E. Miller, Cleveland, Ohio, 2005. Used by permission.

Chapter 9 Sub-Saharan Africa: The Rhythms of Community

31 (Site 1) Polyrhythmic ensemble
"Fante Area: Vocal Band" performed by the Odo ye few korye kuw Vocal Band, recorded by Roger Vetter, Abura Tuakwa, Ghana, 1984, from the recording entitled *Rhythms of Life, Songs of Wisdom: Akan Music from Ghana, West Africa,* SF 40463, provided courtesy of Smithsonian Folkways Recordings. © 1996. Used by permission.

32 (Site 2) Talking drums
"Denkyira Area: Talking Drum" performed by Elizabeth Kumi, appellant, and Joseph Manu, drummer, recorded by Roger Vetter, Abura Tuakwa, Ghana, 1984, from the recording entitled *Rhythms of Life, Songs of Wisdom: Akan Music from Ghana, West Africa,* SF 40463, provided courtesy of Smithsonian Folkways Recordings. © 1996. Used by permission.

33 (Site 3) Palm Wine "Highlife Song"
"Palm-wine highlife song" performed by Koo Nimo and band, recorded by David B. Coplan, Kamasi, Ghana, 1970. Used by permission.

34 (Site 4) **Pygmy song from the Democratic Republic of the Congo**
"Elephant Song" performed by Mbuti Pygmies, from the recording entitled *Music of the Rain Forest Pygmies: The Historic Recordings Made by Colin M. Turnbull,* Lyrichord LYRCD 7157 (original recording, 1961). Used by permission.

CD 2

1 (Site 5) *Mbira dza vadzimu*
Shona ancestral spirit song, *"Nyama musango,"* performed by Elias Kunaka and Kidwell Mudzimirema (Mharadzirwa), recorded by John E. Kaemmer, Jirira, Zimbabwe, 1973. Used by permission.

2 (Site 6) *Akadinda* xylophone
Baganda *akadinda* song *"Gganga aluwa"* ("Gganga escaped with his life") performed by Sheikh Burukan Kiwuuwa and his group of royal *akadinda* musicians, recorded by Peter Cooke, Kidinda Village, Mpigi, Buganda, Uganda, 1987. Used by permission.

3 (Site 7) *Jali* with *kora*
"Kuruntu Kallafa" performed by Salieu Suso with kora, from the recording entitled *Griot: Salieu Suso,* Lyrichord LYRCD 7418, n.d. Used by permission.

4 (Site 8) *Mbube* vocal choir
"Phesheya Mama""(Mama, they are overseas)" sung by the Utrecht Zulu Singing Competition, recorded by Gary Gardner and Helen Kivnick, 1984, from the recording entitled *Let Their Voices Be Heard: Traditional Singing in South Africa.* Rounder 5024, 1987. Used by permission.

Chapter 10 Europe: Harmony and Hierarchy

5 (Site 1) **Byzantine chant**
"Come, Faithful," from the recording entitled *Byzantine Hymns of Christmas,* Society for the Dissemination of National Music, SDNM 101, n.d. Used by permission.

6 (Site 2) *Flamenco*
"Alegrias" performed by Carlos Lomas and Pepe De Malaga, from the recording entitled *Andalusian Flamenco Song and Dance,* Lyrichord LYRCD 7388, n.d. Used by permission.

7 (Site 3) *Balalaika*
"Yablochka," from the recording entitled *Eastern European Folk Heritage Concert: St. Nicholas Balalaika Orchestra,* Private issue, 2003. Used by permission.

8 (Site 4) **Highland bagpipes**
"An Piob Mhor" (Great Highland Bagpipe: Scotland—Highlands), from the recording entitled *Bagpipes of the World: Sean Folson,* Nova Albion Records NAR 5544, 1999. Used by permission.

9 (Site 5) **Union bagpipes**
"Piob Uilleann" (Uilleann or Union Pipes), Ireland, from the recording entitled *Bagpipes of the World: Sean Folson,* Nova Albion Records NAR 5544, 1999. Used by permission.

10 (Site 6) Hurdy gurdy

Medley of traditional tunes performed by Sean Folson, 2003 (private studio recording).

11 (Site 7) Women's chorus

"Harvest Song" (originally published on Balkanton BHA 1293), from the CD to accompany book: Timothy Rice, *Music in Bulgaria: Experiencing Music, Expressing Culture.* New York: Oxford University Press, 2004. Used by permission.

Chapter 11 Caribbean: Musical Energy of Island Peoples

12 (Site 1) *Vodou* ritual

Excerpts from "Bosou Djo Eya (Mayi rhythm)" performed by Societe Jour M'alonge Foc Nan Point Dieu Devant, recorded by David Yih, Carrefour, Haiti, 1987, and "Guantanamo Song (Rara Rhythm, Souther Style)," recorded by Elizabeth McAlister, Port-au-Prince, Haiti, 1993. From the recording entitled *Rhythms of Rapture: Sacred Musics of Haitian Vodou.* SF 40464, provided courtesy of Smithsonian Folkways Recordings. © 1995. Used by permission.

13 (Site 2) *Reggae*

"Torchbearer," performed by Carlos Jones and the Plus Band, from the recording entitled *Roots with Culture,* Little Fish Records LF02912, 2004. Used by permission.

14 (Site 3) *Calypso*

"Money is King" performed by Growling Tiger and the Trans-Caribbean All-Star Orchestra, from the recording entitled *Growling Tiger: High Priest of Mi Minor—Knockdown Calypsos,* Rounder 5006, 1979. Used by permission.

15 (Site 4) Steel band

"Jump Up," performed by the Miami [Ohio] University Steel Band from the recording entitled *One More Soca,* Ramajay Records. Used by permission.

16 (Site 5) Rhyming spiritual

"My Lord Help Me to Pray" performed by Bruce Green, Clifton Green, and Tweedie Gibson, recorded by Peter K. Siegel and Jody Stecher, Nassau, Bahamas, 1965, from the recording entitled *Kneelin' Down Inside the Gate: The Great Rhyming Singers of the Bahamas,* Rounder 5035. Used by permission.

17 (Site 6) Afro-Cuban Derived *Salsa*

"Quitate de la Via Perico," performed by Tolú, from the recording entitled *Bongó de VanGogh,* Tonga Productions TNGCD 8405, 2002. Used by permission.

18 (Site 7) *Merengue*

"Apágame la Vela (Put Out my Candle)" performed by Bienvenido Brens, recorded by Verna Gillis with Ramon Daniel Perez Martinez, 1976, from the recording entitled *Raices Latinas: Smithsonian-Folkways Latino Roots Collection,* SF 40470, provided courtesy of Smithsonian Folkways Recordings. © 2002. Used by permission.

Chapter 12 Central and South America: New World Recipes.

19 **(Site 1) Amazonian Indian chant**

"Nhiok: Okkaikrikti" recorded by Max Peter Baumann, 1988, from the recording entitled *Ritual Music of the Kayapó-Xikrin, Brazil,* SF 40433, provided courtesy of Smithsonian Folkways Recordings. © 1995. Used by permission.

20 **(Site 2) *Sikuri* ensemble**

"Qhantati Urui: Easter Music" performed by the Conimeño Ensemble, recorded by Thomas Turino, Conima, Peru, 1985, from the recording entitled *Mountain Music of Peru: Volume II,* SF 40406, provided courtesy of Smithsonian Folkways Recordings. © 1994. Used by permission.

21 **(Site 3) *Tango***

"El Choclo" (The Ear of Corn): *Tango Criollo* performed by Rene Marino Rivero, recorded by Tiago de Oliveiro Pinto, 1991, from the recording entitled *Raices Latinas: Smithsonian-Folkways Latino Roots Collection,* SF 40470, provided courtesy of Smithsonian Folkways Recordings. © 2002. Used by permission.

22 **(Site 4) *Mariachi***

"Los Arrieros (The Muleteers)" performed by Mariachi Los Camperos, from the recording entitled *Raices Latinas: Smithsonian-Folkways Latino Roots Collection,* SF 40470, provided courtesy of Smithsonian Folkways Recordings. © 2002. Used by permission.

23 **(Site 5) *Samba***

"Agoniza, Mas Nao Morre" "(It suffers but doesn't die)" performed by Nelson Sargento, from the recording entitled *Brazil Roots: Samba.* Rounder CD 5045, 1989. Used by permission.

24 **(Site 6) *Capoeira***

"Saia do Mar Marinheiro" performed by King Zumbi of Palmares/Rei Zumbi dos Palmares (Mestre Moraes), from the recording entitled *Capoeira Angola from Salvador, Brazil,* SF 40465, provided courtesy of Smithsonian Folkways Recordings. © 1996. Used by permission

Chapter 13 North America: Diverse Peoples, Diverse Musics

25 **(Site 1) Cape Breton fiddling**

"E Minor Jigs" performed by Buddy MacMaster, fiddle, and Mac Morin, piano, from the recording entitled *Buddy MacMaster: The Judique Flyer,* Stephen MacDonald Productions, Atlantic Artists SMPCD 1012, n.d. Used by permission.

26 **(Site 2) Ballad singing**

"Edward" performed by Edith B. Price, from the recording entitled *Eight Traditional British-American Ballads from [the] Helen Hartness Flanders Collection,* Middlebury College, 1953. Used by permission.

27 **(Site 3) Old Regular Baptist lined hymn**

"And Must This Body Die," performed by congregation led by Elder Larry Newsome, from the recording entitled *Grace 'Tis a Charming Sound: Pleasant View Old Regular Baptist Church in Worship.* Privately issued CD by Terry E. Miller and members of the Advanced Field and Lab Methods in Ethnomusicology Class, Kent State University, Spring, 2000. Used by permission.

28 **(Site 4) Singing school shape–note music**
"Exhortation" performed by Sacred Harp singers at Hopewell Primitive Baptist Church near Cullman, Alabama, 1971. Recorded by Terry E. Miller. Used by permission.

29 **(Site 5) Bluegrass**
"True Life Blues" performed by Bill Monroe and His Bluegrass Boys, from the recording entitled *Off the Record, Vol. 1: Live Recordings 1956–1969,* SF 40063, provided courtesy of Smithsonian Folkways Recordings. © 1993. Used by permission

30 **(Site 6) African-American spiritual**
"Come and go to that land" recorded by Terry E. Miller at Gethsemene Baptist Church, Cleveland, Ohio, 1986. Used by permission.

31 **(Site 7) African-American Gospel Choir**
"God is Good All the Time" performed by New Hope Baptist Choir, from the recording titled *God is Good: The Total Musical Experience at New Hope Missionary Baptist Church, Akron, Ohio.* Privately issued CD by Terry E. Miller and members of the Advanced Field and Lab Methods in Ethnomusicology Class, Kent State University, Spring, 1998.

32 **(Site 8) Country Blues**
"Penitentiary Blues" performed by Lightnin' Hopkins, recorded by Samuel B. Charters, Houston, Texas, 1959, from the recording entitled *Lightnin' Hopkins,* SF 40019, provided courtesy of Smithsonian Folkways Recordings. © 1990. Used by permission

33 **(Site 9) *Conjunto* from Texas**
"Me Voy, Me Voy" performed by Los Cachorros de Juan Villareal, from the recording entitled *!Conjunto!: Texas-Mexican Border Music,* Rounder CD 6023, 1988. Used by permission.

34 **(Site 10) Cajun music**
"La talle des ronces" performed by Adam and Cyprien Landreneau and Dewey Balfa, from the recording entitled *Lousiana Cajun from the Southwest Prairies Recorded 1964–1967, Volume 2,* Rounder 6002, 1989. Used by permission.

35 **(Site 11) Plains Chippewa: Rock Dance song**
"Rock Dance Song" performed by Pembina Chippewa Singers. Recorded by Nicholas Curchin Peterson Vrooman, Turtle Mountain, North Dakota, 1984, from the recording entitled *Plains Chippewa/Metis Music from Turtle Mountain,* SF 40411, provided courtesy of Smithsonian Folkways Recordings. © 1992. Used by permission

36 **(Site 12) Native American *flute***
"Taos Pueblo Courting Song" performed by John Rainer, Jr., from the recording entitled *Music of New Mexico: Native American Traditions,* SF 40408, provided courtesy of Smithsonian Folkways Recordings. © 1992. Used by permission